Professional Practice in Governance and Public Organizations

The *Professional Practice in Governance and Public Organizations* series features cutting-edge insights and practical guidance for professionals in the areas of economics, politics, public policy, public administration, and international organizations. With concise, accessible volumes, the series explores the latest developments in governance, public lawmaking, organizational and political strategies, institutional policies, policy instruments, public management, and finance. Core topics include decision-making, leadership, and the transformative impact of digitalization.

Each book is authored by practitioners, experts, and leading authorities from public and international organizations, think tanks, and NGOs, ensuring a blend of theoretical depth and real-world applicability. While designed primarily for professionals in these fields, the series also serves as an invaluable resource for students of economics, political science, public policy, and public administration, equipping them with practical guides for their future careers.

Gerda Füricht-Fiegl • Julia Kreyler-Valsky
Alexander Burka
Editors

Handbook on EU Law-making

A Practical Guide

Springer

Editors
Gerda Füricht-Fiegl
University of Applied Sciences Burgenland
Eisenstadt, Austria

Julia Kreyler-Valsky
University of Applied Sciences Burgenland
Eisenstadt, Austria

Alexander Burka
University of Applied Sciences Burgenland
Eisenstadt, Austria

ISSN 2731-9776 ISSN 2731-9784 (electronic)
Professional Practice in Governance and Public Organizations
ISBN 978-3-032-16558-9 ISBN 978-3-032-16559-6 (eBook)
https://doi.org/10.1007/978-3-032-16559-6

This Springer imprint is published by the registered company Springer Nature Switzerland AG
The registered company address is: Gewerbestrasse 11, 6330 Cham, Switzerland

Contents

Contributors

Deniz Alkan Director for European and International Affairs at the State Chancellery of Saarland, Saarbrücken, Germany

Alexander Burka University of Applied Sciences Burgenland, Eisenstadt, Austria

Antonina Cipollone European Commission, Head of Unit Better Regulation & Simplification, Brussels, Belgium

Doris Dialer Consumer Affairs Attaché, Permanent Representation of Austria to the EU, Brussels, Belgium

Founding Member, Innsbruck Center for European Research (ICER), Innsbruck, Austria

Oliver Drewes Managing Partner Pantarhei Europe, Brussels, Belgium

Gerda Füricht-Fiegl University of Applied Sciences Burgenland, Eisenstadt, Austria

Thomas Gloeckel General Secretariat of the Council of the EU, Brussels, Belgium

Anna Guerri Department of Political Science, University of Innsbruck, Innsbruck, Austria

Wolfgang Hiller, Former Director of Impact Assessment and Foresight at the European Parliament Research Service, Brussels, Belgium

Eike Hortsch Head of Division for Europe, Finance and Science at the Saarland State Representation in Berlin, Berlin, Germany

Harald J. Jauk University of Applied Sciences Wiener Neustadt, Wiener Neustadt, Austria

IMC University of Applied Sciences Krems, Krems an der Donau, Austria

Roland Jöbstl Attaché for Climate, Environment and the Atomic Questions Working Party, Permanent Representation of Austria to the EU, Brussels, Belgium

Marina Jovanovic International Institute for Applied Systems Analysis (IIASA), Laxenburg, Austria

Arnold H. Kammel Secretary General of the Federal Ministry of Defence of Austria, Lecturer and Honorary Professor (FH), University of Applied Sciences Burgenland, Eisenstadt, Austria

Peter Kerstens DG for Financial Stability, Financial Services and Capital Markets Union (DG FISMA), European Commission, Brussels, Belgium

Julia Kreyler-Valsky University of Applied Sciences Burgenland, Eisenstadt, Austria

Michael Kudler Austrian Chamber of Labour, Vienna, Austria

Tino Kunert Policy Advisor at the Representation of Saarland to the EU, Brussels, Belgium

Edgar Lenski Deputy Director General for EU Affairs of the German Federal Chancellery, Fellow at the Walter Hallstein-Institute for European Constitutional Law, Humboldt-University Berlin, Berlin, Germany

Lukas Mandl Member of the European Parliament, Brussels, Belgium

Camilla Mariotto Department of Political Science, University of Innsbruck, Innsbruck, Austria

Andreas Maurer Department of Political Science, University of Innsbruck, Innsbruck, Austria

Céline Mias EU Director at the Danish Refugee Council, Brussels, Belgium

Irina Michalowitz Vice President Global Government Relations & Public Policy at DeepL, Palo Alto Networks, Santa Clara, CA, USA

Founder and Advisory Director to IMConsult, Didcot, UK

Sebastián Rodríguez Pérez Rollout Democracy, Córdoba, Spain

Evelyn Regner Member of the European Parliament, Vienna, Austria

Nina Schilling Austrian Federal Ministry for European and International Affairs, Vienna, Austria

Rudolf W. Strohmeier Former General Director European Commission, Brussels, Belgium

CBH Rechsanwälte, Brussels, Belgium

Birgül Tütün-Ince Austrian Federal Railways (ÖBB) and University of Applied Sciences BFI Vienna, Vienna, Austria

Martin Wagner Institute of Law, University of Applied Sciences Wiener Neustadt, Wiener Neustadt, Austria

Bernhard Zeilinger University of Applied Sciences BFI Vienna, Vienna, Austria

Jérémie Zeitoun Attaché at the Permanent Representation of Luxembourg to the EU, Brussels, Belgium

Stefan Zotti DG for Education, Youth, Sport and Culture (EAC), European Commission, Brussels, Belgium

Setting the Scene: Context and Legal Foundations

Understanding the Ordinary Legislative Procedure in EU Lawmaking

Gerda Füricht-Fiegl, Alexander Burka, and Julia Kreyler-Valsky

The EU today is less than a state, but far more than a traditional international organization, able to adopt and implement policies that get to the heart of its Member States (Pollack et al., 2020). Given the principles of multilevel governance, legislative decisions at the EU level do not only involve supranational institutions—such as the European Commission, the European Parliament, and the Council of the EU—but also require interaction with national institutions and governing bodies. Laws adopted at the EU level are binding in the Member States and thus apply to nearly 450 million citizens in 27 countries (as of 2026).

Given the significance of EU lawmaking, it is essential to understand how legislation comes into being. The collaborative and often complex nature of this process varies depending on the policy area in question. The very same EU institutions and national policymakers are oftentimes involved in various lawmaking processes concurrently, and different policy domains require different institutional settings. Rather than a single uniform lawmaking process, there are five main variants: the Ordinary Legislative Procedure (also referred to as the Community Method), the regulatory mode, the distributive mode, policy coordination, and intensive transgovernmentalism (Pollack et al., 2020). Among these, the Ordinary Legislative Procedure (OLP) represents the primary method for adopting binding legislation within the EU. It is therefore the central focus of this handbook.

Although the OLP is formally codified in the EU treaties, its practical implementation has evolved over time through both formal reforms and informal institutional adaptations. These changes sought to streamline the legislative process, enhance transparency, and balance the power of the key legislative actors. One of the most

G. Füricht-Fiegl · A. Burka · J. Kreyler-Valsky (✉)
University of Applied Sciences Burgenland, Eisenstadt, Austria
e-mail: gerda.fuericht-fiegl@hochschule-burgenland.at;
alexander.burka@hochschule-burgenland.at; julia.kreyler-valsky@hochschule-burgenland.at

G. Füricht-Fiegl et al. (eds.), *Handbook on EU Law-making*, Professional Practice in Governance and Public Organizations, https://doi.org/10.1007/978-3-032-16559-6_1

significant developments introduced by the entry into force of the Treaty of Lisbon in 2009 is the redistribution of legislative authority among the EU institutions. While the Council of the EU continues to play a dominant role, the European Parliament now acts as a co-legislator in most policy areas, reflecting the growing importance of democratic accountability in EU governance (Dionigi & Rasmussen, 2019). This represents just one—albeit highly significant—example of the continuous evolution of the EU legislative process and, more broadly, of the modes of cooperation between the EU institutions. Another notable development is the growing importance of the trilogue over the years. These two developments vividly underscore the need for a continuous, systematic analysis and transparent presentation of the EU's legislative process. With this handbook, we seek to advance both objectives by providing a comprehensive and practice-oriented guide to the OLP. It brings together contributions from scholars and practitioners, including experts from the EU institutions directly involved in the legislative process. Our objective is twofold: to enhance the academic understanding of how the OLP functions within the EU's institutional framework, and to offer practical insights into the day-to-day workings of EU lawmaking.

The volume is structured into eight parts, each addressing a key dimension and/or key player of the OLP. It begins by exploring the role of the EU institutions involved, the institutional interplay among the core EU actors and situates them within the broader multilevel governance system. Subsequent chapters focus on additional institutional participants and the influence of external stakeholders, particularly in the context of lobbying and interest representation. The handbook further examines selected policy fields and ongoing or anticipated legislative files, illustrating how the OLP operates across different substantive areas. Finally, it offers reflections on the future of EU lawmaking, considering possible reforms and long-term trends.

By combining theoretical analysis with practical and procedural detail, this volume seeks to equip readers with both the conceptual tools and practical knowledge necessary to engage effectively with the OLP—arguably the cornerstone of democratic decision-making in the European Union.

Part I of this book analyzes the legal framework of the OLP under Art. 288–299 TFEU, focusing on the roles of the EU Commission, the European Parliament, and the Council of the European Union. Furthermore, it highlights the practical shift toward concluding legislation in early readings through informal "trilogues," which, though not regulated by primary EU law, increasingly shape the OLP's application and may influence future treaty provisions.

Part II is dedicated to the European Commission as an initiating force—and traditionally the driving engine—of EU lawmaking. Like the other parts that follow, we preface this section with a scientific review of the institution's role within the OLP, with special focus on its rules of procedure. Our contributors subsequently provide practitioners' insights into the various stakes at play when initiating the OLP process, covering key topics such as the preparatory phase of EC initiatives, the role and function of Cabinets of Commissioners as well as the conflicts of national and international interest at play.

In Part III, the Council's role as a lawmaker within the OLP is discussed and complemented with an analysis of the preparatory bodies in the process, i.e. COREPER I and II as well as Council Working Groups. The function and significance of Council presidencies is examined, followed by a closer look at the way decisions are determined by means of informal coalition-building among Member States.

Part IV on the European Parliament concludes our appraisal of EU bodies involved in the OLP. After a thorough review of the powers as well as constraints the EP faces as a lawmaker, our contributors tackle such crucial topics as the work of the EP's committees and its bodies and how they interact. We also invited renowned representatives of the two largest political groups within the EP—namely the EPP and S&D group—to share their views on the power shift following the 2024 elections and its impact on future policymaking. Their contributions conclude Part IV of this volume.

In the subsequent Part V, we focus on inter-institutional bargaining during the OLP process. The role of the trilogue and its increasing importance is examined, along with practical behind-the-scenes insights on power games and informal determinants of decision-making, such as institutional loyalty and pride, or personal connections. Furthermore, this part contains a view to other institutional players which hold a stake in EU policymaking and regularly make their voices heard in the context of the OLP. These include the European Council, the Committee of the Regions, the European Economic and Social Committee as well as national parliaments and their role in multilevel governance.

It goes without saying that EU law- and decision-making today cannot be assessed comprehensively without casting a light on the manifold and diverse perspectives businesses and civil society bring to the process. Our contributors explain the legal basis as well as ways and strategies these players implement to make their voices heard and tackle topics like lobbying from a business as well as NGO perspective, the need for transparent conduct, and the importance of finding the right tone when campaigning certain interests.

Finally, in Part VII, we delve into selected areas of growing importance when discussing current EU policymaking. Some of these fields are governed by the OLP like the EU's Digital Policy. Others are partly covered by the OLP yet of utmost political relevance, e.g. the EU's policy response to disinformation and foreign interference. The Competitiveness Compass is covered with a view to its impact on policy areas that had been governed by OLP. Lastly, we included social policy as an important and current example of how to balance national sovereignty and EU's social objectives.

We conclude this volume with an outlook on how EU lawmaking will be conducted in the not-too-distant future. Here we focus on the European Commission's better regulation system as a dynamic, adaptive framework that tries to balance evidence-based decision-making with stakeholder inclusivity. A holistic and innovative approach to better regulation, combined with a genuine and engaging consultation system, presents an opportunity to legislate in a way that is more attuned to societal needs and improve the quality of legislation from the moment it is adopted by the Commission.

References

Dionigi, M., & Rasmussen, A. (2019). The Ordinary Legislative Procedure. *Oxford Research Encyclopedia of Politics*. Retrieved June 30, 2025, from https://oxfordre.com/politics/view/10.1093/acrefore/9780190228637.001.0001/acrefore-9780190228637-e-1044

Pollack, M. A., Roederer-Rynning, C., & Young, A. R. (2020). An overview. In *Policy-making in the European Union*. Oxford University Press.

Gerda Füricht-Fiegl is a political scientist at the University of Applied Sciences Burgenland, where she heads the English-taught master's program *European Studies—Management of EU Projects*. She serves as vice-rector for Research and Innovation. Her teaching and research focus on the EU political system and political communication in the EU. She also brings extensive professional experience from the European Commission (DG COMM) and the European Parliament.

Alexander Burka is a professor at the University of Applied Sciences Burgenland and co-founder and managing director of the CIVIC-Institute for International Education in Düsseldorf. He studied at the Universities of Vienna and Helsinki, as well as Free University Berlin, and has worked for numerous national and international institutions in the areas of international competences, civic society, and democracy development. He also authors educational materials on international, political, and EU-related topics.

Julia Kreyler-Valsky is a lecturer at the University of Applied Sciences Burgenland and an expert in equal opportunities. She has held positions with the Austrian Minister for Women's Affairs, the OECD, and the financial sector in Central and Eastern Europe. Her research focuses on inclusive institutional structures and the effectiveness of anti-discrimination policies. Julia holds a Master's in Public Administration (LSE) and a PhD in Sociology (University of Vienna).

Legal Framework of the Ordinary Legislative Procedure in the EU: Scope, Actors and Procedure

A Legal Dogmatic Analysis of the Relevant Primary EU Law

Martin Wagner

Abstract This chapter examines the basic legal framework of the Ordinary Legislative Procedure (OLP), focusing on Art. 288–299 Treaty on the Functioning of the European Union (TFEU). The core provisions (Art. 289 and 294 TFEU) define the main actors, namely the European Commission (Commission), the European Parliament (EP) and the Council of the European Union (Council) and specify their respective roles as well as the procedural steps involved. The analysis reveals that the OLP applies in most cases, although the Treaties do not indicate the practical relevance of its phases. While all phases were frequently applied in the past, an emerging trend in practice can be seen from the recent years: most legislative acts are now concluded in the first or the early second reading due to informal interinstitutional negotiations [mainly the trilogues]. This trend may affect future OLP treaty provisions, particularly as the trilogues are not governed by any primary EU law.

Keywords EU law · TFEU · Legal analysis · Rules of procedure · Scope of application · Informal interinstitutional negotiations · Trilogues

1 Introduction

This chapter addresses the Ordinary Legislative Procedure (OLP) of the EU from a legal perspective with a legal dogmatic approach. Its purpose is to establish the basis for the subsequent chapters in this handbook.

M. Wagner (✉)
Institute of Law, University of Applied Sciences Wiener Neustadt, Wiener Neustadt, Austria
e-mail: martin.wagner@fhwn.ac.at

G. Füricht-Fiegl et al. (eds.), *Handbook on EU Law-making*, Professional Practice in Governance and Public Organizations, https://doi.org/10.1007/978-3-032-16559-6_2

Therefore, the relevant legal provisions regarding the OLP will be presented and examined to understand its main characteristics and its procedural steps. In this context, the special legislative procedure (SLP) of the EU will also be illustrated.

The chapter concludes with a brief consideration of the main actors involved, particularly the European Commission (Commission), the European Parliament (EP) and the Council of the European Union (Council). It outlines their respective roles within the OLP, highlights emerging trends and provides a concise outlook.

2 Types of Procedure

The key legal provisions for the adoption procedure are incorporated in Art. 288–299 of the Treaty on the Functioning of the European Union (TFEU) (OJ C 202, 7.6.2016, pp. 47–200). Due to the focus of this chapter, Art. 289 and 294 TFEU are particularly relevant.

Art. 289 TFEU distinguishes between two types of legislative procedures, that is the OLP in para 1 and the SLP in para 2. The main difference between the two procedures lies in the role of the EP and the Council. Whereas in the OLP, both institutions play an equally important role and jointly adopt legislative acts, in the SLP one of the two institutions adopts a legislative act with the participation of the other institution.

It should to be noted that the SLP or OLP only applies where the Treaties[1] expressly refer to them (ECJ, 2017, para 62).

2.1 Ordinary Legislative Procedure (OLP)

According to Art. 289 para 1 TFEU, the OLP is initiated by a proposal from the Commission, which corresponds to Art. 17 para 2 Treaty on European Union (TEU) (OJ C 202, 7.6.2016, pp. 13–41). The OLP consists in the joint adoption of a regulation, directive or decision by the EP and the Council. Art. 289 para 1 TFEU only outlines the OLP and refers to Art. 294 TFEU, which determines the procedural steps in further detail.

Art. 294 para 1 TFEU specifically stipulates that the OLP applies where reference is made to it in the Treaties. The reference is usually formulated as follows: "(…) the European Parliament and the Council, acting in accordance with the ordinary legislative procedure, (…)".

The comprehensive list in Table 1 shows in which subject areas the OLP applies and outlines its legal foundations.

In general, it can be said that the OLP is the standard and most important method in legislative procedures (Bauerschmidt, 2021, p. 227; Borchardt, 2025, para 530).

Table 1 shows that the OLP applies to at least 85 subject areas. However, this is not an exhaustive list. It needs to be noted in that context that the Treaties determine

[1] According to Art. 1 para 2 TFEU, "Treaties" means the TFEU and the TEU.

Table 1 List—Scope of application of OLP (European Parliament, 2025b)

Nr	TFEU	Subject areas
1.	Art. 14	Services of general economic interest
2.	Art. 15 para 3, second subpara	Procedures for the right of access to documents
3.	Art. 16 para 2, first subpara	Data protection
4.	Art. 18 para 2	Measures to combat discrimination on grounds of nationality
5.	Art. 19 para 2	Basic principles for anti-discrimination incentive measures
6.	Art. 21 para 2	Measures to facilitate the exercise of the right of every citizen of the Union to move and reside freely in the territory of Member States
7.	Art. 24 para 1	Citizens' initiative
8.	Art. 33	Customs cooperation
9.	Art. 42 para 1, Art. 43 para 2	Application of competition rules to the common agricultural policy
10.	Art. 43 para 2	Legislation concerning the common agricultural policy
11.	Art. 46	Free movement of workers
12.	Art. 48 para 1	Internal market—social security measures for Community (Now: European Union (EU)) migrant workers
13.	Art. 50 para 1	Right of establishment
14.	Art. 51 para 2	Exclusion in a Member State of certain activities from the application of provisions on the right of establishment
15.	Art. 52 para 2	Coordination of the provisions laid down by law, regulation or administrative action in Member States providing for special treatment for foreign nationals with regard to the right of establishment
16.	Art. 53 para 1	Coordination of the provisions laid down by law, regulation or administrative action in Member States concerning the taking up and pursuit of activities as self-employed persons and the mutual recognition of qualifications
17.	Art. 56 para 2	Extending provisions on freedom to provide services to service providers who are nationals of a third State and who are established within the Union
18.	Art. 59 para 1	Liberalisation of services in specific sectors
19.	Art. 62	Services
20.	Art. 64 para 2	Adoption of other measures on the movement of capital to and from third countries
21.	Art. 75 para 1	Administrative measures relating to capital movements in connection with preventing and combating crime and terrorism
22.	Art. 77 para 2	Visas, border checks, free movement of nationals of non-member countries, management of external frontiers, absence of controls at internal frontiers
23.	Art. 78 para 2	Asylum, temporary protection or subsidiary protection for nationals of third countries
24.	Art. 79 para 2	Immigration and combating trafficking in persons

(continued)

Table 1 (continued)

Nr	TFEU	Subject areas
25.	Art. 79 para 4	Incentive measures for the integration of nationals of third countries
26.	Art. 81 para 2	Judicial cooperation in civil matters (excluding family law)
27.	Art. 82 para 1, second subpara, and 2, first and second subpara	Judicial cooperation in criminal matters—procedures, cooperation, training, settlement of conflicts, minimum rules for recognition of judgments
28.	Art. 83 para 1, first subpara, and, possibly, 2	Minimum rules concerning the definition of criminal offences and sanctions in the areas of particularly serious crime with a cross-border dimension
29.	Art. 84	Measures to support crime prevention
30.	Art. 85, para 1, second subpara	Eurojust
31.	Art. 85 para 1, third subpara	Arrangements for involving the EP and national parliaments in the evaluation of Eurojust's activities
32.	Art. 87 para 2	Police cooperation (certain aspects)
33.	Art. 88 para 2, first subpara	Europol
34.	Art. 88 para 2, second subpara	Procedures for scrutiny of Europol's activities by EP and national parliaments
35.	Art. 91 para 1	Implementation of the common transport policy
36.	Art. 100 para 2	Sea and air transport
37.	Art. 114 para 1	Measures for the approximation of national provisions which have as their object the establishment and functioning of the internal market to promote the objectives of Art. 26
38.	Art. 116 para 2	Measures to eliminate distortions in the internal market
39.	Art. 118 para 1	Intellectual property except language arrangements for the European intellectual property rights
40.	Art. 121 para 6	Multilateral surveillance
41.	Art. 129 para 3	Modification of the Protocol on the Statutes of the European System of Central Banks (ESCB) and European Central Bank (ECB)
42.	Art. 133	Measures necessary for the use of the euro
43.	Art. 149 para 1	Incentive measures for employment
44.	Art. 153 para 1, except points (c), (d), (f) and (g), and para 2, first, second and forth subpara	Social policy
45.	Art. 157 para 3	Social policy (equal opportunities, equal treatment and equal pay)
46.	Art. 164	European Social Fund
47.	Art. 165 para 4, first indent	Education (excluding recommendations)
48.	Art. 165 para 2, seventh indent, and 4	Sport
49.	Art. 166 para 4	Professional training
50.	Art. 167 para 5, first indent	Culture (excluding recommendations)

(continued)

Table 1 (continued)

Nr	TFEU	Subject areas
51.	Art. 168 para 4	Public health—measures to tackle common safety concerns in the health sphere
52.	Art. 168 para 5	Public health—incentive measures to protect human health and in particular to combat the major cross-border health scourges, and measures to tackle tobacco and alcohol abuse
53.	Art. 169 para 3	Consumer protection
54.	Art. 172 para 1	Trans-European networks
55.	Art. 173 para 3, first subpara	Industry
56.	Art. 175 para 3	Measures in the area of economic and social cohesion
57.	Art. 177 para 1	Structural Funds
58.	Art. 177 para 2	Cohesion Fund
59.	Art. 178 para 1	European Regional Development Fund
60.	Art. 182 para 1, first subpara	Framework Programme for Research
61.	Art. 182 para 5	Implementation of European research area
62.	Art. 183 and Art. 188 para 2	Implementation of the Framework Programme for Research: rules for the participation of undertakings and dissemination of research results
63.	Art. 184 and Art. 188 para 2	Supplementary research programmes for some Member States
64.	Art. 185 and Art. 188 para 2	Participation in research programmes undertaken by several Member States
65.	Art. 189 para 2	Space policy
66.	Art. 192 para 1	Environment (Community measures to achieve environmental objectives except measures of a fiscal nature)
67.	Art. 192 para 3	Environment Action Programme
68.	Art. 194 para 2	Energy, excluding measures of a fiscal nature
69.	Art. 195 para 2	Tourism—measures to complement the action of the Member States in the tourism sector
70.	Art. 196 para 2	Civil protection against natural and man-made disasters
71.	Art. 197 para 2	Administrative cooperation in implementing Union law by Member States
72.	Art. 207 para 2	Commercial policy—implementing measures
73.	Art. 209 para 1	Development cooperation
74.	Art. 212 para 2	Economic, financial and technical cooperation with third countries
75.	Art. 214 para 3	General framework for humanitarian operations
76.	Art. 214 para 5	European Voluntary Humanitarian Aid Corps
77.	Art. 224	Regulations governing political parties and their funding
78.	Art. 257 para 1	Creation of specialised courts
79.	Art. 281 para 2	Modification of Statute of Court of Justice, except Title I and Art. 64

(continued)

Table 1 (continued)

Nr	TFEU	Subject areas
80.	Art. 291 para 3	Procedures for monitoring the exercise of implementing powers
81.	Art. 298 para 2	European Administration
82.	Art. 322 para 1	Adoption of financial rules
83.	Art. 325 para 4	Fight against fraud affecting the Union's financial interests
84.	Art. 336	Staff Regulations of officials and Conditions of Employment of Other Servants of the Union
85.	Art. 338 para 1	Statistics

in different subject areas the option to switch from the SLP to the OLP and provide therefore the so-called bridging clause or passerelle (Borchardt, 2025, para 539; Budischowsky, 2025, para 19; Craig & de Búrca, 2024, p. 165; Palmstorfer, 2025a, para 8).

Art. 48 para 7, second subpara TEU determines in general the following: "Where the (TFEU) provides for legislative acts to be adopted by the Council in accordance with a special legislative procedure, the European Council may adopt a decision allowing for the adoption of such acts in accordance with the ordinary legislative procedure" (Budischowsky, 2025, para 19).

In addition, there are several subject areas with specific bridging clauses, such as judicial cooperation in civil matters (Art. 81 para 3, second subpara TFEU), social policy (Art. 153 para 2, fourth subpara TFEU), environmental policy (Art. 192 para 2, second subpara TFEU) or for provisions of the Treaties in the context of enhanced cooperation (Art. 333 para 2 TFEU) (Palmstorfer, 2025a, para 8).

2.2 *Special Legislative Procedure (SLP)*

According to Art. 289 para 2 TFEU, regulations, directives or decisions can be adopted either (1) by the EP with the participation of the Council[2] or (2) by the Council with the participation of the EP[3] in the course of an SLP. There is no

[2] The SLP subject areas in the TFEU for which the EP requires the Council's participation (consent), are determined in: Art. 223 para 2; Art. 226 para 3; Art. 228 para 4; a special form of SLP in Art. 314 (Böttner, 2022, pp. 70–71; Palmstorfer, 2025a, para 11–12).

[3] The SLP subject areas in the TFEU for which the Council's consultation with the EP is required, are determined in: Art. 21 para 3; Art. 22 para 1; Art. 22 para 2; Art. 23 para 2; Art. 64 para 3; Art. 77 para 3; Art. 81 para 3, first subpara; Art. 83 para 2; Art. 87 para 3, first subpara; Art. 89; Art. 113; Art. 115; Art. 118 para 2; Art. 126 para 14, second subpara; Art. 127 para 6; Art. 153 para 2, third subpara; Art. 182 para 4; Art. 192 para 2, first subpara; Art. 194 para 3; Art. 203; Art. 262; Art. 308 para 3; Art. 311 para 3; Art. 349 para 1 (Böttner, 2022, pp. 72–74; Palmstorfer, 2025a, para 13); the SLP subject areas in the TFEU for which the Council requires the EP's consent, are determined in:

equivalent rule to Art. 294 TFEU for the SLP in the Treaties. Therefore, the individual procedural rules are determined by the provisions of the specific subject areas.

The SLP only applies where the Treaties expressly refer to it (ECJ, 2017, para 62).[4] The reference is typically formulated as follows: "(...) (Council)/(European Parliament), (...) acting in accordance with the special legislative procedure, (...)".

2.3 *Right of Initiative*

According to Art. 289 para 1 TFEU, a proposal from the Commission is required to initiate an OLP.[5] An exception to this general rule is determined in Art. 289 para 4 TFEU. It stipulates that in specific cases—as provided for by the Treaties—legislative acts may be adopted on the initiative of a group of Member States[6] or of the EP,[7] on a recommendation from the European Central Bank[8] (ECB) or at the request of the Court of Justice of the EU[9] (CJEU) or the European Investment Bank[10] (EIB). In such cases, Art. 294 para 2, the second sentence of para 6[11] and para 9, shall not apply.

3 Ordinary Legislative Procedure (OLP)

In Sect. 2, the different types of procedures and their scope of application have been presented in order to understand the variety and complexity of legislative procedures. In the following, the main characteristics and the procedural steps of the OLP will be presented with a focus on the TFEU provisions.

Art. 19 para 1; Art. 25 para 2; Art. 83 para 2; Art. 86 para 1, first subpara; Art. 223 para 1, second subpara; Art. 311 para 4; Art. 312 para 2, first subpara; Art. 352 para 1 (Böttner, 2022, pp. 71–72; Palmstorfer, 2025a, para 14).

[4] For the scope of application of the OLP, see Sect. 2.1, and of the SLP, see Sect. 2.2 (fn).

[5] See Sect. 3.2.2.

[6] See TFEU: Art. 76 point (b) (Böttner, 2022, p. 9 fn 8; Palmstorfer, 2025a, para 26).

[7] See TFEU: Art. 223 para 1; Art. 223 para 2; Art. 226 para 3; Art. 228 para 4 (Böttner, 2022, p. 9 fn 8; Palmstorfer, 2025a, para 27); see also in this context Art. 225 TFEU; Art. 48 para 2 TEU; Art. 48 para 6, first subpara TEU (Palmstorfer, 2025a, para 27).

[8] See TFEU: Art. 129 para 3 (and 4); Art. 219 para 1, first and second subpara, and 2 (Böttner, 2022, p. 9 fn 8; Palmstorfer, 2025a, para 28).

[9] See TFEU: Art. 255 para 2; Art. 257 para 1; Art. 281 para 2 (Böttner, 2022, p. 9 fn 8; Palmstorfer, 2025a, para 29).

[10] See TFEU: Art. 308 para 3 (Böttner, 2022, p. 9 fn 8; Palmstorfer, 2025a, para 30).

[11] See the respective comment of Palmstorfer (2025c, para 85).

3.1 Development of the OLP

The OLP is based on the co-decision procedure, which was established by the Treaty of Maastricht in Art. 189b ex-TEC. The co-decision procedure entered into force on 01.11.1993. The co-decision initially applied mainly to the internal market and some other policies in this context.

Since then, developments took place through the Treaty of Amsterdam (entered into force on 01.05.1999) and the Treaty of Nice (entered into force on 01.02.2003).

The Treaty of Lisbon, which entered into force on 01.12.2009, brought only minor substantial changes in terms of the procedure but gives the EP significantly more power. It also changed the name from co-decision procedure to OLP and extended the scope of application.[12] The new OLP was implemented in Art. 294 TFEU. (Palmstorfer, 2025c, para 11–12)

The OLP is now characterised by the principle of parity between the EP, which is directly elected and represents the EU citizens, and the Council, which represents the governments of the Member States. Legislation can only be adopted with the approval of an identical legal text by both the EP and the Council. (European Parliament, 2025a, p. 6)

3.2 Procedure

The legal text of Art. 294 TFEU determines the procedure of the OLP. It is governed by the procedural[13] principles of (1) conferral (Art. 5 para 1 and 2 TEU), (2) democracy (Art. 9–12 TEU), (3) institutional balance and sincere cooperation (Art. 13 para 2 TEU) and (4) legislative transparency (Art. 15 para 2 and 3 TFEU) (Bauerschmidt, 2021, pp. 213–217).

The main actors in the OLP are the Commission, the EP and the Council which is called the “decision-making triangle”. Furthermore, national parliaments are involved, and certain bodies are consulted. Even though the European Council does not perform legislative functions in the OLP, it provides political guidance. (Bauerschmidt, 2021, p. 217)

Art. 294 TFEU stipulates general procedural rules on the OLP, which are supplemented by the detailed rules of procedure (RoP) of the EP (2025d) and the Council (OJ L 325 (2009/937/EU), 11.12.2009, pp. 35–61).[14]

However, there is the need to further regulate the practical issues of the OLP, which has been done through interinstitutional agreements (IIA) based on Art. 295

[12] See Sect. 2.1.

[13] Regarding the substantive principles for the content of legislative acts, see Bauerschmidt (2021, p. 225).

[14] Due to the focus and the limited scope of this chapter, the RoP of the EP and Council will not be examined here but in other chapters of this handbook.

TFEU (Palmstorfer, 2025d, para 4). The following IIA are particularly relevant for the OLP (European Parliament, 2025a):[15]

- Joint declaration on practical arrangements for the co-decision procedure (Art. 251 of the EC Treaty)[16] (OJ C 145, 30.6.2007, pp. 5–9)
- Framework Agreement on relations between the European Parliament and the European Commission (OJ L 304, 20.11.2010, pp. 47–62)
- Interinstitutional Agreement between the European Parliament, the Council of the European Union and the European Commission on Better Law-Making (OJ L 123, 12.5.2016, pp. 1–14)

3.2.1 OLP: Step by Step

Figure. 1 (flowchart) translates and visualises the procedural steps of the OLP (Art. 294 TFEU).

In practice, the steps are more complex, in particular because of the informal interinstitutional negotiations (trilogues) that are not covered by Fig. 1.[17]

3.2.2 Right of Initiative

The OLP will be initiated by the Commission's proposal (Art. 294 para 2 TFEU),[18] which is adopted by the College of Commissioners after an oral or written procedure. This proposal will simultaneously be sent to the EP and the Council. (European Parliament, 2025a, p. 23)

In case the subject matter is not in the exclusive competence of the EU (Art. 5 para 3 TEU), the Commission will also send the proposal to the national parliaments for the subsidiarity control mechanism[19] (Palmstorfer, 2025c, para 25). Each national parliament has two votes[20] and can issue a reasoned opinion within 8 weeks if it considers the proposal not in compliance with the principle of subsidiarity. The Commission must review the proposal if one third[21] (yellow card) or a majority (orange card) of the national parliaments issue such a reasoned opinion and it has three options to proceed, which are (1) maintaining, (2) amending or (3) withdrawing its proposal. However, if the Commission receives the orange card and decides

[15] Due to the focus and the limited scope of this chapter, the mentioned IIA will not be examined here but in other chapters of this handbook.

[16] There are no primary EU laws that specifically deal with or regulate the trilogues, Borchardt (2025, para 532).

[17] See European Parliament (2025a, pp. 46–47).

[18] See Sect. 2.3.

[19] For further details, see European Parliament (2025a, pp. 20–21) and European Commission (2025).

[20] If the Member State has a bicameral parliamentary system, each chamber has one vote.

[21] The threshold for the subject areas in Art. 76 TFEU is one quarter.

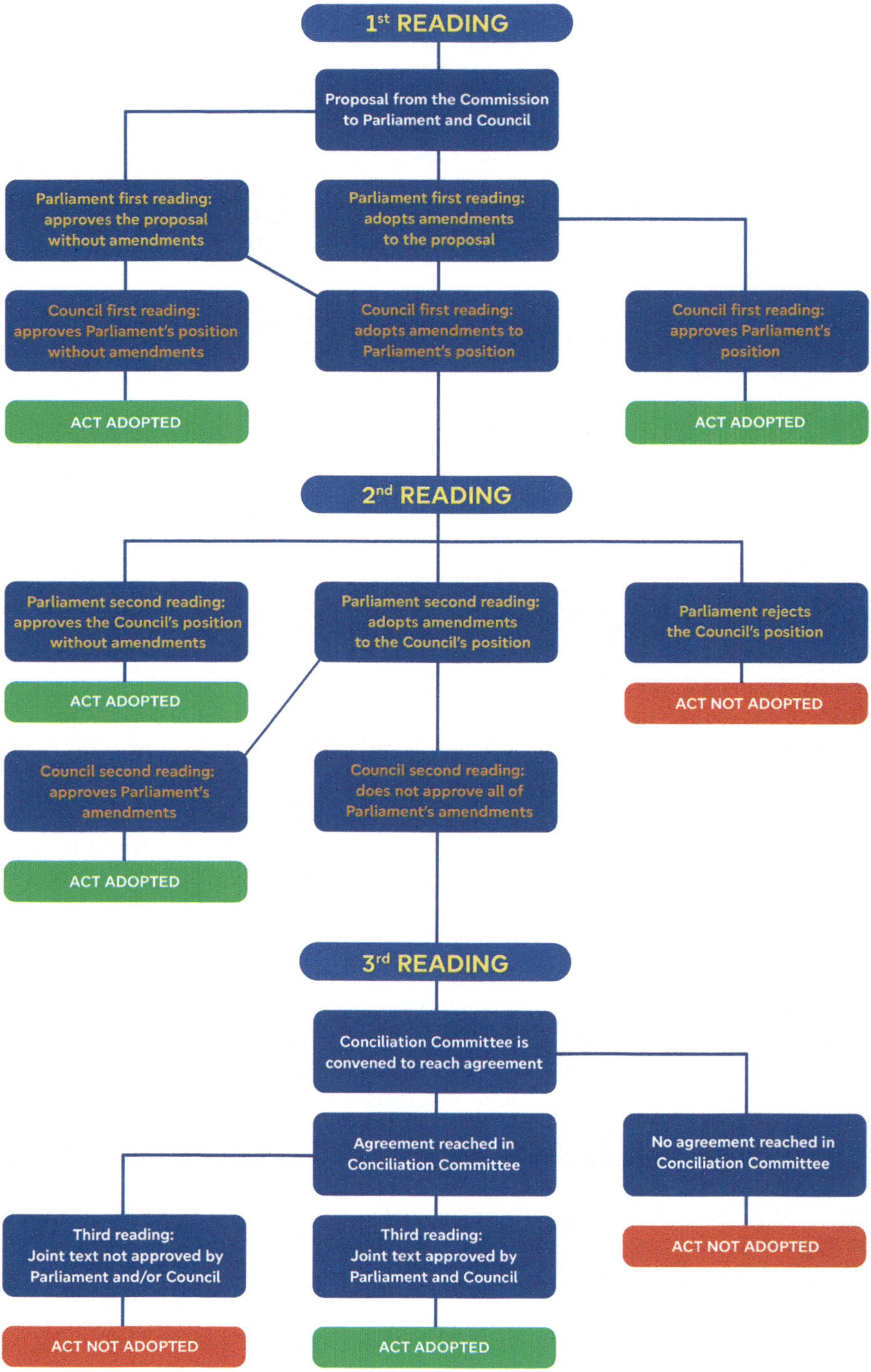

Fig. 1 The OLP—Step by step (European Parliament, 2025c)

to maintain the proposal, this must be justified to the EP and the Council. Subsequently, the EP and the Council vote whether the proposal does comply with the principle of subsidiarity. In cases the two institutions vote for a non-compliance with the required majorities,[22] the proposal will not be further considered. (European Parliament, 2025a, pp. 21–22)

In addition, the Commission also sends the proposal to the European Economic and Social Committee (EESC) and the Committee of the Regions (CoR), if so provided for by the Treaties (European Parliament, 2025a, p. 23).

The Commission can alter its proposal at any time during the procedure, as long as the Council has not acted (Art. 293 Abs. 2 TFEU). This also includes the right to withdraw the proposal[23] (Borchardt, 2025, para 531; Craig & de Búrca, 2024, pp. 161, 165). The Commission regularly exercises this right, with 43 OLP procedures being withdrawn in the 9th legislative term (2019–2024) alone (European Parliament, 2025a, p. 18).

3.2.3 First Reading

After receiving the Commission's proposal, the EP adopts its position and informs the Council accordingly (Art. 294 para 3 TFEU).[24] Most of the Commission proposals will be amended[25] by the EP. In rare cases, the EP adopts the proposal without any amendments or rejects the proposal in its entirety. (Craig & de Búrca, 2024, p. 161; European Parliament, 2025a, p. 26)

The Council can approve the position of the EP (Art. 294 para 4 TFEU).[26] In this case, the legislative act is adopted. If the Council does not approve the position of the EP, it can also adopt a different position[27] at first reading and communicate it to the EP (Art. 294 para 5 TFEU).

In practice, informal interinstitutional negotiations (trilogues[28]) take place before the EP adopts its position at first reading.[29] If an informal agreement is reached, the EP adopts its position accordingly which will be then approved by the Council. Therewith the procedure is concluded at first reading. (European Parliament, 2025a, p. 26)

---

[22] EP: simple majority; Council: 55% majority.

[23] Further details on the right to withdraw a proposal in ECJ (2015, para 83); Palmstorfer (2025b, fn 21–22).

[24] Rules 60–63 of the EP's (2025d) RoP determine the details of the process within the EP at the stage of the first reading, see also European Parliament (2025a, pp. 26–37).

[25] There are no limitations in this regard, Borchardt (2025, para 532).

[26] Further details in the Council Decision of 1 December 2009 adopting the Council's Rules of Procedure (2009/937/EU).

[27] However, the Council's right to amend EC's proposal is limited to a certain extent, see ECJ (2022, para 93).

[28] European Parliament (2025a, pp. 48–49).

[29] See also Borchardt (2025, para 532).

If the EP and the Council do not reach an informal agreement before the EP adopts it first-reading position, the two can still reach an early second-reading agreement. This means that an agreement is found after the EP adopts its first-reading position but before the adoption of the Council's first-reading position. (European Parliament, 2025a, p. 26)

Once the Council has adopted a first-reading position, it will be communicated to the EP with the full reasons. The Commission also fully informs the EP about its position to the Council's first-reading position (Art. 294 para 6 TFEU).

Art. 294 TFEU determines no deadlines or majority rules for the first-reading stage (Borchardt, 2025, para 532; Craig & de Búrca, 2024, p. 161).

3.2.4 Second Reading

If the Council does not approve the first-reading position of the EP, the second-reading phase starts based on the Council's first-reading position.

According to Art. 294 para 7 TFEU, the EP has three options to react on the first-reading position of the Council.[30] Firstly, it can approve the Council's position (or not take a decision[31]) and the act is then adopted based on the wording of the Council's first-reading position. Secondly, the Council's first-reading position can be rejected by a majority of its component members, and the act is then deemed not to be adopted. Thirdly, the EP proposes amendments by a majority of its component members and forwards the amended text to the Council and to the Commission which provides an opinion on the amendments.

Based on Art. 294 para 8 TFEU, the Council can act by a qualified majority[32] and has two options.[33] Firstly, the Council can approve the EP's second-reading position, and the act is adopted. Secondly, the Council can also deny its approval or does not reach the required majority. In such a case, the President of the Council in agreement with the President of the EP convenes a meeting of the Conciliation Committee within 6 weeks.

Art. 294 para 7–8 TFEU determines strict deadlines for the second-reading stage.[34]

[30] Rules 64–70 of the EP's (2025d) RoP determine the details of the process within the EP at the stage of the second reading; see also European Parliament (2025a, pp. 40–42).

[31] The timeframe is 3 months. This has not happened so far, see European Parliament (2025a, p. 40, fn 32).

[32] If the Commission has delivered a negative opinion on the proposed amendments of the EP at the second reading stage, the Council shall act unanimously (Art. 294 para 9 TFEU). A consent of the Commission is not required, see Borchardt (2025, para 533).

[33] Further details in the Council Decision of 1 December 2009 adopting the Council's Rules of Procedure (2009/937/EU).

[34] See also Sect. 3.2.7.

3.2.5 Conciliation

The conciliation phase is regulated in Art. 294 para 10–12 TFEU and is the last chance to come to an agreement on a proposed legislative act (Palmstorfer, 2025c, para 57). The Conciliation Committee (CC) consists of a Council's and an EP's delegation with a number of 27 each. The Council is represented by a minister of each Member State or its representative. The EP delegation consists of 27 members and is chaired by one of the Vice Presidents. In addition, the Commission is represented by the Commissioner who is responsible for the file. (European Parliament, 2025a, p. 43)

The task of the conciliation phase is to reach an agreement, which is a compromise,[35] on a joint text within 6 weeks. This agreement requires a qualified majority of the members of the Council (or their representatives) and a majority of the EP's members (Art. 294 para 10 TFEU).[36]

Since the provided timeframe is relatively short, informal interinstitutional negotiations (trilogues) take place before the CC is formally convened (European Parliament, 2025a, p. 43).

Most of the time, the CC reaches an agreement on a joint text. Since 1999, only two times the CC failed to do so (European Parliament, 2025a, p. 60, fn 47).

The relevance of the conciliation phase has decreased since it was applied in the eighth legislative term for the last time. The vast majority of legislative acts are concluded at the first-reading stage or—much lesser—at the (early) second-reading stage[37] (European Parliament, 2025a, p. 58).

3.2.6 Third Reading

The third reading phase is regulated in Art. 294 para 13 TFEU.[38] According to this provision, the proposed act of the CC shall be deemed to be adopted if the joint text will be approved by the EP and the Council. This requires a majority of the votes cast by the EP and a qualified majority by the Council within 6 weeks. The vote of the two institutions takes place separately and does not allow any further amendments to the joint text of the CC (European Parliament, 2025a, p. 60).

Generally, the EP votes first on the joint text and approves it. The EP however rejected the agreement of the conciliation phase two times. The Council votes

---

[35] See also Borchardt (2025, para 534) and ECJ (2006, para 57–59).

[36] Further details on the process are determined in Rules 76–79 of the EP's (2025d) RoP, see also European Parliament (2025a, p. 43), and in the Council Decision of 1 December 2009 adopting the Council's Rules of Procedure (2009/937/EU).

[37] See also Sect. 4.

[38] Further details on the process are determined in Rules 76–79 of the EP's (2025d) RoP, see also European Parliament (2025a, p. 43), and in the Council Decision of 1 December 2009 adopting the Council's Rules of Procedure (2009/937/EU).

usually after the EP. The Council has never rejected a conciliation's agreement so far. (European Parliament, 2025a, p. 60f, fn 48)

If one of the two institutions fails to agree on the joint text, the proposed act shall be deemed not to have been approved, which brings the OLP to an end. The only option to retry the already proposed issue is to restart the OLP by the Commission in the form of a new proposal. (Palmstorfer, 2025c, para 78)

3.2.7 Deadlines

Art. 294 TFEU determines the deadlines for the OLP. Through an initiative of the respective institution, the 3-month-deadline(s) can be extended by 1 month, and the 6-weeks-deadline(s) can be extended by 2 weeks.[39] The extension does not require the approval of the other institution (Palmstorfer, 2025c, para 79).

3.3 Signing and Publication

Once the provisional agreement has been reached by the respective institutions, the text and the specific wording of this agreement is legal-linguistically finalised, before it is subject to the adoption in plenary (European Parliament, 2025a, p. 62).

After the EP and the Council have formally adopted the agreement at first, second or third reading, the President of the EP and a representative of the rotating presidency of the Council sign the legislative act, as laid out in Art. 297 para 1, first subpara TFEU (European Parliament, 2025a, p. 63).

Once the signing process has been finished, the legislative act will be published in the Official Journal of the European Union (OJ).[40] It needs to be noted that publication is a strict prerequisite for the applicability of the legislation.[41] Legal acts enter into force on the 20th day following their publication, unless agreed otherwise (Art. 297 para 1, third subpara TFEU). (European Parliament, 2025a, p. 64)

4 Comments on the OLP from a Legal Perspective

It can be said that—from a legal perspective—the Commission, the EP and the Council play an equally important role at different levels in the OLP. The Commission has the important right of initiative and is more active at the beginning of the

[39] The way how the deadlines are calculated, in particular, when it starts, is discussed in the literature, such as in Palmstorfer (2025c, para 80–84).

[40] Member States's laws on publication also need to be considered; for Austria, see Stocker and Vcelouch (2025, para 53–59).

[41] See ECJ (2007, 2009).

legislative process, while the EP and the Council become active afterwards in the adoption process, which is from the first reading onwards.

In general, it can be noted that Art. 294 TFEU as the main provision on the OLP contains four phases, which are first reading,[42] second reading,[43] conciliation[44] and third reading.[45] The reader of Art. 294 TFEU and of this chapter could get the impression that all phases are equally relevant or applied in practice, since the legal text does not distinguish or provide any indicators in that respect. In fact, however, this is not the case and has changed over time.

At this point it needs to be highlighted that not every initiative of a legislative act undergoes all OLP stages in order to become a law (Craig & de Búrca, 2024, p. 162). As already outlined, an agreement (or disagreement) can be reached already in the course of the first or second reading. The numbers in Fig. 2 show at which stage legislative acts were concluded between the fifth and the ninth legislative term.

A trend can be derived from the presented numbers in Fig. 2, namely a shift from an OLP that applies more or all phases regularly towards an OLP that predominantly finishes at the first-reading stage.[46] The reasons for this fact are diverse and result from many actions taken by the EP and the Council in the past, in particular informal interinstitutional negotiations (trilogues) (Cabral, 2020, p. 167). However, this practice of trilogues is also critically viewed in the light of a transparent and democratic lawmaking process (Palmstorfer, 2025c, para 86),[47] in particular because (1) decisions/compromises are being made by a small group, (2) lack of transparency,[48] (3) lack of detailed rules on the side of the Commission and the Council (Craig & de Búrca, 2024, p. 164). To overcome this criticism, the involved institutions have set specific steps.[49]

Considering the success rate of laws enacted under the OLP procedure, it can be concluded that only a few of them were nullified in the context of annulment proceeding or preliminary ruling proceeding. Taking the significant number of cases into consideration, it can be ascertained that the few cases of nullification are an indicator for the success and the functionality of the OLP. (Palmstorfer, 2025c, para 87)

Looking ahead, two main areas may be affected by future changes in the treaties, namely the question of (1) who plays what kind of role in the legislative process (stakeholder) and (2) how the process is structured and organised (procedural rules). Looking at the numbers in Fig. 2, it can be assumed that there will be at least

---

[42] See Sect. 3.2.3.

[43] See Sect. 3.2.4.

[44] See Sect. 3.2.5.

[45] See Sect. 3.2.6.

[46] See also European Parliament (2024).

[47] See also Dauner and Sohn (2015) and Craig and de Búrca (2024, pp. 163–164); for a positive critique, see Bauerschmidt (2021, pp. 224–225).

[48] See GC (2018).

[49] See, i.e., Rules 71–75 of the EP's (2025d) RoP; European Parliament (2025a, pp. 56–57).

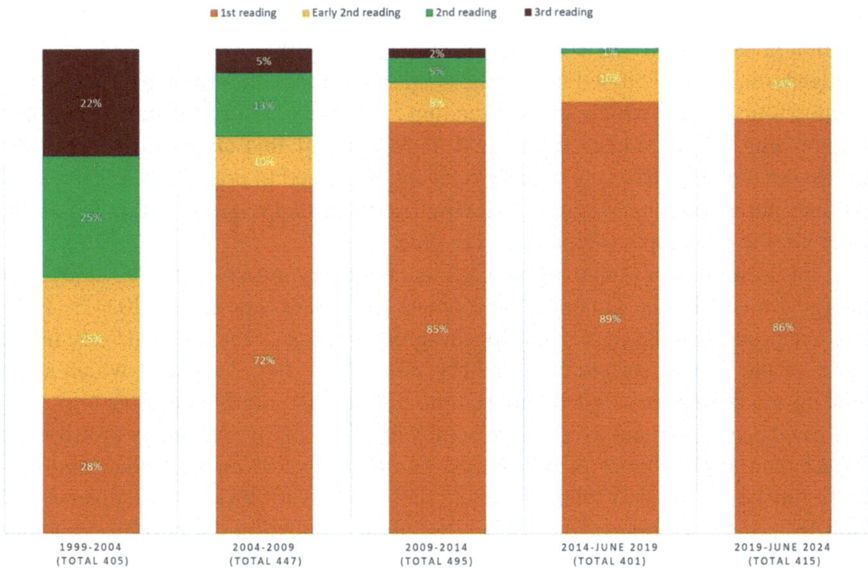

Fig. 2 Activity report—Stage of adoption of OLP files since the fifth legislative term (European Parliament, 2024, p. 24)

adjustments to the procedural rules if it turns out that the second reading, conciliation or third reading become more and more obsolete. Furthermore, it cannot be ruled out that informal interinstitutional negotiations (trilogues) will also be codified in future treaties.

References

Bauerschmidt, J. (2021). The basic principles of the European Union's ordinary legislative procedure. *ERA Forum, 22*(2), 211–229. https://doi.org/10.1007/s12027-021-00671-9

Borchardt, K.-D. (2025). *Die rechtlichen Grundlagen der Europäischen Union: Eine systematische Darstellung für Studium und Praxis* (8. überarbeitete Auflage). UTB Rechtswissenschaften: Vol. 1669. Facultas Verlags- und Buchhandels AG.

Böttner, R. (2022). *Special legislative procedures in the Treaties: Institutional balance and sincere cooperation*. Study requested by the AFCO Committee. Policy Department for Citizens' Rights and Constitutional Affairs, Directorate-General for Internal Policies. https://doi.org/10.2861/004330

Budischowsky, J. (2025). Art. 48 EUV. In *EUV AEUV online—Kommentar zu EUV und AEUV*. Manz Verlag.

Cabral, T. S. (2020). A short guide to the legislative procedure in the European Union. *UNIO—EU Law Journal, 6*(1), 161–180. https://doi.org/10.21814/unio.6.1.2711

Consolidated versions of the Treaty on European Union and the Treaty on the Functioning of the European Union; Consolidated version of the Treaty on European Union; Consolidated version of the Treaty on the Functioning of the European Union Protocols Annexes to the Treaty on the Functioning of the European Union Declarations annexed to the Final Act of the Intergovernmental Conference which adopted the Treaty of Lisbon, signed on 13 December 2007 Tables of equivalences, OJ C 202, 7.6.2016, pp. 1–388. Retrieved from https://eur-lex.europa.eu/legal-content/EN/TXT/?uri=oj:JOC_2016_202_R_0001

Council Decision of 1 December 2009 adopting the Council's Rules of Procedure (2009/937/EU), OJ L 325, 11.12.2009, pp. 35–61. Retrieved from https://eur-lex.europa.eu/legal-content/EN/TXT/PDF/?uri=OJ:JOL_2009_325_R_0035_01

Craig, P. P., & de Búrca, G. (2024). *EU law: Text, cases, and materials* (Eighth edition). Oxford University Press.

Dauner, M., & Sohn, K.-D. (2015). *Gesetzgebung im Trilog: Das Ende der transparenten repräsentativen Demokratie?* cep|Centrum für Europäische Politik. Retrieved from https://www.cep.eu/fileadmin/user_upload/cep.eu/Studien/cepInput_Trilog/cepInput_Gesetzgebung_im_Trilog.pdf

ECJ, C-344/04, IATA and ELFAA (European Court of Justice). (2006). Retrieved from https://curia.europa.eu/juris/showPdf.jsf?text=&docid=57285&pageIndex=0&doclang=EN&mode=lst&dir=&occ=first&part=1&cid=1609496

ECJ, C-161/06, Skoma-Lux sro v Celní ředitelství Olomouc (European Court of Justice). (2007). Retrieved from https://curia.europa.eu/juris/showPdf.jsf?text=&docid=71342&pageIndex=0&doclang=EN&mode=lst&dir=&occ=first&part=1&cid=342817; https://eur-lex.europa.eu/legal-content/EN/TXT/PDF/?uri=CELEX:62006CJ0161

ECJ, C-345/06, Gottfried Heinrich (European Court of Justice). (2009). Retrieved from https://curia.europa.eu/juris/document/document.jsf?text=&docid=77515&pageIndex=0&doclang=EN&mode=lst&dir=&occ=first&part=1&cid=1612648

ECJ, C-409/13, Council v EU Commission (European Court of Justice). (2015). Retrieved from https://curia.europa.eu/juris/document/document.jsf?text=&docid=163659&pageIndex=0&doclang=EN&mode=lst&dir=&occ=first&part=1&cid=249604

ECJ, C-643/15 and C-647/15, Slovak Republick and Hungary v Council (European Court of Justice). (2017). Retrieved from https://curia.europa.eu/juris/document/document.jsf;jsessionid=421633C14B28CD5C9EA08EE676EDD6C9?text=&docid=194081&pageIndex=0&doclang=EN&mode=req&dir=&occ=first&part=1&cid=1803170

ECJ, C-24/20, EU Commission v Council (European Court of Justice). (2022). Retrieved from https://curia.europa.eu/juris/document/document.jsf;jsessionid=5C0727410F5BF56307320578CE76490C?text=&docid=268058&pageIndex=0&doclang=EN&mode=lst&dir=&occ=first&part=1&cid=243620

European Commission. (2025). *Subsidiarity control mechanism*. Retrieved from https://commission.europa.eu/law/law-making-process/adopting-eu-law/relations-national-parliaments/subsidiarity-control-mechanism_en

European Parliament. (2024). *Activity Report: Developments and trends in the ordinary legislative procedure, 2 July 2019–15 July 2024*. Retrieved from https://www.europarl.europa.eu/cmsdata/289669/1305846_EN.pdf

European Parliament. (2025a). *Handbook on the Ordinary Legislative Procedure: A guide to how the European Parliament co-legislates*. Retrieved from https://www.europarl.europa.eu/cmsdata/293152/Handbook%20on%20the%20Ordinary%20legislative%20procedure_January%202025.pdf

European Parliament. (2025b). *List—Scope of application OLP*. Retrieved from https://www.europarl.europa.eu/cmsdata/198103/List_of_legal_bases.pdf

European Parliament. (2025c). *The Ordinary Legislative Procedure: Step by step*. Retrieved from https://www.europarl.europa.eu/cmsdata/293607/Diagram.pdf

European Parliament. (2025d). *Rules of procedure: 10th parliamentary term*. Retrieved from https://www.europarl.europa.eu/doceo/document/RULES-10-2025-01-20-TOC_EN.html

Framework Agreement on relations between the European Parliament and the European Commission, OJ L 304, 20.11.2010, pp. 47–62. Retrieved from https://eur-lex.europa.eu/legal-content/EN/TXT/PDF/?uri=CELEX:32010Q1120(01)

GC, T-540/15, Emilio De Capitani v EU Parliament (General Court of the EU). (2018). Retrieved from https://curia.europa.eu/juris/document/document.jsf?text=&docid=200551&pageIndex=0&doclang=DE&mode=lst&dir=&occ=first&part=1&cid=270289

Interinstitutional Agreement between the European Parliament, the Council of the European Union and the European Commission on Better Law-Making, OJ L 123, 12.5.2016, pp. 1–14. Retrieved from https://eur-lex.europa.eu/legal-content/EN/TXT/PDF/?uri=OJ:L:2016:123:FULL

Joint declaration on practical arrangements for the codecision procedure (Art. 251 of the EC Treaty), OJ C 145, 30.6.2007, pp. 5–9. Retrieved from https://eur-lex.europa.eu/legal-content/EN/TXT/PDF/?uri=CELEX:32007C0630(01)

Palmstorfer, R. (2025a). Art 289 AEUV. In *EUV AEUV online—Kommentar zu EUV und AEUV.* Manz Verlag.

Palmstorfer, R. (2025b). Art 293 AUEV. In *EUV AEUV online—Kommentar zu EUV und AEUV*. Manz Verlag.

Palmstorfer, R. (2025c). Art 294 AUEV. In *EUV AEUV online—Kommentar zu EUV und AEUV*. Manz Verlag.

Palmstorfer, R. (2025d). Art 295 AUEV. In *EUV AEUV online—Kommentar zu EUV und AEUV*. Manz Verlag.

Stocker, E., & Vcelouch, P. (2025). Art 297 AUEV. In *EUV AEUV online—Kommentar zu EUV und AEUV*. Manz Verlag.

Further Reading

Borchardt, K.-D. (2025). *Die rechtlichen Grundlagen der Europäischen Union: Eine systematische Darstellung für Studium und Praxis* (8. überarbeitete Auflage). UTB Rechtswissenschaften: Vol. 1669. Facultas Verlags- und Buchhandels AG.

Cabral, T. S. (2020). A short guide to the legislative procedure in the European Union. *UNIO—EU Law Journal, 6*(1), 161–180. https://doi.org/10.21814/unio.6.1.2711

Craig, P. P., & de Búrca, G. (2024). *EU law: Text, cases, and materials* (Eighth edition). Oxford University Press.

European Parliament. (2024). *Activity report: Developments and trends in the ordinary legislative procedure, 2 July 2019–15 July 2024*. Retrieved from https://www.europarl.europa.eu/cmsdata/289669/1305846_EN.pdf

European Parliament. (2025). *Handbook on the Ordinary Legislative Procedure: A guide to how the European Parliament co-legislates*. Retrieved from https://www.europarl.europa.eu/cmsdata/293152/Handbook%20on%20the%20Ordinary%20legislative%20procedure_January%202025.pdf

Useful Links

CJEU: https://curia.europa.eu/jcms/jcms/j_6/en/

Council: https://www.consilium.europa.eu/en/council-eu/decision-making/ordinary-legislative-procedure/

EU Official Journal: https://eur-lex.europa.eu/oj/direct-access.html?locale=en

EU Parliament: https://www.europarl.europa.eu/olp/en/home

European Law: https://eur-lex.europa.eu/homepage.html?locale=en

Martin Wagner is Head of the Institute of Law at the University of Applied Sciences Wiener Neustadt and a lecturer in higher education. He also passed the Austrian bar exam and works at a commercial law firm in Vienna. In addition to European law, his academic and practical expertise lies in civil, real estate, corporate and higher education law.

Initiating EU Legislation: The European Commission

Inside the Black Box: Agenda-Setting and Internal Coordination in the European Commission

Anna Guerri and Camilla Mariotto

Abstract This chapter examines the internal dynamics underlying the European Commission's agenda-setting power within the European Union's legislative process. While the Commission enjoys a formal first-mover advantage through its exclusive right of legislative initiative, its capacity to shape policy outcomes depends on political, supranational, and bureaucratic factors. The analysis opens the "black box" of the Commission by detailing how legislative proposals emerge from multi-layered decision-making procedures involving the College of Commissioners, the Secretariat-General, and the Directorates-General (DGs). It traces how political priorities, articulated through the Annual Work Programme, are transformed into concrete legislative initiatives through coordination mechanisms, interservice consultations, and hierarchical oversight. This chapter highlights the hybrid nature of the Commission, which combines collective political responsibility with DGs' technical expertise, makes coordination indispensable for coherence, policy effectiveness, and ultimately legislative success.

Keywords Agenda-setting power · European Commission · Directorates-General · Presidentialisation · Rules of procedures · Coordination · Policy preparation

1 Introduction

The European Commission (Commission) occupies a central position in the political system of the European Union (EU). It holds the exclusive right of legislative initiative and serves as arbiter of the entire legislative process, thereby shaping the policy space in which interinstitutional negotiations unfold, even if it cannot ultimately determine outcomes. Through this agenda-setting power, the Commission

A. Guerri (✉) · C. Mariotto (✉)
Department of Political Science, University of Innsbruck, Innsbruck, Austria
e-mail: camilla.mariotto@uibk.ac.at

G. Füricht-Fiegl et al. (eds.), *Handbook on EU Law-making*, Professional Practice in Governance and Public Organizations, https://doi.org/10.1007/978-3-032-16559-6_3

influences how issues are defined, which alternatives are considered, and which Directorates-General (DGs) are involved, making it a key institutional actor in EU policymaking (Senninger et al., 2021; Bauerschmidt, 2021).

The scope of its tasks renders the Commission an exceptionally complex organisation that must combine political priorities with technical expertise. This is also reflected in its hybrid nature as both a central source of political leadership (Peterson, 2008) and the EU's largest administration. Politically, the College of Commissioners, formally a body of equals, decides by majority but generally strives for consensus. Administratively, 50 DGs and horizontal services provide the technical expertise and coordination necessary to translate political priorities into policy output. This dual structure, combining collective political responsibility with DGs' technical expertise, makes coordination indispensable for coherence, policy effectiveness, and ultimately legislative success (Cini, 2002; Senninger et al., 2021; Bauer et al., 2023).

The Commission's agenda-setting power has attracted sustained scholarly attention from organisational, institutional, and policy-oriented perspectives. One interpretation of this broad scholarship emphasises its political entrepreneurship: the Commission raises awareness of new issues, builds coalitions among national governments and stakeholders, and seeks to "upgrade the common interest", thereby deepening European integration (Cini, 2002; Hartlapp et al., 2013; Nugent & Rhinard, 2016, 2019). More recent work extends this perspective by analysing how other actors, such as the European Council through summit conclusions (Moloney & Princen, 2024; Reh et al., 2013) or organised interests through lobbying (Greenwood, 2011), also shape the EU's legislative agenda.

By contrast, this chapter builds upon a much more institutionalist interpretation that examines agenda-setting as a formal process embedded in the EU's legislative procedures, and, in particular, in the procedural rules governing the introduction, discussion, and adoption of legislative initiatives. This strand of the literature, mostly regarding spatial formal models (i.e. Tsebelis & Garrett, 2000; Crombez & Vangerven, 2014), suggests that the Commission has a first-mover advantage derived from its legislative agenda-setting power. Following Crombez (1996), the Commission has the authority to select and propose a policy from a set of feasible possibilities closest to its own preferences, even without the power of gatekeeping. Yet this power remains limited, as both the Council, the European Parliament (EP), and, since the Lisbon Treaty, citizens through the European Citizens' Initiative can request new legislation. Even within this constrained model, scholars continue to recognise the Commission's centrality in shaping EU policy outcomes (Pollack, 2003; Rasmussen, 2007; Bailer, 2014).

Despite this extensive literature, the Commission's internal decision-making structures remain comparatively underexplored, as systematic studies on its intra-organisational dynamics are still scarce. Existing research has examined the role of the president, individual commissioners, and the administrative services (Peterson & Pollack, 2004; Egeberg, 2012; Bauer, 2006), yet scholars consistently note that internal processes remain "obscure" (Kassim et al., 2017, p. 2; see also Egeberg, 2012; Hartlapp et al., 2013; Wille, 2013; Bürgin, 2018). More recent work has begun to illuminate how leadership, coordination mechanisms, and managerial reforms influence the Commission's internal coherence and agenda-setting capacity.

Building on these insights, this chapter seeks to open the "black box" of the Commission's agenda-setting power by examining how its internal coordination mechanisms support the political layer in the formulation of legislative initiatives. To this end, this chapter will examine the internal decision-making procedures of the Commission, detailing how the College of Commissioners and the administrative hierarchy coordinate. The following section analyses how political priorities are translated into legislative proposals, assessing the conditions under which the Commission succeeds in steering the EU's legislative agenda and the limits imposed by the Council and the EP. The final section shifts the focus to the bureaucratic level, exploring how DGs exercise differentiated agenda-setting capacities within the Commission's internal coordination framework. Together, this chapter illustrates that the Commission's agenda-setting power is neither purely political nor purely technical, but emerges from the interaction between hierarchical control, bureaucratic expertise, and interinstitutional negotiation.

2 The Policy Preparation Inside the European Commission

Understanding the Commission's internal decision-making procedures is essential to grasping its agenda-setting power. Although the College of Commissioners formally holds the right of initiative, the translation of political priorities into legislative proposals depends on a multilayered political and administrative process designed to ensure coherence and collective responsibility.

The College of Commissioners, composed of 27 members and chaired by the president, meets weekly—typically on Wednesdays. Each Commissioner is assigned a specific portfolio, the allocation of which reflects both political considerations and individual expertise (Franchino, 2009). The decision to formally propose a legislative act is taken collectively, ideally by consensus. Any commissioner may, however, request a vote. Decisions require an absolute majority, with the president casting the deciding vote in the event of a tie. Abstentions and absences count as negative votes. The ordinary voting rule—the *oral procedure*—occurs by a show of hands, without secret ballots. While the results are confidential, individual votes are recorded in the College minutes. This procedure implies open political deliberation among commissioners and signals a significant level of unresolved internal conflict when votes occur. Nevertheless, under the principle of collegial responsibility, commissioners in the minority are bound to defend the majority position once a decision is taken. Preparatory coordination unfolds in three stages: Special Chefs' meetings among sectoral cabinet members; the weekly Heads of Cabinet meeting (the "Hebdo"), chaired by the Secretariat-General (SG); and finally, the College meeting itself (Hartlapp et al., 2014; Blom-Hansen et al., 2025). This tiered system acts as a clearinghouse to reconcile conflicts before they reach the College, reinforcing the president's capacity—via the SG—to align divergent views and control the policy pipeline (Kassim et al., 2013; Hartlapp et al., 2014).

Three additional modes of decision-making exist. The *written procedure*, initiated by the SG at the request of one or more commissioners, is mainly used for routine administrative matters. Cabinets receive the proposal and may object within a short deadline; if no objections are raised, the measure is deemed adopted. The *empowerment procedure*, by contrast, delegates decision-making authority to individual commissioners in specific policy domains—most prominently agriculture and competition, including anti-dumping cases (Sabathil et al., 2008, p. 39). Although this delegation streamlines decisions, other commissioners may challenge them to safeguard collective responsibility. Finally, under the *delegation procedure*, the College transfers authority to one or more DGs or Heads of Service, allowing for administrative decisions at the DG level.[1]

Before reaching the political level, most legislative work is prepared by the administration through specialised coordinating units. The SG, akin to a prime minister's office but with a more interventionist coordination role, oversees politically salient initiatives and reports directly to the president (Kassim, 2006). Complementary oversight is provided by the Legal Service, DG Budget, and DG Economic and Financial Affairs, which review proposals to ensure legal, financial, and economic consistency (Blom-Hansen et al., 2025).

Over the past two decades, this coordination system has evolved through what scholars describe as the *presidentialisation* of the Commission (Becker et al., 2016; Kassim et al., 2017).[2] Administratively, this process is most evident in the strengthened role of the SG, which has evolved from a guardian of collegiality into a personal service of the presidency. Expanded staff and mandate have enhanced its capacity to steer DG activities and monitor policy coherence (Kassim et al., 2013; Bürgin, 2020). The newly created Regulatory Scrutiny Board (RSB), a semi-independent body that reviews impact assessments, has an effective veto power over proposals, reinforcing hierarchical control over DGs (Blom-Hansen et al., 2025).

These institutional transformations have reshaped internal policymaking. DGs remain the main drivers of legislative drafting, cultivating expertise and stakeholder networks to build the legitimacy of proposals (Hartlapp et al., 2014). Yet their autonomy is increasingly circumscribed by mechanisms of coordination and hierarchical review (Hartlapp et al., 2014; Hustedt & Seyfried, 2016; Candel et al., 2023; Marques et al., 2025).

[1] The procedures are defined by Chapter III "Decision-making procedure" of the Commission Decision (EU) 2024/3080 establishing the Rules of Procedure of the Commission and Amending Decision C(2000) 3614.

[2] Incremental treaty reforms gradually expanded the presidential authority, granting veto rights over national nominees, discretion in portfolio allocation, and stronger agenda-setting powers. Building on these institutional changes, successive presidents, from Prodi and Barroso to Juncker and von der Leyen, constructed internal hierarchies within the College through the creation of executive and standard vice-presidential tiers tasked with coordinating cross-sectoral priorities (Kassim et al., 2013; Hartlapp et al., 2013; Becker et al., 2016; Bürgin, 2020; Bauer et al., 2023).

3 How Policy Priorities Turn into Legislative Proposals

Having outlined the Commission's internal procedures, we now turn to how political priorities are translated into concrete legislative initiatives. Each year, the president and the College of Commissioners set the overall policy agenda through the Annual Work Programme (AWP), which identifies the key reforms the Commission plans to propose over the following 12–18 months in line with the president's political guidelines. The SG, working closely with commissioners, their DGs, and the president's cabinet, coordinates this process. In preparing the AWP, the Commission takes into account the priorities of both the EP and the Council. Despite the AWP listing the most salient reforms, the Commission also initiates numerous additional legislative acts throughout the year.

Empirically, the AWP has proven to be a reliable indicator of the Commission's legislative output. Osnabrügge (2015) finds that the Commission implements more than 94% of its AWP, with 76% of proposals formally introduced within the deadline. This Commission's *technical* capacity, however, is more likely when the EP is not a co-legislator, when national administrations are not involved in implementation (as with directives), and when the planning horizon extends to 18 months.

Yet the Commission's agenda-setting influence is neither automatic nor unconstrained. Kreppel and Oztas (2017) have pointed out, instead, that the Commission falls short in taking advantage effectively of its *political* influence at the agenda-setting stage. They show that the Commission is not entirely free to determine which policy areas receive legislative attention, and that its success rate in securing the adoption of its proposals (67%) is lower than that of national governments (around 80%).

Other studies confirm that the Commission's legislative success varies according to the proposal characteristics, institutional dynamics, and internal coordination mechanisms. Success tends to decline as policy complexity increases (Burns, 2004; Rauh, 2020), when the EP is deeply involved (Rauh, 2020; Thomson & Hosli, 2006), or when decisions within the College are more contested, i.e. through oral procedure (Rauh, 2020; Bickerton et al., 2015; Rasmussen, 2012). Uncertainty about the preferences of the Council or the EP, given by procedural reforms or national elections, also increases the likelihood that proposals are withdrawn or fail (Boranbay-Akan et al., 2017). Conversely, when the Commission's proposals succeed, this may reflect strategic alignment or even fortuitous coincidence rather than autonomous agenda control. As Thomson (2011, p. 19) aptly notes, success can be "an expression of luck rather than power". Indeed, Oztas and Kreppel (2022) find that the Commission most often achieves its objectives when its preferences align, fortuitously or strategically, with those of other institutions such as the EP, the Council, and the European Council.

Still, these findings do not necessarily undermine the Commission's legitimacy as an agenda-setter. The fact that it is most successful when its initiatives reflect the political priorities of democratically elected institutions offers solace, as it can be seen as evidence of responsiveness rather than weakness. Studies also suggest that the College pays attention to issues salient to citizens and civil society actors, prioritising legislative files that resonate with public opinion or NGO activity (Giurcanu & Kostadinova, 2022; Koop et al., 2022). Thus, while the Commission formally controls the legislative pipeline, its practical success depends on the alignment of preferences across institutions and on its own internal coordination capacities.

However, most of the literature reviewed so far treats the Commission as a unitary actor. Relaxing this assumption reveals a more nuanced and complex picture. Rauh (2020) shows that coordination dynamics among DGs and services vary considerably, and that more experienced DGs are better able to anticipate which policies the co-legislators will accept. As a result, their drafts tend to undergo fewer textual changes during the legislative process, indicating a higher degree of the proposal's success. The next section explores how these internally differentiated agenda-setters coordinate their efforts and shape the preparation of legislative proposals within the Commission.

4 Institutional Constraints and Strategic Agency

The DGs are pivotal in preparing policy proposals, with their influence shaped by institutional position, coordination rules, and the strategic use of procedural opportunities (Hartlapp et al., 2013, 2014). Although most initiatives originate within the DGs, their autonomy is increasingly constrained by the Secretariat-General (SG), which acts as administrative gatekeeper and designates the lead DG. By steering this allocation process, the SG aligns initiatives with the College's political agenda while shaping the bureaucratic space within which DGs exercise their agency (Hartlapp et al., 2014).

Once the lead responsibility has been assigned, the lead DG gains significant procedural control and informational leverage over the subsequent drafting process. By determining when and how to involve other DGs, the lead DG can strategically delay or limit internal consultation to pre-empt opposition. Once a legislative draft is established, it becomes the de facto foundation for later negotiations, granting the lead DG strong agenda-setting power. During the mandatory horizontal coordination mechanism, the so-called interservice consultation (ISC), these advantages persist. The limited time and personnel available reduce other DGs' power to provide substantive comments and suggest changes to the draft legislation (Hartlapp et al., 2013; Princen et al., 2025). When the ISC is completed, the lead DG can ultimately and strategically decide if such opinions should be incorporated at the administrative stage or escalated to the political level. The (revised) draft is then discussed by the cabinet of commissioners and finally, in the case of politically salient and controversial files, the College of Commissioners itself. Consequently, while coordination mechanisms impose formal obligations of consultation, they simultaneously create opportunities for strategic agency. A skillful lead DG can exploit procedural rules to advance preferred outcomes and anticipate at which decision-making level a controversial initiative stands the best chance of success (Hartlapp et al., 2014).

Even in the subsequent political coordination process, the substance of proposals largely reflects the lead DG's original draft, as later amendments tend to accommodate rather than weaken the core content.

Several factors shape bargaining among DGs during policy preparation: alignment with horizontal services and other DGs, the policy area's competences, the lead DG's seniority, and interinstitutional dynamics. Horizontal services—the SG, Legal Service, and DG Budget—act as institutional counterweights, endowed with internal veto powers to ensure legal, financial, and procedural coherence (Hartlapp et al., 2014). Their endorsement signals technical robustness, while opposition can block a proposal. DGs that secure their support, or at least neutrality, gain a clear advantage. Additionally, the lead DG can build coalitions with other DGs in order to contrast presidential or horizontal intervention (Hartlapp et al., 2014).

The lead DG's influence also depends on the degree of supranational competence in its policy domain, as areas governed by qualified majority voting offer greater leverage in interinstitutional negotiations. Established DGs with long legislative experience, such as competition or environment, further benefit from stakeholder networks and technical expertise. Finally, anticipation of member state reactions, the preferences of the Council or EP, and interactions with organised interests or epistemic communities influence DGs' internal bargaining strategies (Hartlapp et al., 2014). Thus, they operate not as isolated units but as actors embedded in multi-level governance networks, balancing internal coordination with external political expectations.

5 Conclusions

This chapter has shown that the Commission's agenda-setting power remains central yet conditional within the EU's legislative process. While formal models highlight its first-mover advantage, empirical research reveals that legislative success depends less on unilateral initiative than on the Commission's capacity to anticipate and align with the preferences of the Council and the EP. Proposals advance most successfully when institutional uncertainty is low, the policy is simple, the College's decisions are less contested, and its preferences coincide—strategically or fortuitously—with those of the co-legislators. Coordination dynamics among DGs and services further shape this process: experienced DGs are better able to anticipate co-legislators' acceptance and secure proposals with minimal alteration, thus retaining significant influence despite growing hierarchical oversight by the SG. By opening the "black box" of internal coordination, this chapter has highlighted how political leadership, bureaucratic expertise, and procedural rules jointly shape the EU's legislative agenda.

In sum, the Commission's agenda-setting reflects a hybrid form of power—politically constrained yet strategically adaptive—whose effectiveness lies not in imposing outcomes but in crafting proposals that resonate with the evolving preferences of co-legislators. At the same time, the Commission must also balance its dual role as a political actor, engaging with democratically elected institutions and public expectations, while operating within a dense bureaucratic coordination system that can displace internal political deliberation. This enduring tension between technocratic governance and democratic accountability lies at the core of the Commission's agenda-setting power, shaping both its institutional legitimacy and its capacity to steer the Union's policy agenda.

References

Bailer, S. (2014). An agent dependent on the EU member states? The determinants of the European Commission's legislative success in the European Union. *Journal of European Integration, 36*(1), 37–53. https://doi.org/10.1080/07036337.2013.809342

Bauer, M. W. (2006). Co-managing programme implementation: Conceptualizing the European Commission's role in policy execution. *Journal of European Public Policy, 13*(5), 717–735. https://doi.org/10.1080/13501760600808592

Bauer, M. W., Kassim, H., & Connolly, S. (2023). The quiet transformation of the EU Commission cabinet system. *Journal of European Public Policy, 30*(2), 354–374. https://doi.org/10.1080/13501763.2021.2003423

Bauerschmidt, J. (2021). The basic principles of the European Union's ordinary legislative procedure. *ERA Forum, 22*(2), 211–229. https://doi.org/10.1007/s12027-021-00671-9

Becker, S., Bauer, M. W., Connolly, S., & Kassim, H. (2016). The Commission: Boxed in and constrained, but still an engine of integration. *West European Politics, 39*(5), 1011–1031. https://doi.org/10.1080/01402382.2016.1181870

Bickerton, C. J., Hodson, D., & Puetter, U. (2015). The New Intergovernmentalism: European Integration in the Post-Maastricht Era: The new intergovernmentalism. *Journal of Common Market Studies, 53*(4), 703–722. https://doi.org/10.1111/jcms.12212

Blom-Hansen, J., Skorkjær Binderkrantz, A., Bækgaard, M., Finke, D., Senninger, R., & Serritzlew, S. (2025). *Policy preparation inside the European Commission* (1.1). Oxford University Press. https://doi.org/10.1093/9780198907961.001.0001

Boranbay-Akan, S., König, T., & Osnabrügge, M. (2017). The imperfect agenda-setter: Why do legislative proposals fail in the EU decision-making process? *European Union Politics, 18*(2), 168–187. https://doi.org/10.1177/1465116516674338

Bürgin, A. (2018). Intra- and inter-institutional leadership of the European Commission President: An assessment of Juncker's organizational reforms. *JCMS: Journal of Common Market Studies, 56*(4), 837–853. https://doi.org/10.1111/jcms.12648

Bürgin, A. (2020). The impact of Juncker's reorganization of the European Commission on the internal policy-making process: Evidence from the Energy Union project. *Public Administration, 98*(2), 378–391. https://doi.org/10.1111/padm.12388

Burns, C. (2004). Codecision and the European Commission: A study of declining influence? *Journal of European Public Policy, 11*, 1–18. https://doi.org/10.1080/1350176042000164271

Candel, J. J. L., Princen, S., & Biesbroek, R. (2023). Patterns of coordination in the European Commission: An analysis of interservice consultations around climate change adaptation policy (2007–2018). *Journal of European Public Policy, 30*(1), 104–127. https://doi.org/10.1080/13501763.2021.1983008

Cini, M. (2002). The European Commission: An unelected legislator? *The Journal of Legislative Studies, 8*(4), 14–26. https://doi.org/10.1080/13572330200870002

Crombez, C. (1996). Legislative Procedures in the European Com-munity. *British Journal of Political Science, 26*(02), 199–228. https://doi.org/10.1017/S0007123400000429

Crombez, C., & Vangerven, P. (2014). Procedural models of European Union politics: Contributions and suggestions for improvement. *European Union Politics, 15*(2), 289–308. https://doi.org/10.1177/1465116513517014

Egeberg, M. (2012). Experiments in supranational institution-building: The European Commission as a laboratory. *Journal of European Public Policy, 19*(6), 939–950. https://doi.org/10.1080/13501763.2012.681456

Franchino, F. (2009). Experience and the distribution of portfolio payoffs in the European Commission. *European Journal of Political Research, 48*(1), 1–30. https://doi.org/10.1111/j.1475-6765.2008.00819.x

Giurcanu, M., & Kostadinova, P. (2022). A responsive relationship? Setting the political agenda in the European Union. *Journal of European Public Policy, 29*(9), 1474–1492. https://doi.org/10.1080/13501763.2021.1953113

Greenwood, P. J. (2011). *Interest representation in the European Union*. Palgrave Macmillan.

Hartlapp, M., Metz, J., & Rauh, C. (2013). Linking agenda setting to coordination structures: Bureaucratic politics inside the European Commission. *Journal of European Integration, 35*(4), 425–441. https://doi.org/10.1080/07036337.2012.703663

Hartlapp, M., Metz, J., & Rauh, C. (2014). *Which policy for Europe? Power and conflict inside the European Commission*. Oxford University Press. https://doi.org/10.1093/acprof:oso/9780199688036.001.0001

Hustedt, T., & Seyfried, M. (2016). Co-ordination across internal organizational boundaries: How the EU Commission co-ordinates climate policies. *Journal of European Public Policy, 23*(6), 888–905. https://doi.org/10.1080/13501763.2015.1074605

Kassim, H. (2006). The secretariat general of the European Commission. In G. Edwards & D. Spence (Eds.), *The European Commission* (pp. 75–94). John Harper.

Kassim, H., Peterson, J., Bauer, M. W., Connolly, S., Dehousse, R., Hooghe, L., & Thompson, A. (2013). *The European Commission of the twenty-first century*. Oxford University Press. https://doi.org/10.1093/acprof:oso/9780199599523.001.0001

Kassim, H., Connolly, S., Dehousse, R., Rozenberg, O., & Bendjaballah, S. (2017). Managing the house: The Presidency, agenda control and policy activism in the European Commission. *Journal of European Public Policy, 24*(5), 653–674. https://doi.org/10.1080/13501763.2016.1154590

Koop, C., Reh, C., & Bressanelli, E. (2022). Agenda-setting under pressure: Does domestic politics influence the European Commission? *European Journal of Political Research, 61*(1), 46–66. https://doi.org/10.1111/1475-6765.12438

Kreppel, A., & Oztas, B. (2017). Leading the band or just playing the tune? Reassessing the agenda-setting powers of the European Commission. *Comparative Political Studies, 50*(8), 1118–1150. https://doi.org/10.1177/0010414016666839

Marques, M., Rohde-Liebenau, J., & Graf, L. (2025). Connecting internal and external dynamics in European intersectoral policy coordination—The case of education and employment. *Journal of European Integration, 47*(3), 423–443. https://doi.org/10.1080/07036337.2024.2379425

Moloney, D., & Princen, S. (2024). Assessing the role of the European Council and the European Commission during the migration and COVID-19 crises. *West European Politics, 47*(7), 1556–1587. https://doi.org/10.1080/01402382.2023.2225403

Nugent, N., & Rhinard, M. (2016). Is the European Commission really in decline? *JCMS: Journal of Common Market Studies, 54*(5), 1199–1215. https://doi.org/10.1111/jcms.12358

Nugent, N., & Rhinard, M. (2019). The 'political' roles of the European Commission. *Journal of European Integration, 41*(2), 203–220. https://doi.org/10.1080/07036337.2019.1572135

Osnabrügge, M. (2015). The European Commission and the implementation of its legislative programme. *European Union Politics, 16*(2), 241–261. https://doi.org/10.1177/1465116515573844

Oztas, B., & Kreppel, A. (2022). Power or luck? The limitations of the European Commission's agenda setting power and autonomous policy influence. *Journal of Common Market Studies, 60*(2), 408–426. https://doi.org/10.1111/jcms.13242

Peterson, J. (2008). Enlargement, reform and the European Commission. Weathering a perfect storm? *Journal of European Public Policy, 15*(5), 761–780. https://doi.org/10.1080/13501760802133328

Peterson, J., & Pollack, M. A. (2004). Introduction: Europe, America, Bush. In *Europe, America, Bush*. Routledge.

Pollack, M. A. (2003). *The engines of European integration: Delegation, agency, and agenda setting in the EU*. Oxford University Press.

Princen, S., Polman, D., Candel, J., & Biesbroek, R. (2025). External pressure, bureaucratic politics and policy insiders: The policy shaping influence of internal coordination processes on European Commission Strategies. *Journal of European Public Policy*, 1–24. https://doi.org/10.1080/13501763.2025.2522825

Rasmussen, A. (2007). Challenging the Commission's right of initiative? Conditions for institutional change and stability. *West European Politics, 30*, 244–264. https://doi.org/10.1080/01402380701239707

Rasmussen, A. (2012). Twenty years of co-decision since Maastricht: Inter- and Intrainstitutional implications. *Journal of European Integration, 34*(7), 735–751. https://doi.org/10.1080/07036337.2012.726012

Rauh, C. (2020). One agenda-setter or many? The varying success of policy initiatives by individual Directorates-General of the European Commission 1994–2016. *European Union Politics, 22*(1), 3–24. https://doi.org/10.1177/1465116520961467

Reh, C., Héritier, A., Bressanelli, E., & Koop, C. (2013). The in-formal politics of legislation explaining secluded decision making in the European Union. *Comparative Political Studies, 46*(9), 1112–1142. https://doi.org/10.1177/0010414011426415

Sabathil, G., Joos, K., & Kessler, B. (2008). *The European Commission: An essential guide to the institution, the procedures and the policies*. Kogan Page.

Senninger, R., Finke, D., & Blom-Hansen, J. (2021). Coordination inside government administrations: Lessons from the EU Commission. *Governance, 34*(3), 707–726. https://doi.org/10.1111/gove.12525

Thomson, R. (2011). *Resolving controversy in the European Union: Legislative decision-making before and after enlargement* (1st ed.). Cambridge University Press.

Thomson, R., & Hosli, M. O. (2006). Who has power in the EU? The Commission, Council and Parliament in legislative decision-making*. *Journal of Common Market Studies, 44*(2), 391–417. https://doi.org/10.1111/j.1468-5965.2006.00628.x

Tsebelis, G., & Garrett, G. (2000). Legislative politics in the European Union. *European Union Politics, 1*(1), 9–36. https://doi.org/10.1177/1465116500001001002

Wille, A. (2013). *The normalization of the European Commission: Politics and bureaucracy in the EU executive*. Oxford University Press. https://doi.org/10.1093/acprof:oso/9780199665693.001.0001

Further Reading

Blom-Hansen, J., Skorkjær Binderkrantz, A., Bækgaard, M., Finke, D., Senninger, R., & Serritzlew, S. (2025). *Policy preparation inside the European Commission*. Oxford Scholarship Online Political Science. Oxford University Press. https://doi.org/10.1093/9780198907961.001.0001

Buket, O., & Kreppel, A. (2022). Power or luck? The limitations of the European Commission's agenda setting power and autonomous policy influence. *JCMS: Journal of Common Market Studies, 60*(2), 408–426. https://doi.org/10.1111/jcms.13242

Hartlapp, M., Metz, J., & Rauh, C. (2014). *Which policy for Europe? Power and conflict inside the European Commission*. Oxford University Press.

Rauh, C. (2020). One agenda-setter or many? The varying success of policy initiatives by individual directorates-general of the European Commission 1994–2016. *European Union Politics, 22*(1), 3–24. https://doi.org/10.1177/1465116520961467

Anna Guerri holds a Master's degree in Political Science from the University of Innsbruck, specialising in EU governance and the policymaking dynamics of the European Commission. Her research reflects both academic research and professional experience in regional and European institutions.

Camilla Mariotto is an Assistant Professor of European Politics at the University of Innsbruck. She has published academic articles on the legislative and executive politics of the European Union, with a focus on policy implications. She is co-author of *Balancing Pressures: the Politics of Governing the European Economy.*

The Preparation Phase of the European Commission Proposals: Process, Participation, and Transparency

Peter Kerstens

Abstract This chapter analyses the European Commission's internal process for preparing legislative proposals—the foundation of EU policymaking given the Commission's near-exclusive right of initiative. It traces the sequence from agenda-setting to formal adoption, emphasizing the interaction between political leadership, bureaucratic coordination, and stakeholder participation. The process begins with the political priorities of the President of the Commission, Mission Letters, and annual Work Programmes, which guide policy formulation. Subsequent stages involve public consultations, expert group deliberations, and impact assessments reviewed by the Regulatory Scrutiny Board to ensure evidence-based policymaking. The drafting and inter-service consultation phases reflect complex internal coordination and the balance between technical rigour and political direction. This chapter also evaluates transparency and inclusiveness, highlighting formal mechanisms such as consultations and the Transparency Register alongside informal lobbying and expert exchanges. While larger, better-resourced actors often exert greater influence, transparency reforms and structured participation frameworks have enhanced legitimacy and accountability. Ultimately, this chapter portrays the Commission's preparatory phase as a blend of politics, expertise, and procedure that shapes the trajectory of EU lawmaking and stakeholder engagement.

1 Introduction

The European Commission (Commission) occupies a unique position in the institutional architecture of the European Union (TEU, Art. 17). It holds the near-exclusive right of legislative initiative in most policy areas. This power renders the internal

P. Kerstens (✉)
DG for Financial Stability, Financial Services and Capital Markets Union (DG FISMA), European Commission, Brussels, Belgium
e-mail: Peter.kerstens@ec.europa.eu

G. Füricht-Fiegl et al. (eds.), *Handbook on EU Law-making*, Professional Practice in Governance and Public Organizations, https://doi.org/10.1007/978-3-032-16559-6_4

processes by which Commission proposals are conceived, prepared, and adopted of paramount importance to understanding how EU policy and law is made.

While the Council of the European Union (Council) and the European Parliament (EP) ultimately adopt legislative proposals, typically after substantive amending, the Commission's preparatory phase sets the parameters of debate, defines policy objectives, and frames legislative options. This process is characterized by political and policy preferences and priorities, market or science-based evidence, stakeholder engagement and internal scrutiny mechanisms designed to pursue regulatory quality, proportionality, and coherence across EU policies.

This chapter examines the preparatory phase of Commission proposals from initial agenda-setting, through public consultations, expert group input, the work of the Regulatory Scrutiny Board (cf. European Commission, 2024a), inter-service consultations and the final adoption of proposals by the College of Commissioners. It also evaluates the opportunities for external stakeholders to influence these processes, as well as the effectiveness and transparency of participatory mechanisms in shaping legislative outcomes.

2 From Agenda-Setting to Formal Preparation

2.1 The Agenda-Setting Role of the Commission

Agenda-setting within the European Commission is the earliest and often the most decisive stage for the broad lines and priorities of policymaking. It involves identifying emerging problems, policy gaps or areas where EU action is deemed necessary (Nugent & Rhinard, 2022). These early deliberations are shaped by political priorities articulated in the President of the Commission's political guidelines, issued by a new president, when he or she is nominated and puts together the College of Commissioners, based on nominations by the Member States. While Member States still have the upper hand in deciding who they nominate to sit on the European Commission, the president has very considerable leeway to assign them their respective portfolios, responsibilities, and mission letters. That way the president-designate sets out the main parameters of the Commission's priorities for the forthcoming mandate. Once a new College of Commissioners takes up office, these priorities broadly determine what the European Commission will be focusing on during its 5-year mandate, subject to political imperatives that occur during the mandate and that may require a deviation or adaptation to the policy priorities, as well as continued agenda-setting efforts by the heads of state and government meeting in the European Council. These priorities are then translated into multiannual strategies and a yearly Work Programme that provides a list of topics and proposals that are very likely to come to the Commission's agenda in the years to come.

2.2 Mission Letters

Though not specifically envisaged in the treaties, in recent Colleges of Commissioners the practice has grown for the President-designate of the Commission, after having gained the blessing of the EP when attributing nominee Commissioners their portfolios, to issue them a 'mission letter' with a more or less specific list of guidelines and expectations or instructions of what the president expects the Commissioner-designate to work on in his or her area of assigned responsibility (European Commission, 2024b). This includes the subjects or priorities to be represented in their proposals. These mission letters may bear evidence of commitments or concessions the president-designate made to the heads of state and government or the EP in return for their support for his or her appointment. As such at the earliest moments of agenda-setting, a political process develops that is a function of the relative political powers among the heads of state and government who in common agreement nominate the President of the European Commission, and the relative strength of the political groups in the EP resulting from the most recent EP elections.

This process of developing the president-designate's political priorities typically plays out in the course of late spring in the year of his or her nomination, and in the subsequent summer the elaboration of the Commissioner-designates' mission letters is conducted. The mission letters, which span the portfolios of all Commissioners-designates are themselves the result of both a political and bureaucratic exercise. While the tone and eventual content and priorities of the mission letters are clearly political documents, they are preceded by a process of a more bureaucratic policy forecasting conducted by the Commission's Secretariat-General. Months before a new President of the Commission is nominated the Secretariat-General requests the various Commission departments to make suggestions, in their respective fields of expertise and responsibility, on what the forthcoming College of Commissioners should be focusing on. The decision on which ideas make it to political priorities and are included in the mission letters is very largely determined by the president-designate and his or her private office in collaboration with the Secretariat-General.

Stakeholders that take a close interest in forthcoming European Union policy and legislation should therefore pay close attention to this crucial stage in the policy cycle, which largely takes place before the new College of Commissioners takes office. Whether or not a certain topic is part of the Commission's priorities and the Commissioners' mission letters usually have a determining effect on this topic coming to the Commission political agenda or not. As this process is largely informal, close attention needs to be paid to discussions inside the Commission departments, as well as to how the political cards are stacked in European elections that determine the composition of the EP. Furthermore, national elections determine national majorities or coalitions and the question of who represents the Member States in the Council and the European Council, and therefore need to be monitored closely as well.

An issue that made it to the political priorities and mission letters, is highly likely, to be the subject of a Commission policy or legislative proposal at some point during its mandate.

2.3 *Policy Communications, Green Papers, and White Papers*

Beyond political priorities and mission letters, new and emerging policy fields or broader areas of policy development and regulation often are the subject of policy Green Papers. These documents serve to stimulate discussion and gather feedback on possible directions for future action. Green Papers are not proposals but consultation documents, typically structured around a set of open questions and policy challenges. Their aim is exploratory: to test the political and technical feasibility of EU action and to stir the debate among stakeholders, Member States, and EU institutions.

Following the consultation stage initiated by a Green Paper, the Commission may issue a White Paper outlining specific policy orientations or legislative options. White Papers are more prescriptive than Green Papers, indicating the Commission's preferred course of action and often announcing forthcoming legislative proposals.

In other cases, the Commission may adopt communications—less formal policy documents that articulate strategies, frameworks, or action plans. Communications often serve both internal and external functions: internally, they coordinate Commission departments around common objectives; externally, they signal the Commission's intentions to stakeholders, national authorities, and EU institutions.

In recent years, the issuance of Green Papers and White Papers has declined, and policy communications and digital consultations and targeted stakeholder engagements have become more prominent. Irrespective of the name of the papers, the primary function they have in common is to fine-tune the policy debate and test concrete policy options.

Consultation and stakeholder engagement on the Commission department's more or less developed ideas on how to tackle a certain set of issues is therefore key to the Commission's preparatory work for its proposals.

2.4 *The Commission Work Programme*

Each year the Commission departments, co-ordinated by the Secretariat-General, establish a work programme for the European Commission for the following year. This work programme also provides timing indications for when the items are scheduled to come to the College of Commissioners for adoption. Unless a political imperative or crisis situation determines otherwise, no item will usually be scheduled for adoption by the Commission in a given year unless it is included in the work programme for that respective year. The work programme is an essential document for Commission officials as they schedule forthcoming communications or proposals, and for interested parties as they gain insight on issues scheduled to appear on the Commission agenda and on the timeframe on when to best provide their input.

3 Public Consultations: Mechanisms, Opportunities, and Challenges

3.1 The Consultation Framework

Public consultation is a cornerstone of the Commission's Better Regulation Agenda.[1] It aims to enhance transparency, legitimacy, and the evidence base of EU policy-making by inviting feedback from citizens, businesses, NGOs, academics, and public authorities. The Better Regulation Guidelines establish a 'whole-of-cycle' approach, requiring consultation not only during legislative preparation but also in ex post evaluation and fitness checks (European Commission, 2021).

The Commission employs a variety of consultation instruments:

Roadmaps and Inception Impact Assessments: These outline the problem, objectives, and possible options for action. They are published on the 'Have Your Say' portal, with a minimum 4-week feedback period.

Open Public Consultations: Broad online questionnaires allow stakeholders to comment on policy objectives, options, and impacts. The consultation period usually lasts 12 weeks.

Targeted Consultations: These may take the form of stakeholder workshops, surveys, or bilateral meetings with interest groups and national experts. Often these targeted consultations can be highly technical, so as to seek input for parties with substantial technical expertise in an area.

Feedback on Draft Delegated or Implementing Acts: After the legislative phase, the Commission may invite feedback on draft secondary measures, although oftentimes such feedback is already sought by the regulatory or management committee or authority that assists the Commission in preparing the delegated acts. For example, the area of financial services regulation, which is now largely at EU level, has three supervisory authorities, one for banking, one for securities markets, and one for insurance and pensions. These authorities develop a broad range of highly detailed and technical standards that are incorporated in delegated and implementing acts. These authorities also conduct stakeholder consultations, obviating the need for the Commission to do the same.

[1] See also Chap. 29 of this handbook.

3.2 Opportunities for Stakeholder Influence

Public consultations provide formal channels for external stakeholders to influence the policy formulation stage. Early contributions, especially at the roadmap or the Inception Impact Assessment stage, can shape the framing of the problem and the range of options considered. Later consultations may affect the selection of preferred policy instruments or the calibration of regulatory requirements.

The Commission departments are required to present a summary of the replies received and conclusions drawn in synopsis reports published alongside impact assessments and proposals, enhancing accountability. Unless specifically asked not to publish their reply or when the reply may contain confidential or protected material, the default option is that replies received to a public consultation are made available to the public online.

3.3 Effectiveness and Inclusiveness

Even though these formal opportunities to provide input are available to the general public, larger well-organized stakeholders are claimed to dominate participation. They may even have had a sneak preview at the consultation paper or may have sought to influence its development. Small businesses, trade unions, and civil society groups are often said to face resource constraints that limit their engagement, both quantitatively and qualitatively, especially in highly technical policy fields.

Interest groups, NGOs, and industry associations have developed sophisticated strategies to participate in these processes, including coalition-building, evidence submission, and collective or co-ordinated engagements.[2]

Commission departments often receive dozens of submissions to consultations that can have large amounts of open ended or closed questions. While not all stakeholders are equally well represented or able to answer the questions, it is rare for consultations not to yield answers across the broad spectrum of possible opinions and perspectives that may be held in society on a given subject and the diversity of options of how to tackle it.

The Commission is under no obligation to follow the majority opinion, or the opinions most commonly expressed in the consultation procedure. It is conscious about the fact that on many subjects, society at large may in fact be the silent majority and those with a big or vocal interest in a particular outcome do not necessarily represent a majority view.

While stakeholders may find it hard to determine the actual impact of their individual submissions on the policy decisions taken by the Commission, consultations are vital for the Commission departments to gauge what views are held and how they are expressed and to gain feedback on technical and detailed policy options and

[2] See also Chap. 21 of this handbook.

choices. The results of consultations are utilized to formulate proposals in a way that they most likely fall on fertile ground in the political and legislative debate that will unfold in the Council and in the EP.

It is noteworthy that by the time the Commission departments draft their consultation papers, they may often already have developed ideas on the issues at stake and on possible opinions held by various stakeholders, especially by those who do not wait to make their views known until they are asked. Interest groups and stakeholders on the EU policy scene live in a large echo-chamber of ongoing policy debate, conferences, stakeholder events, industry or civil society working groups and coalitions, and meetings with EU officials both in Brussels and across Member States, where they promote policy debate and try to influence policy formation.

Irrespective of whether they have a direct or demonstrable impact or not on the final policy design by the Commission, stakeholders on any given subject typically cannot afford not to provide a detailed response to a consultation by the Commission. They need to demonstrate that they have made their views heard. Also, during the further legislative process, Member States or the EP will be interested in what they had to say on a given subject and whether their views were reflected or not by the Commission in its proposal.

4 Expert Groups and the Role of Technical Advice

4.1 Composition and Function

Expert groups are another crucial channel through which external stakeholders and national authorities contribute to policy preparation. These groups provide specialized advice, technical expertise, and policy input to the Commission departments. They may be composed of representatives from Member State administrations, EU agencies, academia, civil society, and industry and or a combination thereof (European Commission, 2025).

At the time of writing (autumn 2025), the Commission maintains over 700 registered expert groups, covering most policy domains.

4.2 Stakeholder Representation and Balance

The Commission distinguishes between different types of members: Member State authorities, organizations (e.g. NGOs, industry), individuals appointed in a personal capacity and EU bodies. To prevent dominance by specific interests, the Commission introduced transparency and balance requirements. Each group's membership, mandate, and meeting agendas are published in the Register of Expert Groups.

Nonetheless, questions about representativeness persist. Business representatives remain overrepresented relative to NGOs and trade unions in most policy areas. This can affect both the framing of technical issues and the perceived legitimacy of resulting policies.

4.3 Influence on Drafting

Expert groups can exercise substantial influence during the early drafting phase of proposals, particularly where technical complexity is high and regulatory details are critical. Commission officials often rely on expert groups for evidence, data, and feasibility assessments. In areas like chemicals regulation or food safety, technical advice from expert committees has shaped not only specific standards but also the architecture of regulatory regimes.

However, the degree of influence varies across policy areas. In politically salient domains—such as climate policy or migration—the Commission arguably retains tighter control over drafting and relies more on internal expertise and coordination and political guidance than on external experts. Also, in the area of financial services and digital regulation, the evident imbalance in representation between business and civil society representatives and the demonstrable deregulatory impact this had in the past, led the Commission to keep much tighter control over drafting, even where this comes at the expense of missing out on technical expertise. Relying on technical experts 'on loan' from Member States can and does also compensate for this fact.

4.4 Evaluation of Effectiveness and Transparency

The transparency of expert group operations has improved markedly following criticism from the EP and NGOs. The publication of minutes, documents, and membership details enables scrutiny and fosters public trust. However, the practical accessibility of these materials for non-specialists remains limited. Moreover, as expert groups become more formal and formalistic, detailed policy choices and drafting of technical provisions may shift to informal exchanges between Commission officials and trusted stakeholders and experts outside formal expert groups. This can blur the boundary between technical advice and lobbying.

5 Impact Assessment and Review by the Regulatory Scrutiny Board

5.1 The Role of Impact Assessment

Impact assessment (IA) is a central tool in the Commission's better regulation system. It aims to ensure that legislative proposals are evidence-based, proportionate, and consistent with policy objectives. An IA accompanies most major legislative proposals and non-legislative initiatives with significant economic, social, or environmental effects.

The IA process examines:

- The definition of the problem and the baseline scenario
- The policy objectives and a number of possible options
- The likely impacts (quantitative and qualitative) of the different options
- Stakeholder feedback and consultation results

Impact assessments are prepared by the lead Commission department, either by the team that is responsible for drafting the actual policy proposal, by the team specialized in impact assessments, or by a combination thereof.

5.2 The Regulatory Scrutiny Board

The Regulatory Scrutiny Board (RSB) is an independent body within the Commission that reviews the quality of all impact assessments. It consists of a chair and six members (three internal, three external), appointed for fixed terms to ensure independence.

The RSB assesses IAs according to criteria of clarity, methodological rigour, and compliance with better regulation principles. It may issue a positive, positive with reservations, or negative opinion. A negative opinion requires the Directorate-General (DG) to revise the IA before the proposal can proceed.

Impact assessments are often confused with policy choice. The essence of an impact assessment is that there is a proper definition of a problem that the policy initiative aims to address. It must then, in a rigorous way, evaluate the impact of various policy options or choices, often compared to a baseline scenario of doing nothing (which may in itself have negative impacts, given that there must be a defined problem to start with). However, the IA should not determine the policy choice, as this is ultimately a political decision and process. The purpose of the IA is to make sure that the political or policy decision is informed by a proper analysis of the problem and a comparison in effects, both positive and negative, of considered policy options. That said, it is rare to see that the chosen policy option is not the preferred option according to the IA. This is also the source of criticism of the IA, namely that the policy choice is made first, and that only then the IA is developed to demonstrate that it was the best choice. Methodology, rigour of assessment, and independence of the RSB all aim to guard against this, but critique persists.

5.3 Stakeholder Input in the IA Process

Stakeholders can influence the IAs indirectly through consultations, which inform the identification of impacts and policy options. However, the IA process itself is largely internal, with limited transparency until the final report is published. The publication of the RSB's opinions—together with revised IAs—has improved visibility and transparency.

6 Drafting of the Proposal and Inter-Service Consultation

6.1 Drafting by the Lead Directorate-General

In principle, once the IA and consultation processes are complete, the lead DG drafts the legislative proposal. They may be assisted by the Commission's Legal Service and Secretariat-General (SG). In practice, the drafting of a legislative proposal starts much earlier, especially if the area or the proposals are technically complex and of considerable length. It is not uncommon for legislative proposals to run in the dozens of pages with double or even triple digit numbers of articles.

The Legal Service ensures compliance with the treaties, legal coherence, and clarity of wording. The SG coordinates the consistency with the Commission's strategic priorities and ensures that procedural steps have been fulfilled. Often this is assured through inter-service steering groups, especially where a proposal may affect the policy areas or responsibilities of multiple Commissions services, which is often the case. The SG will then lead the inter-service steering or coordination group so that the lead service can take account of the view of other services, but also make sure it stays aligned with other initiatives already on the statute book or under preparation.

6.2 Inter-Service Consultation

Before a proposal can be submitted to the College of Commissioners, it undergoes inter-service consultation (ISC), a mandatory internal procedure that ensures horizontal coordination across the Commission. All relevant DGs and services review the draft proposal and accompanying IA, providing comments or objections. In case of urgency or political priority, this inter-service consultation process can be replaced by the inter-service steering group process.

The ISC typically lasts 2–4 weeks, depending on the complexity and sensitivity of the proposal. Disagreements between services may be resolved through bilateral meetings or escalated to the Secretariat-General and ultimately to the Commissioners' cabinets if necessary. The ISC is often the final stage where internal political and technical considerations converge.

6.3 Transparency and External Influence

The ISC is a closed process, not accessible to external stakeholders. However, stakeholders can indirectly influence its outcome through continued engagement with Commission departments. In practice, lobbying activity often intensifies at this stage, as actors continue to seek to shape the proposal before it reaches the College. While a legislative proposal usually does not 'leak' into the public domain while it is still in the hands of solely the lead service and possibly the SG and Legal Service, as soon as the inter-service consultation is formally launched and the draft proposal is sent around to other Commission departments, it typically also leaks, often creating a flurry of stakeholder activity. This is an entirely informal process that requires stakeholders to be very much on the ball and rely on well-established lines of communication with Commission departments.

While such interactions raise concerns about unequal access, they also reflect the pluralistic nature of EU policymaking. The Transparency Register (European Commission, 2020) and the publication of high-level meetings between Commissioners, their cabinets, Directors-General, and interest representatives—introduced under the Transparency Initiative—have enhanced accountability, but gaps remain for senior, middle management and desk officer level officials. At this stage in the process, it is almost a given that the proposal will be on the Commission agenda shortly and its main parameters are fixed. However, technical changes that may not interfere with the overall objectives, but that can make a very substantial difference in stakeholders' bottom lines, are possible and not at all rare. Such changes can often effectively be fed in at desk officer or middle management level.

7 Adoption by the College of Commissioners

The culmination of the preparatory phase is the formal adoption of the proposal by the College of Commissioners. The College, composed of all Commissioners under the authority of the president, acts collectively in adopting legislative proposals, which are then transmitted to the Council and the EP for negotiation and adoption.

The decision to include a proposal on the College agenda is taken by the president, based on recommendations from the Secretariat-General. The College's deliberations are collegial but politically guided, ensuring alignment with the Commission's overall priorities and inter-institutional commitments.

The weekly meetings of the College (typically on Wednesday morning, except during EP Plenary Session in Strasbourg when the College meets in Strasbourg on Tuesdays) are prepared by the Heads of the Commissioners' private offices (Cabinet) who typically meet on the Monday preceding the College meeting. If agreement on a proposal is reached at the level of the Heads of the Cabinet, there is normally no debate in the College at all, and the item just features as an A-item (adoption without debate) on the college agenda. The meetings of the Heads of Cabinets are typically prepared in the preceding week by meetings between members of the Cabinets of the Commissioners, organized by proposal/subject matter. It is usually during or following these meetings of members of the Cabinets that last minute changes are brought to a proposal. If everyone agrees or agrees subject to certain requested changes, the item will be scheduled for the meeting of the heads of the Cabinets also as an A-point. If the members of Cabinet cannot 'close' the proposal or 'lift all outstanding reservations or requests for changes', the heads of the Cabinets will take up the issue and if they fail, it will be for the College itself to solve. However, this is rather the exception than the rule.

In fact, many legislative proposals are not on the agenda of the meetings of the College of Commissioners at all, not even as an A-point, but are adopted through written procedure. In a written procedure, which is only possible if there are no outstanding reservations from the inter-service consultation and if the president has not scheduled the item for the College itself to recognize its political importance, the Cabinet of the Commissioner in charge will, through the Secretariat-General, circulate the draft proposal resulting from the inter-service consultation to the private offices of all other Commissioners. Usually, they have one week to react. If no one reacts within the deadline set, the proposal is adopted. If a Cabinet of a Commissioner raises objections or wants to propose a change, the written procedure can be suspended. A solution is found, and the written procedure is restarted, or the issue moves to oral procedure, with a meeting of members of the Cabinets first.

This final stage of the adoption process still provides opportunity for outside influence, either from business, civil society or from Member States or the EP. While it can be impactful, influencing the Commission proposals at this stage is only reserved for stakeholders that are best organized in terms of the strength of their advocacy, and dependent on how closely they are tuned into the process, and how well and timely they can communicate their position or exercise political influence.

Once adopted, the proposal, impact assessment, and synopsis report of the consultation are published on the Commission's website, marking the transition from internal preparation to the inter-institutional legislative process.

8 Evaluating Stakeholder Influence in the Preparation Phase

8.1 Formal Versus Informal Influence

As set out above, stakeholders engage with the Commission through both formal mechanisms (consultations, expert groups) and informal channels (meetings, correspondence, political advocacy). Influence is more pronounced when stakeholders provide credible expertise aligned with the Commission's policy objectives and regulatory culture, or when they represent significant constituencies, and often both.

Informal interactions, often through the Brussels ecosystem, can complement or circumvent formal participation mechanisms. The Commission's Transparency Register aims to ensure that such interactions are recorded and publicly visible.[3] Nevertheless, asymmetries persist between well-resourced actors and diffuse interests.

8.2 Effectiveness of Consultations and Expert Groups

The effectiveness of consultations and expert groups in shaping proposals depends on three key factors: timing, capacity, and responsiveness.

Timing: Early engagement—during the roadmap or inception phase—has greater impact, as policy frames are still malleable. Late-stage consultations tend to refine rather than redefine policy options.

Capacity: Stakeholders with analytical resources and legal expertise can contribute data and evidence that influence impact assessments and option selection.

Responsiveness: The Commission's responsiveness varies across departments and policy areas. In domains with high technical content, expert input may directly shape provisions; in politically sensitive fields, political guidance or alignment with large political factions in the EU legislator tends to dominate.

While the formal commitment to 'consult broadly' is fulfilled, the perception of meaningful impact remains uneven. Some view consultations as mere exercises in procedural legitimacy rather than substantive participation, but this assessment does not do justice to the reality that influence is an ongoing process throughout the policy cycle, rather than a box-ticking exercise during a formal consultation process.

[3] See also Chap. 21 of this handbook.

9 Conclusion

The preparation phase of the Commission proposals represents a complex interplay of political leadership, technical expertise, stakeholder engagement, and internal coordination. From the initial publication of political priorities, mission letters, communications, or green and white papers to the final adoption by the College, each stage reflects the Commission's triple role as both a political actor, as a technical bureaucracy and as guardian of the treaties, responsible for upholding the respect and implementation of the treaties and the EU law flowing from them.

The EU has made significant progress in embedding transparency, evidence, and participation into the legislative preparation process. Public consultations, expert groups, and impact assessments constitute a sophisticated ecosystem for participatory policymaking. Yet, their effectiveness depends not only on informal and procedural openness but also on the timing and substance of stakeholder input.

While large and well-organized actors may exert significant influence, the Commission's efforts to broaden access and transparency measures represent meaningful steps towards more inclusive governance.

All in all, the Commission is a rather transparent institution, notwithstanding procedural complexity, which may make processes hard to navigate for those not familiar with them. Its political priorities and plans for proposals are set out long before the Commission acts, leaving plenty of time and room to help shape policy outcomes.

Most Commission officials are very accessible and open to engage with anyone who wishes to speak to them. Yet finding your way around the Commission and knowing who is working on what and when to engage requires expertise and experience in the EU decision-making process itself. In this respect, the Commission may not be very different from a national administration or regulator. What does set the Commission apart is that the EU is the only body with legislative powers where the legislator itself has no right of initiative. A legislative initiative, bar some exceptions, at the EU level always requires a proposal from the Commission. Influencing the Commission and its proposals requires aspiring influencers to study the Commission, its structures, its authority, its political drivers, its departments, and its people (Nugent & Rhinard, 2022).

References

European Commission. (2020). *Transparency register: Agreement between the European Parliament, the Council and the Commission*. OJ L 422, 15.12.2020. Retrieved from https://www.integritywatch.eu/ecmeetings.php

European Commission. (2021). *Better regulation guidelines*. SWD (2021) 305 final.

European Commission. (2024a). *Regulatory scrutiny board annual report*. Publications Office.

European Commission. (2024b). *List of Commissioners-delegate 2024–2029*. Retrieved from https://commission.europa.eu/about/commission-2024-2029/commissioners-designate-2024-2029_en
European Commission. (2025). *Register of Commission expert groups*. Retrieved from https://ec.europa.eu/transparency/regexpert/
Nugent, N., & Rhinard, M. (2022). *The European Commission* (3rd ed.). Palgrave Macmillan.
Treaty on the European Union (TEU). (2012). Consolidated Version OJ C326/13

Peter Kerstens is a senior official at DG for Financial Stability, Financial Services and Capital Markets Union (DG FISMA) at the European Commission and Advisor on Financial Sector Digitalization and Cybersecurity. With three decades of experience in EU policymaking, he has served in various Commission Cabinets and as Finance Counsellor at the EU Delegation to the United States in Washington DC. He played a key role in shaping the EU's digital finance agenda, including Markets in Crypto-Assets (MiCA) and Digital Operational Resilience Act (DORA), and is a recognized expert in digital transformation and financial technology.

In the Machine Room of Power Broking: Cabinets in the European Commission

Stefan Zotti

Abstract Cabinets, the private offices of Commissioners, serving as their closest political advisors, play a key role in the decision-making process of the European Commission. Over the years, the cabinets have evolved and become more formalised in their composition, particularly in terms of their role between the political and administrative levels of the Commission. Has Walter Hallstein, the first President of the Commission, still been sceptical about this French heritage in the administrative system of the young Commission, fearing that this might allow for excessive national influence on the Commission's policies, the cabinets today are truly European in their composition and role, supporting and facilitating the Commission's internal decision-making process and its interinstitutional work. Three key roles can be identified, namely advising the Commissioners and translating political aims and priorities into legislative proposals and policies which the Commission's services can execute; ensuring the collegiality of decision-making in the European Commission and the coherence among the various policy fields and initiatives in line with the political guidelines of the president and overarching political priorities of the EU; and lastly, organising and ensuring the political support for new initiatives within the Commission as well as from other EU institutions, mainly the Council and the European Parliament.

Keywords European Commission · Commission working methods · Cabinets · Decision-making · EU institutions · Political priorities of the EU · European Commission administration · Strategic advisors

---

The article is based on the private opinion of the author and does not reflect the official position of the European Commission.

S. Zotti (✉)
DG for Education, Youth, Sport and Culture (EAC), European Commission, Brussels, Belgium
e-mail: Stefan.zotti@ec.europa.eu

G. Füricht-Fiegl et al. (eds.), *Handbook on EU Law-making*, Professional Practice in Governance and Public Organizations, https://doi.org/10.1007/978-3-032-16559-6_5

1 Cabinets in the European Commission

1.1 The Cabinet: French Heritage in the European Commission

'The cabinet is where the real power is' (Eppink, 2007, p. 77)—this assumption not only convinced Derk-Jan Eppink to join the cabinets of Commissioners Bolkestein and Kallas but is also a widely shared view among insiders and external stakeholders of the European Commission. It may come as a surprise that, apart from anecdotal evidence, as in Eppink's book (see also: Mérand & Ross, 2024), relatively little research is available on the role of cabinets in the overall decision-making process of the European Commission. This may be related to the mission of cabinets, which, as we will see, focuses primarily on preparing the Commission's political decision-making in the background and ensuring the implementation of these decisions by the Commission's services. However, a lack of comparability with other administrative systems and decision-making mechanisms in national governments may alter the view on the role of cabinets in the European Commission, starting with the terminology.

The term 'cabinet' in the United Kingdom refers to the government itself, more concretely to the decision-making body composed of senior members of the government, mainly the political leaders of the various government departments chaired by the Prime Minister. A similar understanding can be found in the United States, Germany ('Bundeskabinett'), and other countries. The equivalent within the European Commission to this latter sort of 'cabinet' would be the 'College of Commissioners', the most senior decision-making body of the Commission, composed of all Commissioners and chaired by the President of the Commission.

'Cabinets' in the European Commission are rooted in the French system, which has been known as the 'cabinet ministériel' since the 'monarchie de Juillet', the French post-revolutionary kingdom between 1830 and 1848. These cabinets served not only as private offices to the respective ministers, something which is also known in the British system ('private secretaries', 'principal private secretaries') but as a group of politically appointed advisers from within and outside of the public administration, which would support the decision-shaping and -making of the ministers and ensure that the administration follows and implements the political will of the respective minister.

When establishing the first European Commission in 1958 under the leadership of Walter Hallstein, the French system of cabinets, as the personal staff of each Commissioner, was also introduced on the European level, even if Hallstein himself remained rather critical and aware of the risk that this might allow for too strong a national influence of the Commission's work. However, with Emile Noël, a French official serving as the Commission's first Executive Secretary, later referred to as Secretary-General, key working methods developed in line with the French tradition (European Commission et al., 2007, p. 57). These cabinets in earlier times were predominantly composed of nationals of the respective Commissioner, often with a professional background in national administration, in opposition or at least substantial tension with the Commission's services, to ensure coherence in the Commission's collegial decision-making with national interests.

Only the fall of the Santer Commission in 1999, due to a scandal caused by Commissioner Edith Cresson, who appointed a close friend as adviser, leading to allegation of nepotism, led to new rules for the composition of cabinets under Commission President Romano Prodi in 2000, aiming at restricting the influence of Member States through the cabinets, inter alia by ensuring a broader national diversity, limiting the number of cabinet members to six; José Manuel Barroso, with basically the same intention introduced a minimum threshold of at least three members drawn from the Commission services in 2004 (Egeberg & Heskestad, 2010).

These reforms, referred to as 'big bang cabinet reforms' by some scholars (Deckarm, 2016, p. 749), indeed resulted in an effective denationalisation and professionalisation of the cabinets, reduced influence of national governments and a stronger orientation of the cabinet's work towards the Commission's actual task and mission (Deckarm, 2017).

1.2 The Cabinets in Today's European Commission

Cabinets, as the supporting staff of each Commissioner, play a crucial role in linking the political and the administrative level of the European Commission by supporting the individual Commissioner, ensuring collegiality among the Commissioners and communicating the political priorities and decisions to the administrative services, i.e. the Directorates-General under the political responsibility of the respective Commissioner. Over the years, the role of cabinets has been more strictly regulated, and today's 'Working Methods of the European Commission' set out the rules and responsibilities of cabinets, particularly in ensuring the collegiality of Commissioners and working closely with the services in great detail, as will be demonstrated.

In the personal support of the Commissioner, much still depends on the Commissioner's personality and the personal relationship they establish with the cabinet members. In any case, the role of the cabinet in policy shaping and in preparing policy decisions within the portfolio of the Commissioner or on general political matters goes beyond the role of a private office in other political systems or, at least, combines the daily support of the Commissioner's work with a substantial advisory role on the policy itself. Rules concerning the composition, which today also state that at least half of the members must be established Commission officials, just underlines this high level of professional experience and policy competence, which enables the cabinet to be the Commissioner's closest team of advisers, who can drive the development of new policies, together with the respective Commission service.

This hybrid role of cabinets, situated between the political and administrative levels, is also reflected in the hybrid composition of members from within and outside the Commission, placing them at the central point of the Commission's decision-making process. Close to the Commissioner, in permanent contact with all other cabinets and the Commission service(s) under the Commissioner's political responsibility, cabinets play a crucial role in the preparation and implementation of high-level policy decisions, making them most eminent power brokers and deal-makers within the Commission as well as towards the other EU institutions and Member States.

2 Composition of the Cabinets

In her 'Communication from the President to the Commission' on 'Rules governing the composition of the Cabinets of the Members of the Commission and of the Spokesperson's Service' (European Commission, 2024), President Ursula von der Leyen presented the Commissioner with revised regulations on the cabinets, which, compared to previous versions, strengthened the diversity of cabinets even further. As discussed earlier, these rules, since the presidency of Prodi and Barroso, aim to limit national influence on the Commissioner's decision-making and ensure the broadest possible reflection of different views and approaches in the Commission's policy development.

As the general principle, the President underlines that 'Cabinets help Commissioners in carrying out their collegial and portfolio roles. For this reason, their composition should reflect the diversity of the European Union as far as possible, drawing on a wide range of professional experience and ensuring geographic and gender balance' (ibid., p. 2). Focusing on the members, i.e., those persons with an AD status (administrators, principal administrators) and leaving out the administrative and secretarial staff, cabinets of Commissioners have six members, including the Head, the Deputy Head, and one senior expert, while Vice-Presidents, including the High Representative/Vice-President (HR/VP), have nine and the President 12 AD members, also including Head, Deputy and up to two or three senior experts, respectively. Out of these, no less than three members in the case of Commissioner's cabinets, six or seven in the case of the Vice-Presidents' and the President's cabinet, respectively, need to be established officials.

The members of the President's and Vice-Presidents' cabinets must consist of at least five different nationalities, with no more than four or three having the same nationality as the President or Vice-President, respectively. The cabinets of Commissioners shall have members of at least three nationalities, with a maximum of two members from the Commissioner's nationality. To further limit the influence of a single Member State in particular cabinets, the rules also state that either the Head or the Deputy Head must have a nationality different from that of the Commissioner they serve.

As a new rule, to strengthen the female leadership in the Commission, the Communication sets a quota of at least 50% of women among the AD members. In

June 2025, the share of female cabinet members in all 27 cabinets was 56% compared to 44% of male cabinet members.

3 Ensuring Collegiality

The European Commission is a collegial body, as stated in the 'Working Methods' (European Commission, 2019), meaning it 'takes decisions collectively. All Members of the Commission are equal when making decisions and equally accountable for these decisions' (idb., p. 4). Given the complexity and sheer number of decisions to be taken by the Commission every day, cabinets play a key role in preparing and facilitating collective decision-making: 'The Cabinet is actively involved in the process of preparing the meetings of the College during which it expresses the points of view of the Member of the Commission on the various point on which decision is to be taken' (ibd., p. 25).

The College of Commissioners, as the most senior decision-making body of the Commission, in principle meets on a weekly basis, generally on Wednesday mornings, except for weeks when the European Parliaments holds its plenary meetings in Strasbourg, where the College meetings are scheduled for Tuesday afternoon. This weekly College meetings are prepared by a set of weekly preparatory meetings on the cabinets' level, which serve the aim of finding agreement on as many as possible points while at the same time, identifying strategically important and/or politically sensitive issues which would need to be addressed by the Commissioners themselves. This implies that issues, once discussed and agreed upon, should, in principle, not be reopened at a later stage in the process, which lends these meetings at the cabinet level considerable political weight. Obviously, this process requires a very close alignment and open communication between the Commissioners and their cabinets to ensure that the Commissioners see all their points covered in the negotiations held at the cabinet's level.

3.1 Group for External Coordination (EXCO)

The regular circle of preparatory meetings starts already a week before the College meetings (6 days in case the College meets on Tuesday afternoon in Strasbourg) on Wednesday afternoon with the 'Group for External Coordination' (EXCO), a relatively new standing cabinet committee, established under President Von der Leyen in 2019, summoning the external actions experts of all cabinets and is co-chaired by the President's Diplomatic Adviser and the Deputy Head of the HR/VP's cabinet. The main aim of the EXCO is 'to prepare the external aspects of College meetings, to ensure full political coordination and coherence on external action matters and to enhance the working relationship between the Commission and the European External Action Service' (ibd., p. 14). The agenda of the EXCO covers, inter alia, issues such as the coordination of external aspects of internal policies, for example, the clearance of the Commission's position in international climate conferences or other international fora, the coordination of financial support to third countries, or the monitoring of ongoing international negotiations. As with all meetings at the cabinet level, the EXCO is also prepared by a meeting at the services level, bringing together external action experts from all Commissioner services.

3.2 Special Chef Meetings (RSCC)

Thursdays are traditionally reserved for the so-called Special Chef meetings (RSCC—Réunion Spéciale des Chefs de cabinet), thematical meetings to prepare strategic initiatives or new legislative proposals of the Commission. Contrary to the name, these meetings are not attended by the Heads of cabinet but by cabinet members, who mirror the work of other Commissioners and serve as experts in the various policy fields within each cabinet. This explains the need for a broad diversity of professional experience and expertise, which was discussed in the previous part, as basically, every cabinet would need members with legal, economic, external policy and other policy experiences to be able to understand and assess the crucial elements of the issues at stake and to contribute to the negotiations fruitfully.

At the cabinet level, Special Chef meetings are the primary and most important way to contribute to and influence collegial decision-making, ensuring that the crucial political interests of the Commissioners are heard and considered. The RSCC reports to the weekly meeting of the Heads of cabinet and follows the same logic as described above, namely that issues agreed upon at the Special Chef level must not be reopened at a later stage, be it at the level of the Heads of cabinet or in the College itself.

The Special Chef meetings are chaired by the thematically responsible member of the President's cabinet.

3.3 Groupe des Relations Interinstitutionnelles (GRI)

Ensuring collegiality and political coherence is obviously of particular importance in the field of legislation to provide political ownership and support of the whole College for positions taken or adopted during legislative negotiations with the (co-) legislators. Facilitating this coherence is the task of the second standing cabinet committee, the Groupe des Relations Interinstitutionnelles (GRI), which meets every Friday morning and is chaired by the Deputy Head of the President's cabinet.

The GRI is the principal forum for exchanging information on all interinstitutional matters, monitors the development of legislative negotiations, and prepares Commission positions on all aspects of interinstitutional work. The Working Methods underline the key role the GRI plays in the interinstitutional work of the

Commission: 'Established Commission position, and Commission proposals can only be changed by referring an issue back to the Commission through the GRI. Any position papers, statements, letters to other institutions, etc., which may commit the Commission on legislative or other matters must be agreed by the College through the GRI before being presented' (ibd., p. 14).

This gives the GRI a crucial political role in the preparations of the College's meetings, enabling the Commission to effectively enact its right of initiative in legislative processes and ensuring a high level of political coherence in legislative negotiations.

3.4 Heads of Cabinet Meeting (HEBDO)

The cycle of preparatory meetings for the College meetings is concluded by the weekly meeting of the Heads of cabinet, taking place every Monday. Chaired by the Secretary-General of the European Commission, the most senior cabinet members take note of the outcome of the other cabinet-level meetings, solving open issues if necessary and preparing the agenda of the College meeting by going through all agenda points, raising issues of political interest to their Commissioners to reach agreement on as many as possible issues to allow the College of Commissioners to focus their deliberations on key policy initiatives or strategically important legislative files.

This complex and elaborate cycle of preparatory meetings reflects the collegial character of the Commission's decision-making and should allow all Members of the Commission to contribute to the shaping and making of the manifold political decisions to be taken. For the understanding of the cabinet's role in this, it is essential to remember that the cabinets and their members represent the Commissioner they are working for, as the Working Methods underline: 'In all College preparatory meetings, Heads of Cabinet and Cabinet members speak on behalf of their respective Member of the Commission; it is therefore of crucial importance for the functioning of the Commission's decision-making process that Heads of Cabinet and Cabinet members are mandated by their Members of the Commission with a clear line to take' (ibid., p. 7).

4 Cabinets and Commission Services

Historically, the cabinet system has always run the risk of creating a parallel structure to the general administration, thereby decoupling political decision-making from the technical expertise of the administration's experts or even politicising the public administration by involving the political level in the micro-management of the administration's daily work, including personnel decisions.

The Working Methods repeatedly emphasise the shared responsibility for the Commission's functioning: 'The Members of the Commission, the Cabinets and the services are collectively responsible for working closely together to ensure effective implementation of the President's Political Guidelines and the College's priorities' (ibid., p. 23). This cooperation is primarily established between the Commissioner and the Director(s)-General reporting directly to them, which in the daily work includes the cabinets and the policy assistant(s) of the Director-General as first contact point.

Common responsibility, however, must not be misunderstood as diluting the different roles. Quite to the contrary, the 'Working Methods' clarify these roles to facilitate a clear and transparent division of labour between the political and administrative levels. The cabinet shall draw as much as necessary on the assistance of the services while keeping them informed about the College's work and the decisions taken on the political level to steer the services' work. However, 'the Cabinet does not involve itself in the direct management of the services, which is the exclusive responsibility of the Director-General' (ibid., p. 25). This is precisely to prevent the development of parallel structures and blurring of competences. To emphasise the different competencies, the Working Methods introduce a differentiation between 'politically sensitive and/or important acts', for which validation on the political level is required at every stage of the planning and implementation cycle, and 'other acts', which fall under the full responsibility of the Director-General.

The services of the Commission, even if not under the direct operational leadership of the respective Commissioner (contrary to the situation in most Member States), are placed by the President under the political authority of the Commissioner in charge of the portfolio concerned and must work under their political responsibility. This implies an active involvement 'in drawing up the institution's policies and initiatives', which is crucial to the success of any initiatives, given the fact that the technical expertise on the policies is with the services.

Notwithstanding the political responsibility of the respective Commissioner for the service, the 'Working Methods' also clarify that the services 'are coordinated by the Secretariat-General on behalf of the President. To this end, the services apply the guidelines and instructions issued by the President via her Cabinet or the Secretariat-General'. This double responsibility vis-à-vis the Commissioner, on the one hand, and the President/Secretariat-General, on the other, however, is not intended to create parallel chains of command but to ensure the collegiality and coherence of the Commission's policymaking from the service level. This strengthened role of the Secretariat-General in the field of policy coordination also reflects a relatively recent development of stronger, streamlined internal coordination, introduced by the former President of the European Commission (EC), Jean-Claude Juncker under the title of 'new ways of working' to facilitate the functioning of this 'political Commission' in 2014. These new ways 'subordinated the work of Members of the Commission and their cabinets to the delivery of the president's programme through a tier of vice-presidents' (Bauer et al., 2023, p. 363). Though some scholars' view that this new design of the Commission's internal structure (which was in its principles also applied by President Von der Leyen once she took office in 2019) transformed the cabinet system as such might go too far, a certain impact of the increasing centralisation—and be it only through a stronger coordinating role of the Secretariat-General—on the work of the cabinets and the application of the principle of collegiality cannot be ignored.

Commission Services

Within the European Commission, the term *services* refers to the various administrative departments that support the work of the Commissioners and implement EU policies. These include Directorates-General (DGs), which are organised by policy areas, the internal services such as the Legal Service or the Secretariat-General as well as specialised executive agencies. Services are responsible for drafting legislative proposals, implementation of policies, managing EU programmes, and ensuring compliance with EU law. They play a central role in the day-to-day functioning and policy coordination within the Commission.

5 The Power Brokers: Ensuring Policy Coherence and Political Support

Cabinets, as demonstrated, play a crucial role in supporting policy design and decision-making within the European Commission, ensuring the political steering of the services as well as collegiality among the Commissioners. In contrast, the management of the Commission, including the implementation of various policies and programmes, remains under the operational responsibilities of its senior civil officials.

To better understand the role and potential influence of cabinets, it may help to analyse them in line with the Strategic Triangle, a conceptual framework developed by Harvard Kennedy School Professor Mark Moore (1995) to guide public managers in creating public value. It emphasises the interplay between three key dimensions of (public) policymaking: public value proposition, operational capacity, and legitimacy. A successful policy, according to this concept, is, therefore, one that is technically correct, politically supportable, and organisationally implementable in pursuit of its goal.

Starting with the dimension of technical correctness, i.e. the concrete design of the policies and (legal) initiatives, respectively, it became clear that the cabinets support the work of the responsible services, which have the expertise and the key technical knowledge to draft new policies, in so far as the cabinets ensure the coherence of any new initiative with the broader political aims of the Commission as outlined, inter alia in the Political Guidelines of the President, but also with the aims of other, potentially conflicting interests of different policy areas. Political steering of the cabinet, facilitated by the fact that several cabinet members come from the services and therefore benefit from substantial policy understanding, is in this regard focused on translating political priorities into policies, in close cooperation with the service, which is in the lead of the actual drafting of legislative or policy proposals. This drafting, however, happens in close alignment and under the political guidance of the responsible Commissioner. To ensure this feedback, regular meetings are held between the Commissioner, their cabinets and the service(s) on the senior level, to seek the Commissioner steering on new proposals and to inform about the implementation of any strategic initiative. Practically, these discussions are prepared by notes in which the service informs the Commissioner about the envisaged policy initiatives or legislative proposals and based on these notes, the Commissioner and/or their cabinet is able to steer and give the necessary guidance for the service. In short, on the design dimension of policy innovation, cabinets play a crucial role in close cooperation and shared responsibility with services to deliver on the Commission's political priorities.

The third dimension, operational capacity to implement the solution found, is mainly provided by the services; the role of cabinets is therefore limited to alerting the political leadership if, based on a sound assessment of the service, problems concerning implementability could compromise the proposal.

However, the second dimension, namely ensuring the political support for any new initiative, is a last core task of cabinets which has not yet been discussed: Any policy proposal finds itself contested by a multitude of diverging interests from stakeholders within and outside of the Commission, as the means and ends of different policies might be in tension with each other if only one thinks about potential conflicts between environment and industrial policies to name just one. Even if these potential conflicts have been mitigated over the last decade, inter alia through strong mainstreaming of policies in the Political Guidelines of the respective Presidents, which develop and outline the overarching narratives and prioritisations of the Commission's policy aims, it nevertheless needs much effort to internally ensure the common understanding and support of the whole College of Commissioners—particularly due to the collegial decision-making of the Commission, which gives every Commissioner a stake in every policy field.

Furthermore, given that the Commission's legislative proposal has no automatic majority in either the European Parliament or the Council, organising and ensuring political support from the political groups, as well as among the Member States, is of crucial importance for the Commission to succeed and have its legislative agenda adopted. Complementing and adding on the negotiations on the technical level, it falls on the Commissioners and the cabinets to canvass for their proposals in the Member States and the European Parliament, often drawing on the network of their political parties on the European level, which might help to facilitate the exchange between like-minded actors from the different EU institutions. It is the cabinet's responsibility to, therefore, closely monitor developments in the other institutions (and to share their information via the GRI with the whole Commission), to organise meetings, make sure the Commissioner meets the right key players at the right time to shape their decisions and thereby to contribute to ensuring majorities for the Commission proposals with the co-legislators.

The European Union, as a polity with rather specific elements, such as the exclusive right of initiative for the executive branch, a co-legislative process which until today combines classical national with supra-national elements, and an executive branch which in its role and its composition exceeds the traditional understanding of a government, also developed specific instruments and decision-making models to fulfil its mission over the decades. The Commission, combining political and administrative elements to 'promote the general interests of the Union' as stated in the Treaty (Art. 17 TEU), over the years, has developed ways and instruments to balance the various interests of its members, including national views, different policy logics, and political positions. The cabinet plays a key role in these efforts, as it establishes the link between the political and administrative levels, helps to translate politics into policies, and thereby drives the necessary discussions between the Commissioners as well as between the Commission and other EU institutions.

Cabinets ensure the functioning of the European Commission at least in three critical regards: (1) they advise the political leadership, combining political and policy expertise and experiences in themselves, which helps the Commissioner to shape their political aims and priorities and translate these priorities into policy decisions to be executed by the services; (2) in working closely together with all other cabinets, in particular the corresponding Vice-Presidents, and closely monitoring the work in other policy fields, they ensure collegiality decision-making and political coherence of the decisions taken, in line with the Political Guidelines of the President; (3) they organise the political support within the Commission and in the other EU institutions to ensure the adoption of any new policy initiative or legislation.

So, are cabinets indeed the place where the real power is, as Eppink (2007) insinuated in his book? Definitely not, the power in the European Commission is, in any case, vested in the College under the leadership of the President, with many actors, such as the Secretariat-General and the various Commission services, contributing to and supporting the political leadership. However, cabinets indeed play an essential role as power brokers in the background, balancing interests and ensuring effective and efficient decision-making, which allows the European Commission to play the role attributed to it by the Treaty.

References

Bauer, M. W., Kassim, H., & Connolly, S. (2023). The quiet transformation of the EU Commission cabinet system. *Journal of European Public Policy, 30*(2), 354–374.

Deckarm, R. (2016). From national enclaves to supporting offices: An analysis of the 1999 reform of European Commissioners' cabinets. *Journal of Contemporary European Research, 12*(3), 735–752.

Deckarm, R. (2017). The countries they know best: How national principals influence European Commissioners and their cabinets. *Journal of European Public Policy, 24*(3), 447–466.

Egeberg, M., & Heskestad, A. (2010). The denationalization of cabinets in the European Commission. *Journal of Common Market Studies, 48*(4), 775–786.

Eppink, D.-J. (2007). *Life of a European mandarin. Inside the Commission*. Lannoo.
European Commission. (2019). *Communication from the President to the Commission: The working methods of the European Commission*. P(2019)2. European Commission.
European Commission. (2024). *Communication from the President to the Commission: Rules governing the composition of the Cabinets of the Members of the Commission and the Spokesperson's service*. P(2024)7. European Commission.
European Commission, Bitsch, M.-T., Bossuat, G., Bussière, É., Cailleau, J., et al. (2007). *The European Commission 1958–72—History and memories of an institution*. Publications Office.
Mérand, F., & Ross, G. (2024). EU Commission cabinets: Past and present. *Politique Européenne, 84*, 56–73.
Moore, M. H. (1995). *Creating public value. Strategic management in government*. Harvard University Press.

Stefan Zotti is Deputy Head of the Higher Education unit in the European Commission (DG EAC). The former member of the Cabinet of Commissioner Johannes Hahn (Regional Policy) between 2010 and 2013 holds a Doctorate in Catholic Theology and a Master in European Studies. He was Director-General of the OeAD-GmbH (Austrian Agency for International Cooperation in Education and Research) between 2016 and 2018. Since 2013, he has been teaching EU policies at the University of Applied Sciences Burgenland.

Changing Role to Find a Balance: The European Commission Between National and Supra-National Interests

Rudolf W. Strohmeier

Abstract Since its very beginnings, the European Commission had to manoeuvre between the national interests of the Member States and its role to formulate and implement the supra-national Community interest. In defining the latter, it needs to take into account the first without falling into the trap of limiting itself to the lowest common denominator. This is, however, only possible if the Commission knows well the Member States' interests which use many exchanges to influence the Commission.

With the increased powers of the European Parliament both in the legislative process and the composition of the Commission, the correlating increase of party politics has more and more outweighing traditional ways bringing national interests of Member States to the Commission. The parallel process of moving from a Commission College of equals towards a presidential regime has also reduced the possibilities for national influence via individual Commissioners as the formulation of the Community interest is shifting more and more to the President of the European Commission and the political parties supporting him/her.

Keywords Commission College · Commissioner's cabinet · President of the European Commission · Presidential regime · Supra-national interest · Home country

R. W. Strohmeier (✉)
Former General Director European Commission, Brussels, Belgium

CBH Rechtsanwälte, Brussels, Belgium

G. Füricht-Fiegl et al. (eds.), *Handbook on EU Law-making*, Professional Practice in Governance and Public Organizations, https://doi.org/10.1007/978-3-032-16559-6_6

1 The Composition of the Commission College Representing the Interests of the Sending Member States

1.1 The Beginnings of the Commission College

The issue of balancing the tensions between the national interests of Member States and the so-called supra-national (Schneider, 2012) or community interests defined by the European Commission (Commission) has existed from the very beginning of the European integration process.

Already the founding fathers had stipulated in Art. 17 (3) of the Treaty on the European Union (TEU; ex-Art. 214 Treaty on the European Community, TEC) that the members of the Commission have to be personalities offering "full guarantee with regard to their independence". They are neither allowed to take nor to seek instructions from "their" or another government or any other entity. Art. 245 (1), 2. Sentence of the Treaty on the Functioning of the European Union (TFEU; ex-Art. 113 TEC) obliges the Member States to respect the independence of the European Commission and to refrain from influencing it in executing its tasks.

The political reality, however, looked different already when the EC was established.

The German basic idea of a market economy always conflicted with the French, more centrally planned economy orientation. When the first Commission was built, the German government of Konrad Adenauer insisted that the candidate for the post as President of the Commission had to represent the German economic concept. As the French (socialist) Commission candidate Louis Armand wanted to become (Spielenburg & Poidevin, 1994, p. 365) and stayed as uncontested chair of EURATOM, the post of President of the Commission had consequently to fall to a market-oriented candidate to keep the political balance. Two candidates were therefore considered: The German Christian Democrat Walter Hallstein and the Belgian liberal Jean Rey. For reasons of the national interest, the Belgian government gave priority to the also to be decided seat of the European Commission (Belgium {Brussels} and not Luxembourg) and not to the person Jean Rey. That cleared the way for Walter Hallstein (Dumoulin, 2007, p. 56).

It is also nothing new that Member States express expectations on the attribution of dossiers for "their" Commissioner to have at least easier access to dossiers which are of national interests. At service level, it was custom until the 1990s that certain General Directorates (DG) were always run by the same nationality because of the clearly expressed national interest in the policy sector concerned. E.g. DG Agriculture was regarded as a "French" turf, DG Competition as a "German" one.

1.2 The College Situation After Enlargement in 2004

Cleary demonstrating the intention of Member States to keep national influence on the Commission was, however, the non-implementation of the decision of the heads of state and government to reduce the number of Commissioners for the time after the enlargement of the EU in 2004. With this reduction, it was intended to ensure the functioning of the institution Commission as it was regarded impossible to create 20 or more dossiers of equal importance to respond to the principle of a College of equals. Therefore, Art. 17 (5) para 2. TEU, implementing this decision, stipulated explicitly that a College with fewer members than Member States would have to be composed in such a way that the demographic and geographic spectrum of the entirety of Member States would be reflected. But this attempt to guarantee the national interests of Member States in the composition of the Commission was not followed further. In the package agreed with Ireland before its second referendum held in 2009 on the Treaty of Lisbon, the European Council kept the rule "one Commissioner per Member State", based on the provision of Art. 17 (5) TEU, to convince—successfully—the Irish voter. As a consequence, the European Council decided in May 2013 to stick to this decision for the composition of the Commission to be nominated following the EP election 2014 and confirmed it later twice (for the Juncker Commission in 2014 and for the von der Leyen Commission II in 2024).

1.3 The College Dealing with National Interests

To manage the complex interplay between (evident) national and its supra-national obligations is neither intellectually nor politically an easy task for the Commission.

1.3.1 Commission as "Guardian of the Treaties"

The most important role of the Commission is to exercise that of the "Guardian of the Treaties" (Art. 17 (1) 3rd Sentence TEU). By that the Commission is obliged to apply the rules of the treaties independently of the Member States concerned.

This obligation is, however, often disputed, in particular, in cases of state aids, competition law or in the common agricultural policy (CAP). Avoiding to provoke upfront a Member State the College sometimes delays a final decision as it was the case with the Art. 7 TEU procedures against Poland and Hungary where the EP took the Commission 2021 to the European Court of Justice (ECJ) because of not action. In particular by not accepting EU migration laws, voices in these Member States concerned claimed that they want to keep their national identity. Legally speaking, this is a reference to Art. 4 TEU obliging the Commission to respect the national identity of its Member States (Bieber et al., 2016, p. 747) which is politically delicate.

Sometimes the Commission feels even obliged not to apply properly Community law because of the contradicting factual or supposed vital interest of a certain Member State. Most prominent in this respect is the famous quote of President of the Commission Jean-Claude Juncker why the College did not apply the rules of the Stability Mechanism strictly towards Paris: "Because it is France", for which he was heavily criticised, e.g., by the president of the Euro-Group at that time (Mühlauer, 2016).

1.3.2 Balancing the National Interests in the College

Having the privilege to be the only institution to table legislative proposals (Art. 17 (2) TEU) the College of Commissioners in its preparation of files needs to find a fine balance among the different interests of the Member States, as their diverging economic, demographic and geographic situations may lead to different solutions for specific policy sectors.

This phenomenon can actually be observed with regard to/in the case of the Russian war in Ukraine and the resulting policy considerations of Member States located in the East of Europe—e.g. with regard to sanctions or the increase in defence spending—in comparison to those in the Western parts of the Union. It is therefore quite often difficult for the College to balance these interests and to define "the" Community or supra-national interest, which is in most cases not identical with the lowest common denominator. However, if the final result of a legislative text looks like or is factually a compromise formula, then this is usually the result of the situation in the Council which cannot agree with EP's positions typically closer to the Commission proposal than to the Council.

To get the necessary elements for the formulation of the Community interest, the individual Commissioners "shouldn't hand in at the cloakroom" their national identity because otherwise the College would lack the knowledge of the country the Commissioner "knows best"—as the Brussels jargon is for a Commissioner's home country. This profound knowledge is indispensable to avoid tabling proposals which, in political reality, would have no chance to fly—both in the Council and the EP, which would make no political sense and bear the risk of undermining the Commission's credibility. As former President of the Commission José Manuel Barroso (2014, p. 18) formulates: "The Commission is not a Think Tank presenting ideas as provocation (…) but should always seek the balance between the necessary ambition (*note: meant is the Community interest*) and the realistic chance of adoption".

Commissioners need, therefore, to be well informed about "their" home country to contribute to the collective wisdom of the College in defining the community interest. Of course, any information will influence the process of forming a Commissioner's opinion as well as the staff of the Commission.

An important element observed working closely with Commissioners are in this context the personal ambitions of Commissioners for the time after their term at the EU-Commission ends. The German or Austrian experience that having been

Commissioner means "fin de la carrière politique" does not correspond to that of other Member States. Examples of this different reality are, e.g., Peter Mandelson, who became Secretary of State for Business, Innovation and Skills in the UK the day after he left the Commission; Michel Barnier, who became foreign minister and (shortly) even prime minister in France after his term in the Commission; Romano Prodi becoming prime minister of Italy again after his role as President of the Commission. Who wants to keep the option open to come back to the national political scene might be less prepared to "forget" the national interests of his/her home country for the sake of the community interest.

1.3.3 Cabinets and Staff as Contact for Member States

Starting with the Delors Commission, the number of members of a Commissioner's cabinet (or private office) became much bigger than today. This created even more possibilities for Member States and (national) interest groups to interact with Commissioners via the individual cabinet members. This was all the more the case as at that time normally only one cabinet member was not of the Commissioner's nationality allowing the country known best to exchange directly with more or less the entire cabinet depending on the subject the cabinet member was responsible for.

Only since the Prodi Commission (2000–2005), "supra-national" cabinets become more and more the rule. For President Romano Prodi, the cabinets had to ensure a correct application of the principle of collective responsibility (Schlenker, 2019, p. 90), to make them less receptive to national influence. Nevertheless, he had a group of special advisors around him, dominantly of Italian nationality, which internally was called "his Italian Cabinet". This new approach to supra-national cabinets followed the role model of the Austrian Commissioner Franz Fischler's cabinet, where the number of non-Austrians outweighed the Austrians. Interestingly, Fischler took this decision not to counterbalance possible Austrian influence on his cabinet but to get more information about and better contacts to other Member States (Fischler, 2024, p. 128). How successful this approach was is proven by the fact that Fischler—despite his controversial reforms of the agricultural sector (Agenda 2000)—survived the—avoidable (Ludlow, 2014, p. 210 ff.; Roca et al., 2009, p. 209)—resignation of the Santer-College in 1999 before being nominated again for the Prodi Commission because of the support of the EP and the Member States. For the cabinets of the presidents of the Commission, this "supranationalisation" approach started, however, 20 years earlier with the cabinet of President Gaston Thorn (Mangenot, 2014, p. 88 ff.).

More generally speaking about lobbyism in Brussels, van Schendelen (2008, p. 210) concludes that lobby groups "contribute by their upstream of demands and activities to more discursive decision-making and so to the more representative definition of people's welfare". This conclusion could also be applied to the lobbying of Member States; therefore, one could argue that these efforts contribute to the formulation of the community interest.

One important element in this respect is related to the implementation of EU policies. The EU administration has a strong focus on agenda-setting and formulation of policies, not on law implementation of EU-laws, which lays at the Member States level (Young, 2015, p. 51). Member States influencing the Commission during the preparation of a legislative act can contribute to the anticipation of potential implementation problems by that facilitating not only the negotiation of proposals at a later procedural stage and also avoiding frustration of citizens when ultimately confronted with difficult to implement acts.

2 Factors Influencing the European Commission

2.1 The Committee of Regions (CoR)

Introduced by the Treaty of Maastricht in 1994 (Art. 305 ff. TEU; ex-Art. 263 ff. TEC) as "institutionalisation of the 'forth level' of the EU" (Weidenfeld & Jung, 1994, p. 37), the Committee of the Regions (CoR) was intended not only to establish a link between the citizen at local and regional levels and the EU-level (Knemeyer, 1994), but also to influence the legislative process of the EU as nearly three quarters of EU-laws are implemented at the local and regional levels, in particular, in those Member States having a decentralised political system like, e.g., Spain or Germany.

However, the Commission always regarded possibilities to be blocked by the CdR before tabling a proposal with consequences for regions and cities as an unacceptable attack on its right of legislative initiative.

Since the Treaty of Maastricht, representatives of regions can however be nominated by their Member State as member of a Council formation (Title III Art. 16 (2) TEU; ex-Art. 146 TEC). In particular if they are at the same time also Member of the CoR, they have a higher standing in their contacts with the Commission to defend regional and/or national interests.

With the ideas described in the Commission Communication of February 2025 on the new post-2027 Multiannual Financial Framework where EU-funds should be implemented with Member States and regions in the areas of cohesion policy, common agricultural policy, fisheries and maritime policies, home affairs and Trans-European Networks one could imagine, that CoR's consultative role could at least factually upgraded as otherwise proper spending might not be assured.

The creation of the CoR is a good example of pursuing national interests, as the principle of subsidiarity and regional representation at EU-level was an important German interest. It is therefore not surprising that the German Commissioner Schmidhuber in his first mandate was the "father" of the advisory board of the regional and local authorities, established by the Commission in 1998 and proceeding the CoR.

2.2 *The Strengthened Role of the EP*

In the past, the Council of Ministers has been the nearly exclusive decision centre of the European Community (Joos, 1997, p. 65). Today, the EP is practically at equal footing with the Council in legislative matters, due to its increased powers, in particular with regard to the nomination of the Commission but also to its enlarged co-decision competences. In addition, by the parallel building of European Party families, the EP organises itself more than 25 years around party political lines following the introduction of Art. 138a by the Treaty of Maastricht, now Art. 10 (4) TEU. This means that the Commission is not only just influenced by MEPs as such, but needs to take its political majorities (which can depend on the subject) at least at the same footing into consideration for the preparation of its legislative proposals than the Council. It took quite some time for the Commission to accept this political reality. The author remembers a discussion end 2005/early 2006 between the former Secretay General Catherine Day and Vice-President Viviane Reding in which Catherine Day stated that "the Commission is not adapted to party politics". Raunio even notes that the linkage between the national parties represented in the EP—via their national delegations in the party families—has increased by mutual information and control links following the EP has won more powers (Raunio, 2007, p. 255 f.). This too is facilitating nation influence but at the same time defining Community interests at EP level, which might be different from those formulated by the Commission.

Interestingly, Member States have adapted much faster to this new reality as their lobbying efforts focused more and more also towards the EP (Engel & Borrmann, 1991).

The most recent proof of the power of the EP is von der Leyen Commission II political U-turn announcing the "Industrial Green Deal" and abolishing fundamental elements of its former "Green Deal" approach. This happens, e.g., by the various omnibus acts—after the political majority of the EP shifted from centre-left to centre-right (following the EP elections in 2024) as well as the majority in the Council shifted to centre-right—as the majority of national governments (actually 14) are led by European People's party (EPP). Both elements forced the Commission to modify its former policies in line with these new majorities. In cases where the political majorities of EP and Council run parallel, the definition of the Community interest is certainly easier to define for the Commission than the other way round. Perhaps this difficulty led the von der Leyen Commission I to engage NGOs to undertake lobby activities against the interests of industries in some Member States (Beutelsbacher & Bojanowski, 2025). It is, however, disturbing that following that investigation one Commission department paid NGOs to oppose the Mercosur negotiations which are based on a Council mandate and negotiated by another department (Beutelsbacher & Bojanowski, 2025).

2.3 *The Presidencies of the European Council*

Established in 1974, the European Council representing the heads of state and government of the Member States gained increasing influence on the European integration process since the Treaty of Lisbon 2009 turned it into a formal EU institution. On paper its non-legislative function (Art. 15 (1) 2. sentence TEU) and its role of impulse generator and priorities setter (Art. 15 (1) 1st sentence TEU) seem prima facie to limit its influence on the Commission.

Bressanelli et al. (2025) conclude in a recent study that the European Council's increasingly assertive interventions complicate the traditional understanding of the "classic" roles assigned to the EU's legislative players by undermining the possibilities of the Commission to define to the community interest.

In addition, Member States holding the presidency started in 2007 to work together closely in groups of three, called "trios", preparing common agendas for 18 months, which the Commission politically cannot ignore. In this context, the respective presidency of the European Council can pursue also national agendas while preparing and implementing during its presidency those "trio" programmes. A very recent example is the revision of the Passengers Rights Regulations (EU) No 261/2004 and (EU) No 2027/1997, proposed by the Commission already in 2013, but "sleeping" in the Council since 2020. The Polish presidency took it up for its term and pushed it through the Council meeting on 5 June 2025, evidently to help (national) airlines still suffering from the fall out of the Corona crisis and the blockage of the Russian airspace as sanction against Russia after its invasion into Ukraine.

3 Consequences of the Change from a College to a Presidential Commission Structure

Already during the Juncker Commission (2014–2019) the possibilities for Member States and stakeholders to influence the College became less easy due to the centralisation of the Commission decision process.

This was first the result of the increased powers of the EP in view of the Commission's election with the Treaty of Lisbon (Art. 214 TEU) with separate votes on the President elect and the College. Since EP succeeded in March 1999 to bring the Santer Commission down as President Santer respected the French interest to keep Commissioner Edith Cresson instead of firing her (Ludlow, 2014, p. 210 ff.), Fontaine (2009, p. 455 ff.) speaks therefore of the "parliamentarisation" of the political system in the EU starting with the Santer Commission. Subsequently, the EP exercised more and more party-political influence on the Commission which led to the famous "Spitzenkandidat" formula for the nomination of the President of the Commission in the election campaign 2014. In this perspective, the election winner

Jean-Claude Juncker had a double—legal and political—legitimation as president, by the European Council *and* the EP's majority. Being by that procedure no longer "primus inter pares" in the College allowed him to exercise more influence in the formulation of the community interest than his predecessors—at the detriment of the other College members. With this process, a degradation of the individual Commissioners took place, linked not only to the loss of influence with regard to the attributed dossier but also to the pursuit of national interests.

This phenomenon was reinforced by the extremely powerful execution of this new role of the president by Juncker's Head of Cabinet (and later Secretary General) Martin Selmayr. His understanding of his role led to many attributes of him, of which "the secret emperor of the EU" (Müller, 2016) was probably among the nicest and is broadly reported (Robert, 2016). To persue their national interests it became more important for Member States to establish good contacts to Martin Selmayr than to the Commissioners and the DGs under their helmet. The same applied for all other interest groups, including even journalists.

President von der Leyen in her first mandate developed this system further by creating eight Vice-Presidents, of which three became Executive Vice-Presidents. Only those had the DGs under their responsibility, grouped together under the heading of the three subject areas she had made them responsible for. As a result, all the non-executive Commissioners became even less influential and by that less interesting as interlocutors for Member States but also for interest groups. This was aggravated by the fact that having no DG under their control limited their operational capacities and overall knowledge of files.

This trend towards a "presidentialisation" of the European Commission (Ceron et al., 2024, p. 7) or "politicisation" of the European Commission's presidency (Ceron et al., 2025)—contrary to the letter of Art. 17 (6) TEU stipulating the principle of collegiality—was significantly strengthened in the von der Leyen Commission II after the failure of the 2019 process (Kessler, 2024, p. 2). In the 2024 election campaign, von der Leyen benefited from the fact that she was the successful EPP Spitzenkandidat *and* the uncontested choice of the heads of state and government. This position allowed her establishing a clear hierarchical structure of the College with four Vice-Presidents reporting to her and 22—factually—Junior Commissioners or State Secretaries. Already in 2021, the European Federalist in an article published on 21 April 2021 classified the 18 Commissioners in the von der Leyen Commission I not being Vice-Presidents as such. Although the latter are observing now one Directorate General, they stay under the control of the responsible Vice-President of the Commission, steering and coordinating each of the four Commission's priorities as formulated in the most recent Working Methods of the Commission.

To counterbalance this loss of possibilities to pursue national interests in the Commission, the choice of candidates becomes much more important for a Member State. Only heavyweights in terms of competence, political experience and membership in one of the political parties forming the majority in the EP can expect to become a Vice-President exercising influence—also in view of national interests.

4 Conclusion

This new Commission structure has significant repercussions for any effort to influence it—may it be exercised by a Member State to pursue a national interest or any group with a particular interest. Because Junior Commissioners have factually less influence in the College, Member States as well as stakeholders need first to focus on the President and the Vice-Presidents and their respective Cabinets.

Taking further into account, that at the same time the Vice-Presidents represent today four main political families [European Peoples Party (EPP), Progressive Alliance of Socialists and Democrats (S&D), European Conservatives and Reformists (ECR), Liberals (Renew)] capable of building together a stable majority in the EP supporting the President—the Greens are also supporting the von der Leyen Commission but part of the College—it became more important to pursue national interests second with the respective political groups in the EP. All the more as today they are well connected with their national parties in the capitals of the Member States.

The since long-time disputed problem of how to reduce the number of Commissioners as there are not 20 and more meaningful dossiers available could therefore be regarded as factually solved: Commissioners today are only the President and the Vice-Presidents.

References

Barroso, J. M. D. (2014). In Europäische Kommission (Ed.), *Die Europäische Kommission 2004–2014, Eine Bilanz des Präsidenten–Mit ausgewählten Dokumenten*. Amt für Veröffentlichungen der EU.

Beutelsbacher, S., & Bojanowski, A. (2025). *Die Welt 8 June 2025*. Retrieved June 10, 2025, from https://www.welt.de/wirtschaft/plus256222171 8/geheime-verträge-offengelegt-eu-kommission-bezahlte-aktivisten-fuer-klimalobbyismus.html

Bieber, R., Epiney, A., Haag, M., & Kotzur, M. (2016). *Die Europäische Union*. Europarecht und Politik, 12. Aufl., Nomos, Baden-Baden.

Bressanelli, E., Koop, C., Minetto, F., & Reh, C. (2025). *The European Council: Truly the law-maker-in-chief?* CEPS Explainer 2025-03. CEPS.

Ceron, M., Christiansen, T., Dimitrakopoulos, D. G., & Russack, S. (2024). *Is the EU's Spitzenkandidaten procedure fit for the future?* CEPS Explainer 2024-04. CEPS.

Ceron, M., Christiansen, T., & Dimitrakopoulos, D. G. (Eds.). (2025). *The politicisation of the European Commission's presidency: Spitzenkandidaten and beyond*. Palgrave Macmillan.

Dumoulin, M. (2007). In Europäische Kommission (Ed.), *Die Europäische Kommission 1958–1972, Geschichte und Erinnerungen einer Institution* (Vol. 1). Amt für Veröffentlichungen der EU.

Engel, C., & Borrmann, C. (1991). *Vom Konsens zur Mehrheitsentscheidung. EU-Entscheidungsverfahren und nationale Interessenpolitik nach der Einheitlichen Europäischen Akte*. Europa Union Verlag.

Fischler, F. (2024). *Die Kraft der Mitte – Die politische Lebensgeschichte eines Tirolers und Europäers, Ecowing*. Red Bull Media Haus.

Fontaine, P. (2009). *Herzenssache Europa – Eine Zeitreise 1953–2009, Geschichte der Fraktion der Christdemokraten und der Europäischen Volkspartei im Europäischen Parlament*. Editions Racine.
Joos, K. (1997). *Interessenvertretung deutscher Unternehmen bei den Institutionen der Europäischen Union*. Berliner Wissenschafts-Verlag.
Kessler, C. K. (2024). *Is the Spitzenkandidat process a waste of time?* Centre For European Reform. Insight of 3 June 2024.
Knemeyer, F.-L. (1994). *Europa der Regionen – Europa der Kommunen, Wissenschaftliche und politische Bestandsaufnahme und Perspektive*. Nomos Verlagsgesellschaft.
Ludlow, P. (2014). Von einer Liebesheirat zum Showdown: Beziehungen zum Europäischen Parlament. In *Die Europäische Kommission 1986–2000* (Vol. 3). Amt für Veröffentlichungen der EU.
Mangenot, M. (2014). *Die Europäische Kommission 1973–1986* (Vol. 2, pp. 169–180). Amt für Veröffentlichungen der EU.
Mühlauer, A. (2016, June 2). Dijselbloem wirft Juncker Nachgiebigkeit vor. *Süddeutsche Zeitung*.
Müller, P. (2016). Der heimliche Herrscher der EU. *Der Spiegel*, 27.12.2016. Retrieved June 2, 2025.
Raunio, T. (2007). In K. E. Joergensen, M. A. Pollack, & B. Rosamond (Eds.), *Handbook of European Union Politics* (pp. 247–262). Sage.
Roca, P., Rassmussen, A., & Ponzano, P. (2009). *Der Aufbau eines Parlaments: 50 Jahre Geschichte des Europäischen Parlaments 1958–2008*. Europäisches Parlament/Amt für Veröffentlichungen der EU.
Schlenker, D. (2019). *Die Europäische Kommission 1986–2000* (Vol. 2, pp. 86–91). Publications Office of the European Union.
Schneider, H. (2012). *Supranationale Integration – ein zukunftsweisendes Konzept und was daraus geworden ist, Passauer Jean Monnet Papiere 03/2012*. Universität Passau, Jean-Monnet-Lehrstuhl für Europäische Politik.
Spielenburg, D., & Poidevin, R. (1994). *The history of the high authority of the European coal and steel community—Supranationality in operation*. Weidenfeld and Nicolson.
The European Federalist. (2021). Retrieved June 3, 2025, from https://www.foederalist.eu/2021/04/verkleinerung-eu-kommission.html
Van Schendelen, R. (2008). Brussels as the place for lobbying the European Union. In R. De Groof (Ed.), *Brussels and Europe* (p. 197 ff). Academic and Scientific Publishers.
Weidenfeld, W., & Jung, C. (1994). Das Entstehungsgefüge der Europäischen Union: Institutionen, Prozesse und Verfahren. In W. Weidenfeld (Ed.), *Maastricht in der Analyse, Strategien und Optionen für Europa* (p. 11 ff). Bertelsmann Verlag.
Young, A. R. (2015). In H. Wallace, M. A. Pollack, & A. R. Young (Eds.), *Policy-making in the European Union* (7th ed., p. 46 ff). Oxford University Press.

EU-Documents

Communication from the Commission to the European Parliament, the European Council, the Council, the European Economic and Social Committee and the Committee of the Regions, The road to the next multiannual financial framework, COM/2025/46/final of 11.2.2025.
Communication from the President to the Commission—The Working Methods of the European Commission, COM/P(2024)5 of 1.12.2024.
polish-presidency.concilium.europa.eu/en/programme/programme of the presidency, p. 39. Retrieved May 27, 2025. Chancellery of the Prime Minister, Warsaw (2025). Programme of the Polish to the Council of the European Union.

Rudolf W. Strohmeier is a lawyer and economist who built his career in the European Commission. After early roles in the Bavarian representation to the federal government in Bonn, he served in cabinets of Commissioners Schmidhuber and Fischler. Later, he joined DG AGRI and was nominated by the President of the Commission Romano Prodi as his advisor for agriculture, industry as well as research and development. He became Head of Cabinet to Commissioner Viviane Reding, then Deputy Director-General for Research & Innovation, and finally Director-General of the EU Publications Office until 2020.

The Council of the European Union as Co-Legislator

The Council as a Lawmaker

Arnold H. Kammel

Abstract This article sheds light on the role of the Council of the EU within the Ordinary Legislative Procedure (OLP) from an institutional perspective. By doing so, it provides an overview of the role and functioning of the Council as a policy- and lawmaker. It aims to assess its structure, powers and competences and depicts the role of the Council in the OLP. By analysing the relevant Treaty provisions as well as the Rules of Procedure (RoP) of the Council, the article also looks at the practical implementation. It concludes by debating the outlook of the battle between the intergovernmentalist and supranationalist camp.

Keywords Council · Council of Ministers · Council of the European Union · Member States · Legal analysis · Rules of procedure

1 Introduction

The Council (also known as the Council of Ministers or the Council of the European Union) is next to the European Court of Justice, the oldest EU institution explicitly mentioned since the signing of the European Coal and Steel Community Treaty of 1952. The articles 26–30 of the ECSC Treaty[1] specified the role of the Council as the forum of engagement of Member States. With the Treaties of Rome in 1957,

[1] Document 11,951 K/TXT.

A. H. Kammel (✉)
Secretary General of the Federal Ministry of Defence of Austria, Lecturer and Honorary Professor (FH), University of Applied Sciences Burgenland, Eisenstadt, Austria
e-mail: arnold.kammel@hochschule-burgenland.at

G. Füricht-Fiegl et al. (eds.), *Handbook on EU Law-making*, Professional Practice in Governance and Public Organizations, https://doi.org/10.1007/978-3-032-16559-6_7

separate Councils were established for the three Communities. The Merger Treaty[2] of 1967 put an end to the three separate Councils by establishing a single Council as laid out in Art. 1 of the Merger Treaty and so providing the basis for the Council as it is known nowadays in the institutional framework of the EU as a legislative and executive body.

Today, the Council voices the national governments' will. It is composed of representative ministers of the Member States who are empowered to commit the governments of their states and exercise the right to vote on their behalf (Art. 16 (1) and (2) TEU). The major role of the Council consists in safeguarding Member States' interest in the EU decision-making. Thus, it is one of the most 'intergovernmental' institutions (Barnard & Steve, 2014, p. 54).

The formal meetings of the Council usually take place in Brussels; only in April, June, and October does the Council meet in Luxembourg, aside from one informal meeting that is hosted in the country holding the presidency of the Council[3] for the respective half-year term (Art. 1 (3) RoP).

2 Powers of the Council

Art. 16 (1) TEU states that the Council shall jointly with the European Parliament (EP) exercise legislative and budgetary functions and carry out policy-making and coordinating functions as laid down in the Treaties. However, besides this rather technical description of the role and powers of the Council, it exercises important functions in the overall decision- and policy-making of the EU.

According to Craig/de Burca (Ibid., 74) it exercises its powers in seven ways:

First, the Council must approve all legislative proposals from the Commission before they become law. The necessary majorities vary according to the policy domain out of which a law should be passed.

Secondly, the Council can in accordance with Art. 241 TFEU request the Commission by simple majority to undertake studies that the Council considers desirable for achieving the common objectives and to submit to it any appropriate proposals. If the Commission does not deliver, it needs to state the underlying reasons.

Thirdly, according to Art. 290 TFEU the Council can delegate power to the Commission, granting the latter the right to pass further regulations in a given area.

Fourthly, as complexity increases, the Council plays a decisive role in the inter--institutional collaboration between the EP, the Commission, and the Council concerning the legislative agenda and the use of Inter-Institutional Agreements.

---

[2] Official Journal of the European Communities, P 152, July 13, 1967.

[3] See Chap. 9 of this handbook.

Fifthly, the Council in accordance with Art. 314 TFEU plays an important role in defining and adopting the EU's budget, thus defining the scope of activities of EU action in many policy domains.

Sixthly, the Council concludes agreements on behalf of the EU with third states or international organisations as stated in Art. 218 TFEU.

Finally, given the intergovernmental character of the Common Foreign and Security Policy (CFSP) including the Common Security and Defence Policy (CSDP), the Council takes the necessary decisions in that policy domain within the margins of the strategic guidelines provided for by the European Council (Art. 24–26 as well as Art. 42 TEU). Thus, the Council, in the formation of the so-called Political and Security Committee monitors military and civilian operations and also reports back to the Foreign Affairs Council.

Looking at the conclusion of international agreements under the framework of Art. 218 TFEU, a new challenge seems to arise from the perspective of the Council. Until recently, the Council presidency has been keen to maintain a leading role throughout the life of an international agreement, including by adding its signature to the final act. However, in its 2024 landmark case *C-551/21—Commission v Council (Signature d'accords internationaux)*, the European Court of Justice (ECJ) has unexpectedly broken with a long-standing tradition that, after decades of accepted practice, ensured the participation of Member States in the act of signing international agreements on behalf of the EU (Genini, 2024, p. 152). It thus remains to be seen how this will affect the Council's competence regarding Art. 218 TFEU.

Lastly, it is worth mentioning that the Council has been often criticized in terms of its democratic legitimacy as co-legislator. Regarding the so-called democratic deficit of the EU, Art. 10 (2) TEU states that the democratic legitimacy of the Council is based on each individual minister's democratic accountability to the electorate or parliament of each Member State. Thus, it is not surprising that the Council is sometimes referred to as the upper-chamber of a two-chamber legislative system (Barnard & Steve, 2014, p. 54); however, given the fact that the Council has both executive and legislative functions, this comparison only encompasses parts of the functions of the Council. Furthermore, in terms of democratic legitimacy, there is no collective legitimacy as regards the EU as a whole.

3 Configurations and Meetings

The Council does not have a fixed membership, rather it is made up of different ministers depending on the subject matters to be discussed. Thus, it meets in the so-called Council configurations. The European Council adopts, according to Art. 236 lit. a TFEU, by qualified majority, the list of Council configurations.[4] Only the

[4] European Council Decision 2010/594/EU of September 16, 2010, amending the list of Council configurations (OJ L 263, 6.10.2010, 12)

General Affairs Council whose task is to ensure the consistency of the work of the different Council configurations as well as the Foreign Affairs Council that 'elaborates the Union's external action on the basis of strategic guidelines laid down by the European Council and ensures that the Union's action is consistent' are permanently enshrined by the treaties according to Art. 16 (6) TEU.

Currently, ten Council configurations exist, having reduced the number from twenty-two that prevailed in the 1990s (Craig & De Búrca, 2024, p. 71). Annex 1 of the Council's Rules of Procedure (RoP) defines the subject matter for the formations:

- General affairs,
- Foreign affairs,
- Economic and financial affairs,
- Justice and home affairs,
- Employment, social policy, health and consumer affairs,
- Competitiveness (internal market, industry and research),
- Transport, telecommunications and energy,
- Agriculture and fisheries,
- Environment,
- Education, youth and culture.

The conduct of the Council meetings is mainly regulated within the Council's RoP.[5] From a primary law perspective, Art. 16 (8) TEU defines that Council meetings are divided into two parts, i.e. those dealing with legislative and non-legislative acts. The same paragraph also provides for a public meeting whenever the Council meets in its legislative capacity. Art. 3 (6) RoP further defines the agenda of the Council meetings. The first part shall be entitled 'Legislative deliberations' and the second 'Non-legislative activities'.

The items appearing in each part of the provisional agenda shall be divided into *A items* and *B items*. Items for which approval by the Council is possible without discussion shall be entered as A items, but this does not exclude the possibility of any member of the Council or of the Commission expressing an opinion at the time of the approval of these items and having statements included in the minutes. B items are subject to further debate as they include points left over from previous Council meetings, points upon which no agreement was reached in Committee of Permanent Representatives (COREPER) or at working party level or that are too politically sensitive to be settled at a lower level. The results of Council votes are automatically made public when the Council acts as legislator. If a member wants to add an explanatory note to the vote, this note will also be made public, if a legal act is adopted (Art. 9 (2) RoP).

As the Council acts as one legal body, any Council configuration can adopt legislative acts that fall under the remit of another configuration.

[5] Council Decision 2009/937/EU of December 1, 2009, adopting the Council's Rules of Procedure [2009] OJ L325/35, as amended by Council Decision (EU) 2022/1242 of July 18, 2022 [2022] OJ L190/137.

4 Structure of the Council[6]

In order to properly carry out its functions and competences, the work of the Council is organised at three different levels: the ministerial (formal Council) level where decisions are made; the senior official level for the preparation of the Council meetings; and the working groups (bodies/committees) with experts from the national level examining each proposal in preparatory bodies. Furthermore, the work is facilitated by the General Secretariat of the Council as the administrative arm of the Council. In the following subsection, the structure of the Council below the ministerial level will be briefly described.[7]

(a) Committee of Permanent Representatives (COREPER)

The work of the Council is to be prepared by the Committee of Permanent Representatives (COREPER) which shall carry out the tasks assigned to it by the Council. Despite the clear mandate given by Art. 16 (7) TEU and although it does not have the power to formally adopt decisions, it plays an important role in shaping the work and agenda of the Council. It is split into two parts: COREPER I and COREPER II according to policy domains. It is set up by the so-called Permanent Representatives—government officials at ambassadorial level and Deputy Permanent Representatives of the Member States that form the leadership of the Permanent Representation of the Member States to the EU. They meet weekly in Brussels to debate the current EU integration agenda.

(b) Working Groups

Below the COREPER there are roughly 150 working groups which prepare the work of the Council and analyse every legislative proposal coming from the Commission. Working groups are set up by government officials and experts coming from the Member States and preparing the work of the COREPER.

(c) Council General Secretariat

The Council also has its own General Secretariat under the leadership of the Secretary General which provides the necessary administrative service to the European Council, the Council, the COREPER and the Working Parties. It has taken over an important role in preparing the documentation, legal advice, and translation services and preparation of the agendas. Furthermore, the programme of the 18 months trio presidency[8] is also elaborated in close cooperation with the Council General Secretariat. Thus, especially in the more recent years, the role of the Council Secretariat and especially its Secretary General has been further strengthened.

---

[6] This section just provides a rough overview of the bodies below the Council level and will be further analysed in Chap. 8 by Roland Jöbstl.

[7] See also Chap. 8 of this handbook.

[8] See further details on the trio presidency in Chap. 9 of this handbook.

5 Voting in the Council

As a rule in accordance with Art. 16 (3) TEU, the Council acts by qualified majority unless otherwise provided for in the treaties. There are certain policy matters in which the Council votes by simply majority, i.e., 14 out of the 27 Member States (Art. 238 (1) TFEU), which is mainly used for procedural matters or unanimously, as, e.g., Art. 314 TFEU sets out as the rule in taxation matters.

However, given the various enlargement rounds and treaty revisions, qualified majority voting (QMV) has been extended mainly in the area of Title V of the TFEU in the area of freedom security and justice and unanimous decisions have been reduced. Unanimity is still required on matters which Member States consider to be sensitive, such as Common Foreign and Security Policy (CFSP), citizenship, EU membership, harmonisation of national legislation on indirect taxation, EU finances, certain areas of justice and home affairs as well as harmonisation of national legislation in the field of social security and social protection. Nonetheless, external factors such as the current (Status October 2025) geopolitical developments also contribute to an "opening" of those areas. In order to foster EU's strategic autonomy in defence, the Commission has proposed various new instruments under the internal market rules and thus circumventing the strong intergovernmental character of security and defence policy of the EU.

In 2017 a new voting mechanism has been implemented. Traditionally, the Council reached a majority by the so-called 'weighted votes system', meaning that the votes per Member States were calculated proportionally on the basis of its inhabitants. With the Lisbon Treaty and after a transition period between 2014 and 2017, a double majority criterion based on the number of Member States and the population of the Union has been defined by Art. 16 (4) TEU. In fact, the introduction of this new demographic element has relatively increased the weight of the largest Member States within the Council (Baratta, 2024, p. 159).

As from 1 November 2014 and in accordance with Art. 238 (3) lit. a TFEU a qualified majority shall be defined as at least 55% of the members of the Council, comprising at least fifteen of them and representing Member States comprising at least 65% of the population of the Union. The two conditions are cumulative and need to be fulfilled in order to obtain a majority otherwise the proposal is rejected. Abstentions are considered equivalent to negative votes as they do not contribute to the formation of a majority. The right to vote has to be exercised by the Minister in charge of the portfolio. In case of absence, it may be transferred to a Deputy Minister/State Secretary or potentially to the Permanent Representative according to the constitutional requirements of the respective Member State.

A blocking minority must include at least four Council members, failing which the qualified majority shall be deemed attained.

In order to safeguard Member States' interests when opposing the approval of certain legislative initiatives, the so-called Ioannina mechanism has been put in place. It enabled countries representing at least three quarters of the EU's population or at least three quarters of the number of Member States required to form a blocking minority, to block the vote for a Council act by qualified majority, in order to try to find a solution within a reasonable space of time. From April 1, 2017, the new rule of qualified majority became compulsory. The activating percentage of the 'Ioannina compromise' was reduced to at least 55% of the EU's population or at least 55% of the number of Member States required to constitute a blocking minority.

Votings in general take place during the physical Council meetings. Art. 11 RoP states that the Council shall vote on the initiative of its president. The members of the Council shall vote in the order of the Member States laid down in the list of successive presidencies, beginning with the member who, according to that order, follows the member holding the office of president (Ibid. para. 3). During the Covid pandemic, Art. 12 RoP was amended in order to facilitate voting on urgent matters in written form where the Council unanimously decides to use that procedure or where COREPER decides to use that procedure in accordance with the voting rule applicable for the adoption of the Council acts concerned. In special circumstances, the president may also propose the use of that procedure.[9]

The text of the acts adopted by the Council and that of the acts adopted by the EP and the Council in accordance with the ordinary legislative procedure shall be signed by the president in office at the time of their adoption and by the Secretary-General (Art. 15 RoP).

Qualified Majority Voting
In accordance with Art. 238 (3) lit. a TFEU a qualified majority shall be defined as at least 55% of the members of the Council, comprising at least fifteen of them and representing Member States comprising at least 65% of the population of the Union.

6 Council Presidencies[10]

The meetings of the Council are chaired on a six-monthly basis by each member state according to a rotational system. According to Art. 16 (9) TEU the presidency of Council configuration shall be held with the conditions established in accordance with Art. 236 lit. b TFEU. Every country takes its turn. This means that every Member State—irrespective of its size and relative influence within the European family—holds the presidency of the Council. The turn comes every 13-and-a-half year. In order to ensure the consistency and continuity between presidencies, groups of three states set up their trio programme which is endorsed by the General Affairs Council after holding a public debate on it. Except for the Foreign Affairs Council that is chaired by the High Representative of the Union for Foreign Affairs and Security Policy that is also at the same time Vice-President of the Commission (HR/VP), it is up to the presidency to plan and chair the meetings in the Council and its

[9] Council Decision (EU) 2022/1242 of July 18, 2022 [2022} OJ L190/137.

[10] See also Chap. 9 of this handbook.

Table 1 List of Council presidencies 2025–2030; Trios marked in different colours

Poland	January-June	2025
Denmark	July-December	2025
Cyprus	January-June	2026
Ireland	July-December	2026
Lithuania	January-June	2027
Greece	July-December	2027
Italy	January-June	2028
Latvia	July-December	2028
Luxembourg	January-June	2029
Netherlands	July-December	2029
Slovakia	January-June	2030
Malta	July-December	2030

preparatory bodies. The presidency ensures that discussions are conducted properly and that the Council's rules of procedure and working methods are correctly applied.

It also organises various formal and informal meetings and gatherings in Brussels and in the country of the rotating presidency.

The presidency represents the Council in relations with the other EU institutions, particularly with the Commission and the EP. Its role is to try and reach agreement on legislative files through trilogues, informal negotiation meetings, and Conciliation Committee meetings. The current list of the trio presidencies has been approved by the Council in 2016[11] and foresees the Council relations until 2030. The current and upcoming presidencies are as follows Table 1:

7 The Council in the Ordinary Legislative Procedure

As mentioned above, with the introduction of the co-decision procedure as the OLP, the Council acts as a co-legislator together with the EP. Analysing Art. 294 TFEU, the term *Council* is mentioned twenty-one times. More specifically, the Council receives the proposal of the Commission together with the EP. It then awaits the positioning of the EP after the first reading of the EP. There are two possible reactions by the Council taking into consideration the voting rules as stated before: it

[11] Council Decision (EU) 2016/1316 of 26 July 2016 amending Decision 2009/908/EU, laying down measures for the implementation of the European Council Decision on the exercise of the Presidency of the Council, and on the chairmanship of preparatory bodies of the Council, OJ L208/42.

either accepts the EP's position, thus the text will be adopted correspondingly to the position of the EP. Or it rejects the EP's position, so subsequently it shall adopt its position at first reading and communicate it to the EP stating the reasons that led to the Council's position.

Within three months, the EP returns to the Council in three possible ways. It either approves the Council position and thus creates new law. It rejects, by a majority of its component members, the Council's position at first reading, thus not adopting the proposed act or proposes, by majority, new amendments that will be scrutinised by the Council and the Commission. After again an up to three months period, the Council by qualified majority may approve all amendments, thus the text is being adopted or it does not approve the amendments leading to the situation that the President of the Council has to set up the *Conciliation Committee (CC)*. In the case of a negative opinion of the Commission on certain amendments, the Council needs to act by unanimity.

According to Art. 294 (10) TFEU the CC being set up by an equal number of members of the EP and the Council or its respective members has the task of reaching agreement on a joint text, by a qualified majority of the members of the Council or their representatives and by a majority of the members representing the EP within 6 weeks of its being convened, on the basis of the positions of the EP and the Council at second reading.

If no agreement can be reached within 6 weeks, the legal act has failed. If a text is agreed by the CC, it is again a six-week period within which the Council has to adopt the legislative act by qualified majority. The respective deadlines of 3 months and 6 weeks can be extended by a maximum of 1 month or 2 weeks, respectively, if Council and EP initiate such an extension.

As shown, the Lisbon Treaty has moved the co-decision procedure to an equal forum for decision-making between Council and EP, putting both at equal footing in terms of their decision-making capacities.[12]

8 Conclusion

Despite the continuous strengthening of the role of the EP in the EU decision-making with every respective treaty reform, the Council remains the fulcrum of policy and lawmaking in the European Union (Hayes-Renshaw & Wallace, 2006, p. 321). No key decision regarding the development of the European integration process happens without the approval of the Council and thus the Member States as the Council strives to accommodate as many national interests as possible (Akse, 2020, p. 58). In *realpolitical* terms it seems that as a consequence of the multitude of challenges the EU is facing, the Council, following the example of the European Council, has taken over a leadership role and thus in the interinstitutional setup its

[12] See also Chap. 2 of this handbook.

role has been further strengthened. However, as indicated in the context of the conclusion of international agreements, the supranational institutions, i.e. the Commission as well as the European Court of Justice, try to counterbalance those attempts. It needs to be seen whether the complexity of the international environment in which the EU needs to position itself as a strong and reliable partner fosters the interinstitutional cohesion or leads to more fragmentation which again will be benefitting more the intergovernmental character of the EU integration process as Member States remain the "Masters of the Treaties".

References

Akse, E. (Ed.). (2020). *How the EU institutions work. Your handbook and guide to EU decision-making*. John Harper Publishing.

Baratta, R. (2024). *Institutions of EU law*. Wolters Kluwer.

Barnard, C., & Steve, P. (Eds.) (2014). European Union Law, Oxford.

Craig, P., & De Búrca, G. (2024). *EU law. Text, cases and materials* (8th ed.). Oxford University Press.

Genini, D. (2024). Breaking a Tradition: How Signing of Agreements Is No Longer a Matter for the Council. In: *European Papers*, Vol. 9, 2024, No 1, European Forum, Insight of 25 June 2024, 145–152.

Hayes-Renshaw, F., & Wallace, H. (2006). *The Council of Ministers* (2nd ed.). Palgrave.

Arnold H. Kammel is Secretary General and Director General for Defence Policy at the Austrian Federal Ministry of Defence. He studied Law, Political Science and European Studies in Graz, Alcalá de Henares (Madrid), Vienna and Eisenstadt. Since 2010 he has been lecturing in the Master's study programme "European Studies – Management of EU projects" at the Hochschule Burgenland in the fields of European Law, Institutions and Policies and was awarded the title Honorary Professor (FH).

The Council's Engine Room: Understanding COREPER and Its Working Parties

Roland Jöbstl

Abstract This chapter analyses the role of preparatory bodies within the decision-making framework of the Council of the European Union, and its role in the Ordinary Legislative Procedure (OLP). Focusing on COREPER and the Council Working Parties, it examines their respective legal bases, institutional structures and functional responsibilities. Particular attention is given to the procedural interaction between technical and political levels of negotiation, the formal and informal practices that shape preparatory work and the organisation of meetings. By highlighting the significance of preparatory processes in the legislative cycle, the chapter provides an overview of the internal mechanisms that enable effective decision-making within the Council. The analysis draws on primary legal documents and practical insights, offering a practitioners perspective engaged in EU legislative affairs.

Keywords Antici · Council · Preparatory bodies of the Council · COREPER I · COREPER II · Mertens · Working Parties

1 Introduction

The Council of the European Union (Council) plays a central role in the EU's general decision-making and specific role in the legislative procedure. Through the Council the Member States act jointly as co-legislator. This chapter aims to explore the structure and functions of its preparatory bodies, especially COREPER I and II, as well as the Council Working Parties, showing how their structure and tasks contribute to shape EU decision-making.

The Council, as one of the formal EU institutions, also called "the Council of Ministers", brings together ministers and officials from the Member States. The

R. Jöbstl (✉)
Attaché for Climate, Environment and the Atomic Questions Working Party, Permanent Representation of Austria to the EU, Brussels, Belgium
e-mail: roland.joebstl@gmail.com

G. Füricht-Fiegl et al. (eds.), *Handbook on EU Law-making*, Professional Practice in Governance and Public Organizations, https://doi.org/10.1007/978-3-032-16559-6_8

Council is not to be confused with the European Council, which is the meeting of the heads of states. While the Council meets regularly and is also the formal decision-making body on the side of the Member States, without the preceding steps of filtering, analysis and identification of key questions of political importance by the preparatory bodies, the Council would not be able to handle the volume and complexity of today's political processes.

This chapter discusses characteristics of the Council and the logic of the preparatory bodies. The chapter focusses on work at ambassador level with the Permanent Representatives (PR) and its Deputy (DPR) and bodies at attaché level and discusses the interaction of those processes along an example of a legislative procedure under qualified majority.

2 Reminder: The Council of the European Union

The Council is one.

The preparatory bodies serve the decision-making of the Council, as discussed in the comments of the Council's Rules of Procedure (CRP) (Council of the European Union: General Secretariat of the Council (GSC), 2022) (Council, 2022, excerpt by the author):

> The Council is a single legal entity, which may meet in different configurations (Agriculture and Fisheries, Environment, etc.) according to the subject matter dealt with (Art. 2(1) CRP). [...] Three consequences follow from the fact that the Council is a single legal entity. Firstly, a legal act concerning any subject falling within the Union's competence can be adopted by any Council configuration. [...] Secondly, because the Council is a single legal entity, there is no hierarchy among the different Council configurations. [...] Thirdly, since the Council is a single legal entity, the office of the presidency of the Council is also a single office. Thus, the rules applicable to the presidency apply to any person chairing one of the Council configurations, including the Foreign Affairs configuration, or, as appropriate, one of the Council's preparatory bodies, unless the CRP specify otherwise (Article 1(5) 2nd subpara CRP).

The basic principles of the Council also apply for the preparatory bodies. As it is the Council and only the Council that can adopt items of a legal matter for Member States, items discussed, positions taken by any of the preparatory bodies might have procedural implications and political importance but are always depending on the Council as formal and final decision-making body. Therefore, those preparatory bodies mirror the Council's logics and serve to provide orientation on next steps, expected majorities and intended voting behaviour. Yet, while Council configurations may differ in competence and political power, once an item is adopted the legal nature does not differ depending on where, when and how it was adopted.

2.1 *Composition and Participants (Council Configurations, Ministers, Presidency)*

As laid out in the previous chapter the Council Decision on the Council's Rules of Procedure establishes currently ten formations[1] of the Council. As this structure does not necessarily correspond to the structure of governments or the allocated competences of ministers in Member States, there might be one minister participating in multiple Council formations as well as multiple ministers participating in a single Council meeting.

Generally, Member States are to be represented by the Head of Delegation (HoD) at the Council meetings at ministerial level. This is largely the case with Member States usually being represented by one or more members of the central government, usually minister, vice-minister, deputy-minister or state secretary (Council of the European Union: General Secretariat of the Council (GSC), 2022). CRP defines that ministers are to be substituted by the relevant PR or DPR: "*A member of the Council who is prevented from attending a meeting may arrange to be represented (Art. 4 CRP). In practice, that member is represented by the Permanent Representative or his or her Deputy*".

For the HoD to represent the Member States, delegations include a whole team of people, supporting and facilitating the Council proceedings. The minister is supported and accompanied usually by staff from his cabinet including personal aides or spokespersons. As first Deputy to the ministers, the Permanent Representative (PR) or Deputy Permanent Representative (DPR) plus their team (Antici, Mertens) represent the Member States, make interventions, and follow the discussions in the first row. Furthermore, the delegations include the attachés responsible for the files and relevant technical questions and reporting, as well as senior officials (General Directors, Directors) and experts on EU affairs and coordination units from capitals to follow Council discussions.

2.2 *Formal and Informal Processes Within Council Meetings*

In addition to formal items of the Council meetings set in the agenda, Council meetings do entail other less formal processes. Several Council formations include a ministerial lunch in their provisional agendas, typically framed as working or informal lunch events to exchange with high representatives of third countries or international organisations. These informal lunches are more common in Councils with external or thematic focus and must not address ongoing legislative processes. In addition to those items of the Council agenda, Council meetings are also often used by Member States to arrange bilateral and multilateral meetings at the margins of the Council. These informal meetings are organised by the individual Member

[1] See details in Chap. 7 of this handbook.

States including thematic pre-meetings of groups of like-minded member states, e.g. „Friends of Renewables "or the „Green Growth Group "or meetings organised around the party affiliation of ministers and might include participation of Commission representatives, Members of the EP (MEP) or other actors. Furthermore, bilateral meetings are usually organised in parallel to the Council meetings to facilitate a direct exchange of ministers with the relevant Commissioners and/or other Member States, discussing items of joint interest or concern. Each of those informal settings is, to differing degrees, mirrored at preparatory level as part of the run-up and as follow-up to those meetings.

3 Council Preparatory Bodies

While the Council is empowered to and in emergency situations can take decisions without preparation by other bodies, it is the norm that its work is prepared by the Committee of Permanent Representatives of the governments of the Member States to the European Union (COREPER, derived from French ***Co****mité des* ***rep****résentants* ***per****manents*) after having been discussed by one of more than 150, in many cases highly specialised, working parties and committees, known as the "Council preparatory bodies". The Council's website distinguishes the preparatory bodies into two main categories (Website of the General Secretariat of the Council (GSC), n.d.) (Council, 2025):

I. *Committees set up by the treaties, intergovernmental decisions or by Council act—mostly permanent and often with an appointed or elected chairperson.*
II. *Committees and working parties set up by* COREPER*—dealing with specific subjects and chaired by the delegate of the country holding the rotating presidency of the Council of the EU.*

In addition, temporary "ad hoc" bodies can be created for a specific purpose defined in a mandate. These ad hoc bodies cease to exist when their task is fulfilled. The majority of preparatory bodies are Council Working parties set up and reporting to one of the COREPERs including the Antici and Mertens Groups. Central for foreign affairs is the Political and Security Committee (PSC) within the category of Committees established by the treaties. Committees and Groups established by Council Act include the Special Committee on Agriculture (SCA) and, as a recent addition, the Working Party on the United Kingdom (WPUK), which was established after the Brexit. A current list of preparatory bodies can be found with the General Secretariat of the Council for 2025 (Website of the General Secretariat of the Council (GSC), n.d.).

3.1 The Permanent Representatives Committee (COREPER I and II)

At the heart of the Council's preparatory work is the COREPER. Divided into COREPER I and COREPER II, this body ensures that political and technical issues are refined before reaching the ministerial level. The following section analyses COREPER structure, tasks, participants and working practices. The essential task of COREPER is to prepare the Council's work; this especially means coordinating and filtering legislative and policy discussions before they reach the Council (Art. 19 CRP). COREPER II deals with general affairs, foreign affairs, economic and financial affairs and justice and home affairs and is attended by the ambassadors assigned to be PR. COREPER I handles technical areas like agriculture, environment, transport, employment, telecommunications and is attended by the DPR.

3.1.1 Legal Foundation and Institutional Role

The principle "the Council is one" applies also to the work of preparatory bodies, meaning that COREPER as the general and central preparatory body, while meeting in two formations I + II, is also one. While having traditional clear allocation of policy fields and responsibilities for the preparation of different Council configurations, there can be a deviation from the norm. Art. 19 of the CRP (Council Rules of Procedure, 2009) lays out the mandate of the COREPER:

> *Article 19 Coreper, committees and working parties.*
>
> *1. Coreper shall be responsible for preparing the work of all the* meetings *of the Council and for carrying out the tasks assigned to it by the Council. It shall in any case [19] ensure consistency of the European Union's policies and actions and see to it that the following principles and rules are observed:*
>
> *(a) the principles of legality, subsidiarity, proportionality and providing reasons for acts*
> *(b) rules establishing the powers of Union institutions, bodies, offices and agencies*
> *(c) budgetary provisions*
> *(d) rules on procedure, transparency and the quality of drafting*

This means that the COREPER is the last level of discussion by civil servants, before the Council with its ministerial and political responsibility and nature is handling an item. In most situations it is a matter of filtering, preparing and coordination, sometimes in a very procedural, "technocratic" manner, also within the Member States. At the same time COREPER allows a probing of the political sensitivities of certain questions by Member States without forcing decision, allows for a non-public discussion of key political questions and provides a last step of escalation, before something is brought up to the ministerial level.

3.1.2 Structure: COREPER I versus COREPER II

COREPER I and COREPER II are each responsible for preparing different Council configurations and policy areas (Website of the General Secretariat of the Council (GSC), n.d.) (Council, 2025).

COREPER I prepares the work of six Council configurations:

- agriculture and fisheries (AGRIFISH) (only financial issues or technical measures on veterinary, phytosanitary or food legislation as agricultural issues are prepared by the Special Committee on Agriculture (SCA)),
- competitiveness (COMPET),
- education, youth, culture and sport (EYCS),
- employment, social policy, health and consumer affairs (EPSCO),
- environment (ENVI),
- transport, telecommunications and energy (TTE).

COREPER II prepares the work of four Council configurations:

- economic and financial affairs (ECOFIN),
- foreign affairs (FAC),
- general affairs (GAC) including the preparations of the European Council (EUCO),
- justice and home affairs (JHA).

The distinction between COREPER I and COREPER II lies in the nature of the issues and Council configurations they prepare. COREPER I deals with rather sectoral, internal and socio-economic policies, often more technical and legislative in nature, such as environment, transport, energy, employment and internal markets. Its focus is on the EU's internal functioning and sector-specific regulation that directly affects citizens and businesses.

By contrast, COREPER II discusses issues of political, external or cross-cutting nature such as foreign affairs, economic governance and justice. It also deals with matters affecting the EU as a political entity, including institutional issues, international relations and broader governance topics including the EU budget. This distinction reflects the different levels of political oversight and strategic importance of the files handled by each committee. For both formations, the representatives are tasked with wide range of topics bringing in a horizontal perspective of a Member States key concerns across different policy areas.

The two COREPER formations (I and II) usually meet every week for full-day or half-day sessions on Wednesdays, with additional COREPER I meetings regularly added on Fridays. The usual agenda of a COREPER meeting includes an extensive list of items from different topics within its remit. The discussion of an individual agenda item can take anything from less than 5 min, e.g. preparation of a Council agenda without any delegation taking the floor, to a regular single-table round of 1 h extending to full-day meetings hashing out extensive compromise packages for political agreements. Contrary to most Council meetings COREPER is non-public, requiring same-day reporting for capitals to receive information about the outcomes and discussions.

3.1.3 Participants: Permanent Representatives, Deputy Permanent Representatives, Attachés

At COREPER the participants include a reduced set of participants per Member States compared to Council meetings. In COREPER II Member States are represented by the PR and Antici complemented by attachés and in COREPER I by DPR and Mertens complemented by attachés.

The wide range of subjects that both COREPER formations are responsible for creates a special dynamic for those meetings. The PR (and DPRs), leading the debate in COREPER, are still public servants but already in a strong proximity to the political decision-making. Different from the ministerial level, they are still receiving political instructions from the capitals of the Member States but due to the assigned responsibility of ensuring consistency, legality, subsidiarity and proportionality they are in many instances given a certain margin of manoeuvre and bring in their perspective on a Member States position across policy fields.

The Antici and Mertens are the closest aids of their ambassadors, substituting the ambassadors in COREPER also when taking the floor, but generally acting as the logistical, technical and on many occasions political right hands of them as well.

As elaborated in the section above, as COREPER handles a plethora of topics and items, ambassadors and their closest aides stay in the meeting and attachés rotate in-and-out for their respective dossiers. Attachés take up the role of „technical "experts negotiating and preparing the files in the working parties, responsible for the note taking during the COREPER meetings and adding context and further explanation to discussions and instructions.

This leads to the common pattern that, while ministers might bring in their political priorities and attachés might have a technical focus on the content from the perspective of the responsible ministry, in COREPER ambassadors have the possibility to bring in a cross-cutting and horizontal perspective on a dossier in the current political picture. Also, as COREPER ambassadors are usually embedded in the structures of the Ministry of Foreign Affairs or in some Member States assigned from the chancellery or prime minister, this perspective of the head of government or central government does shape the specific discussions in COREPER.

3.1.4 Tasks: Political Preparation of Council Decisions

Aside from the overall responsibilities of COREPER (Art 19, para. 1 CRP) and further procedural competences (para. 3 setting up of working groups, para. 7 CRP on procedural decisions) Art. 19, para. 2 CRP lays out the essence of the COREPER activities.

> 2. All items on the agenda for a Council meeting shall be examined in advance by Coreper unless the latter decides otherwise. Coreper shall endeavour to reach agreement at its level to be submitted to the Council for adoption. It shall ensure adequate presentation of the dossiers to the Council and, where appropriate, shall present guidelines, options or suggested solutions.

This means everything that can be pre-agreed by COREPER should be and will be prepared for adoption as non-discussion (A-item) by any Council formation. Anything that is not yet ready for Council shall be filtered and subjected to further discussions on more technical level or moved to a later stage. Everything that is put as discussion point (B-item) for the Council must be pre-assessed and pre-digested to identify the key options, conflicts and possible solutions for political debate. The work put in by the chairing presidency in identifying and presenting those key options together with structured questions significantly shapes the debate and potentially the outcomes. It is quite common for ambassadors to be able to refrain from taking the floor if they don't have major concerns or do not add to the debate. Building on the preparatory work of the working party, ambassadors usually take a speaking time of 2–10 min. This means that, while at working party level a whole day of discussion allows delegations to extensively take the floor on technical aspects, the discussion at COREPER requires a massive reduction and prioritisation of concerns at play for each Member State, but also a simplification of the discussions towards support and alignment with the solutions of the presidency or rejection and seeking a group of like-minded Member States to chart out alternative approaches.

3.2 Council Working Parties

3.2.1 Legal Basis and Institutional Framework

Most Working Parties are set up based on Art. 19 para. 3 of the CRP (Council Rules of Procedure, 2009) (Council, 2022), especially those dealing with specific subjects and chaired by the delegate of the country holding the rotating presidency of the Council, e.g., competition, energy, transport, environment, etc. For new topics or topics requiring the participation of multiple or different participants per Member States ad hoc working parties can be established with a specific mandate. Working parties in the remit of one of the ten Council formations make up the majority of preparatory bodies, with AGRIFISH „leading "with 46 different working party formations, corresponding to almost 1/3 of all formations, followed by 38 under FAC. Yet, working party formations differ significantly in the frequency of the meetings. The ENVI Council has only two regular working party formations (WP Environment and WP International Environment Issues) but tends to have multiple meetings per week, while other working parties, e.g., Atomic Questions under GAC, meet only monthly.

3.2.2 Structure and Types and Participants: Attachés, National Experts, Council Secretariat, Presidency Chairs

The majority of working parties are chaired by officials of the Member State of the current rotating presidency,[2] but some have a fixed chair elected or appointed among the members, are chaired by a representative of the High Representative of the Union for Foreign Affairs and Security Policy (common in the foreign affairs field), and some working parties on technical expertise being chaired by the General Secretariat of the Council (GSC). At working party level, member states are usually represented by attachés and/or national experts. The chair is supported by staff from the GCS, if necessary, including the Council Legal Service. Furthermore, the Commission usually participates in Council working parties, especially when discussing a legislative proposal. In matters where the Commission has no formal role or items are purely in the competence of Member States participation might be limited to Council-only.

In the spirit of a multi-lingual union, Member States request and pay for interpretation at working-party- and COREPER-level. Documents are usually provided in English or another working language of the Union.

3.2.3 Tasks and Responsibilities: Drafting and Technical Preparation, Reporting

The tasks of the working parties generally include the following steps:

- Examination of the proposal or document.
- Possible amendments or revisions.
- Further approval or identification of items to be discussed at the next level, e.g., COREPER.

Each of those steps might be split up into multiple sub-steps of the course of multiple weeks, or all of them concluded within the same meeting. Usually,

[2] See Chap. 9 of this handbook.

especially when discussing legislative proposals by the Commission, the examination starts with a presentation of the proposal and the impact assessment by the Commission, rounds of written questions and answers by the Commission. Depending on the complexity of the proposal this first examination might take less than 4 or more than 10 meetings. If Member States are given the possibility to provide written questions or comments, due to the deadlines a period of 1–4 weeks might be needed between reverting to the issue.

When a proposal or document needs changes to be discussed or presented to the next level in rare instances those might be done in the same meeting as the examination. In most cases these next steps are done after a period for written comments and presented in a follow-up meeting by the presidency, usually after consultation with the concerned member states and Commission. Again, based on the complexity of the issue this might be done in an iterative manner with multiple revisions until a discussion at the next level is possible. Drafting is usually done by the presidency, often supported by the Commission but also drawing on written comments and drafting proposals put forward by Member States. Sometimes this is done during the meeting but usually in the follow-up or run-up to meetings, allowing the presidency to have a well-informed picture of possible compromises, solutions, and landing zones. Technical preparations by the presidency usually include a formal call for written comments issued via the GSC, in many instances also include more or less extensive bilateral exchanges with concerned Member States and the Commission.

For simple procedures or dossiers, it might be sufficient to present the document including possible changes to the working party once and directly forward it to the COREPER. In complicated cases, it might be required or requested that during the revising of the text, a dossier is brought up to COREPER for political guidance, be it on the process or on content, only to revert back to the level of the working party for further preparations.

Each of those steps needs some kind of examination and assessment by the responsible authorities and experts in the Member States and attachés to report back on the state and progress of discussions. The detail of reporting differs between dossiers and Member States, sometimes limited to oral reports, other instances requiring extensive written reports with additional enquiries among member states, Commission and/or presidency.

Generally, the Working Party shows a certain iterative nature in examining, commenting, drafting, compromising over documents to ensure that all aspects are covered and member states are able to take a position and make a decision.

4 Interplay Between Working Parties, COREPER and the Council

4.1 Vertical Workflow: From Technical to Political to Ministerial Level

The functioning of the Council relies on a carefully coordinated process linking Working Parties, COREPER and Council meetings. This section illustrates the flow of legislative work between these bodies and highlights mechanisms that ensure efficiency and coherence in the decision-making process.

The schematic Fig. 1 shows a simplified overview of the most essential steps from the publication of a legal proposal by the Commission to the formal adoption by the Council, which subsequently is followed by the publication in the Official Journal of the EU for its entry into force. The figure focusses on the perspective of the Council and its preparatory bodies of the Working Party (WP) and COREPER.

Formally, the role of the Commission is rather limited as the central responsibility is the publication of the proposal, reflecting the Commissions of the right of initiative and the right to withdraw a proposal if the central objectives and elements of the proposal are lost in the negotiations of the co-legislators (Council and EP). In practice, the Commission as author of the proposal has a very integral role in supporting and facilitating the negotiations, being extensively requested to explain, justify, but also help with re-drafting if changes are deemed necessary.

The working party does the footwork on the Council side to examine and amend the proposal to form the Council's position and is essential towards the final phase of the negotiations to find compromises with the EP's position. The key steps on the Council side and its preparatory bodies include the presentation of the proposal by the Commission, an exchange of views and a policy debate in Council, usually prepared by COREPER on the outline of the questions and key issues, and, most essential, the Council position as set out in the General Approach and the formal adoption by the Council.

As political agreements in first reading following the process of a trilogue have become the most common procedures for the ordinary legislative procedure, this

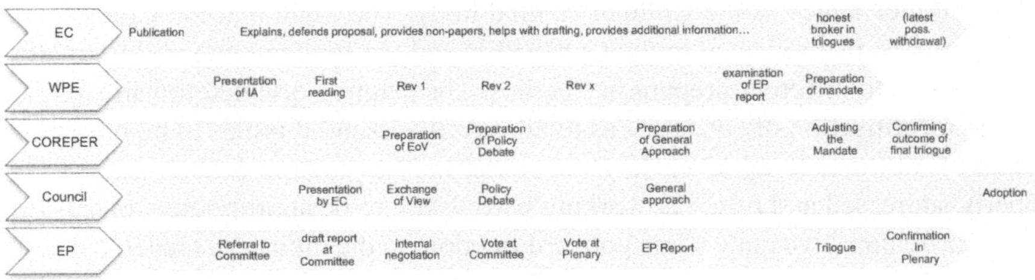

Fig. 1 Key steps from publication to adoption of a legislative proposal by the Commission, the Council and its preparatory bodies of the Working Party on Environment (WPE) and the COREPER and the EP in the scenario of a political agreement via trilogue

example also follows this logic. The formalised but informal processes of agreeing to the Council's position set out as General Approach (GA) by the Council have become the norm to prepare for the negotiations with the EP ahead of trilogues.[3] It needs to be noted that the GA is a political agreement without an explicit legal basis in the EU Treaties, but a procedural practice that has developed over the last decades to streamline negotiation processes. The key documents in those steps are the revised presidency texts (REV 1, 2, etc.), which are elaborated in the working party, reflecting the gradual development of the draft text towards a text with the necessary majority. The preparation of the GA is then done by COREPER ahead of the Council meeting and to prepare for an adoption of the GA in Council.

As soon as the EP has on their side adopted a negotiation mandate, the dossier and the EP's position, as presented in the EP's report, are examined in the working party to identify possibly agreements, disagreements or compromise options to be included in a negotiation mandate for the COREPER. In this phase the key documents for technical work are the so-called 4-column-documents, a working document used in Council negotiations to track and compare positions on a legislative proposal, containing the original text of the Commission proposal, the EP's position, the GA and possible comments and compromises. In case of a successful agreement with the EP, this working document is compiled and transformed into a revised document or report to be adopted by EP in its first reading.

Contrary to the GA, which is in most cases adopted as part of a Council meeting, the revised negotiation mandates and the potential confirmation of the outcome of the trilogues are confirmed by COREPER, in order for the EP to adopt a revised first-reading position that is subsequently formally adopted by the Council, usually as an A-item.

5 Conclusion

This chapter gives insight into the legal basics, structures and interlinkages of the Council's preparatory bodies as part of the EU's legislative procedure. A key observation is that, while the preparatory bodies differ in content and practices, they all serve the Council as the formal decision-making body and generally apply the same logics and mechanics as the Council as final body. The logic that the Council is a single entity is also reflected in the COREPER and the fundamental ability to allocate a dossier to different preparatory bodies. The setup is oriented towards reduction and prioritisation of concerns, as to allow only essential issues to be put on the agenda of the ministerial level. In most cases, this requires technical issues to be properly addressed and raised at working party level, to be appropriately discussed. While the treaties give quite some political freedom to the ministerial level to decide based on political considerations, COREPER does ensure a political filtering and

[3] See Chaps. 16 and 17 of this handbook.

adds horizontal and cross-sectoral perspective to the process. The widespread use of the political agreements in first reading via trilogues has also fully shaped the processes of the preparatory bodies. To which extent this will find further formalisation is yet to be observed.

References

Council of the European Union: General Secretariat of the Council (GSC). (2022). *Comments on the council's rules of procedure*. Publications Office of the European Union. https://data.europa.eu/doi/10.2860/682589

Council Rules of Procedure: Consolidated text: Council Decision of 1 December 2009 adopting the Council's Rules of Procedure (2009/937/EU) http://data.europa.eu/eli/dec/2009/937/2025-01-01

Website of the General Secretariat of the Council (GSC): https://www.consilium.europa.eu/en/council-eu/preparatory-bodies/)

Roland Jöbstl works as Attaché for the Austrian Federal Ministry of Agriculture and Forestry, Climate and Environmental Protection, Regions and Water Management engaged in the lawmaking and daily processes of decision-making of the EU. With professional experience in the European Parliament, civil society, special interest group, federal and regional environmental administration, he focuses on the practical implications of internal logics and mechanisms of EU institutions and legislative procedures.

Chairing the Council: The Role of the Rotating Presidency in EU Lawmaking

Thomas Gloeckel

Abstract This article examines the role of the rotating Presidency of the Council of the European Union in the EU lawmaking process, focusing on its function as a facilitator within the Ordinary Legislative Procedure (OLP). Adopting a chronological, practical and functional lens, the chapter explores how the presidency prepares, manages, and steers legislative work—without holding formal decision-making power. It highlights the evolution of the presidency in light of treaty reforms, institutional developments and the increased complexity of legislative negotiations. Emphasis is placed on the need for strategic planning, administrative coordination and the cultivation of trust among institutional actors. The chapter also analyses the tools at the presidency's disposal, including both formal procedural instruments and a growing set of informal working methods and digital coordination tools that support negotiation, compromise-building, and agenda management. As presidencies due to the system of rotation now occur only every 13.5 years for each Member State, capacity-building, structured learning and trio cooperation are essential. In an era marked by digitalisation, institutional interdependence and geopolitical uncertainty, the rotating presidency plays a vital role in ensuring procedural continuity, consensus-building and legislative progress across the Union.

Keywords Rotating presidency of the Council · Council of the European Union · EU legislative process · Interinstitutional coordination · Trio system · Informal working methods · Institutional continuity

---

T. Gloeckel (✉)
General Secretariat of the Council of the EU, Brussels, Belgium
e-mail: Thomas.gloeckel@consilium.europa.eu

G. Füricht-Fiegl et al. (eds.), *Handbook on EU Law-making*, Professional Practice in Governance and Public Organizations, https://doi.org/10.1007/978-3-032-16559-6_9

1 Introduction

This article explores the role of the rotating Presidency of the Council of the European Union (Council) in the EU lawmaking process from a practical perspective. It examines how the presidency prepares, manages, and steers legislation under the Ordinary Legislative Procedure (OLP), while also setting priorities and shaping the Council's legislative agenda.

Established in 1958, the presidency—held for 6 months by each Member State—embodies institutional continuity and Member State equality, ensuring every Member State periodically leads the Council's work. Beyond procedure, it serves a political and symbolic function: bringing the Council closer to citizens, giving the EU a "national face" for 6 months and making the Union more visible. Since the Lisbon Treaty (2009), presidencies work in 18-month "trios[1]" to ensure continuity and each presiding over all Council formations except the Foreign Affairs Council (FAC), chaired by the High Representative pursuant to Art. 18 (3) TEU. The Political and Security Committee (PSC) and Common Foreign and Security Policy (CFSP)/ Common Security and Defence Policy CFSP/CSDP working groups are chaired by the European External Action Service (EEAS).[2]

Although the presidency does not legislate, it plays a pivotal facilitative role—chairing meetings, brokering compromises, ensuring continuity, and representing the Council in trilogues—all grounded in Art. 16 (9) TEU and the Council's Rules of Procedure 2009/937/EU. In this capacity, it is a key agenda-setter, influencing the pace and prioritisation of files.

With an average 13.5-year interval between mandates, most national officials lack prior experience and rely on the General Secretariat of the Council (GSC), structured training, and peer exchange. In today's fast-paced, digitalised environment, the presidency acts as a procedural engine—mobilising Member States and institutions to reach compromises and projecting the Union's work into the public sphere of the presiding Member State and beyond.

2 Historical and Institutional Evolution of the Presidency

The rotating presidency has undergone significant transformation shaped by treaty reforms, institutional adaptation, and practical evolution. While once a dominant legislative actor, the presidency now functions within a more structured and multilateral framework.

---

[1] The *trios* of the Council of the EU are groups of three consecutive rotating presidencies that cooperate on a joint 18-month program to ensure continuity and coherence in the Council's legislative and policy agenda. See Chap. 23 of this handbook.

[2] See current and upcoming presidencies in Chap. 7 of this handbook.

The Lisbon Treaty introduced key institutional changes: the creation of the European Council as an EU institution of its own with a permanent president, the High Representative's role as chair of the Foreign Affairs Council and the establishment of the EEAS. These reforms reduced the external representational role of the presidency, while enhancing the EU's coherence in external action. Simultaneously, the Lisbon Treaty institutionalised the presidency trio system, facilitating medium-term coordination and continuity across legislative cycles.

The OLP has also matured. The European Parliament (EP) now acts as co-legislator in almost all policy areas and legislative timelines have shortened. First-reading agreements are now the norm, with informal trilogues as the main forum for political negotiations. Much of the preparatory work occurs in the so-called Informal Technical Meetings (ITM), enabling faster convergence on compromise texts.

Presidencies are now expected to coordinate increasingly complex, cross-sectoral files—such as the European Green Deal or Simplification—requiring horizontal coordination and strategic prioritisation. Digital tools from video conferences to collaborative web-based drafting tools have further reshaped negotiation dynamics, requiring presidencies to operate with procedural precision and adaptability.

In this environment, Member States—particularly those with limited administrative resources—rely on institutionalised learning, GSC support and peer exchanges to build capacity. The role of the presidency has evolved into that of a procedural facilitator and strategic coordinator within a co-legislative, digitally enabled Union.

3 What Is Expected from a Presidency?

The rotating Presidency of the Council of the EU is both an institutional function and a strategic task. While it offers visibility to the presiding Member State, its primary purpose is to serve the Council by facilitating legislative work and maintaining procedural continuity.

The presidency chairs Council configurations and preparatory bodies, ensures the smooth functioning of the Council, organises formal and informal meetings and represents the Council in interinstitutional negotiations—particularly with the EP and the Commission. It does not exercise executive power over the EU but functions as an honest broker among Member States, coordinating positions and enabling decision-making across policy areas.

Empirical practice has shown that an effective presidency is marked by:

- *Impartiality*, ensuring that national preferences do not influence consensus-building,
- *Competence*, in steering files at all levels of decision-making,
- *Credibility*, built through professional conduct and consistent follow-up,
- *Strategic communication*, to clarify the presidency's facilitating role and manage perceptions domestically and in Brussels,

- *Continuity*, through coordination within the trio system and across institutional cycles,
- *Trust*, as the presidency has no decision-making power of its own and must rely on the confidence of other actors.

Managing domestic expectations is a core challenge. While the presidency may highlight EU initiatives aligned with national interests, its role is not to promote a national agenda but to act inclusively for the benefit of all Member States.

The presidency also requires significant administrative coordination. Preparation typically starts years in advance and involves central ministries, permanent representations and often subnational actors, enhancing national capacity for engaging in EU decision-making well beyond the six-month term.

4 Preparation Phase: The Time Before Taking Office

The Council presidency's effectiveness is shaped by a preparation phase starting 18 to 36 months in advance, involving financial and human resources from national budgets and ensuring institutional readiness for the six-month term. Preparation serves strategic and operational purposes: engaging ministries, setting coordination structures, managing expectations, and fostering interinstitutional ties. With each Member State holding the presidency only once every 13.5 years, limited institutional memory makes training, documentation and peer learning essential.

4.1 Strategic and Operational Preparation

Presidency preparation focuses on building institutional capacity and procedural fluency. Most Member States set up central coordination units—often in the Prime Minister's Office or Ministry of European Affairs—mirrored by teams in their Permanent Representation in Brussels. The GSC provides handbooks, training and simulations, complemented by support from EU institutions, training bodies and previous presidencies. With most personnel being first-timers, structured knowledge transfer via trio partners, documentation and training is essential.

4.2 Building the Team: Brussels-Based and Capital-Based Structures

The presidency functions through a dual system: one part based in Brussels, one in the national capital. Effective co-ordination between the two is critical for managing complex, fast-paced legislative processes.

Brussels-Based Component: COREPER Teams At the heart of the Brussels-based operation are the Permanent Representations and their two political cores: COREPER II, led by the Permanent Representative (ambassadors) and supported by the Antici Group, and COREPER I, led by the Deputy Permanent Representatives and supported by the Mertens Group.[3] They are the central actors in policy planning, coordination and compromise-building.

During the presidency, these teams:

- Coordinate horizontal planning across Council formations,
- Draft compromises and guide working parties,
- Prepare and debrief trilogues and informal technical meetings (ITMs),
- Manage cross-cutting political trade-offs and procedural bottlenecks.

Given their proximity to decision-making and accumulated experience, these groups also serve as informal mentors and institutional memory hubs.

Capital-Based Component: Political Direction and Expertise In the capital, a presidency coordination unit steers the overall strategy and political coherence. It is supported by EU desks in line ministries, which provide substantive input on legislative files.

Responsibilities typically include:

- Drafting trio and presidency programmes,
- Advising on sensitive national positions,
- Preparing ministers for Council meetings,
- Supporting Brussels teams with legal and technical expertise,
- Ensuring policy consistency with national objectives.

Communication between the capital and Brussels is continuous, relying on videoconferences, shared documents and direct coordination.

Presidency performance depends on how well these two components work in tandem. Poor coordination—delayed instructions, inconsistent messaging or unclear mandates—can quickly erode credibility. Conversely, tight internal alignment enhances agility and responsiveness.

4.3 Building Trust

Trust is a precondition for an effective presidency. As an honest broker, the presidency must be perceived as impartial and competent—qualities that enable it to secure negotiating mandates and guide legislative progress. Trust-building starts well before taking office and requires systematic outreach. Key partners include:

[3] See Chap. 8 of this handbook.

- Member States: for alliance-building and political support,
- The Commission: for technical expertise and legislative insights,
- The EP: for smooth trilogue negotiations,
- The GSC: for procedural guidance and operational support.

Personal contacts and mutual familiarity matter. Regular interaction through bilateral visits, informal consultations and trio coordination lays the groundwork for a presidency capable of navigating complex interinstitutional dynamics.

4.4 Setting Priorities: From Strategic Agenda to Presidency Programme

High-Level Calendar The presidency calendar, submitted at least 7 months before the presidency starts, structures the semester's political and legislative rhythm. Prepared in coordination with the GSC, it includes European Council meetings, third-country summits, Council meetings, COREPER sessions, EP plenaries and informal ministerial meetings. Though subject to updates, it is central to resource allocation and agenda management.

Indicative Agendas Each Council configuration develops indicative agendas, which define the presidency's legislative and policy priorities. Drafted by the incoming presidency in cooperation with the GSC, the Commission and the EEAS (for FAC), they are finalised shortly before the term begins. These agendas provide transparency, ensure institutional coordination and allow the presidency to influence the sequencing of files.

The presidency's agenda is primarily shaped by the following sources:

- Trio programme,
- National presidency programme,
- European Council strategic agenda,
- Commission work programme,
- Inherited legislative files,
- External events and crises.

Engagement with the EP In the preparatory phase, "speed-dating" meetings between incoming Permanent Representatives and EP committee chairs have become common practice. These informal exchanges serve to align expectations, identify priority files and establish rapport before trilogue negotiations begin.

Domestic Political Considerations National politics can also influence the presidency's approach. Governments may avoid sensitive files if national elections coincide with the presidency or may use the semester to spotlight consensual EU achievements. Navigating this balance requires careful planning and political judgement.

5 Execution Phase: Role in the Ordinary Legislative Procedure

Once in office, the rotating presidency enters the execution phase, managing legislative files under the OLP, which constitutes the core of EU lawmaking. Each presidency begins its six-month term on either 1 January or 1 July. The presidency does not take decisions but facilitates negotiations, builds consensus and brokers inter-institutional agreements.

5.1 Phase I: General Planning of a File

Strategic management begins with a comprehensive mapping of legislative proposals, both inherited and newly announced in the Commission work programme. This is carried out in coordination with the GSC and the Commission. Files are assessed based on political sensitivity, technical complexity and urgency.

A clear hierarchy of files is established, enabling backward planning from desired outcomes, such as securing a general approach at a particular Council. Milestones are plotted in reverse. This means: identification of relevant COREPER meetings, deadlines for agenda setting (typically 3 weeks before Council) and timing of substantive discussions.

5.2 Phase II: Reaching a Council Mandate

In this phase, the presidency acts as a broker, steering Council bodies through iterative technical and political discussions. The working party, which is chaired by a presidency official, is the primary forum for line-by-line examination or thematic clustering of proposals, depending on the presidency's approach. While formal positions cannot be adopted at this level, consensus-building begins here.[4]

The presidency, through the working party chair, ensures comprehensive examination of the text—even politically sensitive elements—and explores delegations' positions informally to avoid future deadlocks. Delegations are encouraged to submit comments or drafting suggestions in writing. This practice fosters ownership of the emerging compromise and enhances approval prospects.

Once technical discussion reaches maturity, the presidency determines when to escalate the file to COREPER, where political guidance is consolidated. Here, the presidency often employs a "package approach," bundling trade-offs across interrelated issues to accommodate diverse interests and create a viable Council position. The presidency designs and presents such packages to optimise consensus.

[4] See Chap. 8 of this handbook.

For Council meetings, the presidency—based on Member State input—decides whether to expose unresolved issues to ministerial negotiation or present a pre-agreed proposal. This choice often depends on the Council formation's working culture. Regardless of the approach, early and transparent communication with delegations remains essential.

5.3 *Phase III: Trilogue Negotiations*

Once the Council has adopted a negotiation mandate—typically via a general approach or a COREPER mandate—the presidency enters informal negotiations (so-called trilogue phase) with the EP and the Commission. At this stage, the presidency becomes the sole Council negotiator, shifting from a collegial role to one of representation and discretion.

Although bound by the Council mandate, the presidency decides how and when to engage the EP, navigating political dynamics while remaining in regular contact with delegations. Updates are provided through COREPER or relevant working parties and feedback may lead to revised mandates.

EP's scheduling of trilogues often compresses timelines, requiring presidencies to reinforce negotiation teams. While Permanent Representatives, in some cases ministers, usually lead, the presidency may delegate negotiation responsibilities to Antici/Mertens members or working party chairs. These chairs are vital during this phase, acting as liaisons between the negotiation table and delegations, ensuring continuity and coherence.

Negotiations occur at multiple levels. Political trilogues—frequently led by ambassadors or ministers of the presidency—are supplemented by preparatory ITMs, where compromise texts are refined. A notable innovation here is the Trilogue Table Editor (TTE), a joint digital tool of the Council and EP that facilitates real-time co-editing and traceability of changes. While the TTE enhances procedural efficiency and transparency, its success hinges on the trust and collaboration among negotiators.

6 Structural and Procedural Tools at the Presidency's Disposal

Although the rotating presidency holds no legislative voting power, it commands a robust procedural toolbox. These tools—formal and informal—enable the presidency to structure negotiations, frame compromises, manage institutional interactions and influence the pace and sequencing of files. Effective use of this toolbox often determines whether a legislative file advances or stalls.

6.1 Formal Tools: From Agenda Management to Compromise Drafting and Package Deals

The presidency's internal operation rests on close coordination with the GSC following agreed protocols for agenda setting, document circulation and the drafting of confidential briefings. Briefings have to be concise, standardised and typically in English or French. Deadlines are strictly enforced and workflows designed to maintain version control, confidentiality and procedural discipline.

A core formal prerogative of the presidency is controlling the Council's internal calendar. It decides when and how to convene working parties, COREPER and Council configurations. This control extends to agenda planning, a powerful tool influencing the pace and visibility of files.

In EU decision-making, Council and COREPER agendas categorise items. Council items are classified as 'A' points, which are agreed at the COREPER level and adopted without discussion or 'B' points, which are scheduled for political discussion, often to resolve unresolved issues or seek ministerial guidance. In COREPER, 'I' points refer to non-discussion items, such as procedural decisions, while 'II' points require substantive political discussion. This categorisation allows the presidency to prioritise files, manage expectations and send political signals effectively.

The drafting of presidency compromise texts is another critical tool. These texts evolve throughout negotiations, gradually integrating national sensitivities, technical clarifications and political trade-offs. Their quality—both legal and political—is decisive for acceptance in COREPER and ultimately in the Council.

In trilogues, the presidency uses the TTE to prepare four-column documents comparing institutional positions and possible compromises, enabling real-time coordination and helping delegations anticipate landing zones.[5]

Compromises frequently take the form of package deals, bundled solutions that allow political trade-offs across issues. These packages help balance competing interests by offering all sides something, without granting any delegation or the EP everything. This method also helps move past technical stalemates by shifting focus to political priorities.

6.2 Informal Tools: Brokering Consensus and Building Coalitions

In parallel to formal procedures, the presidency exercises informal influence through diplomacy and strategic engagement. Key informal tools include:

- *Informal ministerial meetings* for candid political exchanges,

[5] See Chap. 21 of this handbook.

- *Bilateral consultations* with pivotal Member States to test ideas and build coalitions,
- *Head of delegation meetings* during trilogues, involving only core negotiators from the three institutions,
- *Side meetings* with EP rapporteurs and Commission officials to explore options discreetly,
- *Shuttle diplomacy* in Council preparatory bodies—especially COREPER—to bridge divides.

Much depends on the chair's political instinct, ability to manage ambiguity in drafting and skill in building coalitions that hold together under pressure.

6.3 The Role of the Trio: Continuity and Cross-Presidency Coordination

The establishment of presidency trios under the Lisbon Treaty enhances continuity and coherence in the Council's legislative work. In this format, three successive rotating presidencies cooperate over 18 months to develop a joint programme of priorities and timelines, presented as a single draft to the General Affairs Council at least 1 month before the first term begins. The drafting process involves consultation with the President of the European Council, the High Representative (as President of the Foreign Affairs Council) and the Commission, with GSC coordination and support.

The 18-month programme facilitates sequencing of files across presidencies, enabling structured progress on dossiers not concluded within a single term and helping manage institutional memory in complex negotiations.

Beyond procedure, the trio format fosters early coordination among partners with differing priorities, mirroring the inclusive, neutral role expected once in office. Exposure to these divergences develops key competences such as impartiality, coalition-building and accommodating diverse interests.

While the trio system does not replace national responsibility, it provides a coordination framework that strengthens the Council's resilience and supports coherent legislative planning.

7 Forward-Looking Reflections: Adapting the Presidency Role to a Changing Landscape

The role of the rotating presidency of the Council is subject to constant evolution. Institutional reforms, technological advancements and an increasingly complex geopolitical environment have significantly influenced both the expectations placed on presidencies and the tools they require to deliver effectively. In this context, forward-looking reflection is not only desirable but essential to maintain the relevance, legitimacy and functionality of the presidency in the EU's lawmaking process.

7.1 *Shrinking Rotation Cycle, Shrinking Institutional Memory*

The fixed rotation system, whereby each Member State assumes the presidency every 13.5 years, reinforces institutional equality and allows for broad participation. However, it also presents structural challenges in terms of continuity and experience retention. The long interval between successive presidencies by the same Member State often results in the loss of practical know-how, particularly when key individuals have moved on from relevant roles. This discontinuity can weaken institutional memory and necessitates more robust preparatory mechanisms.

To mitigate these effects, Member States increasingly rely on systematic knowledge management tools, including standardised internal procedures, briefing templates and document repositories. The GSC plays a pivotal role in facilitating continuity by capturing lessons learnt and supporting incoming presidencies in adapting best practices.

7.2 *Digitalisation and Negotiation Efficiency*

The digital transformation of the Council's working methods has accelerated since the COVID-19 pandemic. Digital tools now underpin legislative coordination and interinstitutional negotiations. Notably, ITMs—while outside formal procedural structures—have gained strategic importance in aligning positions on complex files before trilogues. Their growing prevalence reflects the need for efficient, informal dialogue in a compressed six-month legislative window, but also raises questions about procedural transparency and inclusiveness.

The development and use of platforms such as the TTE now streamlines the drafting of compromise texts by allowing real-time collaboration between the co-legislators and the Commission. These tools increase the precision and speed of negotiations, reduce the margin of error and improve coherence.

However, the benefits of digitalisation are not evenly distributed. Variations in digital capacity between Member States, institutions and delegations risk disadvantaging less-resourced actors. Ensuring adequate training, equal access to tools and shared standards for digital governance is vital to maintain fairness, efficiency and legitimacy in an increasingly technology-mediated negotiation environment.

7.3 Crisis, Geopolitics and Strategic Agility

Recent years have demonstrated that crisis and disruption are no longer peripheral to the EU's legislative process, but integral to it. The COVID-19 pandemic, Russia's war of aggression against Ukraine and energy and migration crises have profoundly reshaped the Union's policy agenda. In such a context, the presidency must demonstrate a high degree of strategic agility and the capacity to revise legislative priorities, respond to unforeseen developments and implement decisions under time pressure while preserving procedural integrity.

This evolving role necessitates close coordination with the European Council (EUCO), whose strategic decisions increasingly guide the political orientation of the Council's work. The rotating presidency plays a key role in translating EUCO conclusions into operational agendas, primarily through the General Affairs Council (GAC), which it chairs. Ensuring coherence between political-level guidance and Council-level implementation requires foresight, rapid internal coordination mechanisms and closer alignment with Commission contingency planning and legislative programming.

The capacity to react effectively in times of crisis—while maintaining inclusiveness, legal rigour and institutional balance—is becoming a defining feature of a successful presidency. Future presidencies are therefore expected to rely more on foresight capacity, flexible agenda-setting and strong interinstitutional coordination.

8 Conclusion

The rotating presidency of the Council of the European Union remains a cornerstone of the Union's legislative machinery. While it does not "run the EU", it plays a vital facilitative role by chairing the Council and its preparatory bodies, structuring debate, building consensus and representing the Council in interinstitutional negotiations. As such, the presidency operates not as a solitary actor, but as a key player in a collective, multi-institutional process—highly dependent on the actions, cooperation and responsiveness of Member States, the Commission, the EP and the European Council.

The strength of the presidency lies in its convening power, neutrality and procedural control. Yet its effectiveness is constrained by structural realities: It holds no legislative vote, its mandate is brief (6 months) and its success hinges on others' willingness to engage and compromise. Internally, the presidency requires seamless coordination between capital-based and Brussels-based teams. Externally, it depends on active collaboration with institutional partners and national delegations. A successful presidency is therefore both a national and collective achievement, demanding not just leadership, but service.

Presidencies today face a demanding environment characterised by thematic overload, heightened institutional expectations and an unpredictable geopolitical landscape. They must define clear priorities aligned with the Union's strategic agenda, communicate effectively, manage legislative complexity and remain resilient in the face of crises. Informal working practices and digital tools are increasingly central, but must be supported by political judgement, administrative readiness and trust-building.

Ultimately, holding the presidency is a transformative opportunity for Member States. It reinforces EU ownership, sharpens administrative capacity and fosters a deeper European perspective. Much like the Erasmus programme opens minds at the individual level, the presidency expands institutional horizons. It is not merely a rotating duty, it is a strategic act of co-ownership in shaping Europe's legal and political future.

References

Legal and Institutional Sources

Council Decision (EU) 2016/1316. (2016, August 2). *Official Journal of the European Union L 208*. https://eur-lex.europa.eu/legal-content/EN/TXT/PDF/?uri=CELEX:32016D1316&qid=1751886632099

Council's Rules of Procedure. (2009, December 11). Council Decision 2009/937/EU of 1 December 2009 adopting the Council's Rules of Procedure, Official Journal of the European Union L 325.

Treaty on European Union. (2016, June 7). *Official Journal of the European Union C 202*. https://eur-lex.europa.eu/legal-content/EN/TXT/?uri=oj:JOC_2016_202_R_0001

Treaty on the Functioning of the European Union. (2016, June 7). *Official Journal of the European Union, C 202*. https://eur-lex.europa.eu/legal-content/EN/TXT/?uri=oj:JOC_2016_202_R_0001

Joint Declaration on Legislative Priorities (latest version available from the European Parliament, the Council and the Commission; Council document ST-6808-2025-INIT).

Institutional and Practical Guides

Council of the EU. The decision-making process in the Council, Council of the EU website.

European Commission. Better Regulation Toolbox (notably sections on interinstitutional cooperation and co-decision).

European Parliament. Code of Conduct for Trilogue Negotiations.

General Secretariat of the Council (GSC). Presidency Handbook.

Further Reading

1. General Secretariat of the Council (GSC). Comments on the Council's Rules of Procedure, latest edition. An essential interpretative guide for understanding the formal and informal tools available to the Presidency under the Rules of Procedure.
2. Van Hecke, S., Bursens, P., & Wolfs, W. (Eds.). (2022). *The European council and the council: New Intergovernmentalism and institutional change*. Palgrave Macmillan. Offers a broader institutional context, particularly on how the rotating Presidency fits into the EU's evolving governance architecture.

Thomas Gloeckel has over 20 years of experience at the General Secretariat of the Council of the EU, where he currently prepares future presidencies for their tasks, coordinating briefing programmes and supporting presidency officials. He has also gained significant experience in various Austrian ministries, including as an attaché at the Austrian Permanent Representation to the EU, where he was responsible for transport, innovation and technology. In 2018, he was seconded to the Austrian presidency, working in the office of the Special Representative. Additionally, he lectures at the University of Applied Sciences Burgenland.

Shaping Decisions in the Council of the EU: Coalition-Building Among Member States

Gerda Füricht-Fiegl and Nina Schilling

Abstract This article sheds light on decision-making in the Council of the European Union. Under the shadow of qualified majority voting, no single member state can prevail alone. Coalition-building is the Council's operating logic. These coalitions are not random, but structured by factors such as geography, policy interests, or shared relations with external actors. The importance of alliances in the Council has grown in times of uncertainty, be it external (e.g. Ukraine war) or internal, like growing support for anti-EU parties, as shown by recent election results in numerous EU member states.

Against this background we are focusing on coalition-building among certain member states by taking the role of bottom-up regional groups (BURGs) of EU member states as an example. BURGs are informal coalitions outside the EU's treaty framework that aim to increase their members' influence within it.

Currently (as of October 2025), seventeen BURGs have been identified, ranging from the much-researched and discussed *Franco-German Cooperation* to recently formed cooperation such as *Friends of the Western Balkans*. What is evident is that BURG members cooperate more with each other than with outsiders, suggesting that BURGs provide an additional layer of coordination. This effect varies across policy areas: it is strongest in economic, digital, and foreign policy issues, and weaker in areas where cross-group cooperation is already widespread, like agriculture. In addition, ideological distance on European integration reduces intra-BURG cooperation, though overall levels remain high.

G. Füricht-Fiegl (✉)
University of Applied Sciences Burgenland, Eisenstadt, Austria
e-mail: gerda.fuericht-fiegl@hochschule-burgenland.at

N. Schilling (✉)
Austrian Federal Ministry for European and International Affairs, Vienna, Austria

G. Füricht-Fiegl et al. (eds.), *Handbook on EU Law-making*, Professional Practice in Governance and Public Organizations, https://doi.org/10.1007/978-3-032-16559-6_10

In sum, BURGs are linked to meaningful but conditional patterns of coordination. They are less independent drivers of behaviour than arenas that reinforce existing ties, shaped by geography and political preferences.

Keywords Decision-making in the Council of the EU · Coalition-building · COREPER · Regional groups · Regional formats · Bottom-up regional groups of EU member states · BURG

1 Introduction

"Decisions shall be taken as openly as possible and as closely as possible to the citizen". (Art. 10 (3) TEU). This guiding principle, reinforced by the Lisbon Treaty in 2009, requires the Council of the European Union to deliberate and vote in public when exercising its legislative function (Art. 15 (2)-(3) TFEU; Art. 16 (8) TEU). Voting records and legislative debates are now accessible through official registers and live streams, projecting an image of openness. Formal displays illuminate only a fraction of the decision-making process. The substantive negotiations, where compromises are forged and outcomes effectively determined, continue to unfold in COREPER,[1] working groups, and informal settings far from public scrutiny. In this sense, Council decision-making remains a paradox. It gets ever more transparent in appearance yet remains stubbornly opaque in practice. In other words: you can see the show, but not the rehearsal.

A second paradox lies in the Council's decision-making culture itself. Although the treaties establish qualified majority voting as the default, the Council overwhelmingly favours consensus. Most dossiers are resolved in working groups or COREPER long before reaching ministerial level, making formal votes the exception rather than the rule (von Ondarza & Rehbaum, 2024). When votes do occur, they often signal not unity but division, registering national preferences where compromise has failed (Elster, 1998). In recent years this dynamic has become more visible. Hungary, for example, has repeatedly used its veto to block sanctions against Russia, joint EU statements, and the launch of Ukraine's accession talks. Voting has thus become more politically charged, especially on sensitive issues such as foreign politics and the rule of law.

Consequently, the central question is no longer only how decisions are made, but who cooperates with whom to make them possible. Knowing how cooperation is structured within the Council is central to understanding how political decisions are reached (Johansson, 2021, p. 6). As Huhe et al. (2022, p. 1) state, "(c)ooperation is a leitmotif of scholarship on EU politics". Previous scholarship has produced a rich

[1] See Chap. 8 of this handbook.

body of work on coalition-building in the Council. Classic studies highlight the role of voting rules, institutional structures, and negotiation norms (e.g. Hayes-Renshaw & Wallace, 2006; Lewis, 2010). More recent contributions have mapped patterns of cooperation across enlargements and in the light of Brexit, showing how shifts in membership composition alter alignments and blocking coalitions (e.g. Grech, 2021; Johansson, 2021; Naurin & Lindahl, 2010). This research has demonstrated that cooperation in the Council is not random, but structured by factors such as geography, policy interests, or shared relations with external actors (Häge, 2012; Huhe et al., 2018, 2022).

The importance of these alliances has grown in the wake of Europe's recent crises. The 2015 refugee crisis not only fractured solidarity among member states but also reshaped domestic politics across the Union. Examples include Poland's 2015 parliamentary elections, the 2016 Brexit referendum, Germany's 2017 federal elections and Italy's 2018 general elections. These electoral shifts empowered governments critical of deeper EU integration and fuelled fragmentation within the EU (Applebaum, 2024). Regional alignments became more visible as states came together to defend shared positions. The Visegrád Group, for instance, emerged as a vocal bloc opposing refugee quotas and asylum reform, projecting themselves as a "coalition of the unwilling". More recently, however, shifts in government in Poland (October 2023) paved the way for the revival of the Weimar Triangle, this time as a distinctly pro-European platform for Franco-German-Polish coordination on security and foreign policy. This contrast illustrates how regional groups can function both as instruments of fragmentation and as vehicles for renewed integration.

Against this background the effect of regional groups of EU member states, whose proclaimed goal it is to push common interests in the EU, on EU decision-making is of interest. Regional groups are not homogeneous actors, but consist of governments with distinct national interests, political priorities, and ideological orientations. The way in which these interests are aggregated within a regional group may shape both the coherence of the group and its ability to influence decision-making in the Council. Cooper and Fabbrini (2022) define "bottom-up regional groups (BURGs)" as informal yet regularized cooperation formats between geographically proximate EU member states, which operate outside the EU's institutional framework but aim to strengthen the collective influence of their members within it. Unlike ad hoc coalitions such as the former Frugal Four, BURGs are characterized by continuity, geographic clustering, and a shared political identity that extends beyond single-issue cooperation.

This article aims to provide a clearer understanding of decision-making and coalition-building in the Council of the EU.

2 Decision-Making in the Council of the European Union[2]

The Council is not only one of the Union's two co-legislators, but also the key forum where national interests are bargained, compromises struck, and European policies shaped. While treaty provisions define formal procedures, most outcomes are determined by the interplay of institutional rules, informal practices, and coalition dynamics. Formally, decision-making in most EU policy areas is subject to qualified majority rule. Yet in practice, consensus remains the prevailing norm, and unanimity is still common in politically sensitive domains (Häge, 2012, p. 481). The Council voting records often mask this reality: when all member states agree, a vote serves as little more than symbolic confirmation.

2.1 *Decision-Making Rules and Procedures in the Council*

The rules governing decision-making in the Council are codified in the EU treaties. They take shape through institutional practice and informal norms.

2.1.1 Legal Provisions

The rules governing decision-making in the Council are codified primarily in Art. 16(4) of the Treaty on European Union (TEU) and Art. 238 of the Treaty on the Functioning of the European Union (TFEU). These provisions establish the procedures for both qualified majority voting (QMV) and unanimity, depending on the policy area. Under the Ordinary Legislative Procedure (OLP), which applies to the majority of EU policy domains, the Council adopts decisions by qualified majority.[3]

2.1.2 Institutional Practice in the Council

Most legislative and policy decisions are prepared well in advance of ministerial meetings through a multi-layered system of working parties, specialized committees and the Committee of Permanent Representatives (COREPER).[4] This practice highlights the Council as both a bureaucratic machine and a political negotiation arena, where consensus is often forged long before formal votes are taken.

In addition to this institutional hierarchy, decision-making in the Council is also marked by informal and procedural practices deeply rooted in its political culture. One such practice is consensus decision-making, whereby no formal vote is taken,

[2] Text passages from sections 2 and 3 are taken from the author's master's thesis (Schilling, 2025).

[3] See details in Chap. 7 of this handbook.

[4] See details in Chap. 8 of this handbook.

and all member states informally agree or choose not to object. Another is the "silence procedure", widely used in the Council's preparatory bodies, especially COREPER, and for the adoption of Council conclusions. A proposal can be considered adopted if no member state raises an objection within a specified deadline, facilitating the swift approval of non-controversial matters.

Abstention, too, plays a strategic role: in votes requiring unanimity, abstentions do not block adoption, allowing member states to express reservations without casting a negative vote and thereby preserving the appearance of unity (Art. 238(4) TFEU).

Institutional practice thus demonstrates that Council decision-making is a process rather than an event. Decisions are gradually shaped through technical work in committees, filtered through COREPER, and ratified by ministers. Informal norms of consensus and trust play a decisive role, ensuring that the Council maintains legitimacy and cohesion even under the rules of QMV. These same dynamics also create the conditions under which member states coordinate with allies and like-minded partners.

3 Coalitions in Council decision-making

As mentioned above: as decisions in the Council are primarily made through QMV, individual member states rarely have the power to assert their national interests alone. To shape outcomes effectively, they must form alliances with other states. Tallberg (2008) highlights the importance of pre-agreement phases, in which informal coordination occurs prior to official negotiations as an increasingly common feature of Council dynamics. As a result, coalition-building and the ability to convince and coordinate with others are essential elements of Council negotiations.

These negotiations are typically conducted in the "shadow of the vote", meaning that discussions are strategically shaped by expectations about the likely voting outcome. Negotiations proceed until there is sufficient confidence that a winning coalition has emerged and that the Council presidency's compromise will not be obstructed (Kleinowski, 2025, p. 515). Thus, coalition-building is not a one-time event but occurs throughout all stages of the decision-making process. As the literature shows, the determinants of coalition-building behaviour are manifold. We group them into four categories:

1. *Interest-Based Coalitions.*

Similarity in member states' policy preferences fosters coalition-building and cooperative tie formation in the Council, particularly in high-stakes contexts, thereby shaping network dynamics and enhancing bargaining leverage (Huhe et al., 2018; Leifeld & Schneider, 2012; Sabatier & Weible, 2007).

2. *Network Coalitions.*

The Council constitutes a deeply institutionalized arena for negotiation, characterized by frequent, standardized interactions, and long-term cooperation among member states. These conditions create a favourable ground for network effects driven by socialization and trust and therefore member states are more likely to form stable, effective coalitions (Huhe et al., 2018). These networks become more valuable as more like-minded states join, creating a network effect. One advantage of an institutional setting is that it can make cooperation more effective, as governments can use existing structures, networks, and routines that help communication and coordination in the beginning (Ruse, 2013, p. 45).

3. *Geographic Proximity.*

Coalitions of neighbouring states are a dominating pattern in coalition-building within the Council (Naurin, 2015). Due to multiple factors, such as history, geographic closeness often goes along with cultural and linguistic similarities. Neighbouring states typically maintain close ties, collaborate on cross-border initiatives, and operate within established institutional frameworks (Ruse, 2012). Studies have found that coalition patterns follow a North–South as well as a North–South–East or centre–periphery divide (see Elgström et al., 2001; Plechanovová, 2011; Veen, 2010). For instance, the Eurozone crisis fuelled North–South economic tensions, while the refugee crisis is often said to have triggered an East–West split over migration (Schäffer, 2020). Geographical divergence leads to varying geopolitical priorities, national interests, availability of resources, security concerns, and approaches to regional stability and order. Consequently, neighbours are incentivized to push for their interests together in the Council to have more voting power.

4. *Coalitions Based on Common Political Ideology.*

Findings on the effect of party ideology on the coalition-building dynamics are inconclusive. Supporters of the ideology hypothesis argue that member states' cleavages follow two dimensions, namely the socioeconomic left–right axis (Hix, 1999) and the stance on European integration. The left–right dimension primarily captures party positions regarding state involvement in the economy but also positions on morality-based issues (e.g. abortion, same-sex marriage). Importantly, the economic left–right dimension is analytically distinct from the pro- versus anti-European integration dimension (Huhe et al., 2022, p. 81). A party's support for EU integration does not necessarily correlate with its position on economic policy. This is reflected in the affiliation of national parties in the European parties or groups in the EP. For instance, right-national-conservative parties can be found either within the European Conservatives and Reformers group (ECR) or in the Patriots for Europe group (PfE). While the ECR advocates a stronger pro-European stance, the PfE is clearly anti-European.

Other scholars (e.g. Hosli & Arnold, 2007; Tallberg & Johansson, 2008) do not identify empirically convincing evidence for such an argument. States with governments of different ideological leanings regularly cooperate with each other. Huhe et al. (2022) find that party ideology only indirectly and relatively weakly affects the formation of alliances in the Council.

Ideological congruence may affect cooperation through its impact on the position on specific policy issues, which can be the more immediate cause of cooperation.

3.1 Regional Alliances of Member States

While alliances and initiatives of selected Member States aimed at increasing cooperation in various areas have always been an inherent part of the EU (e.g. the Benelux group established in 1944), an increase in the formation of these intra-EU sub-groupings can be observed since the 1990s. As multiple crises have affected the EU in the last decades, unanimity and consensus between the member states are put to the test now more than ever. Member States started to form alliances to push for their specific interests.

Sub-groupings within multilateral organizations have been referred to with various terms, like "minilateralism" (Fritsch, 1988; Kobrin, 1995), while all sharing the same basic characteristics. Minilateralism is understood as the building of informal, voluntary and non-binding alliances between states within multilateral organizations. A particular form of minilateral alliances is the concept of regional groups of EU Member States, introduced by Cooper and Fabbrini (2022). Focusing on the European Union, the authors identify several regional forums in which member states cooperate with one another outside the EU institutional framework (Cooper & Fabbrini, 2022, p. 949). While these groups differ in several aspects, such as number of member states, areas of cooperation or the level of institutionalization, they all represent forms of bottom-up cooperation that operate at an intermediate level between individual member states and the broader EU framework. "Intra-EU Bottom-Up Regional Groups" (BURGs) according to Cooper and Fabbrini (2022, p. 953) meet the following five criteria:

- there is some sort of institutionalized, meaning regular, cooperation (ad hoc issue-based coalitions are therefore not included),
- they are currently active,
- all participating states are EU Member States,
- they are institutionally separate from the EU framework (no EU macro-regional strategies) and
- the countries forming a BURG share geographical proximity.

"Bottom-up" means that these regional groups differ from other member states by forming a separate "grassroots" group. They are not institutionalized by EU law, but self-organized by states themselves. Cooper and Fabbrini (2022) identify thirteen regional groups of Member States fulfilling the above-mentioned criteria. Since Cooper and Fabbrini's research, new BURGs have emerged in response to recent geopolitical developments. We identified four additional regional groups (Atlantic Four, Central Five, Trilateral AT-HR-SI, and the Friends of the Western Balkans) so that we currently count *seventeen BURGs*.

Table 1 List of BURGs

BURG	Countries involved	Est.	Purpose	Institutional features
Benelux	Belgium, Luxembourg, Netherlands	1944	Politico-economic union	Customs Union (1944); Parliamentary Assembly (1955); Economic Union (1958); Benelux Court of Justice (1965); Benelux Union (2008)
France-German Cooperation	France, Germany	1963	Political cooperation	Élysée Treaty (1963); Aachen Treaty (2019); Franco-German Parliamentary Assembly
Iberian Summit	Portugal, Spain	1983	Political dialogue	Bilateral summit of prime ministers
Visegrád Group	Czechia, Hungary, Poland, Slovakia	1991	Political cooperation	Ministerial meetings and summits of leaders; Visegrad Fund (2000); Interparliamentary cooperation (2003)
Baltic Assembly	Estonia, Latvia, Lithuania	1991	Political cooperation	Baltic Assembly (1991); Baltic Council of Ministers (1994)
Weimar Triangle	France, Germany, Poland	1991	Political dialogue	Meetings of foreign ministers, occasional summits of leaders
Salzburg Forum	Austria, Bulgaria, Croatia, Czechia, Hungary, Poland, Romania, Slovakia, Slovenia	2000	Home affairs cooperation	Meetings of interior ministers (2x/yr.); Meetings of police chiefs; meetings on margins of EU
Nordic-Baltic Six	Denmark, Estonia, Finland, Latvia, Lithuania, Sweden	2004	Policy coordination	Ministerial meetings in proximity to EU meetings
Central European Defence Cooperation	Austria, Croatia, Czechia, Slovakia, Hungary, Slovenia (Poland: observer)	2010	Military collaboration, migration control	Meetings of defence ministers
EuroMed	Cyprus, France, Greece, Italy, Malta, Portugal, Spain, and since 2021 also Slovenia, and Croatia	2013	Political cooperation	Ministerial meetings; South EU Summit of national leaders
Slavkov/Austerlitz Triangle	Austria, Czechia, Slovakia	2015	Political cooperation	Summits of leaders

BURG	Countries involved	Est.	Purpose	Institutional features
Three Seas Initiative	Austria, Bulgaria, Croatia, Czechia, Estonia, Hungary, Latvia, Lithuania, Poland, Romania, Slovakia, Slovenia	2016	Cooperation on North-South infrastructure, economics, energy, transport, business	Annual summits of national presidents; business forum
New Hanseatic League	Denmark, Estonia, Finland, Ireland, Latvia, Lithuania, Netherlands, Sweden	2018	Economic policy coordination	Meetings of finance ministers
French-Italian cooperation	France, Italy	2023	Political cooperation	Quirinale Treaty (2023)
Atlantic Four	France, Ireland, Portugal, Spain	2023	Ministerial meetings (e.g. Porto 2023)—emerging BURG!	Atlantic Strategy Ministerial Declaration (2023)
Central Five	Austria, Czechia, Slovakia, Hungary, Slovenia	2020	Political cooperation and dialogue	Meetings of foreign ministers
Trilaterale AT-HR-SI	Austria, Croatia, Slovenia	2012	Political cooperation	Ministerial meetings, summits of national presidents
Friends of the Western Balkans	Austria, Greece, Italy, Croatia, Slovakia, Slovenia, Czechia	2023	Political cooperation	Göttweig Declaration (2023)

Source: Cooper and Fabbrini (2022), pp. 957–958; Own

BURGs represent a highly heterogeneous phenomenon, varying significantly along key dimensions. Importantly, BURGs are not static or pre-defined. Their nature can shift over time, dissolve after negotiations conclude or re-emerge around new policy questions.

3.1.1 BURGs and Coalition-Building

BURGs are informal arrangements of Member States that operate outside the EU's formal treaty-based structures. Initiated by national governments, they may serve as platforms for consultation, information exchange, and the coordination of positions on EU policy issues. BURGs can enhance the visibility and influence of their members, especially smaller states, by enabling them to pre-align positions before engaging in formal negotiations within the Council framework. Coalition-building is a key mechanism through which member states increase their bargaining power. BURGs provide an arena for pre-negotiation alignment, enabling member states to pool resources, share information, and coordinate strategies within the Council preparatory bodies. In the context of qualified majority voting (QMV), a coherent BURG position can signal unity and increase leverage in formal negotiations.

In this respect, BURGs explain coalition dynamics very effectively. First, BURGs often emerge among states with similar policy preferences, especially in areas where common interests are both salient and contested. For instance, Northern European countries frequently form working groups on issues like fiscal discipline or digital regulation. These shared preferences provide a functional rationale for cooperation within a BURG, as aligned member states can coordinate positions and amplify their influence in Council negotiations.

Second, BURGs are sustained and reinforced through network effects. Frequent interaction in Council working groups, informal bilateral consultations, and shared participation in sub-regional forums foster trust and familiarity within the broader European institution. Over time, institutional socialization leads to more structured coordination, even in the absence of formal alliance mechanisms. Ongoing exchange and mutual support help BURGs to become more stable and important.

Third, geographic proximity plays a foundational role in the emergence of BURGs. States with shared borders or close regional ties often face similar geopolitical challenges or cross-border issues (e.g., migration, energy infrastructure, or regional development), which encourage them to coordinate informally. Proximity also facilitates practical cooperation through shared languages, historical ties, and compatible administrative cultures.

Fourth, political-ideological alignment can contribute to the cohesion of BURGs, particularly in debates on value-loaded or identity-based issues.

3.2 Three BURGs Under Scrutiny

In our empirical study on the cooperation within BURGs, we focused primarily on three of the seventeen BURGs (Visegrád Group, Nordic-Baltic Six, and EuroMed).[5] In addition to what's already said before, the evidence indicates variation across policy areas. The BURG effect is strongest within the Transport, Telecommunications and Energy Council (TTE) and the Economic & Financial Affairs Council (ECOFIN), where technical complexity and sectoral expertise make early alignment valuable, and in the Foreign Affairs Council (FAC), where high political salience creates incentives for regional coordination. By contrast, the effect is

[5] The study was conducted as part of the author's master's thesis (Schilling, 2025). Methodologically, it adopted a network-analytic approach. It drew on three waves of the Negotiations in the Council of the EU (NCEU) survey (2015, 2018, 2021), in which officials and diplomats reported their cooperation ties (Naurin et al., 2022). BURG membership was operationalized as a key explanatory variable, and ideological alignment was measured through the party affiliation of heads of government. Cooperation networks were modelled with Exponential Random Graph Models (ERGMs) to estimate tie formation, and fixed-effects linear models were used to evaluate cooperation intensity within BURGs.

weaker in the Environment Council (ENVI) and the Agriculture & Fisheries Council (AGRIFISH). In the preparatory bodies COREPER I and II the effect is comparatively weak, reflecting COREPER's role as a brokerage arena where bargaining cuts across regional or functional lines. This mirrors earlier findings that coalitions in the Council tend to be functional and issue-specific rather than permanent voting blocs (Häge, 2012; Warntjen, 2010). BURGs provide useful platforms for coordination in some domains but cannot be regarded as universal or overriding determinants of cooperation in the Council.

When it comes to the role of ideology, the impact is modest against the generally high baseline of cooperation, but the pattern suggests that divergent positions on European integration can complicate coordination even within otherwise cohesive groups. This is consistent with the argument that the "integration cleavage" has become a dominant structuring principle in European politics (Hooghe & Marks, 2018), and with evidence from Council research showing that Eurosceptic governments are less willing to compromise (Schimmelfennig, 2019). The findings also confirm that the economic left–right dimension is analytically distinct from the pro- versus anti-European integration dimension (Huhe et al., 2022, p. 81). This points to limits in the capacity of BURGs to act as unified actors when their members' governments are divided over the future direction of the Union.

4 Conclusion and Outlook

As the EU faces volatile geopolitical and domestic challenges, the Council's capacity to build compromise is a decisive test of its ability to act. Building on the paradoxes of Council transparency and consensus, we have shown in our article that while formal rules codified in the treaties set the framework, the real dynamics unfold in preparatory bodies such as COREPER and working groups, where informal practices, trust, and the pursuit of consensus dominate. Coalition formation thus emerges less as a single event than as an incremental process embedded in networks of repeated interaction.

Our analysis also highlighted that cooperation is structured along several dimensions: similarity of policy interests, network effects, geographical proximity and ideological orientation. These factors jointly explain why member states rarely act in isolation and instead rely on alliances to shape Council outcomes.

Regional cooperation formats represent one particular expression of this broader logic. Bottom-up regional groups (BURGs) illustrate how proximity, common preferences, and repeated interaction crystallize into informal but regularized platforms for pre-negotiation alignment. While BURGs can enhance leverage and visibility, their effect varies across policy areas. The double-edged nature of BURGs exemplifies both the potential and the limits of such coalitions: they can reinforce cooperation and amplify member states' voices, but they cannot replace the broader consensus that remains indispensable for the Union's ability to act.

Looking ahead, the future of coalition-building in the Council will be shaped by the Union's evolving political environment. Enlargement, domestic shifts in member states, and external crises will continue to alter alignments. Whether these formats become drivers of integration, stabilizers of regional voices, or new lines of division will depend on political context.

References

Applebaum, A. (2024). *Autocracy, Inc.: The dictators who want to run the world*. Doubleday.

Cooper, I., & Fabbrini, F. (2022). Regional Groups in the European Union: Mapping an Unexplored Form of Differentiation. *European Papers - A Journal on Law and Integration, 7*(2), 949–968. https://doi.org/10.15166/2499-8249/588

Elgström, O., Bjuruf, B., Johansson, J., & Sannerstedt, A. (2001). Coalitions in European Union Negotiations. *Scandinavian Political Studies, 24*(2), 111–128.

Elster, J. (1998). Deliberation and constitution making. In J. Elster (Ed.), *Deliberative Democracy* (pp. 97–122). Cambridge University Press.

Fritsch, W. (1988). *The new minilateralism and developing countries*. http://www.econ.puc-rio.br/uploads/adm/trabalhos/files/td208.pdf

Grech, P. D. (2021). Power in the Council of the EU: organizing theory, a new index, and Brexit. *Social Choice and Welfare, 56*, 223–258. https://doi.org/10.1007/s00355-020-01273-z

Häge, F. M. (2012). Coalition Building and Consensus in the Council of the European Union. *British Journal of Political Science, 43*, 481–504. https://doi.org/10.1017/S0007123412000439

Hayes-Renshaw, F., & Wallace, H. (2006). *The Council of Ministers*. Palgrave.

Hix, S. (1999). Dimensions and Alignments in European Union Politics: Cognitive Constraints and Partisan Responses. *European Journal of Political Research, 35*(1), 69–106. https://doi.org/10.1111/1475-6765.00442

Hooghe, L., & Marks, G. (2018). Cleavage theory meets Europe's crises: Lipset, Rokkan, and the transnational cleavage. *Journal of European Public Policy, 25*(1), 109–135. https://doi.org/10.1080/13501763.2017.1310279

Hosli, M. & Arnold, C. (2007). *The Importance of Actor Cleavages in Negotiating the European Constitutional Treaty, European Governance Papers, No. C-07-03*.

Huhe, N., Naurin, D., & Thomson, R. (2018). The evolution of political networks: Evidence from the Council of the European Union. *European Union Politics, 19*(1), 25–51. https://doi.org/10.1177/1465116517740228113

Huhe, N., Thomson, R., Arregui, J., & Naurin, D. (2022). Intergovernmental cooperation networks, national policy positions and partisan ideologies: longitudinal evidence from the Council of the European Union. *Journal of European Public Policy, 29*(1), 78–96. https://doi.org/10.1080/13501763.2021.1991980

Johansson, M. (2021). Explaining cooperation in the council of the EU before and after the Brexit referendum. *Politics and Governance, 9*(1), 5–15. https://doi.org/10.17645/pag.v9i1.3709

Kleinowski, M. (2025). Post-Brexit council: Winners and losers after the UK's withdrawal from the EU. *Journal of European Integration, 47*(4), 513–533. https://doi.org/10.1080/07036337.2024.2385035

Kobrin, S. J. (1995). Regional integration in a globally networked economy. *Transnational Corporations, 4*(2), 15–33.

Leifeld, P., & Schneider, V. (2012). Information Exchange in Policy Networks. *American Journal of Political Science, 56*(3), 731–744. https://doi.org/10.1111/j.1540-5907.2011.00580.x

Lewis, J. (2010). How institutional environments facilitate co-operative negotiation styles in EU decision-making. *Journal of European Public Policy, 17*(5), 648–664. https://doi.org/10.1080/13501761003748591

Naurin, D. (2015). *The councils of the EU: Intergovernmental bargaining in a supranational polity* (4th ed., pp. 135–158). European Union. https://doi.org/10.4324/9781315735399-6

Naurin, D., & Lindahl, R. (2010). Out in the cold? flexible integration and the political status of Euro opt-outs. *European Union Politics, 11*(4), 485–509. https://doi.org/10.1177/1465116510382463
Naurin, D., Johansson, M., Lindahl, R., & Larsson, O. (2022). *The Negotiations in the Council of the European Union Dataset (Version 2) [Data set]*. University of Gothenburg. https://doi.org/10.5878/6cry-c634
Plechanovová, B. (2011). The EU Council enlarged: North-South-East or core-periphery? *European Union Politics, 12*(1), 87–106. https://doi.org/10.1177/1465116510390720
Ruse, I. (2012). The Bargaining Power of Territorially Constituted Institutionalised Coalitions in EU Council Negotiations. *Journal of Contemporary European Research, 8*(3), 319–339. https://doi.org/10.30950/jcer.v8i3.394
Ruse, I. (2013). *(Why) do neighbours cooperate?: institutionalised coalitions and bargaining power in EU council negotiations*. Budrich UniPress Ltd..
Sabatier, P. A., & Weible, C. M. (2007). The advocacy coalition: Innovations and clarifications. In P. A. Sabatier (Ed.), *Theories of the policy process* (pp. 189–220). WestviewPress.
Schäffer, S. (2020). A New Model for European Governance. *Der Donauraum, 60*(1-2), 27–44. https://doi.org/10.7767/dedo.2020.60.1-2.27
Schilling, N. (2025). *Regional groups of EU member states and their influence on decision-making in the Council of the EU*. Master's thesis at the University of Applied Sciences Burgenland.
Schimmelfennig, F. (2019). The Choice for Differentiated Europe: An Intergovernmentalist Theoretical Framework. *Comparative European Politics, 17*(2), 176–191. https://doi.org/10.1057/s41295-019-00166-5
Tallberg, J. (2008). Bargaining power in the European Council. *Journal of Common Market Studies, 46*(3), 685–708. https://doi.org/10.1111/j.1468-5965.2008.00798.x
Tallberg, J., & Johansson, K. M. (2008). Party Politics in the European Council. *Journal of European Public Policy, 15*(8).
Veen, T. (2010, June 23-26). *Actor Alignments in the Council of the European Union: On Stability and Determinants*, Paper of ECPR conference on EU Politics, Porto, Portugal.
von Ondarza, N., & Rehbaum, D. (2024). Rat der Europäischen Union. In *Jahrbuch der Europäischen Integration 2024* (pp. 103–110). Nomos Verlagsgesellschaft GmbH & KG. https://doi.org/10.5771/9783748940845-103
Warntjen, A. (2010). Between bargaining and deliberation: decision-making in the Council of the European Union. *Journal of European Public Policy.* https://doi.org/10.1080/13501761003748641

Gerda Füricht-Fiegl is a political scientist at the University of Applied Sciences Burgenland, where she heads the English-taught master's programme European Studies—Management of EU Projects. She serves as Vice-Rector for Research and Innovation. Her teaching and research focus on the EU political system and political communication in the EU. She also brings extensive professional experience from the European Commission (DG COMM) and the European Parliament.

Nina Schilling is a graduate of the master's programme European Studies—Management of EU Projects at the University of Applied Sciences Burgenland. She holds a bachelor's degree in political science from the University of Vienna and is currently working for the Austrian Federal Ministry for European and International Affairs.

The European Parliament as Co-legislator

The European Parliament and Legislation: Power potentials and challenges

Andreas Maurer

Abstract The European Parliament (EP), the EU's only directly elected institution, has evolved from a deliberative forum into a powerful interinstitutional actor. Its powers to influence executive appointments, authorize legislation, and shape the Union's political architecture are substantial. Yet, structural features of the EU's multilevel system hinder effective communication and representation. Treaty constraints also limit the EP's ability to counterbalance the Council, the European Council, and the Commission within the framework of the current treaty foundations.

Keywords European Parliament · Legislation · Legitimation · Control function · Policy-making function · Interaction function

1 Introduction: The Institutional Framework of the European Parliament

"On Wednesday, the European Parliament decided to introduce deterrent images on cigarette packs".[1] "European car manufacturers will have to comply with stricter climate regulations for new cars from 2020. [...] This was decided by the EU Parliament in Strasbourg on Tuesday".[2] Comparable news was rare 10 years ago; it would have been unthinkable 20 years ago. Behind both pieces of news lies a now

[1] "Brussels introduces warning pictures on tobacco packages", Frankfurter Allgemeine Zeitung, No. 49, 27 February 2014, 1.

[2] "Stricter CO2 requirements for cars", Frankfurter Allgemeine Zeitung, No. 48, 26 February 2014, 10.

A. Maurer (✉)
Department of Political Science, University of Innsbruck, Innsbruck, Austria
e-mail: andreas.maurer@uibk.ac.at

G. Füricht-Fiegl et al. (eds.), *Handbook on EU Law-making*, Professional Practice in Governance and Public Organizations, https://doi.org/10.1007/978-3-032-16559-6_11

common segment of the Ordinary Legislative Procedure (OLP): Following the adoption of amendments to the Commission proposal, the responsible parliamentary committee approaches the Council and negotiates a compromise on an equal footing with the Council presidency as the representative of the Member States in the so-called trilogues. This procedure is probably the most obvious sign of the upgrading of a parliament that has gradually gained shaping competences through the last EU treaty reforms of Maastricht (1993), Amsterdam (1999), Nice (2003), and Lisbon (2009) (Maurer, 2002; Maurer & Wessels, 2003). Today, the EP is comparable to traditional working parliaments and is even better equipped than most national parliaments in the EU in terms of its autonomy of action, power of definition, and enforcement. It is a strong parliament that has largely emancipated itself from the founding European idea of Monnet, Adenauer, and de Gasperi. In the 1950s, the heads of state were only prepared to grant a parliamentary assembly with delegates from the national parliaments a few rights of consultation and control over the Commission.

Today, the EP plays an active role in shaping EU integration. Its powers have steadily expanded through treaty reforms and interinstitutional agreements. Beyond the unresolved issue of its seat, the EP regulates its internal affairs autonomously. As a directly elected body, it represents the citizens of EU Member States—not a singular European demos. Reflecting the Union's hybrid nature, the EP contributes to building an "ever closer union" but defies conventional typologies of parliaments or assemblies (Judge & Earnshaw, 2011).

The EU derives legitimacy from its Member States and from direct elections to the EP. This dual democratic foundation links national governments (via the Council and European Council) with the EP as the representative of EU citizens. This concept of dual legitimacy (Scoffoni, 1992; Maurer, 2003) captures how sovereign and quasi-governmental authority is democratically anchored and continuously evolving. This shared legitimacy also shapes the Commission's investiture, jointly determined by the EP and member states (Hobolt, 2014).

The EP's functions in political and legal control of the Commission and the Council, participation in the generation of European law, and the articulation of trans-European interests have expanded over the last 70 years to include more and more policy areas (Maurer et al., 2025; Brack & Costa, 2018; Corbett et al., 2016; Dialer et al., 2015; Maurer & Dietmar, 2005). Its role as an actor that is not only subject to the EU system, but also shapes the EU system, has been considerably enhanced. The consequences of this progressive involvement of the EP interact with the use of its traditional representational services and the resulting interaction and communication functions. Due to its multidimensional orientation as a controller of the executives (Commission, European Council, Council, European Central Bank), the EP acts as information provider, co-legislator, informal agenda-setter, and mirror of highly aggregated social conflicts, which has only been expressed since the 1990s. As a forum for political groups, the EP aggregates social interests, ideas, wishes, fears, and strategies for action. Within the interinstitutional structure of the EU institutions, on the other hand, the EP tends to operate as a largely unified actor that attempts to secure its functional profiles primarily in the areas of legislation, executive control (Madatali et al., 2025), and system design, without losing sight of parliamentary functions in the fields of representation and interaction.

The EP cannot be mapped onto Walter Bagehot's model of Westminster parliaments without significant adjustments. First, the EU lacks traditional government-opposition dynamics that would support a "state-analogous" interpretation of the EP as a partisan arena. Second, the EU's institutional system does not separate legislative and executive powers in the classical sense. Third, the EP's function is not to control or support a European government. Fourth, the EP's role is confined to specific policy phases, as the EU does not possess universal competence. Its functions are therefore concentrated within a limited issue-specific policy cycle (Maurer, 2002).

2 European Elections and the Composition of the EP

Since 1958, MEPs have expanded from 148 to 751 as EU members have joined. A maximum of 751 MEPs make up the EP. After Brexit (January 2020), the total number was reduced to 705, with 46 of the 73 British seats reserved for EU enlargements and 27 seats for 14 under-represented EU electorates. The right to vote and stand as a candidate in the EP elections for Union citizens residing in a Member State of which they are not nationals is enshrined in Art. 20 and 22 TFEU and specified in Council Directive 93/109/EC. The literature calls European elections "secondary elections" or "by-elections" (Niedermayer, 2014; Reif & Schmitt, 1980), whose issues and political significance nevertheless stem from national politics: opposition and smaller parties often gain more support than national elections. European elections are still composed of national elections and serve as a test election to punish national government policy.

The European elections from 6 to 9 June 2024 confirmed the rightward shift of the party-political spectrum within the EU and the EP that has been observed for a good ten years: in terms of content or—in relation to the functional scope of EU integration—the right-wing conservative and far-right parliamentary groups repeatedly set the pace towards a repressive and isolationist European policy, especially in the areas of asylum, migration, and external border control policy. So far, the Christian Democratic and conservative parties in the European People's Party (EPP) only formed random alliances with the groups further to the right. Institutionally, the shift to the right in European migration policy discourse was accompanied by a corresponding shift in the party and parliamentary group policy coordination system, which opened the possibility for the EPP to form selective coordination alliances with the right-wing nationalist and right-wing extremist parliamentary groups in other policy areas (e.g. environmental and climate policy, industrial and economic policy, or social and labour market policy) (Table 1).

The EPP Group and the S&D Group no longer have the majority needed to form a grand coalition. They are now 40 MEPs short, meaning that they have to rely on at least one of the other groups. If it does not want to vote with the S&D, the EPP

Table 1 Composition of the European Parliament 2014–2024

	EPP	S&D	ALDE/ RENEW	ECR	Greens/ EFA	The Left	EFDD	ENF/ID/ PfE/ESN	NA
1 June 2014	220	191	68	70	50	52	48	0	52
1 July 2019	182	154	108	62	74	41	0	73 ID	57
July 2024	188	136	77	78	53	46	0	84 PfE 25 ESN	33
Profits and losses 2009/2014	−54	−4	−15	13	−8	17	17	36	19
Profits and losses 2014/2019	−38	−37	40	−8	24	−11	−48	73	5
Profits and losses 2019/2024	4	−18	−31	16	−21	5	0	38	−27

Source: Own presentation. Legend: EPP—Group of the European People's Party (Christian Democrats), S&D—Group of the Progressive Alliance of Socialists and Democrats, ALDE—Group of the Alliance of Liberals and Democrats for Europe, Renew Europe, The Left—Group of the Left, Greens/EFA—Group of the Greens/European Free Alliance, ECR—Group of European Conservatives and Reformists, EFDD—Europe of Freedom and Direct Democracy Group (2014–2019), ENF—Europe of Nations and Freedom Group (2014–2019), ID—Identity and Democracy Group, PfE—Patriots for Europe Group, ESN—Europe of Sovereign Nations Group, NA—Non-attached Member; Status: Constituent sitting of the tenth EP on 23 July 2024

Table 2 Alternative coalition options 2024–2029 compared to 2019–2024

"Centre-left"	Cumulative coalition strength	"Centre-right"	Cumulative coalition strength
2019–2024			
S&D	20.5%	EPP	24.23%
+ greens	30.50%	+ ECR	32.49%
+ RENEW	44.88%	+ RENEW	46.87%
50 per cent and more			
+ the left	50.34%	+ greens	56.86%
2024–2029			
S&D	18.94%	EPP	26.04%
+ greens	26.32%	+ ECR	36.90%
+ RENEW	37.04%	+ PfE	48.57%
+ the left	43.45%		
50 per cent and more			
–	–	+ ESN	52.04%

Source: Own calculation based on Maurer (2002, 2012)

will be forced to form a centre-right coalition with the ECR and RENEW or with the two far-right groups. Conversely, for the first time since the introduction of direct elections in 1979, it will be impossible for the S&D to form an alternative, progressive majority with the Greens, Liberals and the Left without or against the EPP (Table 2). And even with the arithmetically possible tripartite alliances, a comfortable majority that impresses the Council or the Commission is not a given: It can be assumed that in the event of an emerging cooperation between the EPP and the

ECR—on migration, climate, or environmental policy—some Christian Democratic parties will turn away from the Western European bloc.

In any case, the development of parliamentary majorities observed in the ninth legislative period for legislative acts that were discussed under the leadership of the Environment (ENVI) and Justice and Home Affairs (LIBE) committees clearly shows that the EP has increasingly decided with extremely narrow majorities from 2023 onwards. Whereas in the first 4 years, voting results were almost always achieved in which the moderate pro-European camp remained largely united and gathered large majorities of over 450 MEPs, from mid-2023 onwards there were repeatedly slim majorities in which the two camps were increasingly hostile to each other along the left-right axis. This narrowing of the consensus corridor of the more or less "pro-European" parties and parliamentary groups is also being exploited by the far-right and Eurosceptic groups in the new, tenth legislative period to realize the ideologically desired regression in the policy areas in question (Figs. 1 and 2).

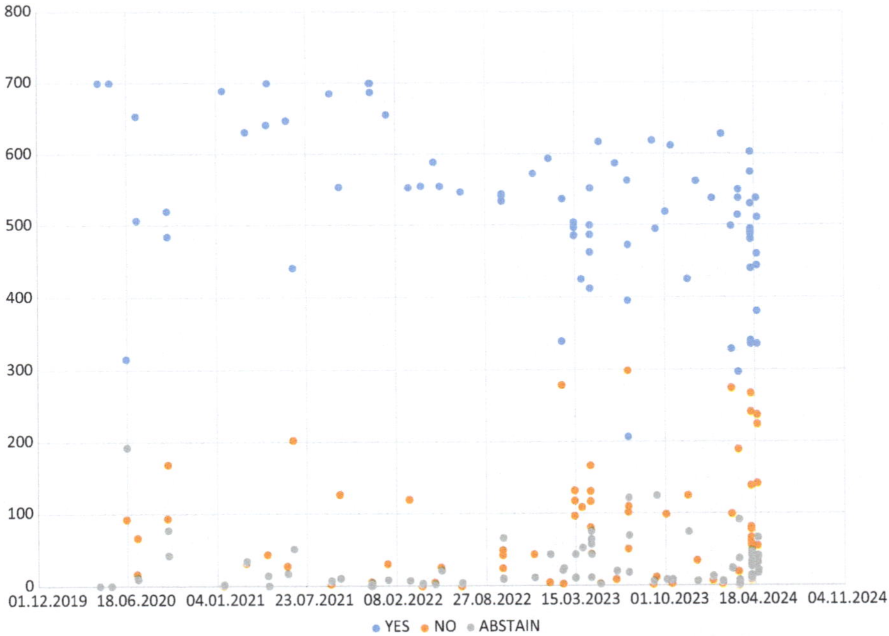

Fig. 1 Legislative plenary votes of the ENVI Committee of the European Parliament (2019–2024). *Source*: Own calculation based on data from the Legislative Observatory; checked, supplemented, and corrected using the parliamentary voting records

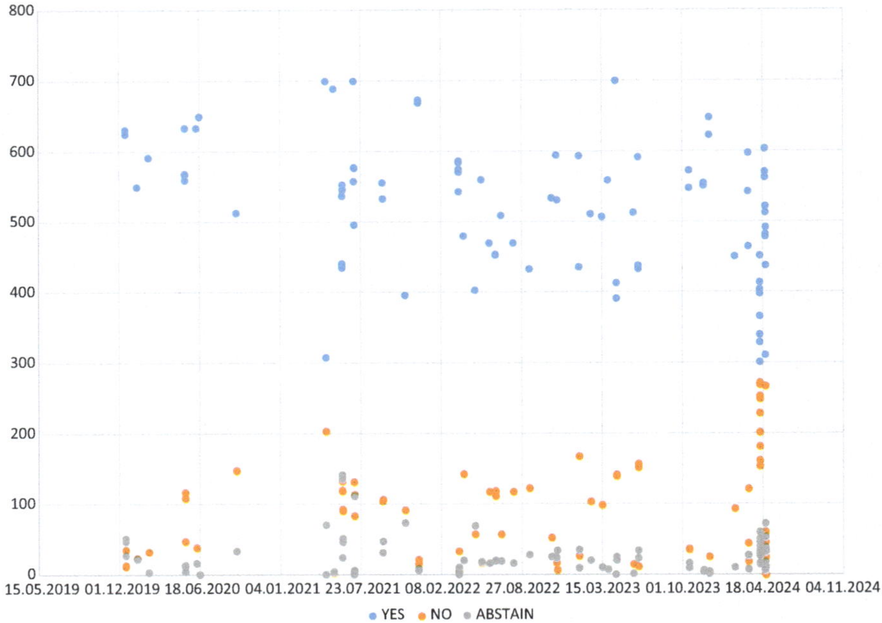

Fig. 2 Legislative plenary votes of the LIBE Committee of the European Parliament (2019–2024). *Source*: Own calculation based on data from the Legislative Observatory; checked, supplemented and corrected using the parliamentary voting records

3 The Parliamentary Groups

Since the ECSC, MEPs have allied politically rather than nationally (Piodi, 2007, pp. 7–11). These political groups nominate rapporteurs, propose agendas, distribute speaking time, and designate committee chairs, thereby shaping parliamentary activity. Dedicated EP financing is also provided. EP groups are not related to government formation, unlike party groups in national parliaments, because EU executive and legislative authority are legitimated separately (Hix, 2005). Political groups negotiate EP majorities without established alliances (Ahrens et al., 2022). Group cohesion is vital, but individual defections do not threaten institutional stability or executive continuity (Hix & Lord, 1997, p. 118).

Political groups have voted more consistently than national contingents since the first legislative term (1979–1984) (Hix et al., 2006). MEPs record their votes in an annex to the minutes. Political parties have become more united while "member" or "sending" nations have become less important (Hix & Noury, 2009). However, EP groups vote less evenly than national parliament groups (Hix et al., 2006, p. 119). The groups do not have to support a majority government. The ultimate weapon of the vote of confidence, which generates a comparatively high degree of unity in national systems, is only available to a limited extent in the EU (Diermeier & Feddersen, 1998). The groups have limited tools to guarantee disciplined voting. EP groupings are more unified than US parties (Hix et al., 2006, p. 117ff.). A unique EP "work-sharing contract" contributes to this (Cox & McCubbins, 1993): Ordinary

MEPs ("backbenchers") help the parliamentary group by actively participating in committees and providing specialist knowledge on new legislative initiatives. In exchange, the group leadership ensures that "their" MEPs' actions are voted on uniformly and that group and parliament seats are distributed fairly. This implicit agreement accelerates EP decision-making and positions political parties as reliable partners for other European institutions (Raunio, 1997, p. 27).

4 Parliamentary Committees and Rapporteurs

The EP belongs to the type of working parliament (Steffani, 1979, p. 96). Accordingly, the EP's legislative and supervisory core competences are exercised in the parliamentary committees. The resolutions and decisions of the plenary sessions are preceded by content preparation and political coordination in the committees (Roger & Winzen, 2015). The committees set up for all European policy areas generate the EP position on all legislative proposals and also represent these directly to the Council and the Commission in the trilogue[3] of the ordinary legislative procedure (OLP).

As part of the exercise of the EP's legislative and budgetary powers, the committees are responsible for commenting on proposals for new legislation submitted by the Commission and on common positions and other documents submitted by the Council. They prepare the EP's part-sessions by drawing up reports on legislative proposals or own-initiative reports. In this sense, they play a key role in the EU's legislative process. When a proposal is submitted to the EP by the Commission or the Council, it is forwarded by the secretariat of the Bureau to the lead committee and, in most cases, to two or three other committees that give their opinion. The committees can also request to issue an opinion themselves or decide whether they wish to accept the invitation to issue an opinion. As co-advising committees, they can submit amendments but may not vote on the entire bill. Subject to approval by the Conference of Presidents, the committees may draw up own-initiative reports on any subject within their remit and put them to the vote in plenary.

Proposals for and amendments to draft legislative acts and a large number of its own-initiative resolutions are drafted by rapporteurs. The rapporteurs are appointed in committee at the suggestion of the group coordinators. The rapporteurs bear the main responsibility for drawing up the parliamentary report on "their" dossier, for amending it as part of the committee's internal deliberations up to the formal vote on the committee draft, for presenting it in the parliamentary plenary, and, in the case of legislative procedures, for defending it vis-à-vis the Council and the Commission (Benedetto, 2005)[4]. To this end, they conduct informal preliminary

[3] See Chap. 16 of this handbook.

[4] According to Rule 75 RoP—Conduct of negotiations (since July 2025), Parliament's negotiating team shall be led by the rapporteur and shall be presided over by the Chair of the committee responsible or by a Vice-Chair designated by the Chair, who may not be a shadow rapporteur for the report concerned. If neither the Chair nor a Vice-Chair can attend a specific negotiation meeting with the Council and the Commission ("trilogue"), the Chair shall inform the President before the meeting takes place that the negotiating team will be exceptionally presided over by the rapporteur at that trilogue.

negotiations with the Commission and with representatives of the Council presidency, as well as with interest groups and non-governmental organizations affected by the proposed measure. Rapporteurs usually invite the shadow rapporteurs of the other political groups to talks before the first debate in committee in order to explore possible lines of conflict and agreement.[5]

The committees of the EP are hardly comparable to those in the national parliaments of the EU member states (Bowler & Farell, 1995): Here too, the lack of a unified executive supported by a governing majority in parliament means that MEPs and political groups meet at committee level in an interplay between conflict and cooperation. Most committee members are very consensus-oriented. It is not uncommon for fault lines to run within the parliamentary groups, between national delegations, or individual parties within the parliamentary groups, each with their own specific interests. Political group affiliation takes a back seat, particularly when the EP wants to push through draft legislation and amendments vis-à-vis the Council: In the first reading phase of the OLP, the EP enters the subsequent trilogue negotiations with publicly agreed starting positions from the committees (Roederer-Rynning & Greenwood, 2015). The Council and Commission have three strategically useful pieces of information at their disposal: Firstly, the initial motions of the rapporteurs as well as the competing amendments of the other MEPs; secondly, the compromise motions agreed between the MEPs; and thirdly, the majorities behind the compromises finally agreed. By contrast, when entering the trilogue negotiations, the EP has neither reliable information about the opinion in the Council nor about the Commission's position on this. This informational asymmetry between EP and Council positions in this phase of the OLP contributes significantly to the fact that the committees attempt to vote on EP's motions with majorities that are far above the majority thresholds required by the treaty. This is the only way they can present a strong, united front to the Council. Weak majorities, on the other hand, quickly signal to the Council which changes position by individual political groups or MEPs can water down the parliamentary position.

5 Legislative Politics and Policy-Making Functions

In the EU institutional system, the division of competences between the Council and EP is not based on the type of decision-making procedure or the quality of the regulations, but—in accordance with the historically grown, path- and interest-dependent integration—depending on the competences successively assigned to the EU in the individual policy areas and thus as a result of the EU's requirements profile, which has grown over time. The catalogue of parliamentary participation options for legislative and quasi-legislative measures of the EU ranges from

[5] See further details in Chap. 12 of this handbook.

consultation to equal participation in the OLP (Art. 294 TFEU) to the necessity of a positive "consent" with an absolute majority of MEPs (Art. 218 and 207 TFEU).

As a rule, the obligatory consultation procedure is as follows: The Commission forwards its legislative proposal to the EP for an opinion. The President of the EP refers the proposal to the relevant parliamentary committee for discussion, which then draws up a motion for a resolution with a report. If the plenary adopts the motion for a resolution and submits amendments to the Commission proposal, the consultation procedure is concluded. If the EP votes on a legislative resolution, the Council is not bound by its content. However, the Council cannot take action without an opinion from the EP. The Council's failure to consult the EP constitutes a breach of essential procedural requirements, which can lead to an action for annulment before the European Court of Justice (ECJ) (Nicoll, 1988).

"The European Parliament shall act jointly with the Council of Ministers as legislator and shall exercise budgetary powers jointly with it". In this short and concise sentence, Art. 14 TEU outlines the central position of the EP in the decision-making structure of the EU. The wording is probably the clearest expression of its policy-making function (Nickel, 2003, p. 501). The basis for exercising this function is the codecision or OLP under Art. 294 TFEU, in which EP and the Council negotiate and decide jointly on the adoption of European secondary legislation on an equal footing. The special character of the procedure lies in the inter-organizational negotiation of compromises. The procedure consisted of a maximum of four readings until the entry into force of the Amsterdam Treaty and three readings since then (Fitzmaurice, 1988). The EP's right to table amendments to the Commission's draft text has significant consequences for the entire decision-making process. The decision of the MEPs determines the majority with which the Council can approve or amend the draft legislation. In addition, the strengthening of the EP resulting from the OLP is characterized by two things: firstly, the EP and the Council bear equal responsibility for the authorization or rejection of a legislative act, as co-legislators to a certain extent, analogous to bicameral systems. And secondly, from the second reading onwards, only EP, but not the Council of Ministers, can bring down the planned legislative act by means of a rejection decision by a majority of its members. The basic process is subject to numerous procedural specifications (Maurer, 2003; Dialer et al., 2015, pp. 219–224; European Parliament, 2017, 2018): Firstly, the three-month and six-week deadlines can be extended by a maximum of 1 month and 2 weeks, respectively, at the initiative of one of the two legislative bodies. Secondly, all three bodies are entitled to agree on details of their cooperation within the framework of interinstitutional agreements. And thirdly, the first reading of the EP is preceded by the mechanism of review and possible rebuke of the Commission proposal by the national parliaments.

The early agreements reached at first and second reading through informal conciliation procedures within the framework of the so-called trilogues[6] deserve particular academic and political attention (Judge & Earnshaw, 2011). The basis for

[6] See Chaps. 16 and 17 of this handbook.

this is the possibility, which has existed since the Amsterdam Treaty (1999), of concluding an OLP at the first reading stage. This option was first made explicit in the Joint Declaration on the practical arrangements for the codecision procedure, according to which the three institutions "shall cooperate in good faith throughout the procedure in order to bring their positions as close as possible to each other and, where appropriate, to enable the act to be adopted at an early stage of the procedure" (European Parliament, 1999). In practice, this procedure begins immediately after the vote on the parliamentary report, including the amendments to the Commission proposal and the draft legislative resolution at committee level. Before the report is forwarded to the plenary for a vote, the committees formulate a negotiating mandate for the rapporteur on the basis of their draft text. The EP delegation entrusted with conducting the negotiations is then made up of the rapporteur, the committee chair, and the shadow rapporteurs of the other political groups, which attempts to negotiate a compromise with the Council presidency and representatives of the Commission in the trilogue. If this is successful, the lead EP committee amends its draft text accordingly and then submits it to the plenary for a vote. If the plenary confirms the changes agreed in the trilogue, the dossier is deemed to be "completed at first reading". The so-called "early second readings" are a variant of this trilogue procedure. Here, the EP votes on the committee's report at first reading and then allows its delegation to conduct informal negotiations with the Council presidency before its first reading. If an agreement is reached at this stage, the Council adopts the draft text at its first reading, whereupon the EP formally confirms the decision at its second reading.

The Lisbon Treaty has extended the scope of application of the OLP from 45 (Treaty of Nice) to 85 case-specific powers of action. These include almost all individual provisions in justice and home affairs policy, the framework decisions on agricultural and fisheries policy, trade policy, partial aspects of economic policy coordination, and the new policy areas of civil protection and administrative cooperation. According to Art. 289 TFEU, the OLP is limited to the adoption of regulations, directives, or decisions adopted on a proposal from the Commission, on the initiative of a group of Member States, on a recommendation from the European Central Bank (ECB), or at the request of the Court of Justice (ECJ). The effective implementation is subject to particular restrictions in two areas. For example, Art. 48 TFEU provides for an "emergency brake" procedure for social security measures for workers moving within the Community: If even one Member State considers that the measures concerned affect fundamental aspects of its social security system, in particular its scope, costs, or financial structure, or its financial equilibrium, it may request that the matter be referred to the European Council. The OLP is then suspended. The European Council must refer the matter back to the Council within a period of 4 months in order to continue the procedure or request the Commission to submit a new proposal. A comparable procedure, but with a different outcome, can be applied in judicial cooperation in criminal matters in accordance with Art. 82 (1) and 82 (2) TFEU. Here, too, the measure in question is referred to the European Council if a Member State is of the opinion that a corresponding draft law would affect fundamental aspects of its criminal justice system. If the European Council does not take a corresponding decision within the four-month period, or if the new legislative procedure initiated at its request is not completed within 12 months, enhanced cooperation shall be established for this dossier if at least one third of the Member States are prepared to do so.[7]

5.1 The Consent Procedure: More Than "Take It or Leave It"

The consent procedure was introduced by the SEA in 1987 for accessions to the EU and the conclusion of association agreements and extended by the Maastricht Treaty to other policy areas of a "quasi-constitutional nature". Formally, the procedure does not give the EP any opportunity to participate substantially in the adoption of the intended Council decision. It is therefore also regarded as "a cruder form of codecision in that there is no scope for Parliament to put forward amendments to the measure in question" (Corbett et al., 2000, p. 204). The necessity of a parliamentary vote of approval in the "absence" of a treaty-based right of participation in the run-up to negotiations allows indirect influence on the draft texts by delaying the vote: The "power to delay is open-ended, clear-cut and beyond doubt; either the Parliament grants its assent or it doesn't" (Westlake, 1994, p. 151), which has been used in practice. The consent procedure can effectively compensate for the lack of participation rights in foreign and human rights policy (Gosalbo Bono, 1992). The Lisbon Treaty broadened the scope of the consent procedure to include Council decisions of major importance for the organization of the EU as well as all international agreements: Since the Treaty of Lisbon, EP's consent is also required for decisions on the immediate convening of an intergovernmental conference to amend the treaties (Art. 48 (3) TEU), the initiation of enhanced cooperation (Art. 329 TFEU); the application of the rounding-off of competences, which enables the EU to take measures not provided for in the treaties in order to achieve the objectives set out therein (Art. 352 TFEU); the decision on the application of a general "bridging clause" for the transition from unanimity to qualified majority voting (Art. 48 para. 7 (1) TEU) or from the special to the OLP (Art. 48 para. 7 (2) TEU); agreements concluded in the course of a Member State's accession to the EU (Art. 50 TEU) and decisions

---

[7]The Council's measures on the right of residence with regard to passports and identity cards, social security and social insurance, the right to vote and stand as a candidate in local elections and EP elections, the facilitation of diplomatic and consular protection, measures on capital movements with third countries, tax harmonization and corporation tax remain excluded from the COT even after the entry into force of the Lisbon Treaty, on language arrangements for legal titles, on minimum requirements for social security and the protection of workers on termination of employment contracts and on the employment conditions of third-country nationals, on environmental policy measures with financial provisions, on land-use planning, land-use and water management issues, on measures affecting a Member State's choice between different energy sources and on provisions of a fiscal nature. Measures on aspects of family law with cross-border implications are also excluded from the CDR. The number of 112 remaining powers of action of the Council that require the "non-involvement" of Parliament thus remains relatively high.

that enable the scope of application of specific legal bases to be extended (e.g. on the European Public Prosecutor or on judicial cooperation in criminal matters; Art. 82 (2d) TFEU).[8]

Regarding international agreements, Art. 218 (3) TFEU extends the list of cases in which the EP's consent is required to all "agreements in areas to which [...] the ordinary legislative procedure [...] applies". Since, as a result of the Lisbon Treaty reform—for the first time since 1958—all Common Commercial Policy measures are adopted in accordance with the OLP and Art. 218 TFEU does not contain any provisions to the contrary, EP's consent has been required for the conclusion of all bilateral, plurilateral, and multilateral trade agreements since 2009 (Devuyst, 2013). In the 2010 framework agreement, the EP and the Commission agreed on a de facto right of consultation for the upstream phases of issuing a parliamentary co-mandate to the Commission for the commencement of negotiations and their implementation (Maurer, 2015; Rosen, 2016): In accordance with the treaty provisions of Art. 207 (3) and 218 TFEU, the Council authorizes the Commission to open negotiations for trade agreements. The Commission is then responsible for conducting the negotiations in consultation with the Trade Policy Committee (TPC) appointed by the Council. According to Art. 218 (10) TFEU, "the European Parliament [...] shall be immediately and fully informed [...] at all stages of the procedure". The Commission is therefore legally obliged to inform the EP regularly and to the same extent as it informs the TPC (Art. 207 (3) (3) TFEU) about the status of the negotiations. The EP assumes that the phrases "all stages of the procedure" and "state of negotiations" cover all stages of the decision-making cycle; from the Commission's first recommendations to the Council to the granting of the mandate and its implementation through to the conclusion of the agreement. Indeed, in the 2010 framework agreement on cooperation between the EP and the Commission, the Commission agreed to inform the EP "promptly and comprehensively at all stages of the negotiation and conclusion of international agreements, including the establishment of negotiating directives", whereby the information "shall be provided in sufficient time to enable [the EP] to express its views and the Commission to take account, as far as possible, of the views of the Parliament" (European Parliament & European Commission, 2010).

6 The Implementation of Parliamentary Powers

The overview of the treaty-based foundation of procedures in the EU shows that parliamentary policy-making and control competences have been considerably expanded since the beginning of EU integration. However, the remaining deficits

[8] The Maastricht Treaty initially extended the scope of the consent procedure to the rules on the right of residence (Art. 21 TFEU), to measures on the allocation of specific tasks to the ECB for the supervision of credit institutions (Art. 127 TFEU) and amendments to the Statute of the European System of Central Banks (Art. 129 TFEU) as well as to provisions on the tasks, objectives, and organization of the Structural and Cohesion Funds (Art. 177 TFEU).

are obvious. Despite the Treaty of Lisbon, there is still a lack of justification as to which aspects are decisive for the differentiation of parliamentary participation rights. Looking at the development of the participation rights available to the EP under primary law, a slow but constant expansion can be observed. The relative extent of the EP's "non-participation" in the Council's policy-making rights has gradually decreased since 1958 (from 72.09% at the time of the EEC Treaty to 34.9% with the entry into force of the Lisbon Treaty 2009). The absolute increase in "non-participation" was partially compensated for by the introduction of the cooperation procedure (1987–2009) and the OLP. The allocation of the EP's incentives to (co)legislate and thus to ensure parliamentary-democratic responsibility lags behind the primary-law justification of legal bases in this regard. Only since the Single European Act (SEA) in 1987, but to a much greater extent since the Maastricht and Lisbon Treaties, has the EP been able to assert its codecision rights for policies transferred to the EU.

Raw data on the effective use of participation procedures (Dialer et al., 2015) illustrate the trend observed since the entry into force of the Maastricht Treaty of the EP concentrating on legislative activities at the expense of simple, non-legislative self-referrals, initiatives, and urgencies: Whereas in 1993 the EP was involved in only 48.44% of all acts of the Council in one of the legislative procedures in question, this proportion was already 60.05% in 1999 and was almost 70% in 2007. If the largely routine administrative acts of the Council in agricultural, fisheries, and customs tariff policy are excluded, the EP participation rate rises firstly to around 90% in general and the share of the cooperation and codecision procedure from 30.87% (for all Council acts) to around 75%. The comparison between the relative increase and decrease rates of decision-making procedures due to treaty reforms and the actual utilization rates of the available procedural provisions thus provides information on the quantitatively measurable success or failure of the gradual parliamentarization of the EU decision-making system: Until 2014, the "non-involvement" of the EP was reduced both in the context of the further development of the EU treaties and in the context of treaty implementation. Nevertheless, the use of the "parliamentary" procedures—cooperation and codecision or OLP—is lower in relation to the total of all legal acts adopted by the Council or by EP and the Council than their relative increase in importance following the treaty reforms would have suggested. Finally, the drastic increase in consent procedures since the entry into force of the Lisbon Treaty is striking. While the share of this procedure fluctuated between 0.5% and 3% of all Council acts until 2009, it was almost 25% in 2014. In this area, the procedural treaty reforms have had a direct and massive impact in favour of the EP. However, the relative decline in parliamentary legislative procedures since 2014 is also striking. The parliamentary quota for all legislative acts is now at a level that roughly corresponds to the period after the entry into force of the SEA in 1987. This relative decline in parliament-intensive procedures can be explained, firstly, by the implementation of subsidiarity demanded by the Member States: since 2009, the Commission has proposed fewer legislative acts than in the 1980s and 1990s. However, the decline in legislative work in general does not explain the low proportion of parliamentary work. In fact, despite its prayerful commitment to “less but better legislation”, the Council has not been deterred from massively expanding the normative category of legislative decisions and adopting more and more measures—bypassing the EP. The main areas affected are economic, monetary, establishment, tax, migration, and asylum policy. In addition, since the Treaty of Lisbon, the Council has increasingly made use of legislative acts in CFSP, in which the member states document the Council’s executive power to issue regulations (Figs. 3, 4 and 5).

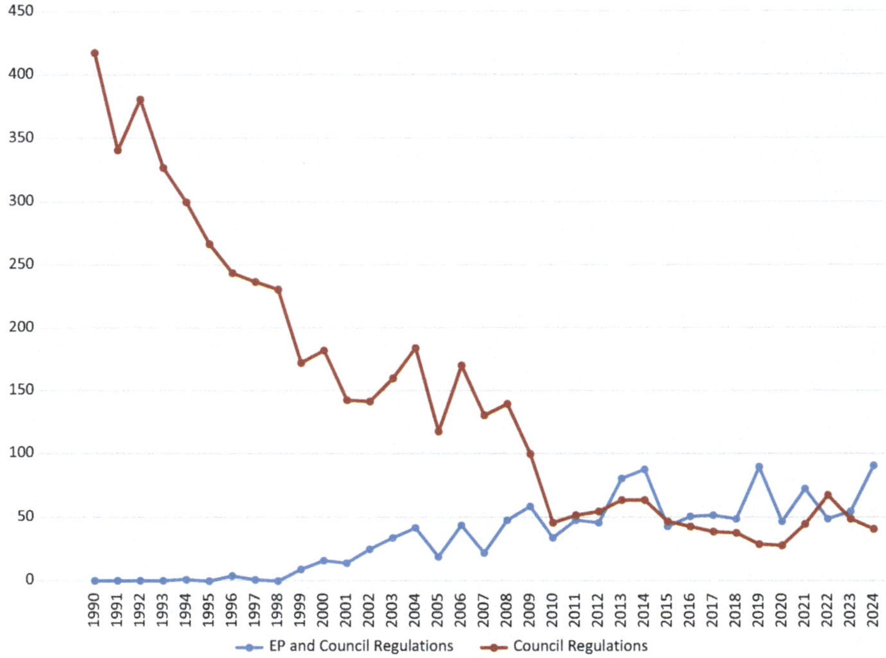

Fig. 3 No. of adopted regulations (per year) 1990–2024. *Source*: Own calculation based on data from the Legislative Observatory and EUR-Lex

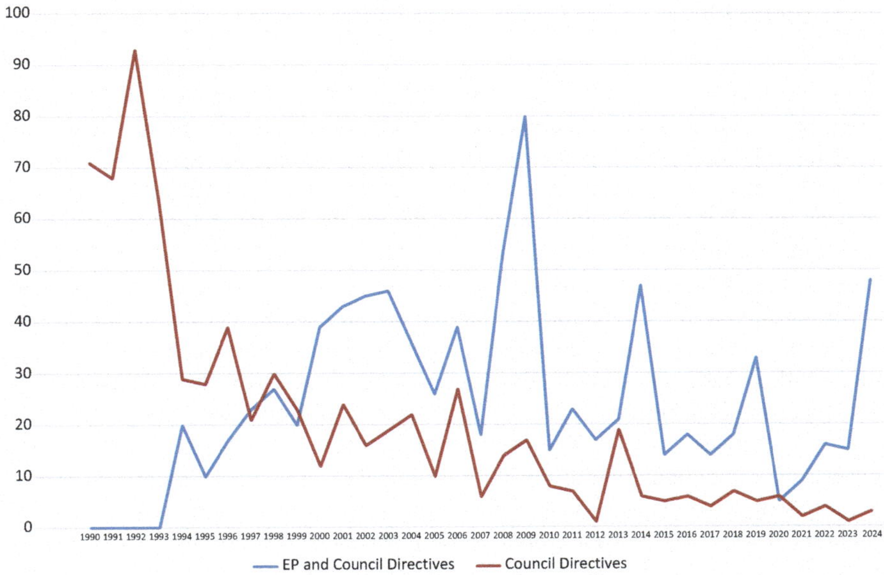

Fig. 4 No. of adopted directives (per year) 1990–2024. *Source*: Own calculation based on data from the Legislative Observatory and EUR-Lex

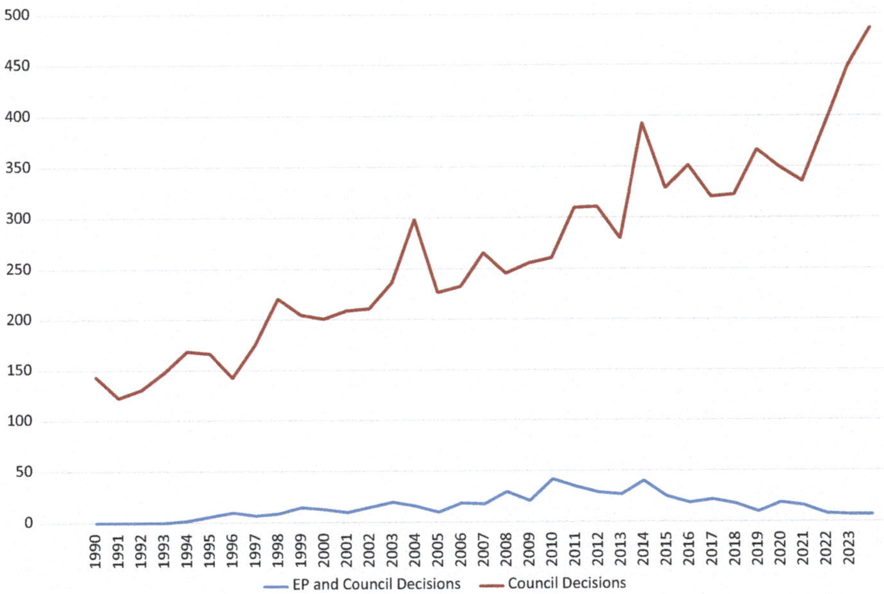

Fig. 5 No. of adopted decisions (per year) 1990–2024. *Source*: Own calculation based on data from the Legislative Observatory and EUR-Lex

7 Conclusion

European citizens still find it difficult to come to terms with the only supranational parliament in the world; a parliament that, unlike national parliaments, can act much more autonomously vis-à-vis the executives. This autonomy of action is the secret of the EP's success and its fate: the EP is not divided into "governing majority" and "opposition". The EP acts independently vis-à-vis the executive bodies of the EU; with changing, often large, cross-party majorities. The majority requirements for voting in the EP do not allow otherwise and thus implicitly produce a considerable communication and identification deficit. Although the EP is strong as an institution, it still comes across as inauthentic, alien, or apolitical and technocratic. What voters will probably also miss in the future is news from Brussels or Strasbourg as to whether the majority has prevailed against the opposition, who has prevailed in the clash between social democratic-progressive and Christian democratic-conservative. In anticipation of this party-political dispute, most voters continue to decide who they will vote for in the EP. It is precisely because of the lack of a clearly hierarchical and party-politicized relationship between the legislature and the executive branch that the EP can form autonomous decision-making preferences and implement them effectively in the interinstitutional procedures. However, the price of this strength should not be underestimated. The EP's power can hardly be conveyed to the EU's national civil societies, which are generally divided along party-political lines.

References

Ahrens, P., Elomäki, A., & Kantola, J. (Eds.). (2022). *European Parliament's political groups in turbulent times*. Palgrave Macmillan.

Benedetto, G. (2005). Rapporteurs as legislative entrepreneurs: The dynamics of the codecision procedure in Europe's parliament. *Journal of European Public Policy, 12*(1), 67–88.

Brack, N., & Costa, O. (eds.). (2018). The European Parliament through the lens of legislative studies: recent debates and new perspectives, Journal of Legislative Studies, Vol. 24, No. 1/2018 (Special issue).

Bowler, S., & Farell, D. (1995). The organizing of the European Parliament, committees, specialization and co-ordination. *British Journal of Political Science, 25*(1), 219–243.

Corbett, R., Jacobs, F., & Shackleton, M. (2000). *The European Parliament* (4th ed.). London.

Corbett, R., Jacobs, F., & Neville, D. (2016). *The European Parliament* (9th ed.). London, John Harper.

Cox, G. & McCubbins, M. (1993). *Legislative leviathan*, Stanford.

Devuyst, Y. (2013). The European Parliament and international trade agreements. Practice after the Lisbon treaty. In I. Govaere, E. Lannon, P. Van Elsuwege, & S. Adam (Eds.), *The European Union in the world, essays in honor of Marc Maresceau* (pp. 172–189). Brill.

Dialer, D., Maurer, A., & Richter, M. (2015). *Handbuch zum Europäischen Parlament*. Baden-Baden.

Diermeier, D., & Feddersen, T. (1998). Cohesion in legislatures and the vote of confidence procedure. *American Political Science Review, 92*(3), 611–621.

European Parliament. (1999). European Parliament, Resolution on the joint declaration regarding the practical arrangements for the new codecision procedure (Article 251 EC Treaty), Official Journal No. C 279, 1 October 1999.

European Parliament. (2017). *Manual on the Ordinary Legislative Procedure*, edited by DG Internal Policies of the Union, Directorate for Legislative Coordination and Conciliation - Conciliation and Co-decision Unit, Brussels, November 2017.

European Parliament. (2018, May). *Collection of the most important legal acts relating to the Rules of Procedure*, Brussels.

European Parliament, & European Commission. (2010). *Framework Agreement on relations between the European Parliament and the European Commission*, OJ L 304, 20.11.2010.

Fitzmaurice, J. (1988). An analysis of the European Community's cooperation procedure. *Journal of Common Market Studies, 26*(4), 389–400.

Gosalbo Bono, R. (1992). The international powers of the European Parliament, the democratic deficit and the treaty on European Union. *Yearbook of European Law, 12*, 85–138.

Hix, S., & Lord, C. (1997). Political Parties in the European Union, Basingstoke.

Hix, S. (2005). *The political system of the European Union* (2nd ed.).

Hix, S., & Noury, A. (2009). After enlargement: Voting behavior in the sixth European Parliament. *Legislative Studies Quarterly, XXXIV*(2), 159–174.

Hix, S., Noury, A., & Roland, G. (2006). Democratic politics in the European Parliament,.

Hobolt, S. B. (2014). A vote for the president? The role of Spitzenkandidaten in the 2014 European Parliament elections. *Journal of European Public Policy, 21*(10), 1528–1540.

Judge, D., & Earnshaw, D. (2011). Relay actors and Codecision first Reading agreements in the European Parliament: The case of the advanced therapies regulation. *European Journal of Public Policy, 18*(1), 53–71.

Madatali, H. A., Eisele, K., Jansen, T., & Tenhunen, S. (2025). *The European Parliament's oversight powers: Tools to scrutinise the European Commission*. European Parliament. https://doi.org/10.2861/1182026

Maurer, A. (2002). *Parliamentary democracy in the European Union. The contribution of the European Parliament and the National Parliaments*. Nomos.

Maurer, A. (2003). The legislative powers and impact of the European Parliament. *Journal of Common Market Studies, 35*(2), 227–247.

Maurer, A., & Wessels, W. (2003). Das Europäische Parlament nach Amsterdam und Nizza: Akteur,Arena oder Alibi?, Baden-Baden, Nomos.

Maurer, A. (2012). Parlamente in der EU, Stuttgart/Wien, UTB/Facultas 2012

Maurer, A. (2015). *Comparative study on access to classified documents and confidentiality rules in international trade negotiations*. European Parliament. https://doi.org/10.2861/846769

Maurer, A., & Dietmar, N. (Eds.). (2005). *The European Parliament. Supranationality, representation and legitimation*. Nomos.

Maurer, A., Dialer, D., & Karas, O. (2025). *Das Europäische Parlament* (2nd ed.). Nomos.

Nickel, D. (2003). Das Europäische Parlament als Legislativorgan - zum neuen institutionellen Design nach der Europäischen Verfassung. *Integration, 26*(4), 501–509.

Nicoll, W. (1988). Le dialogue législatif entre le Parlement et la Commission: la procédure de renvoi en commission du Parlement européen. *Revue du Marché Commun, 316*, 240–242.

Niedermayer, O. (2014). Still a national by-election? The election to the European Parliament on may 25, 2014. *Zeitschrift für Parlamentsfragen, 45*(3), 523–546.

Piodi, F. (Ed.). (2007). *Vers un Parlement unique. L'influence de l'Assemblée commune de la CECA sur les Traités de Rome*. (Parlement européen - CARDOC).

Raunio, T. (1997). *The European Perspective: Transnational Party Groups in the 1989–1994 European Parliament*, Aldershot 1997.

Reif, K., & Schmitt, H. (1980). Nine second-order national elections - a conceptual framework for the analysis of European election results. *European Journal of Political Research, 8*(1), 3–44.

Roederer-Rynning, C., & Greenwood, J. (2015). The culture of trilogues. *Journal of European Public Policy, 22*(8), 1148–1165.

Roger, L., & Winzen, T. (2015). Party groups and committee negotiations in the European Parliament: Outside attention and the anticipation of plenary conflict. *Journal of European Public Policy, 22*(3), 391–408.

Rosen, G. (2016). The impact of norms on political decision-making: How to account for the European Parliament's empowerment in EU external trade policy. *Journal of European Public Policy, 24*(10), 1450–1470.

Scoffoni, G. (1992). Les relations entre le Parlement européen et les parlements nationaux et le renforcement de la légitimité démocratique de la Communauté, in: Cahiers de Droit Européen, Vol. 28 No. 1-2/1992, 22–41.

Steffani, W. (1979). *Parlamentarische und präsidentielle Demokratie*. Leske & Budrich.

Westlake, M. (1994). *A modern guide to the European Parliament*. Pinter.

Andreas Maurer Dipl.Pol. (Frankfurt am Main), MA/D.E.E.A. (College of Europe Bruges), Dr.rer.soc. (Gießen) has been Professor of Political Science and Politics of European Integration since September 2013 at Innsbruck University. Previously he worked at the Institute for European Politics, Bonn, the University of Cologne, the Trans European Policy Studies Association—TEPSA, Brussels, and the German Institute for International and Security Affairs (SWP). Advisor to the European Constitutional Convention, the Conference of Presidents and Speakers of Parliaments of the EU and the Conference of Committees Specialized in EU Affairs of the EU (COSAC). Seconded and contract officer of the European Parliament's Committee on International Trade.

Committees at Work: The Operational Core of EU Lawmaking

Tino Kunert and Birgül Tütün-Ince

Abstract Committees play a central role in the European Parliament's (EP) policy-making process as they prepare the ground for plenary decisions. Within this framework, the rapporteurs, the coordinators, and the shadow rapporteurs hold key positions that shape the outcome of the legislative process. This chapter offers a comprehensive analysis of the committee functions and examines the procedural and political power dynamics embedded in the EP's internal decision-making structures.

Keywords Conference of Committee Chairs (CCC) · Shadow-rapporteur · Conference of Presidents (CoP) · Coordinators · Accredited parliamentary assistants (APAs) · Points mechanism · Urgent procedure · Simplified procedure

1 Introduction

Behind the visible plenary debates of the European Parliament (EP) lies a complex, methodical, and often underestimated machinery of decision-making: the parliamentary committees. These committees are not merely administrative bodies; they are dynamic arenas where political negotiation, expertise, and compromise converge to shape the EU's legislative agenda. Rapporteurs, shadow rapporteurs, and coordinators within these committees are instrumental in drafting reports, negotiating amendments, and building consensus across political groups, ensuring that

T. Kunert (✉)
Policy Advisor at the Representation of Saarland to the EU, Brussels, Belgium
e-mail: t.kunert@europa.saarland.de

B. Tütün-Ince (✉)
Austrian Federal Railways (ÖBB) and University of Applied Sciences BFI Vienna, Vienna, Austria
e-mail: birguel.tuetuen-ince@fh-vie.ac.at

G. Füricht-Fiegl et al. (eds.), *Handbook on EU Law-making*, Professional Practice in Governance and Public Organizations, https://doi.org/10.1007/978-3-032-16559-6_12

diverse perspectives are reflected in legislative outcomes before it reaches the plenary.

The structured processes within committees, as outlined in the Rules of Procedure (RoP), are essential for the effective functioning of the Ordinary Legislative Procedure (OLP). Committees not only scrutinize legislative proposals but also act as a bridge between EU institutions, member states, and civil society, fostering transparency and accountability.

This article highlights the crucial role of EP committees in shaping EU legislation and their broader impact on democratic governance. By examining their procedures, responsibilities, and influence, this study aims to provide a deeper understanding of how committees anchor the EP's legislative power and contribute to the EU's institutional continuity and policy making.

2 The Legislative Path: From Commission Proposal to Committee Referral

2.1 Initial Stage of the Ordinary Legislative Procedure

Committees serve as the EP's engines of policy formulation. Rapporteurs, coordinators and shadow rapporteurs play pivotal roles in drafting reports, negotiating amendments, coordinating political group positions and shaping the compromises that ultimately reach the plenary. Before any legislative proposal is debated in plenary, it passes through a highly structured committee process laid down in the Rules of Procedure (RoP), which define the organisation, decision-making practices and division of responsibilities within committees. Understanding these procedures is essential for grasping the institutional dynamics of the Ordinary Legislative Procedure (OLP). Against this backdrop, this section outlines how a legislative file enters the parliamentary phase of the OLP and the procedural steps that precede its formal referral to a committee.

The OLP currently applies to around 90 legal bases (European Parliament, n.d.-a) under the Lisbon Treaty. Once the College of Commissioners adopts a legislative proposal, it is published on EUR-Lex as a COM document, usually accompanied by an impact assessment. At the same time, the file is transmitted to the Presidents of the European Parliament and the Council, to the national parliaments and, where applicable, to the Committee of Regions and the Economic and Social Committee. When responding to a legislative proposal from the Commission, the EP and the Council have three main options: reject it, adopt it without amendment, or submit amendments (Rule 60(1) RoP). The last option is 'the normal one', embodying democratic participation, but it also requires substantial procedural work, as explored here.

While the Council documents its amendments in a 'general approach', the EP drafts a legislative resolution based on the report(s) by the responsible committee(s).

2.2 *Determination of Committee Responsibility*

Before a committee can begin its substantive work on a legislative or non-legislative file, the competent committee must be designated, along with any others entitled to deliver opinions. This requires clarifying which of the 22 standing committees, subcommittees and the two special committees currently in place (European Parliament, n.d.-b) in the EP are responsible for drafting the report (lead committee) or an opinion on the matter (opinion-giving-committee).

In accordance with Rule 48(1) RoP the « Unit for Reception and Referral of Official Documents » in the Directorate-General for the presidency assesses each legislative proposal—mainly on the basis of Annex VI—and recommends a referral to a lead committee or, where appropriate—up to three committees acting jointly (Rule 59 RoP). It may also propose opinion-giving committees to the president. The president reviews and informs all committees and political groups of the decision in an internal document. If doubts arise, the Conference of Committee Chairs (CCC) may be asked to issue a recommendation (Rule 48(3) RoP), also the president remains free to take the decision deemed appropriate.

Rule 217(2–3) RoP further clarifies that "if two or more standing committees are competent to deal with a matter, one shall be designated as the committee responsible and the others as committees asked for opinions." However, no more than three committees may be seized simultaneously and joint decision-making is only permitted under Rule 59 RoP.

In most cases, a legislative proposal can theoretically be assigned to a committee as the body primarily responsible (Rule 48(1) RoP in conjunction with Annex VI RoP). This lead committee drafts the report and prepares amendment proposals.

In practice, however, referrals to a single committee are rare. Legislative proposals often affect several policy fields and thus engage the competence of different committees. Those substantially concerned, but not primarily responsible, are designated as opinion-giving committees (Rule 57(1) RoP).

Although rule 217(2) RoP suggests that no more than three committees should deal with a legislative proposal simultaneously, there is no strict limit to the number of opinion-giving committees.

Until the 2024 revision of the Rules of Procedure, committees could issue different types of opinions. A "simple" opinion could be voted down by the responsible committee without consequence, which often hindered constructive cooperation and wasted resources. Committees not in a leading role therefore sought alternative forms of participation, resulting in lengthy procedural disputes involving the CCC, the CoP and coordinators.

At the opposite end, the "exclusive" opinion model obliged the lead committee to adopt the opinion-giving committee's text without changes, which undermined coherence and occasionally weakened EP's position in interinstitutional negotiations.

The revised introduce a single form of opinion for committees with shared competences. Amendments submitted by opinion-giving committees must be put to the cote in the lead committee but need not be adopted verbatim (Rule 57(5) RoP). This approach ensures inclusiveness and flexibility, allowing relevant input to be integrated without compromising legislative consistency.

Under the former RoP, competence conflicts were often informally resolved by integrating the rapporteur of an opinion-giving committee into the rapporteurs' team of the lead committee – a practice informally indicated by a '+' sign, allowing participation in trilogue negotiations, although this practice was never formally recorded in official documents. This type of procedure is only documented if the rapporteur has stated this in a 'short justification' of his opinion. Rule 57(8) RoP now codifies this arrangement by permitting the chair and rapporteur of the opinion-giving committee to participate in lead committee and preparatory or shadow meetings in an advisory capacity, while excluding direct trilogue participation. The previously informal "+" right has thus been partially formalised but clearly limited.

The Conference of Committee Chairs (CCC) (European Parliament, n.d.-c)

The CCC composed of the chairs of all standing and special committees (Rule 29 par. 1 RoP), elects its own chair for a two-and-a-half-year term.[1] It serves as a key discussion and coordination forum among committees adressing cross-cutting issues. The recently revised RoP (2024) strengthen the CCC's role in mediating between committees and handling requests for cooperation. It also proposes solutions to settle competence disputes.

The CCC also organises hearings of Commissioners-designate, reviews delegated and implementing acts and contributes to the Commission's annual work programme.

The CCC meets every Tuesday afternoon during a plenary-sessions in Strasbourg.

2.2.1 Joint Committee Procedure (Rule 59 RoP)

In cases where a proposal falls within the remit of several committees, without one competence prevailing Rule 59 RoP allows a joint committee procedure involving up to three committees. Each appoints "its own" rapporteur and shadow rapporteurs, who jointly draft one single text together to be examined and voted on by all committees involved (Rule 59(2) RoP).

[1] Re-election is possible, as the current chair of the CCC, Bernd Lange (S&D, Germany, Chair of the Committee on International Trade, INTA), has already been chair of the CCC since February 2022 in the previous, 9th term of the EP.

In such a procedure, it is also possible to assign referrals to opinion-giving committees. Example: on the proposal for a regulation on circularity requirements for vehicle design and management of end-of-life vehicles the Committee on Environment, Public Health and Food Safety (ENVI) and the Committee on Internal Market and Consumer Protection (IMCO) work jointly as committees in the lead while the Committee on Transport and Tourism (TRAN) delivers an opinion.

The report is adopted in a joint voting session and is deemed adopted only if approved by all involved committees.

Where more than three committees are substantially concerned, Rule 59 RoP no longer applies. In such cases, a different mechanism is foreseen under Rule 214 RoP.

2.2.2 Temporary Legislative Committees (Rule 214 RoP)

As an exceptional mechanism, Rule 214 RoP allows the establishment of a temporary legislative committee when more than three standing committees are substantially concerned, and no single competence prevails. The reference to this mechanism 'as a last resort' indicates that it should be used only in exceptional cases.

The CCC's negotiated proposal forms the basis for the CoP's decision, which then requires plenary approval.

The procedure, introduced at the beginning of the 10th parliamentary term, has not yet been applied but may gain relevance for large legislative packages in the future, such as those related to the post-2028 Multiannual Financial Framework (MFF).

2.3 Dispute Settlement on Referrals

To ensure clarity and fairness in allocating competences, the RoP provide a mechanism for contesting referral decisions. A committee or political group may contest the president's decision before the CoP within two weeks, providing a justification and an alternative referral based on Annex VI (Rule 48(2) RoP). A committee not authorised to deliver an opinion may request such authorisation from the CCC.

The CoP may decide directly or seek a recommendation from the CCC. The CoP's final decision—or, if unchallenged, the president's initial decision—becomes binding (Rule 48(3) RoP).

The Conference of Presidents (CoP, Rules 26 f. RoP) (European Parliament, n.d.-c)

The CoP consists of the President of the EP and the chairs of all political groups and a representative of the non-attached MEPs participates without voting rights. The CoP is responsible for the organisation of EP's business and legislative planning, including the timetable and agendas of plenary

(continued)

sittings (Rule 27/2) RoP). In addition, it decides on challenges to referral decisions and may authorise special scrutiny hearings with Commissioners on major political issues.

The CoP is chaired by the President of the EP[2] and usually meets in Brussels on Thursday mornings before a Strasbourg week and again during plenary weeks. Its agenda, prepared in advance by the Secretary-General and the political groups' secretaries-general, aims to facilitate compromise and ensure efficient proceedings.

2.4 *Announcement of Referrals*

The decision on referrals is announced at the next plenary session, provided that the legislative proposal has been received in all official languages (Rule 48(5) RoP). The announcement is made in writing and recorded in the minutes under "Documents received", indicating the responsible committee and any committees asked for opinions.

Even for uncontroversial files, approximately one month may pass between the Commission's adoption and EP's formal announcement, largely because plenary sessions take place only one week per month.

2.5 *Procedural Variants for Accelerated Legislative Handling*

In addition to the standard workflow, the Rules of Procedure provide several procedural variants to accelerate or simplify committee work, especially for files linked to current political priorities. In the simplified procedure under Rule 52 RoP, the committee chair schedules an initial exchange of views on the Commission proposal. After this debate, the chair may either propose adoption without amendments (Rule (1) RoP) or set a deadline for submitting amendments (Rule 52 (2) RoP). In this case, there is no need to draw up a draft report or appoint a team of rapporteurs. The submitted amendments are voted on at the next committee meeting, and those adopted are forwarded to plenary as a draft resolution. This simplified approach, particularly when applied to opinions under Rule 52 (3) RoP, helps opinion-giving committees to manage tight timeframes more efficiently.

The most far-reaching acceleration is provided by the urgent procedure under Rule 170 RoP, reserved for cases of 'unforeseeable developments'. As this significantly limits the EP's right to full participation, any Commission request to apply it must include a detailed justification and be approved by a simple majority in plenary. Once granted, the accelerated and simplified procedures are combined for further processing. In exceptional cases, the written report may even be replaced by an oral one (Rule 170 (6) RoP).

[2] The current chair is Roberta Metsola (EPP, Malta).

3 The Appointment of the (Co-)rapporteurs and Shadows

3.1 Procedure in the Coordinators Meeting

After a referral, the committee chair places the legislative proposal under the item « Referrals » on the agenda of the coordinators' meeting to determine which political group will appoint the rapporteur (Rule 51(2) and 220(2) RoP). One of the main tasks of the committee secretariat is to monitor referrals from the president and inform the chair accordingly.

Referrals are dealt with in a fixed order: legislative reports and opinions, non-legislative reports and opinions, and own-initiative requests. If the chair and secretariat consider that a referral has been omitted, the matter may be raised at the next coordinators' meeting.

In urgent cases, the committee chair may act on behalf of the committee and seek coordinators' approval through a written procedure. Unless objections are raised within a short deadline, silence is deemed consent, and the issue is placed on the agenda of the following meeting for formal confirmation.

Committee Coordinators, Rule 220 RoP

Each political group may designate one of its members in a committee as coordinator (Rule 220(1) RoP). The specific procedures for this designation are laid down in the internal rules of each political group. Typically, coordinators must be full members of the committee and are elected within their group's working group at the beginning and midpoint of the parliamentary term.

Coordinators are among the first positions to be filled in a new committee and play a central role in organising its work. They propose candidates for the positions chair and vice-chair positions, chair their political group's internal working group, and meet in camera to coordinate the committee's further work. Their responsibilities managing referrals, selecting topics for own initiative reports and hearings, commissioning studies or requesting support from other parliamentary services, and deciding on committee missions.

If a vote is required, coordinators' votes are weighted according to the share of votes held by their political group (Rule 220(2) RoP).

Although the coordinators of a committee should strive to reach a consensus on all matters (Rule 220(2) RoP), each committee applies its own internal rules for cases where no agreement can be found. Where no consensus is reached, coordinators may decide by secret ballot on the allocation of rapporteurships (Rule 220(3) RoP).

These regulations are not comprehensively documented in writing, differ in some details, but are generally based on a points system: At the start of the parliamentary term, each full member of a committee contributes an equal number of points to their political group's account. Example: The Committee on Culture and Education (CULT) has 30 members, each member is worth 2.5 points, resulting in the following points total for the political groups at the beginning of the parliamentary term: e.g. EPP 8 Members (× 2,5 points) = 20 points, S&D 6 Members (× 2,5 points) = 15 points.

Reports and opinions are then assigned fixed point values (e.g. 2.5 points for a legislative report, 2 points for a non-legislative report, 1 point for a legislative opinion and 0.5 point for a non-legislative opinion).

In this case, coordinators will be asked two questions in the following order during a referral in the coordinators meeting:

1. Do the coordinators agree to draw up a [legislative report] for (European Parliament, n.d.-b; European Parliament, 2025) point[s]?
2. Appoint a group providing the rapporteur.

If no consensus is reached, the group with the highest remaining balance is awarded the file. In this respect, it can be crucial when exactly a referral is called up in the course of a meeting for such a distribution. The political group that is appointed will have the corresponding point value deducted from their account immediately in any case.

Alternatively, an auction system has been adopted in other committees, whereby two variants are also used here in a two-stage process. Either the coordinators first assign a point value to a specific matter that is to be referred and then allocate it at this value to a political group that can (still) spend this point value. Or, first, a simple yes or no decision is taken on whether the committee wishes to take action on a matter, and if yes, in a second step, the political groups compete for it in an auction.

In all cases, the coordinator plays a key strategic role that extends beyond the individual committee meeting. First, the coordinator must have an overview of which matters are of interest to a political group and which Member of the European Parliament (MEP) of their working group is capable and willing to take on the role of rapporteur. In addition, the workload should be distributed fairly evenly among the regular members of a committee.

In some cases, coordinators 'save' points to secure high-profile legislative files that their group "must have". Despite these negotiations, cooperation and mutual understanding between coordinators of different groups remain essential to maintaining trust and efficiency in committee work. In general, a rapporteur's team consisting of the rapporteur and shadow rapporteurs is formed for every matter referred to a committee, for both reports and opinions.[3]

With the two-stage distribution described in the coordinators' meeting, a situation may arise in which the coordinators agree that their committee should take a position, but none of them is willing to spend points from their group's balance. In

[3] See the TRAN Committee's *Work in Progress* database on the EP website: https://www.europarl.europa.eu/committees/en/tran/documents/work-in-progress. The shadows of rapporteur teams are not listed in the procedural file but can be found only by searching for the relevant item under *Work in Progress* on the respective committee pages.

such cases – mainly concerning opinions – Rule 57(1) RoP allows the committee to send its views "in the form of a letter from the chair". The matter is therefore referred to the chair, with no points deducted from the political group to which the chair belongs. The chair cannot be penalised for the coordinators‘ "unwillingness". The chair drafts the letter with support from the committee secretariat, ensuring that it reflects the committee's majority view. Often, coordinators are consulted informally, similar to shadow rapporteurs, before finalising the text.

3.2 Co-rapporteurship and Shadow Rapporteurs

For complex or politically sensitive files, a committee may request authorisation from the CoP to appoint up to three co-rapporteurs within the same committee (Rule 54(1) RoP). Such requests are usually preceded by consultation with coordinators. When a point system is used, the total value of the report is divided proportionally among co- rapporteurs. In our example, for a co-report with two co-rapporteurs for a legislative report: 2.5 points: 2 rapporteurs = 1.25 points per co-rapporteur.

All political groups in the committee that have not been assigned a rapporteur's role may appoint a shadow rapporteur for a given file (Rule 54(1) RoP). While optional, declining to do so generally reduces a group's influence in shaping compromises. Waiving this right only makes sense if a political group wishes to avoid constructive participation in the legislative proposal because it intends to reject the proposal from the outset and in any case, regardless of the outcome of parliamentary deliberations.

3.3 Procedure in the Working Groups

Working groups, chaired by the respective coordinators, meet during parliamentary weeks to plan future referrals and assign rapporteurships to individual MEPs. Strategies for upcoming future referrals are briefly coordinated here, and the assigned referrals are allocated to an individual MEP. In principle, it is up to the coordinator to decide alone on the allocation to a specific colleague in the working group.

In allocating files, coordinators consider members' expertise, workload, seniority, and prior commitments, ensuring a balanced distribution among active members. In rare cases, it may happen that nobody wants to take on a matter. In such cases, the coordinator takes over the file and is assisted in drafting the text by a political advisor working for the political group‘s secretariat and responsible for the relevant committee. In addition, the Policy Department of Directorate-General for Internal Policies of the Union (DG IPOL) provides analytical briefings, expert hearings and studies to support committees and rapporteurs in ensuring substantive quality and legal consistency.

Assistants, Advisors, Administrators: Distinct Roles in the EP
Accredited parliamentary assistants (APAs) serve individual MEPs, supporting them in drafting reports, opinions or amendments, organising meetings, and advising on voting decisions. APAs function as crucial information filters and act as the MEPs' "eyes and ears".

Political group advisors work for entire political groups, focusing on cross-committee coordination and strategic positioning. They tend to be more experienced professionals who draft amendments, negotiate with other groups to build majorities, and coordinate their group's overall stance across different committees. The advisors are assigned exclusively to specific committees and thus policy areas.

Committee administrators work in the committee secretariat and are non-political servants who provide procedural and technical support to committee chairs and all committee members regardless of political affiliation.

Both the political groups and the committee secretariats have "assistants", who are responsible in particular for ensuring that organisational processes run smoothly and for preparing meetings and events.

4 Obligations of the Rapporteur

According to Rule 56(1) RoP, the rapporteur is responsible for drafting the committee report and presenting it to the EP. The rapporteur manages the entire legislative process, from the initial drafting stage to interinstitutional trilogue negotiations, acting on behalf of the committee chair, who usually presides over the trilogues (Rule 75(1) RoP).

In preparing the draft report, the rapporteur relies heavily on external expertise. This is gathered through exchanges with expert stakeholders and public hearings organised together with the political group and the committee. Increasingly, rapporteurs also use social media to invite brief input or comments from stakeholders. Once the rapporteur is announced publicly, stakeholders often reach out proactively to present their views or request direct dialogue.

In this context, strict ethical and transparency standards apply to ensure the integrity of the legislative process.

4.1 Conflicts of Interest

The « Code of Conduct for Members of the European Parliament Regarding Integrity and Transparency » (European Parliament, 2023) (Annex 1 to the RoP) aims to ensure that MEPs "act solely in the public interest" (Art. 1 (b)). According to Art. 4(5), only those MEPs who have submitted a publicly accessible declaration of private interests may be appointed as rapporteurs or shadow rapporteurs. Any remunerated activity exceeding €5,000 per year must be declared, including the names of the entities providing such income. Moreover, Art. 3 establishes a general duty to disclose and resolve any conflicts of interest.

4.2 Transparency Requirements

Pursuant to its Art. 3(5) (shadow-)rapporteurs must separately declare for each report whether a conflict of interest could exist. Furthermore, rapporteurs must list organisations and individuals from whom they have received contributions as well as the range of external expertise and opinions received in an annex to their reports. This list is published with the report after committee adoption (Art. 7). According to this, MEPs should „only meet interest representatives that are entered in the transparency register (European Union, 2021).

These procedural and ethical standards form the framework within which rapporteurs and shadow rapporteurs perform their legislative work. The following section outlines how the drafting phase is organised in practice — from the planning of the timetable to the adoption of the committee report.

5 Drafting Phase of the Committee Report

5.1 Determining the Timetable

The drafting phase represents the core of the committee's work, during which the rapporteur translates political priorities into draft reports and compromise texts. Before drafting the report, the rapporteur agrees a timetable with the committee secretariat and, informally, with the shadow rapporteurs. At a minimum, this includes the submission of the draft report, the first exchange of views, its presentation, and the committee vote. In complex files, rapporteurs may table working documents prior to the draft report to structure the political discussion (Rule 55 RoP).

The committee chair sets the deadline amendments—typically one parliamentary working week—after consulting the secretariat and the rapporteur. Sufficient time must be allowed between each stage to ensure that both the draft report and all amendments are available in every language. In addition, all opinions from opinion-giving committees must be received before the committee vote so they can be taken into account during compromise negotiations and in the preparation of the voting list.

Ideally, MEP offices agree informally on a 'save the date' for a shadow rapporteur' meeting after the amendment deadline to discuss potential compromises efficiently (Table 1).

Table 1 OLP procedure at committee stage (European Parliament, 2025)

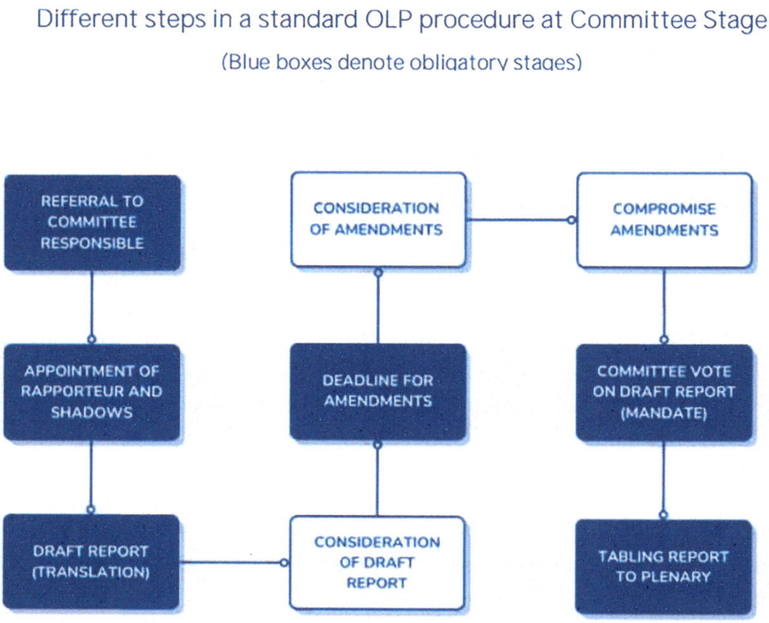

5.2 *Voting in Committee, Rule 224 RoP*

Upon completion of the drafting phase, the committee proceeds to the voting stage, where the compromises reached among political groups are formally adopted as the committee's position. This stage serves as a key intermediary step in the ordinary legislative procedure (OLP), as it defines the committee's formal stance before the report moves to plenary.

During the committee stage, the chair — usually acting on the rapporteur's proposal — sets a deadline for amendments, which must be signed or co-signed by full or substitute members of the committee. In exceptional circumstances, the chair may still accept compromise or individual amendments after the deadline, for example in cases of technical issues (Rule 188(4) RoP). Oral amendments may also be introduced during the vote, unless one-twentieth of members object (Rule 187(6) in conjunction with Rule 225 RoP).

Prior to the vote, the rapporteur and shadow rapporteurs often hold informal "shadows meetings" to align political positions and prepare compromise amendments supported by several groups. Each shadow rapporteur then gives a voting recommendation to their respective political group, which serves as guidance during the vote.

The responsible committee ultimately adopts its report — incorporating the agreed amendments to the Commission proposal—by simple majority, with the final vote taken by roll call. After its adoption in committee, the report proceeds to the next stage of the parliamentary process.

5.3 From Committee Vote to Interinstitutional Negotiations

Once the responsible committee adopts its legislative report, it becomes the EP's first-reading position under Art. 294 TFEU. The text is forwarded to plenary and serves as the basis for the informal trilogues with the Council of the EU and the European Commission. During these negotiations, the rapporteur—supported by the committee chair, the Secretariat and DG IPOL's Policy Departments—represents EP's mandate. This stage ensures that compromises reached in trilogues remain faithful to the committee's decision and politically accountable to the plenary.

6 The Practical Significance of Committees

In the context of the OLP, committees serve as the Parliament's main decision-shaping bodies, where most of the substantive work is carried out. In practice, committees matter far beyond their formal powers. Many MEPs remain in the same committee for several years, which creates continuity, deep expertise and a strong sense of ownership over legislative files. This stability also explains why committee seats are highly contested within political groups and national delegations. Being a full member of a committee with a steady flow of legislative proposals—such as IMCO, ENVI, EMPL, ITRE or LIBE—offers visibly more influence and visibility than serving in committees with a lighter legislative agenda, such as CULT or FEMM[4]. These internal dynamics shape the daily work of MEPs and determine their access to key files and negotiations. For that reason, committees are not only the institutional backbone of the Parliament, but also the places where political influence is built, maintained and exercised.

Committees can also shape policy outcomes beyond formal legislative files. Through persistent political signaling—via own-initiative reports, implementation reports or repeated amendment requests—they often succeed in placing issues on the Commission's agenda. Over time, such continuity can contribute to new proposals or adjustments in existing EU policies, illustrating the broader influence

[4]
- IMCO: Committee on Internal Market and Consumer Protection.
- ENVI: Committee on Environment, Climate and Food Safety.
- EMPL: Committee on Employment and Social Affairs.
- ITRE: Committee on Industry, Research and Energy.
- LIBE: Committee on Civil Liberties, Justice and Home Affairs.
- CULT: Committee on Culture and Education.
- FEMM: Committee on Women´s Right and Gender Equality.

committees exercise within the institutional system. As a result, committees anchor both the Parliament's institutional continuity and its capacity to shape European policy outcomes.

7 Conclusion

This article has explored the central role of committees within the European Parliament (EP), emphasizing their function as the primary engines of legislative and policy making in the EU. From the structured processes of the Ordinary Legislative Procedure (OLP) to the intricate dynamics of referrals, rapporteur appointments, and interinstitutional negotiations, committees are shown to be the backbone of the EP's legislative work. Their ability to integrate expertise, mediate political differences, and ensure transparency underscores their critical importance in shaping European policy outcomes. Beyond formal legislative files, committees also influence the EU's agenda through political signaling and continuity, demonstrating their broader impact on institutional governance.

Looking ahead, the future of committee work will be shaped by the evolving political landscape following the 2024 EP elections. New power dynamics within the EP are likely to influence the composition of committees, the allocation of key roles, and the negotiation of legislative priorities. These changes may bring shifts in voting patterns, the formation of coalitions, and the balance of influence among political groups. As the EU faces pressing challenges such as climate change, digital transformation, and geopolitical instability, the committees' ability to adapt and maintain their effectiveness will be crucial.

References

European Parliament. (2023). *Rules of Procedure of the European Parliament*, https://www.europarl.europa.eu/doceo/document/RULES-9-2023-11-01-ANN-01_EN.html, last accessed: 20.10.25.

European Parliament. (2025). *Handbook on the Ordinary Legislative Procedure*, https://www.europarl.europa.eu/cmsdata/297417/Handbook%20on%20the%20Ordinary%20legislative%20procedure_March%202025_EN.pdf, last accessed: 25.10.25.

European Parliament. (n.d.-a). *List of legal bases providing for the ordinary legislative procedure in the Treaty of Lisbon*; https://www.europarl.europa.eu/cmsdata/198025/List_of_legal_bases.pdf. European Parliament, last accessed: 25.10.25.

European Parliament. (n.d.-b). *List of Committees*, https://www.europarl.europa.eu/committees/en/about/list-of-committees, last accessed: 25.10.25.

European Parliament. (n.d.-c). *Conference of Committee Chairs*, https://www.europarl.europa.eu/committees/en/about/conference-of-committee-chairs, last accessed: 20.10.25.

European Union. (2021). *Interinstitutional Agreement between the European Parliament, the Council of the European Union and the European Commission on a mandatory transparency register*, https://eur-lex.europa.eu/legal-content/EN/TXT/HTML/?uri=CELEX:32021Q0611(01), last accessed: 25.10.25.

Tino Kunert has been a policy advisor for internal affairs, justice, agriculture, the environment, digital affairs and media at the Saarland State Representation to the EU since November 2024. From 2009 to 2024, he was a parliamentary assistant in the European Parliament, where he served as office manager for the coordinator and chair of the CULT Committee. He was also a member of the rbb Broadcasting Council (2001-2010) and the ARD Programme Advisory Board (2003-2010), where he served as chairman from 2007 to 2010.

Birgül Tütün-Ince is a lecturer in political science at the University of Applied Sciences bfi Vienna. She previously worked in the European Parliament as an Accredited Parliamentary Assistant (APA), advising on employment and social affiars. At ÖBB (Austrian Federal Railways), she represents the company in the Community of European Railway and Infrastructure Companies (CER) and serves as a member of the Sectoral Social Dialogue Committee for Railways. Her academic and professional expertise centres on EU employment and social affairs, social dialogue, and the interface between European policymaking and national implementation.

How It Works: The European Parliament's Political Bodies and Members

Wolfgang Hiller

Abstract The European Parliament (EP) with its 720 directly elected members (MEPs) emanating from 27 Member States decides jointly with the Council of the European Union (Council) on EU law and the EU budget and scrutinises the executive. For this to happen in an orderly and efficient way, the EP has set up a complex internal structure in which elected Members of the European Parliament play a central role.

To understand how these structures work, it is essential to look at the role of individual MEPs and the EP's bodies and organisation, including the president, the plenary, political groups and governing bodies, and how they interact with individual MEPs and their work in committees and inter-parliamentary delegations.

Furthermore, it is worthwhile to grasp the importance of the support structures that elected MEPs avail of individually and collectively, and how they can profit from special bodies such as intergroups and other tools to broaden their knowledge of subjects they are called upon to decide.

Keywords MEP · Individual members · Political groups · Committee · Delegation · Plenary · President · BUREAU · Conference of Presidents (CoP) · Quaestors · Conference of Committee Chairs (CCC) · Conference of Delegation Chairs (CDC) · Intergroups

W. Hiller (✉)
Former Director of Impact Assessment and Foresight at the European Parliament Research Service, Brussels, Belgium
e-mail: Whiller0811@gmail.com

G. Füricht-Fiegl et al. (eds.), *Handbook on EU Law-making*, Professional Practice in Governance and Public Organizations, https://doi.org/10.1007/978-3-032-16559-6_13

1 Introduction

The European Parliament (EP) is the only directly elected body of the European Union. With origins going back to the 1950s and the founding treaties of the European Communities, its size and powers have, however, evolved considerably over time.[1]

It now serves as EU co-legislator and budgetary authority, together with the Council of the European Union (Council) and controls the EU executive. It provides democratic legitimisation and contributes to decision-making at the level of the EU.

With its 720 members representing around 450 million citizens across the 27 EU Member States, it is one of the biggest parliaments worldwide and the only multinational parliamentary assembly in the world entirely elected by direct universal suffrage.

As a large parliamentary institution with its individual members emanating from over 200 individual parties and national political groupings, the effective organisation of its workings in 24 official languages is, however, a complex undertaking. This requires well-organised structures that guarantee individual members their right to exercise their mandate fully while ensuring that the capacity of the institution to take speedy and efficient decisions is equally maintained.

To this end, the EP has set up political and administrative bodies and detailed working mechanisms which co-ordinate and lead the work of its members. They are codified in the EP's Rules of Procedure (RoP).[2]

2 The Individual Members

Any examination of EP's 'key actors' must begin with its individual members (Richard Corbett, 2024, p. 49). They are a diverse group of people, with a great variety of backgrounds, and the ones that shape the institution.[3]

2.1 How Are MEPs Selected

Since the first direct elections in 1979, the Members of the European Parliament (MEPs) are elected in the (currently) 27 Member States every 5 years.

---

[1] See also Chap. 11 of this handbook.

[2] The EP's Rules of Procedure are adopted by plenary with a qualified majority and govern all aspects of the internal setup of the EP and its proceedings. It is one of the duties of the president to make sure that these rules are duly respected.

[3] Part 4 of the book 'The European Parliament', written by Richard Corbett et al., gives an overview on the role of individual members within the EP, of their background and their rights and obligations. (Corbett, 2024).

In its tenth term (2024–2029), the EP has 720 seats/members, 38.5% of them are women.

The seat allocation is established by the EU treaties and is reviewed regularly following major events such as enlargements and Brexit, notably.

Each Member State returns a set number of MEP; from six, in smaller Member States like Malta, Luxembourg, and Cyprus, to ninety-six in Germany, the largest. While countries with larger populations thus return more seats than smaller ones, the principle of 'degressive proportionality' ensures, however, that more seats per capita go to less populous Member States.

National electoral laws and traditions largely govern European elections, but there are some common EU rules laid down in the Electoral Act of 1976.

2.2 *The Work of MEPs*

The duties of elected MEPs are diverse. Their overall purpose, however, is to represent the citizens who have elected them.

As EU lawmakers, they take part in the proceedings of the EP in many forms. They are full and substitute members of parliamentary committees, interparliamentary delegations, and other bodies of the house.

They influence EU policy and decisions through active participation in debates and votes.

The daily life of MEPs can be challenging as they must divide their attention between constituents, debates in political groups, as well as negotiations and votes in committees and plenary sessions.

As the EP's calendar is organised into group weeks, committee weeks, plenary sessions, and constituent weeks, most MEPs spend one or two weeks in Brussels where political groups and committees meet, one week in Strasbourg, which is the official seat of the EP and where its monthly plenary sessions take place, and one week in their home country where they have been elected.[4]

2.3 *Member's Political Rights and Obligations*

MEPs are entitled to be members of parliamentary committees and delegations, can join political groups and benefit from a variety of financial, administrative, and content-related support provided by the EP's administration. This includes the possibility to set up private offices with parliamentary assistants both in Brussels and their home country.

[4] See Calendar 2026 (as example): https://www.europarl.europa.eu/sedcms/documents/PRIORITY_INFO/1497/Calendar%202026_EN.pdf.

While MEPs cannot be sanctioned for absence, they are expected to attend the meetings of committees, delegations, and the plenary and of the political group they belong to.

Most importantly, members, inter alia, can take part in debates, propose amendments to legislative and non-legislative texts, and have the right to vote.

While it is true that the EP has a long tradition to seek compromise, decision-making in a complex political environment within an increasingly divided political landscape cannot rely solely on informal and formal bargaining processes but also requires frequent voting.

Voting thus takes place at different stages of the various proceedings—like the Ordinary Legislative Procedure (OLP)—at the level of committee work, in plenary and in political groups as well. Voting in this context is an essential part of political work. It is both a personal right and an obligation.

Each MEP votes individually and personally (Thornstraa, 2012, p. 24). Nevertheless, in practice, members who are part of a political group mostly follow voting instructions agreed previously at the level of their respective groups. Apart from special circumstances, such voting instructions are largely respected despite their legally unbinding character.

2.4 *Consultations with Stakeholders, Citizens and the Media*

To be able to contribute effectively to the political agenda, MEPs keep contact and consult regularly with stakeholders and the citizens they represent and set up and maintain a multitude of networks within and outside of the EP.

Within the EP they co-operate and negotiate with other MEPs of their own political group, the committees and delegations they sit in, and consult and speak with parliamentary support services and other entities of the EP.

They also are in regular contact with representatives of the European Commission (Commission) and other EU institutions and bodies as well as with NGOs, interest groups and other stakeholders both at European and national level.

Finally, as there is a legitimate interest by the media and the public in their work, MEPs are investing in communication activities and tend to be keen on good relations with the media and their representatives both in Brussels and Strasbourg as well as at home. However, this is not enough. To remain politically visible, they tend to be present also on social media and inform the public and their constituents proactively about their work through other means including newsletters and events.

2.5 *The Need to Specialise and Other Challenges*

Citizens rightly expect their political representatives to be able to cover all policy areas. Lawmaking in modern times is, however, a highly complicated business and generally calls for specialised knowledge of the subject matters under discussion.

As it is, however, impossible to be expert in all policy fields, MEPs can draw on a variety of input from inside and outside their institution.

Consultations with stakeholders are useful tools in this regard, as are impact assessments which, as a rule, must accompany legislative and non-legislative proposals of the Commission with substantial impact. Members in practice thus get a large amount of solicited and unsolicited advice including sometimes very concrete suggestions by external actors (companies, NGOs and interest groups, as well as in some cases by national and regional or local authorities), on how to amend legislative and non-legislative proposals and how to vote. In addition, they can rely on the support of the EP's services and their own private offices to structure and evaluate all this information and to conclude.

Participation in intergroups is another way to deepen knowledge about a specific policy area or a file. Intergroups are not official EP bodies but are recognised by the EP as fora for informal exchanges of views on issues across different political groups and for contact between members and civil society. Subjects covered by EP intergroups range from animal welfare to mental health and from space policy to the special interests of small- and medium-sized enterprises (SMEs).

However, it is not only complexity but the sheer amount of legislation and other parliamentary work that suggests it to be a good idea to share workloads and responsibilities amongst like-minded partners. This is why most MEPs join a political group, and this is also, in a similar vein, why there are parliamentary committees, delegations, and working groups, where specialisation and sharing of workloads and responsibility, based on mutual trust and interest, can be organised.

Another challenge in the life of an MEP is the need to divide working time wisely between Brussels, Strasbourg, and their constituencies back home.

While this may seem trivial at first, in practice it is not. MEPs face contradictory expectations at home and at their work environment at European level.

EU politicians should be visible and present with their electorate in their home country, to listen and hear their concerns, which is an essential condition for having a chance to get re-elected. At the same time, they are expected to be fully engaged in committee work and other parliamentary activities in Brussels and Strasbourg. To this end, they should constantly relate to stakeholders, peers and experts linked to the policy fields they are engaged in, to gain recognition, standing and visibility as an effective political operator at European level.

3 Political Groups

In the EP, members do not sit in national delegations, but according to their political affinities in transnational groups. Such groups must comprise members elected from at least one quarter of the Member States as well as at least 23 members.

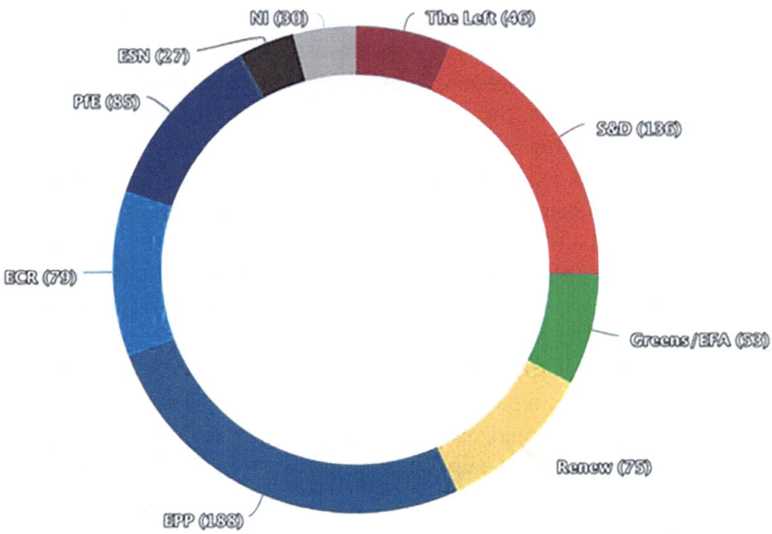

Fig. 1 Political groups: size. *Source*: EP Infographics, EP Facts and Figures, EPRS, European Parliament, September 2025

The number of groups and their size may vary over time. At the time of writing this article,[5] there were eight political groups. They are:

- Group of the European People's Party (Christian Democrats) (EPP).
- Group of the Progressive Alliance of Socialists and Democrats in the European Parliament (S&D).
- Patriots for Europe (PfE).
- European Conservatives and Reformists Group (ECR).
- Renew Europe Group (Renew).
- Group of the Greens/European Free Alliance (Greens/EFA).
- The Left Group in the European Parliament (GUE/NGL).
- Europe of Sovereign Nations Group (ESN).

Only 30 MEPs (out of 720) were non-attached and not affiliated with any of these groups (Fig. 1).

While membership in a political group is not obligatory, most MEPs nevertheless join one, as working as a non-attached MEP is generally more complicated and disadvantageous.

This is because political groups play a key role in the EP by setting the agenda, selecting rapporteurs, and allocating speaking time. They are also closely linked

[5] Script completed in September 2025.

with the election of office holders in the EP as well as with the organisation of work in plenary and committees alike.

They allow exchanges between like-minded colleagues as well as sharing of expertise and responsibilities and provide practical support for their members in plenary and committees.

Most importantly, however, political groups are important places for negotiation where complexity is reduced by finding compromises and common positions that form the basis for further negotiations and compromises with other political groups at a later stage. This is thus an important step for reaching a common position of the EP, which is essential if the EP wants to exercise political leverage vis-a-vis its co-decision partner, the Council, later in the process.

As a reminder: the EP in the OLP is co-legislator. EP and Council therefore need to agree on a joint text, for EU law to be adopted. The more the EP is united in its negotiating position, the stronger is its position vis-a-vis the Member States and the Commission in trilogues and other talks leading to agreements between these negotiating partners.[6]

However, how do political groups work?

They hold regular meetings during the week before the part-session and in part-session weeks, as well as workshops and seminars, some of them taking place right before parliamentary committees meet.

The group leader represents the group in the Conference of Presidents (CoP) and to the outside world, group coordinators in turn represent the group's committee members in parliamentary committees, thus linking political group work with the work of committees.

Political groups also avail of a secretariat, to support their members throughout all phases of their political work.

4 Parliamentary Committees

Committee work is an essential part of parliamentary life. In fact, a parliamentary committee is where most of the EP's legislative and scrutiny-related work is carried out and where plenary decisions are prepared. Apart from voting in plenary, committee work is the main core business for every MEP.

To do this best, MEPs are divided up among 22 standing committees specialising in the different policy areas. They vary in size and range from 25 to 90 MEPs.[7]

In addition, the EP regularly sets up subcommittees and special temporary committees to deal with specific issues and is entitled to create formal committees of inquiry and even legislative temporary committees, to consider legally binding acts or a pre-legislative strategic document. The latter can be established if the subject

[6] See also Chap. 16 of this handbook.

[7] Data in September 2025.

matter touches upon the competence of various standing committees and enables effective pooling of expertise from different committees for a restricted period and limited to a specific file (Fig. 2).

All committees have a chair, vice-chairs, and a secretariat and reflect the political composition of the plenary and the EP as a whole. The chair and the vice-chairs form the Bureau of the committee. Their term of office is two and a half years.

To enhance coordination, political groups nominate one of their committee members as their committee coordinator. Together, usually at the margins of committee meetings, the Bureau and the coordinators regularly meet, to organise the committee's work and to bring forward proposals on important committee matters such as agendas of hearings or the distribution of files. These meetings are called coordinators meetings.

Time frame	MEPs	Special committees	
Jul 1994 - Jul 1995	41	EMPT	Temporary committee on employment
Dec 1995 - Jul 1996	17	TRANSIT	Inquiry into the Community Transit System
Jul 1996 - Feb 1997	19	BSE	Temporary committee of inquiry into BSE
Jul 1996 - Mar 1997	17	TRANSIT	Inquiry into the Community Transit System
Apr 1997 - Nov 1997	20	BSE2	Temporary committee (BSE)
Jul 2000 - Sep 2001	36	ECHE	Temporary committee "ECHELON"
Dec 2000 - Nov 2001	36	GENE	Human genetics
Jan 2002 - Dec 2002	30	FIAP	Foot and mouth disease
Nov 2003 - Apr 2004	44	MARE	Improving safety at sea
Oct 2004 - Jun 2005	50	FINP	Policy challenges and budgetary means of the enlarged Union 2007-2013
Jan 2006 - Feb 2007	46	TDIP	Alleged use of European countries by the CIA for the transport and illegal detention of prisoners
Jan 2006 - Jun 2007	22	EQUI	Crisis of the Equitable Life Assurance Society
Apr 2007 - Feb 2009	60	CLIM	Climate Change
Oct 2009 - Jul 2011	45	CRIS	Financial, Economic and Social Crisis
Jun 2010 - Jun 2011	50	SURE	Policy Challenges Committee
Mar 2012 - Oct 2013	45	CRIM	Organised Crime, Corruption and Money Laundering
Feb 2015 - Nov 2015	45	TAXE	Tax Rulings and Other Measures Similar in Nature or Effect
Dec 2015 - Aug 2016	45	TAX2	Tax Rulings and Other Measures Similar in Nature or Effect (TAXE 2)
Sep 2017 - Nov 2018	30	TERR	Terrorism
Feb 2018 - Dec 2018	30	PEST	EU authorisation procedure for pesticides
Mar 2018 - Mar 2019	45	TAX3	Financial crimes, tax evasion and tax avoidance
Sep 2020 - Mar 2022	34	INGE	Foreign Interference in all Democratic Processes in the European Union, including Disinformation
Sep 2020 - Mar 2022	34	AIDA	Artificial Intelligence in a Digital Age
Sep 2020 - Mar 2022	34	BECA	Beating Cancer
Mar 2022 - Aug 2023	33	ING2	Special Committee on foreign interference and disinformation, and on strengthening integrity in the EP
Mar 2022 - Jul 2023	38	COVI	COVID-19 pandemic: lessons learned and recommendations for the future
Jan 2025 - Ongoing	33	HOUS	Housing Crisis in the EU
Jan 2025 - Ongoing	33	EUDS	European Democracy Shield

Fig. 2 Special committees of the European Parliament since July 1994. *Source*: EP Infographics, EP Facts and Figures, EPRS, European Parliament, September 2025

Committee coordinators are powerful actors within the EP. However, coordinators de jure only make proposals, and it is up to the full committee to accept or reject these proposals. In situations where coordinators reach decisions with a large political majority, their proposals are, however, seldom contested.

While this is not the place to describe in detail how committees conduct parliamentary business on an everyday basis, it is, however, important to remember that committees choose amongst their members rapporteurs whose task is to steer legislative and non-legislative files through committee, plenary and, where applicable, jointly with the committee chair, and sometimes a Vice-President, through trilogues and other negotiations with Council and Commission. Rapporteurs thus are the ones who lead the process, together with shadow rapporteurs, nominated by and representing political groups. Rapporteurs are the ones who draft EP's reports and who are called upon to forge compromises on amendments or other texts so that a final report with the position of the EP can be adopted and eventually enacted as law.[8]

5 Inter-Parliamentary Delegations

Similarly to committees, the EP also sets up inter-parliamentary delegations. Their purpose is to seek to maintain and deepen relations with parliaments and parliamentarians from countries, regions and organisations outside the EU.

At the time of writing,[9] the EP had 48 standing delegations engaged in 'parliamentary diplomacy'.

They fall into three types: (a) inter-parliamentary delegations and delegations to joint parliamentary committees, (b) parliamentary cooperation committees, and (c) multilateral parliamentary assemblies.

The EP also sends a delegation to the joint assembly set up under the agreement between the African, Caribbean, and Pacific states and the EU.

Similarly to committees, each delegation elects a chair and vice-chairs, forming the Bureau. Their term of office is two and a half years.

6 The Plenary

While political groups, committees, and other bodies of the EP are instrumental for preparing decisions, the plenary is the place where they are enacted. Plenary sittings are therefore of special importance and represent the highlight and the culmination of all parliamentary activity as such. They take place in Strasbourg every month

[8] On rapporteurs, see also Chap. 11 of this handbook.

[9] Data in September 2025.

(except August). Such a ‘part-session’ lasts 4 days from Monday to Thursday. Additional part-sessions are held in Brussels.

Being at the end of the parliamentary process, they are the place where the result of the legislative work done in committee and in the political groups is presented and where final decisions are taken.

6.1 How It Works

Plenary sessions are chaired by the President or one of the 14 Vice-Presidents of the EP.[10]

During the session, the chair calls upon speakers and ensures that the proceedings are properly conducted. He or she also directs the voting procedure, putting amendments and legislative resolutions to the vote and announces the results. The president’s authority ensures that the votes, which can be long and complex, proceed at a rapid pace.

The agenda of the sittings is decided at the beginning of each part-session, on proposal by the Conference of Presidents after previous preparation taking place in several steps. In practice, political groups decide which issues will be discussed in plenary and they are also the ones that can table amendments to the committee reports to be put to the vote or put forward resolutions on important issues.

It is also political groups who distribute speaking time amongst their members and try to coordinate the way they vote. Nevertheless, as MPEs exercise a free and independent mandate, they cannot formally be obliged to vote in a particular way.

As far as seating arrangements are concerned, the places assigned to MEPs in the chamber are decided by political affiliation, from left to right, representing the whole spectrum of ideological tendencies in the EU. MEPs not affiliated with any political group (non-attached MEPs) are also grouped together.

In plenary, political groups play a major role; the right of individual members and their possibility to influence proceedings at this stage is limited. All MEPs are, however, expected to be present at debates on topical issues and notably at votes, be they on draft legislative acts or on any other matter.

6.2 A Forum for Transparency and Debate

Plenary proceedings are the EPs main window to the world. When MEPs gather for debates and votes in Strasbourg, representatives of other EU institutions, journalists and stakeholders follow in person or online.

[10] On the president and its 14 vice-presidents, see also Chap. 11 of this handbook.

Apart from the elected MEPs, the Commission and the Council also take part in the sittings. If the EP so requests, the representatives of the two institutions may be called upon to make declarations or to give an account of their activities (The European Parliament, 2025).

Plenary sessions, as most committee meetings, are public. Journalists and citizens can directly follow proceedings live from the gallery or, more conveniently, online from the office or from home through web-streaming. The public can therefore experience in real time what EU representatives say in the EP and how they vote. While final texts may still need to undergo some legal verification processes, the essential result of voting is thus known right away.

While debating and voting legislative files in plenary are important moments of EU lawmaking, plenary, however, is much more. It is also a venue where scrutiny of the EU executive takes place and debates on topical issues are held. Ahead of the European Elections 2024, for example, the EP invited heads of states and governments to the Strasbourg chamber for a series of debates on the 'Future of Europe'.[11]

In a similar way, since 2010, plenary is also where Presidents of the European Commission deliver their State of the Union address each year in September. This address serves as an essential tool for the Commission's accountability to the EP, aimed at making the EU-level priorities more transparent while also communicating these priorities to the public (Baraník, 2025).

For those interested in observing democracy in action, the EPs plenary offers a vibrant and energetic setting, especially during votes.

7 The Governing Bodies

The political bodies of the EP coordinate and lead all political and administrative activities of the institution.

They comprise the Bureau, the Conference of Presidents (CoP), the five quaestors, the Conference of Committee Chairs (CCC), and the Conference of Delegation Chairs (CDC). The term of office of the president, the vice-presidents and the quaestors, as well as of the committee and delegation chairs, is two and a half years.

7.1 The President

The President of the European Parliament is elected from the MEPs for a renewable term of two and a half years.

[11] See also the briefing by Ralf Drachenberg et al. from the European Parliament Research Service entitled 'This is Europe' debates in the European Parliament 2022-2024, available on Parliament's Think Tank pages.

He/she represents the EP vis-à-vis the outside world and in its relations with the other EU institutions, oversees the debates in plenary, and ensures that the EP's RoP are adhered to.

As a tradition, the President of the EP, at the beginning of every European Council meeting, sets out the EP's point of view on items on the agenda and other topical subjects of concern to the EP.

The president also has several important protocollary powers such as signing the EU budget, after it has been adopted by the EP and rendering it thus operational. He/she also co-signs all legislative acts adopted under the ordinary legislative procedure, together with the President of the Council.

When electing a president, the EP also chooses 14 vice-presidents who can replace the president.

7.2 *The Bureau*

The Bureau is the governing body in the EP responsible for administrative, financial, staff and organisational matters. It is responsible for all matters relating to the internal running of the EP, prepares the preliminary draft estimates of the EP's expenditure, and appoints senior staff of the institution, including its Secretary-General.

Members of the Bureau are the President of the EP, the 14 Vice-Presidents and the five quaestors. The quaestors are members of the Bureau in an advisory capacity.

The Bureau generally meets once a month.

7.3 *The Conference of Presidents*

The Conference of Presidents (CoP) is the political body in the EP responsible for the organisation of EP's business and legislative planning as well as for relations with other EU institutions, the national parliaments and non-EU countries. It prepares the EP's timetable and plenary sitting agendas and allocates seats in the chamber.

The CoP is composed of the President of the European Parliament and the political group chairs. One representative of the non-attached MEPs is also entitled to attend its meetings, but without the right to vote. The chair of the Conference of Committee Chairs (CCC) is also regularly invited.

The CoP generally meets twice a month and takes its decisions by consensus or by weighted vote based on the number of MEPs in each political group.

7.4 *The Quaestors*

The College of Quaestors is the EP body responsible for administrative and financial matters that directly affect MEPs.

There are five quaestors, elected for two and a half years. They are also members of the Bureau, exercising an advisory role.

The quaestors generally meet once a month.

7.5 *The Conference of Committee Chairs*

The Conference of Committee Chairs (CCC) is the political body in the EP that coordinates work between committees.

It consists of the chairs of all the standing and temporary committees and generally meets once a month in Strasbourg during plenary sittings.

It makes recommendations to the CoP on matters concerning committees' work and advises the CoP if there is disagreement as to which committee should be responsible.

The Bureau and CoP may delegate certain tasks to the CCC.

7.6 *The Conference of Delegation Chairs*

The Conference of Delegation Chairs (CDC) is the political body in the EP that coordinates the work of EP's standing delegations and ensures that the delegations work efficiently and in coordination with Parliament's other structures.

Members of the CDC are the chairs of the EP's 48 standing delegations and of the three committees that work on international relations: the Committees on Foreign Affairs (AFET), Development (DEVE) and International Trade (INTA).

They in general meet once a month during Strasbourg sessions, where they discuss issues and challenges common to the delegations.

8 The Secretariat and Other Support Structures for MEPs and Parliamentary Bodies

Parliamentary actors and bodies can draw on a broad range of administrative and content-related support.

Support structures include the MEP's private offices, the political groups, and the Secretariat of the European Parliament with its various services.

While some of the services of the Secretariat of the EP are rather of administrative or technical nature, others are political and serve MEPs and parliamentary bodies such as committees or the plenary more directly when dealing with parliamentary business such as reports and amendments.

These services are provided, inter alia, through committee secretariats, translation and interpretation services but also comprise support from lawyer-linguists who check the linguistic and legal quality of proposed and adopted legal texts.

Individual MEPs can also rely on the European Parliament Research Service (EPRS) with the library and its Members Research Service that answers directly to requests from individual members.

Parliamentary committees, on the other hand, work more closely with the EPRS Directorate for Impact Assessment, the policy departments and other research entities such as the Economic Governance Unit (EGOV) or with STOA (Panel for the future of Science & Technology). These services provide a wide range of support for parliamentary actors. The Directorate for Impact Assessment, for example, supports evidence-based and anticipatory policy-making through ex-ante and ex-post evaluations, European added-value work and other activities for MEPs and committees. All this is designed to enhance the capacity of MEPs and committees to make informed decisions on EU initiatives and proposals from the Commission and its own policy initiatives as well.

9 Conclusion

The European Parliament is a complex institution with many actors and bodies but where its 720 individual members (MEPs) are key for shaping EU legislation and policies for the citizen they represent. Nevertheless, to function effectively, such a large and diverse institution needs an organisational structure that coordinates, bundles and leads the many activities unfolding. To this end, various bodies—political groups, committees, delegations, plenary sessions, and governing bodies led by the president—have been set up to help the EP prosper.

While transnational political groups, parliamentary committees, and delegations as well as governing bodies are essential for the organisation of the political work of the house, individual members can be really influential too, similar to their role in the US Congress, both with regard to shaping legislation as rapporteur, shadow rapporteur or as office holder in a committee, working group or a delegation or via other roles and functions in political groups or the governing bodies of the institution as a whole.

In view of the size of the institution and the sheer volume of work, specialisation and sharing of work and responsibilities is, however, key. This is why the EP functions best when individual members and EP's bodies work together, in the interest of the citizens elected MEPs are called upon to represent.

References

Baraník, K. (2025, September 18). *2025 State of the Union address. Purpose, historical significance and overview of the Union addresses since 2010.* Retrieved from EP Think Tank, EPRS, European Parliament.

Dialer, D., Maurer, A., Richter, M. (2015). *Handbuch zum Europäischen Parlament.* Nomos Verlag.

Drachenberg, R. (2024, April). *'This is Europe' debates in the European Parliament, 2022-2024.* Retrieved from EP Think Tank, EPRS, European Parliament.

European Parliament. (2025, September 18). *Intergroups at the European Parliament.* Retrieved from The European Parliament Website.

Kobusek, T. V. (2025, May). *Factsheets of the European Union. The European Parliament: Organisation and Operation.* Retrieved from EP Think Tank.

Corbett, R., Jacobs, F., Neville, D., Cernoch, P. (2024). *The European Parliament, 10th ed. 2024.* John Harper Publishing.

Sabbati, G. (2024, 11). *European Parliament: Facts and figures.* Retrieved from EP Think Tank, EPRS, European Parliament.

Soldwisch, I. (2021). *Das Europaeische Parlament 1979-2004.* Verlag W. Kohlhammer.

The European Parliament. (2025a, September). *How plenary works.* Retrieved from The European Parliament Website.

The European Parliament. (2025b, September). *Rules of Procedure of the European Parliament, Tenth parliamentary term - July 2025.*

Think Tank. (n.d.). The documents that help shape new EU legislation. Retrieved from Think Tank European Parliament.

Thornstraa, D. (2012). *Inside the European Parliament: A guide to the parliamentary and administrative structures.* OPPD, Office for the Promotion of Parliamentary Democracy, European Parliament, DG EXPO.

Further Readings

Readers with special interest in the EP will find a huge source of inspiration in Richard Corbett's book on The European Parliament (Richard Corbett, 2024). This book which he has written jointly with other practitioners and friends with intimate knowledge of the Parliament is now available in its tenth updated edition.

The other piece of resource on the EP not to be missed is Doris Dialer's 'Handbuch zum Europäischen Parlament' (in German) (Doris Dialer, 2015). This is another very readable book giving a comprehensive overview on the EP, its position in the institutional landscape of the European Union, its structure and its functioning.

For a more dynamic perspective, consider accessing the EP's own knowledge sources for up-to-date articles, studies, and other contributions. For this purpose, interested readers can look up the European Parliament Think Tank pages (Think Tank. The documents that help shape new EU legislation), which provide a huge variety of institutional and topical contributions on practically all areas of EU policy, written and researched by EP's services themselves (European Parliament Think Tank pages can easily be accessed via the Internet. They provide a wealth of up-to-date and publicly available knowledge on all institutional issues as well as practically all subject areas Parliament deals with. They also provide useful Infographics and similar material.).

Wolfgang Hiller is the former Director for Impact Assessment and Foresight of the European Parliament Research Service (EPRS). He retired in 2025. Before becoming director, he worked inter alia in a political group, in the European Commission, as Head of the EP liaison office in Vienna, the Cabinet of the Secretary-General and as Head of the secretariat of the Conference of Presidents. He is committed to evidence-based policy-making and keen on protecting democracy, fundamental rights and the rule of law.

EU Elections and Implications for the OLP: Power Shift After the EU Elections 2024

Evelyn Regner and Michael Kudler

Abstract The 2024 European elections marked a significant shift in the balance of power within the European Parliament (EP), with broad implications for the Ordinary Legislative Procedure (OLP) and the future of democratic lawmaking in the EU. This chapter analyses how the European People's Party (EPP) emerged in a dominant strategic position and how its alliances, often times with far-right forces, have reshaped both interinstitutional dynamics and legislative practices. It examines the increasing use of emergency instruments such as Art. 122 TFEU and the rise of Omnibus legislative packages, which reflect a wider paradigm shift: from cooperative, consensus-driven policymaking to a more technocratic and top-down approach. These developments pose risks to the institutional balance and democratic legitimacy of EU governance. While the critique focuses on recent EPP strategies, the underlying message is a broader call to safeguard democratic processes. The chapter concludes with a reflection on the role of constructive pro-European cooperation as the only sustainable path forward in the face of current political, institutional and societal challenges.

Keywords European Parliament · European elections 2024 · European People's Party · Emergency Law · Omnibus Legislation · Deregulation · Democratic legitimacy

---

E. Regner (✉)
Member of the European Parliament, Vienna, Austria
e-mail: evelyn.regner@europarl.europa.eu

M. Kudler (✉)
Austrian Chamber of Labour, Vienna, Austria
e-mail: michael.kudler@akwien.at

G. Füricht-Fiegl et al. (eds.), *Handbook on EU Law-making*, Professional Practice in Governance and Public Organizations, https://doi.org/10.1007/978-3-032-16559-6_14

Remark from the editors: The guiding principle of this book is to provide its readers with valuable insights into how the practice of EU policy-making is conducted in very concrete terms. In order to meet this objective for the chapter on the implications of the 2024 elections to the European Parliament, we therefore invited two renowned representatives of the two largest political groups in the EP to share their perspectives on the power shift that followed the elections. We are pleased to incorporate this unique perspective into this part, presenting the naturally somewhat opposing views of two political practitioners in this handbook.

1 Introduction

The political landscape across Europe is undergoing a shift to the right, and the European Parliament (EP) is no exception. The 2024 European elections have significantly altered the composition of the EP, disrupting long-standing majority dynamics. These changes have not remained confined to the EP but have rippled through the EU's institutional framework, most notably impacting the functioning of the Ordinary Legislative Procedure (OLP), the central mechanism by which European legislation is adopted. This chapter analyses recent developments in EU lawmaking, offering context and perspective to better understand their implications for the broader trajectory of the European project. It concludes with a forward-looking reflection and a warning about the risks posed to democratic governance.

Section 2 examines how the European People's Party (EPP) emerged from the 2024 elections in the most strategically advantageous position. Section 3 expands the focus beyond the EP to consider the broader interplay among the EU institutions involved in the OLP, exploring how shifting parliamentary majorities have influenced interinstitutional dynamics. Section 4 addresses a key structural development in EU lawmaking: the increasing use of emergency legal instruments, particularly Art. 122 TFEU, which sheds light on evolving procedural norms. Finally, Section 5 draws these threads together by illustrating how new political priorities, enabled by a reconfigured power balance, are reshaping the legislative agenda, often at the expense of previously established democratic consensus.

2 Strategic Realignment After the 2024 Elections

This section explores the composition of the EP after the 2024 elections and how new majorities have disrupted long-established power structures.

Before 2024, functional majorities could only be built among pro-European forces, which despite ideological differences were united by a shared commitment to the European project. Dialogue and compromise were not just virtues but necessities. That has changed after the EU elections 2024. While the far right achieved the largest relative gains in the 2024 elections, significantly increasing their parliamentary presence, it was ultimately the European People's Party (EPP) that emerged in the strongest strategic position. By situating itself between the pro-European centre and the far-right bloc, the EPP gained the ability to align with either side to form majorities. While publicly maintaining a pro-European image, the EPP has in practice exploited its strategic positioning to consolidate influence, placing mounting pressure on the foundations of parliamentary integrity.

To understand the significance of this shift, we must first look at the pre-election setup. The pro-European coalition consisting of the EPP, the Progressive Alliance of Socialists and Democrats (S&D), the Greens, Renew Europe, and sometimes The Left relied on mutual support to secure majorities. Without consensus, nothing passed. Even coalition agreements existed, namely between EPP, S&D and Renew (EEP Group et al., 2022). This setup fostered a culture of negotiation, compromise and constructive policymaking. A firewall towards the extreme right groups was established and kept by all of these groups most of the time, in EU jargon often referred to as the 'cordon sanitaire'.

Some early signs of shifting alliances became visible during the mid-term reshuffling of leadership positions in the EP, developments further shaped by the aftermath of Brexit in 2020. The UK's departure meant the loss of a political heavyweight, and notably, one with a substantial number of progressive Members of the EP (MEPs). This absence was felt in the redistribution of roles: during the reshuffle, the EPP backed a candidate from the ECR for a Vice-President position (Robert Zile), instead of supporting one from the Greens (Marcel Kolaja). This decision created a new power constellation within the Bureau of the EP (Bureau).[1] In this setting, a narrow majority could be formed by EPP, Renew and the European Conservatives and Reformists (ECR) (European Parliament, 2022) with the president's double vote (President of the EP: Roberta Metsola from EPP) tipping the balance in 50:50 situations against S&D, Greens and The Left. This dynamic was limited to the Bureau and did not apply in plenary or committee settings before 2024 elections. Nonetheless, it already revealed a pattern: on key political decisions, the centrist groups EPP and also Renew would rather align with the right-wing ECR than with its former progressive allies.

The 2024 election results marked a decisive turn to the right in the entire House. Far-right MEPs increased from 118 to 187, distributed across the ECR and two new groups, Patriots for Europe Group (PfE) and Europe of Sovereign Nations Group (ESN), the latter largely comprising German members from 'Alternative für Deutschland' (AfD). The pro-European groups (The Left, Greens/EFA, S&D and Renew) fell from 343 to 312 seats (out of 719 seats in total). While these numbers may appear to show only a modest shift, the impact on institutional dynamics is profound. The EPP, with just nine additional seats, gained strategic control over parliamentary majorities.

[1] The Bureau of the European Parliament lays down the rules for the EP, including the yearly budget, staff and organisational decisions. It consists of the President of the European Parliament, the 14 Vice-Presidents and the five Quaestors (who have no voting rights in the Bureau), who all are elected by the Members of the European Parliament for a period of two and a half years. (European Parliament, n.d.).

To understand how the EPP gained this pivotal role and emerged as the strategic powerbroker in the new parliamentary landscape, we must examine the situation in the outgoing EP as depicted in Fig. 1. The progressive bloc held a solid majority of 491 seats, 139 seats above the threshold for an absolute majority. With the political group of The Left on board, this majority grew to 528 out of 705 seats. The far right, with only 127 seats, was not only practically irrelevant; it also was largely kept out of decision-making due to the firewall put in place by the pro-European forces. From the EPP's perspective, siding with the progressive coalition wasn't optional, it was the only viable path in the plenary. A hypothetical alliance with the far right would have resulted in 305 seats, far short of an absolute majority. The EPP had to remain loyal to the pro-European coalition if not out of conviction out of sheer pragmatism.

That is no longer the case as can be seen in Fig. 2. In the current parliamentary configuration, the pro-European bloc (excluding the EPP) has 312 seats, not enough to form a majority without EPP support. Meanwhile, the strengthened far-right bloc provides the EPP with an alternative route to a majority. This has given the EPP

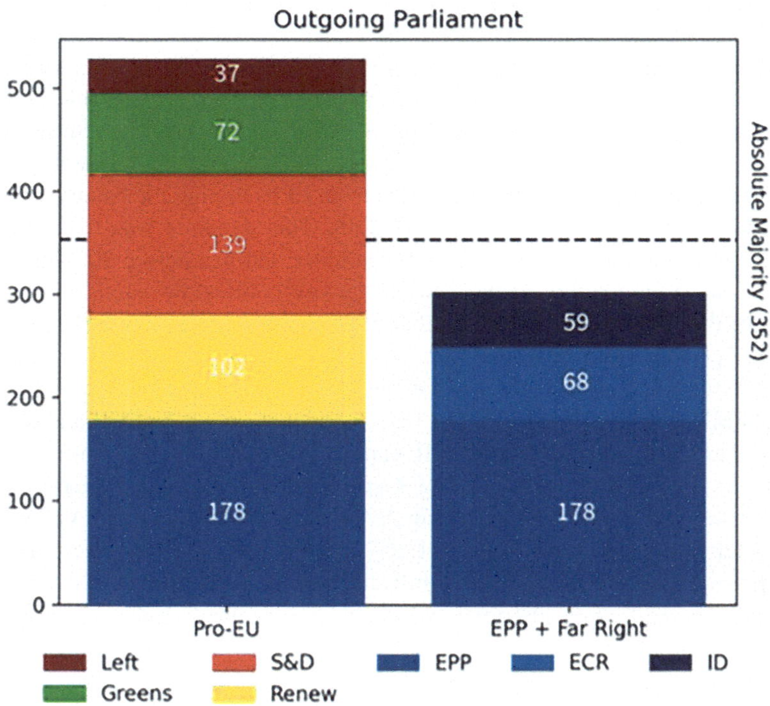

Fig. 1 Parliamentary majorities before the 2024 elections. *Source*: data provided by the EP (European Parliament, EPRS 2024a)

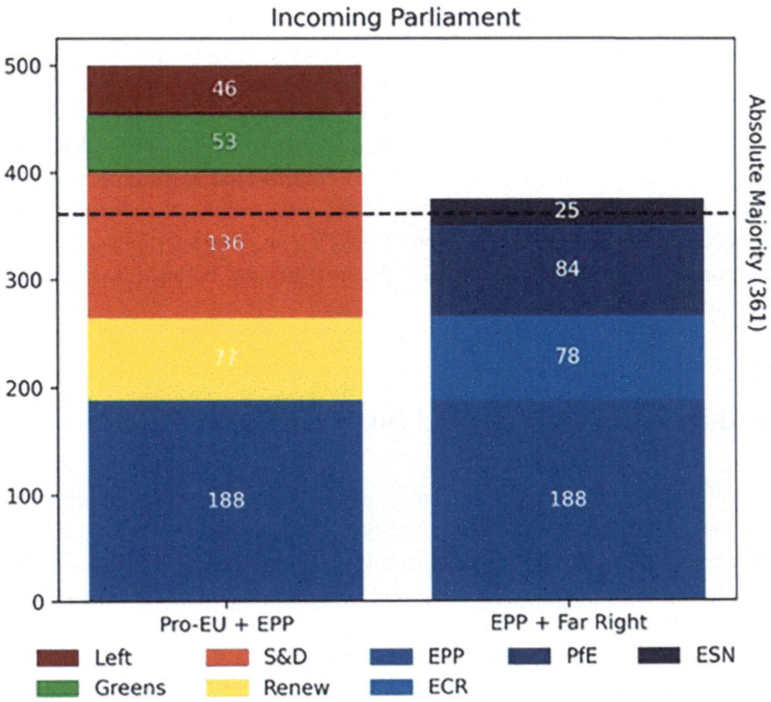

Fig. 2 Parliamentary majorities after the 2024 Elections. *Source*: data provided by the EP (European Parliament, EPRS 2024b)

leverage to play both sides, demanding concessions while holding the balance of power.[2]

This is not just hypothetical: it is already happening in practice. The EPP has increasingly broken away from its previous commitments to the pro-European coalition, choosing instead to align with far-right forces when convenient. One example here was the vote on the 2025 budget. The report had been jointly prepared by the EPP and S&D within the framework of the progressive majority and a compromise had been agreed upon. However, during the plenary vote, amendments originating from the far right, partly identical to earlier EPP proposals that had not made it into the compromise, were reintroduced, for example AM 32 report (Sanchez & Furet, 2024) and voting results (European Parliament, 2024b), 45 and 46 (Jungbluth et al., 2024) and some tabled by a mix of Members from EPP, ECR and Renew, for example number 69 (Herbst, 2024). This latter amendment, for example, was ultimately adopted with the combined votes of the EPP, Renew and the far right, effectively overturning the pro-European agreement as the final vote led to a

[2] Here needs to be noted that the former far-right party 'ID' split into two after the 2024 elections, namely 'Patriots for Europe' (PfE) and 'Europe of Sovereign Nations' (ESN).

rejection of the proposal (European Parliament, 2024c). In doing so, the EPP broke its prior commitment not to reopen the compromise during the plenary stage.

What used to be constructive dialogue has been replaced by distrust. As the just mentioned example shows, at least some promises made by the EPP are abandoned and its credibility as a coalition partner has diminished significantly. With Roberta Metsola as President of the EP, the EPP also controls the institution's leadership. Later sections will detail the implications of this power concentration. In our opinion it is becoming clearer with each vote: the EPP can no longer be seen as the pro-European anchor it once was, and the EP's institutional balance has been deeply compromised.

3 Eroding Balance: OLP and Interinstitutional Shifts

The 2024 election results carry consequences that reach far beyond political alignments as they have fundamentally altered how the OLP functions in practice. The legislative framework comprising the Commission, EP and Council was constructed as a carefully balanced system of checks and balances. Each institution was intended to counterbalance the others, ensuring no single actor could dominate the legislative process. Today, this equilibrium is under increasing strain, as partisan strategies begin to overshadow institutional cooperation and democratic safeguards.

As the only directly elected institution of the European Union, the EP holds a unique and vital role: it serves as the voice of EU citizens in the legislative process. Its primary responsibility is to ensure that the will of the electorate is reflected in European law. To fulfil this role, it must work with the Council to build compromises that reconcile public interests with those of the Member States represented by their ministers. This balance is at the core of the EU's democratic legitimacy. Collaboration among the three institutions, namely the Commission, the EP and the Council, is thus essential to ensuring that legislation is not only effective but democratically grounded.

The OLP is the EU's standard procedure for adopting legislative acts.[3] It officially begins with the Commission, which drafts a proposal and submits it to both the EP and the Council. Each institution can propose amendments, and a final agreement is typically reached through a trilogue, meaning an informal negotiation involving all three bodies. Less often discussed is how the Commission selects which proposals to advance. While the European Council sets broad political priorities, the EP and civil society also exert significant influence through own-initiative reports, grassroots mobilisation and sustained public pressure. Social partners, in particular, have played a key role in shaping progressive policy directions, as illustrated by, but not limited to, initiatives like the European Pillar of Social Rights

[3] See Chap. 2 of this handbook.

(European Commission, 2017) or the Pay Transparency Directive (European Union, 2023a).

However, the system can only function effectively when power is genuinely balanced across institutions. Currently, that balance is slipping. The European People's Party (EPP) not only controls the EP but also holds the presidency of the Commission, where Ursula von der Leyen has consolidated authority under a noticeably more top-down and centralised leadership model (Wax & Vinocour, 2025). Meanwhile, the Council is gradually aligning itself with EPP-led positions due to the number of national leaders stemming from the conservative group. This growing concentration of power within a single political group risks weakening the institutional independence that safeguards EU democracy and threatens the constructive tension that should underpin the legislative process.

More broadly, there is a noticeable trend of the co-legislators giving up their powers to the Commission through delegated acts as within the due diligence proposals.[4] This shift allows the Commission to take on greater responsibility not only in drafting secondary legislation but also in outsourcing key tasks to private entities. A recent example is the due diligence legislation, which will be discussed further in a later section. In this case, the Commission tasked EFRAG, the European Financial Reporting Advisory Group, a private association, with defining the criteria for small and medium-sized enterprises (SMEs). It is yet another example of how legislative responsibility is increasingly being moved away from democratic institutions and into the hands of non-elected actors.

These institutional shifts, set in motion and accelerated by the results of the 2024 European elections, have had tangible effects on the daily reality of EU policymaking. What used to be defined by pluralistic cooperation has now given way to increasingly unilateral approaches. The agenda has undergone a striking transformation: once-flagship initiatives like the Green Deal (European Commission, 2019)[5] and the Just Transition (European Commission, 2020)[6] have been side-lined or even replaced by a focus on competitiveness (see Competitiveness Compass) and simplification (European Commission 2025a, b).[7] In concrete terms, this has meant greater influence for corporate stakeholders already before the start of official procedures in one-sided expert groups, while trade unions, consumer protection and non-governmental organisations have been noticeably marginalised and even put under active pressure. Already at the earliest stages, when deciding which proposals move forward and how, they are often shaped by corporate interests operating behind the scenes (Transparency International EU, n.d.). Vice-President of the Commission Henna Virkkunen for example has had meetings with 84 companies,

[4] See here especially Art. 34 of Directive (EU) 2024/1760 (European Commission, 2024).

[5] The 'Green Deal' is a term coined to describe a package of measures, including legislation, to address the ongoing climate crisis by the EU while boosting the economy and competitiveness.

[6] The so-called Just Transition refers to the need to ensure that every citizen in the EU is taken care of during the ongoing big societal and economic transformations resulting from the climate crisis and its mitigation measures like the Green Deal (see footnote above).

[7] Guised by so-called Omnibus proposals.

yet only 9 with NGOs since her nomination in 2024 (Transparency International EU, n.d.). This growing influence signals what could be described as a creeping privatisation of the legislative process. The EPP's dominance has not only altered the internal balance of power, but it has also reshaped both the tone and the substance of EU legislative work and widely opened the doors to unchecked corporate influence.[8]

4 EU Emergency Law and the Rise of Article 122 TFEU

The shift in the EU's legislative culture has not come overnight. Long before the 2024 elections, a specific legal pathway had been increasingly used to circumvent the traditional co-legislative process: Art. 122 of the Treaty on the Functioning of the European Union (TFEU). This provision grants the Council and the Commission the power to adopt non-legislative acts in emergency situations without the involvement of the EP. While the legal bases have existed since the Treaty of Rome and were designed to enable swift action in exceptional circumstances, their use in recent years reflects a notable shift in the style of EU lawmaking.

The legal instrument itself is not problematic per se. Throughout EU history, Art. 122 TFEU and its predecessors have been activated in moments of acute crisis, such as during the financial and energy emergencies of the past decades. In fact, the number of acts adopted under this article today is not unprecedented when compared to earlier periods (European Parliament DG IPOL, 2023). What has changed, however, is the nature of the measures being adopted and the credibility of the rationale provided. Increasingly, Art. 122 TFEU is being used to introduce far-reaching and long-term policy instruments without a clear demonstration of urgency. This development has triggered institutional friction and mounting frustration within the EP. Already before the 2024 elections.

One of the most significant recent examples is the establishment of the NextGenerationEU (NGEU) recovery fund in 2020. Conceived as a central response to the COVID-19 crisis, this ambitious financial instrument was adopted without meaningful parliamentary involvement. Although justified under emergency powers, the nature and scope of the measure suggest it went beyond the original intent of Art. 122 TFEU. A similar pattern was repeated in 2022, when the EU responded rapidly to the Russian invasion of Ukraine. Again, the EP found itself side-lined at key moments in the decision-making process which was not necessary for the sake of fast action.

The use of emergency mechanisms is not inherently illegitimate. They serve an essential purpose in times of urgent need. But when applied to decisions with long-term structural implications, the use of these instruments raises questions about democratic legitimacy and institutional accountability. What we are witnessing is

[8] A list of cases to be found at Corporate Europe Observatory (Corporate Europe Observatory, n.d.).

not an increase in absolute frequency but a shift in how and why Art. 122 TFEU is being applied.

From the EP's perspective, this trend is troubling. As the representative body of EU citizens, it must be more than a spectator in the legislative process. Its exclusion, even in exceptional cases, should remain a rare and well-justified exception. In a healthy institutional framework, urgency cannot become a blanket justification for side-lining democratic deliberation. A Union that takes its democratic mandate seriously must ensure that all legislative pathways, including those under emergency law, are used transparently, proportionately and only when genuinely necessary.

5 Omnibus and the Deregulation Agenda

The ongoing shift in institutional power, linked to the EPP's strengthened position after the 2024 European elections, could produce tangible political consequences: namely, the targeted dismantling of legislation under the pretext of simplification. The current legislative term reflects a paradigm shift in EU lawmaking away from an inclusive, democratic engagement and towards a technocratic, top-down mode of governance. Within this new landscape, 'competitiveness' and 'simplification' have emerged as dominant narratives. In practice, these terms function less as administrative necessities and more as political instruments. Under the von der Leyen Commission II, they have been mobilised to advance a deregulatory agenda closely aligned with the EPP's priorities (European Peoples Party, 2025; Corporate Europe Observatory, n.d.). Legislation adopted during the previous term, often after extensive negotiations and democratic deliberation, is now being reopened, in some cases barely a year after its adoption (see European Deforestation Regulation later). These revisions do not respond to genuine administrative shortcomings but rather serve explicit political aims (European Peoples Party, 2025; Corporate Europe Observatory, n.d.). The latest example is the EPP, via a simple letter, getting the Commission to scrap the 'Green Claims Directive' aimed at combatting greenwashing (Abnett, 2025; Di Sario, 2025). What is becoming increasingly clear from these examples is that these objectives are being pursued at the expense of the institutional integrity of the EU and the democratic legitimacy of the OLP by 'simply' bypassing them.

5.1 EUDR: Testing the New Majority

A prominent example of this strategy is the attempted revision of the European Deforestation Regulation (EUDR) in late 2024 (European Union 2023b; European Commission, 2024). Originally adopted in 2023, the regulation was scheduled for full implementation by 30 December 2024. However, as the implementation deadline approached, it became clear that key infrastructure, most notably the Commission's centralised information system, would not be operational in time. In response, the Commission proposed a targeted revision: a twelve-month delay in the regulation's application, without altering its substantive provisions.

Time pressure led the EP to initiate an urgent procedure under Rule 170 of its Rules of Procedure (RoP).[9] While the scope of the procedure was meant to remain narrow, the EPP unexpectedly tabled sweeping amendments. Chief among them was the introduction of a 'no-risk' category, which would effectively exempt certain countries, particularly within the EU, from many of the regulation's requirements. The proposed exemption risked undermining the regulation's environmental credibility, opening the door to greenwashing and creating unfair competitive advantages at the expense of the Global South.

The controversial amendments were adopted with support from the EPP and far-right MEPs. During the vote, a technical issue prevented several Members of the EP from casting their votes. Despite this irregularity, EP President Roberta Metsola declined the S&D Group's formal request to repeat the vote. While the Council later rejected the EPP's changes in trilogue negotiations ultimately approving only the initial delay, the episode could serve as a revealing case study of how the new majorities in the EP are being used to attempt structural rollbacks of progressive legislation.

5.2 *Omnibus: From Precedent to Playbook*

Rather than reconsidering its approach, the EPP expanded it. Having tested the waters with the EUDR, the group launched a broader initiative under a new label: 'Omnibus'. Technically, an Omnibus package refers to a single legislative act that amends multiple pieces of existing legislation within the same legal act. In practice, it has become synonymous with a new wave of deregulation under the current Commission. The first Omnibus package, known as Omnibus I, targeted recently adopted rules on corporate due diligence and Environmental, Social and Governance (ESG) reporting. It proposed exempting all small and medium-sized enterprises (SMEs) with fewer than 1000 employees from reporting obligations, framed as relief for SMEs, but in reality, benefiting large multinational corporations operating under SME thresholds. Genuine sources of bureaucratic burden such as significant national divergences in the implementation of identical EU legislation remained unaddressed. Practical solutions like harmonised forms across Member States have received little support from those who most vocally demand less bureaucracy.

[9] EP Rule 170 concerns the urgent procedure, allowing for a decision to be taken rapidly due to unforeseen developments or to meet legally required deadlines. Requests for urgency can be initiated by various parliamentary bodies, the Commission or the Council, and are announced in the EP, followed by a vote on the request itself. If approved, the matter receives priority, and a decision is made based on committee reports or, exceptionally, without one, using simplified procedures where appropriate. (European Parliament, 2024a).

As with the EUDR, the EP once again resorted to urgent procedure, this time to delay the application of certain provisions through what became known as the 'Stop-the-Clock' Directive (European Union, 2025). However, the use of urgent procedure in this case was even more contentious. Rule 170 of the EP's RoP requires the presence of 'unforeseen circumstances'. Previous examples for the use of this rule include legislation to mitigate the COVID-19 crisis. However, in the case of this due diligence legislation, similar unforeseen circumstances making urgent action necessary do not seem to exist. In addition, many Member States and private actors had already invested heavily in compliance with the new laws and were on track for the foreseen deadlines. Despite objections, the majority of EPP and the far-right groups pushed forward with the vote, which passed in the EP on 1 April 2025. The Council followed suit and adopted the measure on 14 April.

This use of Omnibus packages represents a fundamental change in EU lawmaking. Urgent procedures are no longer the exception but appear to be evolving into a procedural norm for deregulation, all while the legislative grounds for urgent procedures are extended far beyond their meaning. Provisions that were debated, negotiated and democratically adopted are being reopened and reinterpreted in the name of competitiveness. While this strategy may be politically expedient, it raises critical concerns about institutional integrity and the long-term reliability of the legislative process. With additional Omnibus packages already in development targeting areas such as InvestEU, the Common Agricultural Policy (CAP) and possibly the General Data Protection Regulation (GDPR), the implications for EU governance, and the rule of law, are profound.

6 Conclusion

The current legislative term has brought to the surface developments that had been quietly advancing for several years. What initially emerged as a gradual shift in legislative culture marked by an increased reliance on emergency legal instruments has now culminated in a systematic reorientation of EU lawmaking. This transformation, made possible by the reconfigured institutional power balance following the 2024 European elections, reflects not only procedural change but a broader political paradigm shift.

Today, we are witnessing troubling developments: democratically adopted legislation is being reopened, changed or even dismantled in response to demands from corporate interests. Long-standing partners of the EPP within the pro-European coalition have found themselves marginalised, and agreements are increasingly undermined. In this environment, trust and reliability, once hallmarks of inter-group cooperation, have eroded. The role of the pro-European coalition within the legislative process risks shifting from consensus building to containment and damage control.

Being pro-European has never meant uniformity of opinion. On the contrary, it has always required the ability to work constructively across ideological lines, to find common ground through negotiation and dialogue. This was the strength of the pro-European coalition in the previous terms: a commitment to shared democratic values despite policy differences. In contrast, the far right seeks not to reform the Union, but to weaken or dismantle it entirely. Its disregard for the rule of law, minority rights and cultural coexistence strikes at the heart of what Europe stands for.

The analysis outlined in this chapter highlights the EPP's conduct not as a matter of partisan politics, but as a reflection of deeper institutional concerns. This is not political point scoring but a pronounced warning about the state of our democratic institutions. Those who enable the dismantling of democratic consensus for short-term political gains risk undermining the very framework that sustains our Union. History has repeatedly shown that the misuse of emergency instruments and the erosion of democratic procedures ultimately benefit anti-democratic actors, often to the detriment of those who first made such compromises.

Europe is facing multiple crises—geopolitical, environmental and economic—but perhaps none is more urgent than the current democratic crisis. Yet, history has shown that the European project often finds its greatest momentum in times of challenge. If we can use this moment to reassert our foundational values, the Union can emerge stronger.

References

Abnett, K. (2025, June 23). EU halts talks on law tackling companies‘ fake ‘green‘ claims. *Reuters*, retrieved: September 2025, https://www.reuters.com/sustainability/climate-energy/eu-halts-talks-law-tackling-companies-fake-green-claims-2025-06-23/

Corporate Europe Observatory. (n.d.). retrieved: September 2025, https://corporateeurope.org/en/deregulation-watch

Di Sario, F., The Parliament. (2025, July 8). How the axing of a tiny green law solidifies the EPP‘s grip on EU politics. retrieved: September 2025, https://www.theparliamentmagazine.eu/news/article/demise-of-eu-greenwashing-law-shows-epps-emerging-dominance

EEP Group, S&D Group, Renew Europe Group. (2022). *Mid-term agreement of 2022*, https://app.box.com/s/9b9pbjxs8kvpxa8yovzmti7oeq6w7tpy

European Commission. (2017). *European Pillar of Social Rights*. https://employment-social-affairs.ec.europa.eu/policies-and-activities/european-pillar-social-rights-building-fairer-and-more-inclusive-european-union_en

European Commission. (2019). *The European Green Deal*, retrieved, 10 September 2025, https://commission.europa.eu/strategy-and-policy/priorities-2019-2024/european-green-deal_en

European Commission. (2020). *The Just Transition Mechanisms: Make sure that no one is left behind*. https://commission.europa.eu/strategy-and-policy/priorities-2019-2024/european-green-deal/finance-and-green-deal/just-transition-mechanism_en

European Commission. (2024, October 2). *Commission strengthens support for EU Deforestation Regulation implementation and proposes extra 12 months of phasing-in time, responding to calls by global partners*. https://ec.europa.eu/commission/presscorner/detail/en/ip_24_5009

European Commission. (2025a). *Competitiveness Compass*: https://commission.europa.eu/topics/eu-competitiveness/competitiveness-compass_en

European Commission. (2025b). *Simplification and Implementation*. https://commission.europa.eu/law/law-making-process/better-regulation/simplification-and-implementation_en

European Parliament DG IPOL. (2023). *The use of Article 122 - Institutional implications and impact.* https://www.europarl.europa.eu/RegData/etudes/STUD/2023/753307/IPOL_STU(2023)753307_EN.pdf
European Parliament. (2022, January 19). *Parliaments new Vice-Presidents and Quaesters.* https://www.europarl.europa.eu/news/en/press-room/20220114IPR21013/parliament-s-new-vice-presidents-and-quaestors
European Parliament, EPRS. (2024a). *Facts and Figures, April 2024.* https://www.europarl.europa.eu/RegData/etudes/BRIE/2024/760403/EPRS_BRI(2024)760403_EN.pdf
European Parliament, EPRS. (2024b). *Facts and Figures, November 2024.* https://www.europarl.europa.eu/RegData/etudes/BRIE/2024/766234/EPRS_BRI(2024)766234_EN.pdf
European Parliament. (2024a). *Rule 170, Rules of Procedure.* https://www.europarl.europa.eu/doceo/document/RULES-10-2024-07-16-RULE-170_EN.html
European Parliament (2024b, October 23). *Minutes - results of roll-call votes.* https://www.europarl.europa.eu/doceo/document/PV-10-2024-10-23-RCV_EN.html#170175
European Parliament. (2024c). *Voting results of AM 69 to the General budget of the European Union for the financial year 2025.* https://www.europarl.europa.eu/doceo/document/PV-10-2024-10-23-RCV_EN.html#170175
European Parliament. (n.d.). *Organisation and rules.* https://www.europarl.europa.eu/about-parliament/en/organisation-and-rules/organisation/political-bodies
European Peoples Party. (2025). *Our priorities for 2025*, retrieved: September 2025, https://www.epp.eu/papers/our-priorities-for-2025
European Union. (2023a). *Directive (EU) 2023/970 to strengthen the the application of the principle of equal pay for equal work or work of equal value between men and women through pay transparency and enforcement mechanisms.* https://eur-lex.europa.eu/eli/dir/2023/970/oj/eng
European Union. (2023b). *Regulation (EU) 2023/1115 on the making available on the Union market and the export from the Union of certain commodities and products associated with deforestation and forest degradation and repealing Regulation (EU) No 995/2010.* https://eur-lex.europa.eu/legal-content/EN/TXT/?uri=CELEX%3A02023R1115-20241226
European Union. (2024). *Directive (EU) 2024/1760 on corporate sustainability due diligence and amending Directive (EU) 2019/1937 and Regulation (EU) 2023/2859.* https://eur-lex.europa.eu/eli/dir/2024/1760/oj/eng
European Union. (2025). *"Stop-the-clock"- Directive. Directive (EU) 2025/794.* https://eur-lex.europa.eu/eli/dir/2025/794/oj/eng
Herbst, N. (2024, October 18). *Amendment 69 to the General budget of the European Union for the financial year 2025—all sections 2024/0176(BUD)*, https://www.europarl.europa.eu/doceo/document/A-10-2024-0008-AM-069-069_EN.pdf
Jungbluth, A., Tyszka, S., Anderson C. (2024, October 17). *Amendments 45 & 46 to the General budget of the European Union for the financial year 2025—all sections 2024/0176(BUD)*, https://www.europarl.europa.eu/doceo/document/A-10-2024-0008-AM-040-049_EN.pdf
Sanchez, J., Furet, A. (2024, October 17). *Amendment 32 to the General budget of the European Union for the financial year 2025—all sections 2024/0176(BUD)*, https://www.europarl.europa.eu/doceo/document/A-10-2024-0008-AM-031-039_EN.pdf
Transparency International EU, Integrity Watch EU project, https://integritywatch.eu/ecmeetings.php?commission=vonderleyen2.
Wax, E., Vinocur, N. (2025, February 20). Ursula von der Leyen tightens her grip on power, *Politico*. Retrieved: Sepetember 10, 2025: https://www.politico.eu/article/ursula-von-der-leyen-power-grab-european-commission-executive-power-backlash/

Further Readings

Broniecki, P., & Høyland, B. (2025, January 13). *What unites the right in the European Parliament?* Retrieved June 17, 2025, from LSE EUROPP Blog: https://blogs.lse.ac.uk/europpblog/2025/01/13/what-unites-the-right-in-the-european-parliament/

Chamon, M. (2023, February 1). *The rise of Article 122 TFEU - On crisis measures and the paradigm change*. Retrieved 05 13, 2025, from Verfassungsblog: https://verfassungsblog.de/the-rise-of-article-122-tfeu

Guillot, L. (2024, November 14). *EPP accused of allying with far right to weaken deforestation rules*. Retrieved July 17, 2025, from Politico: https://www.politico.eu/article/epp-far-right-deforestation-rules-lawmakers-proposal-socialists-climate-change/

Lázara, A. V. (2024, December 13). *Op-ed: Navigating the gap between efficiency and transparency with the EU's emergency powers*. Preuzeto 17. July 2025 iz The Parliament: https://www.theparliamentmagazine.eu/news/article/oped-article-122-and-the-eus-emergency-powers-navigating-the-gap-between-efficiency-and-transparency

Evelyn Regner has been a member of the European Parliament for the Social Democratic Party of Austria (SPÖ) since 2009. She served as Vice-President from 2022 to 2024 and headed the Austrian Trade Union Federation's Brussels office before her mandate. Regner chairs the Mercosur Delegation and is a member of the ECON committee, a substitute member in EMPL and FISC. A strong advocate for workers' rights and gender equality, she played a key role in the EU Pay Transparency Directive.

Michael Kudler is an IT project manager for digitalisation at the Austrian Chamber of Labour. He studied computer science at the Technical University of Vienna and has a strong commitment to combining technical expertise with democratic and social advocacy. Kudler previously served as a trainee in the office of MEP Evelyn Regner, contributed as a founding member and technology lead at Palumba EU and sat on the board of HOSI Wien from 2019 to 2024.

The 2024 Elections to the European Parliament and Its Political and Practical Implications

Lukas Mandl

Abstract The article examines the implications of the new composition of the European Parliament (EP) following the 2024 elections, focusing not only on legislative processes but also on the formation of the new European Commission College and the policies pursued by its members. While the likelihood of significant reforms, such as those introduced through the "Omnibus" packages, has increased due to stronger centrist majorities, the risk of setbacks, disruptions, and destabilisation has simultaneously risen as a result of the expanded and more active parliamentary groups representing far-left and far-right extremists. The author firmly opposes yielding to extremist forces and advocates for the establishment of robust coalitions of the willing to ensure stability and progress.

Keywords European Elections 2024 · Omnibus Legislation · Appointing new Commission · European People's party

Remark from the editors: The guiding principle of this book is to provide its readers with valuable insights into how the practice of EU policy-making is conducted in very concrete terms. In order to meet this objective for the chapter on the implications of the 2024 elections to the European Parliament, we therefore invited two renowned representatives of the two largest political groups in the EP to share their perspectives on the power shift that followed the elections. We are pleased to incorporate this unique perspective into this part, presenting the naturally somewhat opposing views of two political practitioners in this handbook.

L. Mandl (✉)
Member of the European Parliament, Brussels, Belgium
e-mail: Lukas.mandl@europarl.europa.eu

G. Füricht-Fiegl et al. (eds.), *Handbook on EU Law-making*, Professional Practice in Governance and Public Organizations, https://doi.org/10.1007/978-3-032-16559-6_15

1 Introduction: A Personal Viewpoint

While writing this, I am travelling by car through rural Pakistan with a security guide, our driver, and a colleague who, like me, serves as a Member of the European Parliament (MEP)—he for Poland, I for Austria. We are both committed to the European integration, and I believe missions like this one strengthen that commitment, especially in a region where historic rivals still lack peace and where we are reminded daily how fragile freedom, peace, and prosperity remain.

Parliamentarism is, to me, one of history's most decisive innovations and our greatest step towards replacing political violence with dialogue. Since 1979, Europe has handled its challenges through parliamentary means, a core element of its success story. This achievement must not be underestimated in a time when democratic values, institutions, and rituals face real threats, and when we have so much to lose.

The above-mentioned colleague is affiliated with the Group of the Progressive Alliance of Socialists and Democrats in the EP (S&D) as I am with the Group of the European People's Party (EPP). We act with unity in our encounters with Pakistani officials as well as people affected by crises, in a few weeks, however, we will find ourselves once again in a heated plenary session of the EP. That is, on the one hand, good, since the Hemicycle in Strasbourg is the place where the political conflict resolution of our time belongs. On the other hand, it is of concern, since the political heat in Europe has increased in recent times, and if the political system becomes overheated, it will affect European citizens negatively.

Before the last EP elections in 2024, forecasts had shown the risk of a shift to far-right extremism. This outlook might have helped to avoid that from becoming reality. In any case, it did not happen. But it took some time until the engaged public embraced this view. The reason apparently is the loss of political mandate within groups to the left of the Renew Group in the sitting order of the EP. The largest gain was that of the Group of the EPP.

Since the very matter of this article is meant to be the Ordinary Legislative Procedure (OLP), it is clear that several references to the European Commission (Commission) are inevitable in order to provide a holistic picture.

2 European Commission's Approach

The Commission's structure puts a lot of power in the hands of the President of the Commission. Under the current President Ursula von der Leyen, this power is used more precisely than before. Involvement and even interventions in portfolios of members of the College are daily practice. In the second mandate (2024–2029) this is even more the case than in the first one. This reality thus entails a huge responsibility for the president herself for the results of EU policies.

The leadership style of Ursula von der Leyen is neither highly visionary nor servant. It could be classified as rather cool-opportunistic. One must not underestimate that approach. Angela Merkel led Germany in a similar way for more than a decade and a half. Its key characteristic is to try to do things right, rather than to reflect for too long on what could be right. Von der Leyen's approach means getting done what is the obvious wish of many, rather than trying to persuade only a few. When it comes to legislation, the approach shows itself through attempted tactical alliances with probable majorities in the EP, for example on the Omnibus I package as will be laid out.

While the global political landscape shows a lot of red-headed, almost toxic, policymaking, von der Leyen's coolness can be seen as the better alternative. The opportunistic part has led to Commission proposals in the last mandate that have achieved tight majorities but harmed Europe's economy severely. During the last mandate (2019–2024), crisis management worked effectively, particularly in response to Putin's war of aggression and other security threats, yet regulatory policymaking fell short, as illustrated by the "EU Corporate Sustainability Due Diligence Directive" (CSDDD), drafted during that period and now in need of significant revision.

3 The EP's Role in Appointing the New Commission

A large number of decisions in the EP have been taken which may not have led to the perfect compromise, many with the support of MEPs from the EPP. We should not absolve the EPP of this historical fact but instead strive to improve our politics for the future. EPP MEPs behaviour in negotiations is first and foremost a constructive one: A Commission proposal that is for the major part not appreciated can be amended, but the negotiations feel rather like an up-hill exercise. Compromise is neither simple nor easy. With the different majorities, we can now use the improved make-up of the current Parliament to our favour and endeavour for better compromise.

In 2024 five weeks passed after the EP elections before MEPs voted in favour of a second term of Ursula von der Leyen as President of the Commission. During these five weeks it seemed as if the president spent more time with the elected representatives than in all the five years of her first mandate.

When the European Council—where the Member States' governments gather and form a second chamber of the EU's lawmaking process—confronted the EP with only one person nominated for the position of the President of the Commission, the choice was only between *Yes* or *No*. Accordingly, most MEPs tried to influence the policy agenda of the single candidate Ursula von der Leyen.

4 Political and Practical Implications

Given her tactical flexibility and the absence of a strongly fixed policy agenda, von der Leyen is likely to adjust her plans in response to shifting dynamics within the EP. Recent electoral outcomes suggest that majorities favouring a stronger focus on economic growth and prosperity are now more plausible. After a mandate marked by extensive EU-level intervention, many voters appear to have sought a change in direction.

And von der Leyen has started to deliver: First, the composition of the new College and the mission letters outlining the portfolios for its members were promising.

Secondly, the proposals on the responsibilities of von der Leyen II Commission (2024– 2029) and the Commissioners set the right priorities. After the EP had taken early stop-the-clock decisions in order to avoid harmful regulations from the past to be set into force, the Commission was brave enough to create a name for a whole framework of deregulation proposals. The name itself—"Omnibus"—is not exactly made for parliamentary work in terms of public communication. But the content has so far to be seen as positive from my personal perspective.

Instead of constructively engaging in the matter with respect for democratic majorities, parts of the parliamentary spectrum left of the Renew–Group started to target the expression of "deregulation" and therefore the sense for its necessity. They wanted only "simplification" to take place. A new language to cause division among MEPs from the so-called "Platform" Groups (EPP, S&D, Renew) was born. I remember a working lunch in Strasbourg in preparation for the Danish Council Presidency (July 2025–December 2025) led by the Minister of European Affairs from Denmark, Marie Bjerre (from Venstre, the liberal party of Denmark, which is part of the EP's Renew Group), where nearly each parliamentary group was represented with one member. While the Danish Presidency under the social-democratic Prime Minister Mette Frederiksen has been fully instrumental in terms of deregulation, and also in other fields such as migration, numerous colleagues from left groups showed a lack of understanding given the parliamentary circumstances and the matter itself.

And this is what matters: "Content, content, content", as our Group Chairman and EPP President, Manfred Weber, frequently states (Weber, 2025). When I have mentioned above the large responsibility that comes with von der Leyen's ruling habits, one must not forget that the EPP—after winning the EP elections—has more responsibility to deliver than before. That includes not only the parliamentary group, but also the EPP in the College of the Commission and the Council, concretely the heads of Member States' governments.

Listening to European citizens not only in Austria, but all across the European Union, it is clear that the EU must deliver—for the economy, as well as in the face of evolving challenges like the "demographic winter", among other topics. So, it is the right decision to focus on content.

Figures show a quite stable parliamentary workflow for the Platform-Groups. 88% of the roll-call votes[1] are taken with majorities including the major parts of EPP, S&D, and Renew, as an article released in Politico in September 2025 shows

[1] A roll-call vote in the EP is a voting method where each MEP's vote is recorded individually by name. It's typically used when requested by a political group or required for key legislative decisions to ensure transparency and accountability.

(Cokelaere & Griera, 2025). But as stated above, the heat in the Hemicycle continues to increase anyway. From my perspective there are two main reasons: The first is that the obstructive hostility of the three extreme groups in the EP (The Left, Patriots for Europe, and Europe of Sovereign Nations) has become more pronounced in the new mandate and is now less absent from the actual parliamentary procedures.

A second reason may be that the S&D Group does not always uphold the Platform understanding when decisions become sensitive or involve a secret ballot, as seen with the Omnibus I package. This group, as well as the Greens, often follow lines that could be called "tactics, tactics, tactics", or even worse "ideology, ideology, ideology". I see the Renew-Group and the ECR-Group somewhere in limbo between content-oriented reliability and the various other approaches.

When the EP in autumn 2025 took the decision to send the first Omnibus package to the trilogue, negotiations between EP and Council began, supported by the Commission, I was in favour of it. As a parliamentarian by heart, I want to see things deliberated on in the plenary. But for the sake of the pace and predictability that the vast majority of Europeans demand from us, we should have acted with a majority for a quick start of the trilogue negotiations. Within the EP, the first Omnibus package had been negotiated on the Committee level deeply and extensively.[2] I was strongly involved myself as a member of the Committee on Legal Affairs.

The vote failed. With a very small number of votes missing, just nine, we once again presented to the Europeans and the world the impression that we would be slow and weak in decision-making. The objection to the immediate start of the trilogue had been signed beforehand, among others, by 31 S&D MEPs. These 31 S&D MEPs, presumably many others from the group who voted in silence, many from the ECR who stated it publicly, and no doubt countless other MEPs from the three extreme groups voted against the trilogue mandate.

Why? We will never know for sure. Because the ballot was secret. What was the reason for that? The far-right extremists gathered enough signatures to make the ballot secret. Will their voters be upset and turn them down, because it is them who constantly claim a lack of transparency in all EU affairs? Probably not, because most of them will never know. Would the direct trilogue mandate have worked if the ballot had been transparent instead of secret? Most probably yes.

This is one example of the extremists using the parliamentary toolbox more than ever. Another example is the confidence votes against the College of Commissioners that by now have become habit for the extremists in 2025.

Until July 2025 I had not experienced a single confidence vote since entering the EP in 2017. The last one had been against Jean-Claude Juncker in 2014. That time 101 out of 751 Members had voted against Juncker. Populism was on the rise, as

[2] In the EP, committees negotiate legislative files by appointing a *rapporteur* and *shadow rapporteurs* who draft, amend, and negotiate the text with political groups. Once the committee reaches an internal compromise, it votes on the final text, which then goes to the full Parliament for adoption.

"Brexit" and other events afterwards proved. But it was still contained. 13.4% voted against the President of the Commission. 61.4% voted for him.

Why could we call these actions populism? This expression made it through decades of political science, and also political practice, to become the marker for politics that exploits problems rather than solving them, leading to destruction instead of constructive solutions. Some would even connect populism with demagogy. During a remarkable stage interview during the Milken Institute's Global Conference 2025, Tony Blair stated: "I always say about populists, populists don't invent grievances. They may exploit them, but the grievances are usually real, and therefore you're going to deal with it, whether it's stagnant wages or issues to do with anxiety over cultural change". (Milken Institute, 2025).

Do not get me wrong: There is nothing wrong with criticising an executive body such as the European Commission. Quite the opposite: Such criticism is among the first and foremost duties of a proper parliamentarian. There would also be nothing wrong with getting rid of a truly bad administration which would cause harm or would have fallen apart from common sense or proper conduct. To act when it is really needed is among the duties of a responsible parliament. Though along with this responsibility comes the duty to contribute to proper solutions. A colleague once shared an insight from Spain: In the Spanish parliament, a motion of no-confidence has to be constructive; meaning it must come along with a proposal for an alternative administration. The same is true for Germany. This is a technical precaution against the populistic misuse of the severe instrument of confidence votes. Our parliamentary rules and procedures on the European level do not yet know such precautions. Consequently, between July and October 2025 I had to cast my vote during secret ballots not once or twice, but three times in confidence votes against Ursula von der Leyen's College. Within just over 3 months this sharp tool had been used more often than in decades before.

The polarisation within contemporary societies, particularly within the political sphere, may not be the sole factor contributing to the observed phenomenon, but it is undoubtedly a significant one. Some colleagues have explained to me how the precarious state of France's political system plays a contributory role. While this assertion may be true, it does not necessarily contradict the explanation rooted in polarisation—a dynamic that has been deliberately exacerbated by adversaries of Europe through strategies and tactics associated with hybrid warfare. This polarisation has been further intensified by populist actors, who have opportunistically exploited it to advance their own short-term political agendas.

A particularly alarming moment occurred in September 2025, when representatives of extremist factions from both ends of the political spectrum—the PfE-Group (Patriots for Europe) on the far-right and "The Left" Group on the far-left—took the floor consecutively to present their respective motions of no-confidence. Despite their daily posturing as ideological opposites and their overt mutual antagonism, they collaborated openly in a display of politics, which could be seen as destructive.

Why those actions could be characterised as "destructive", even though one could harbour reservations about the policies and political approach of President von der Leyen, including those referenced above? The answer lies in the current state of global affairs, which is marked by profound unpredictability and instability. In this context, the European Union stands as a rare bastion of stability and predictability when compared to other regions of the world. The challenges it faces can and should be addressed through rational and measured parliamentary processes, grounded in acceptable proposals from the Commission. At a time when a new global order is emerging, destabilising the European Union by plunging it into prolonged periods of crisis-driven change management would be detrimental to both Europe and its citizens. Such destabilisation aligns precisely with the objectives of Europe's adversaries and serves to empower populist movements at all levels of governance—regardless of whether they identify as "left" or "right".

During the July 2025 vote exactly half of the EP had von der Leyen's back: Out of 720 MEPs 360 voted for her College (50.0%), 171 were against (23.8%). In October 2025 it was once 378 (52.5%) and once 383 (53.2%) against once 179 (24.9%) and 133 votes (18.5%).

These events provide us with manifold indications for the years to come; here are the three most important ones when it comes to the future of the legislative procedures:

First: One can count on roughly one half of the chamber when it comes to questions of long-term responsibility and reliability, seeking constructive compromises in decision making on behalf of Europe and its citizens. That is not much. But it is enough to spur positive change in those fields where better legislation is needed, or those where a certain withdrawal from regulation is needed.

Second: Roughly a quarter of the EP is ready to, metaphorically speaking, set the European house on fire for the sake of short-term gains or for the benefit of powers who seek to weaken our civilisation. That is concerning, especially because there is another quarter in a limbo; but logics as well as history show it would be wrong to give in to populism and allow lazy compromises to happen, or worse.

Third: The extremists' groups in the EP are more active than before. While during the last two mandates I have personally experienced how extremists were rather absent when it came to formal procedures, they now take advantage of the parliamentary toolbox as much as they can. (This has also been revealed through their secret ballot for the above-mentioned vote on the trilogue mandate of the first Omnibus package.) This will not change, it has to be taken it into account.

One can only recommend to the President of the Commission to finally stay away from any reluctance in putting far-reaching proposals on the table. First and foremost, her College has to observe Montesquieu's principle: "Useless laws weaken the necessary laws".

The following quote from Tony Blair in the above-mentioned stage interview is a well-phrased guideline for the Commission's President and her College: "You know, it's getting things done. I mean, anyone who's ever been in government knows the toughest thing is to get anything done. And I remember this came home to me when I was in Downing Street and, you know, I'd won a big landslide victory, I was the most powerful person in the country. I thought, you know, if I take a decision in Downing Street, you know something's going to happen. And after about a year, I realised nothing happened. The system just absorbed this pressure for change and somehow killed it off. And if you look at, for example, the rise of President Trump here, I think it's got a lot to do with people wanting things moving. They want action. They want things to go, so you've got to—if you're in serious politics, you've got to understand the appeal of your—of the people on the opposite side of politics, and you've got to respond to it". (Milken Institute, 2025).

The upcoming proposals by the Commission will have to be elaborated and presented without any fear of future confidence votes or any other extremists' action of whatever kind. They will have to be fit for purpose, meaning able to tackle the major challenges of our times. Here are seven of them:

1) The "Demographic Winter"

Europe will have to create better conditions for children as well as opportunities for the elderly. Europe urgently needs labour migration and at the same time avoid illegal migration. Many of these requirements can only be met by a multi-level-approach. That is one of the reasons why it is a bad idea to upset the municipalities and the regions of Europe with the first proposal for the new Multiannual Financial Framework (MFF for the period 2028+). This has to be amended. The asylum and migration pact has to be fully implemented and further developed. Here it will be important to nudge certain Member State governments to the right priority setting.

2) Integration

As the first of Tony Blair's quotes above tells: "Populists don't invent grievances. They may exploit them". It is true that integration in our civilisation model has failed in many regards. Ronald Reagan stated: "You can go to live in France, but you cannot become a Frenchman. You can go to live in Germany or Turkey or Japan, but you cannot become a German, a Turk, or a Japanese. But anyone, from any corner of the Earth, can come to live in America and become an American". (Reagen, 1989). As much as we know this is, for the time being, not true for the America under the current presidential administration; but we have to make it a pattern for Europe!

3) External Security Threats

Grosso modo, this has been von der Leyen's priority during the last mandate; the Commission facilitated significant progress. Facing extremists' behaviour and the risks of "fatigue" it will be of utmost importance to increase the pace of defence spending and the depths of cooperation among the Member States.

4) Single Market

Here the President of the Commission has made several excellent remarks in her State of the Union (SOTU) speech 2025: She emphasised the Single Market is not yet finished. She said: "The IMF [International Monetary Fund] estimates that the internal barriers within the Single Market are equivalent to a 45% tariff on goods. And a 110% tariff on services. Just think of what we are missing out on. And, as underscored by the Letta report, the Single Market remains incomplete, mostly in three domains: finance, energy, and telecommunications. We need clear political deadlines. This is why we will present a Single Market Roadmap to 2028. On capital, services, energy, telecoms, the 28th regime and the fifth freedom for knowledge and innovation. Only what gets measured, gets done". (von der Leyen, 2025) This will have to be delivered. I am convinced major parts of the EP will support this pathway, since it will make prosperity happen, create jobs and open opportunities for generations to come.

5) Risk Diversification

In autumn 2025 China restricted rare earth exports when it comes to their use for military purposes. This is one of many wake-up calls, one of the latest, and a very concerning one. While I think we have to talk not only about China, but also with China, in the sense of remaining in exchange, we have to diversify the risks in supply chains not only with China but with other major powers, too. Europe must become able to help and defend itself.

6) Enlargement

The European Union is stuck in the by far longest period of time in its history without any accession. The last one was that of Croatia in 2013—a very successful one indeed, for everyone! During this period one Member State left the Union. One of the decisive questions regarding von der Leyen's leadership is whether she will make the accession of the six Western Balkans countries happen or at least prepare their accession to be realised very soon. Furthermore, the steps for the countries of the Eastern partnership and deepening the relations with Switzerland, Norway, and the UK, as well as considering the aspirations of Iceland, will be historically more important than many other policy areas.

7) Treaty Reform

For pragmatic reasons the next treaty reform is not being discussed openly or behind closed doors; even though the European Union has not made a treaty reform for a longer period of time than ever before. While treaty reform is the natural thing to reform, adapt, and shape the structure to be fit for future purpose, the main sentiment in the majority of the Member States' capitals might be one of fear. But fear and anxiety will not lead anywhere; at least not anywhere good.

So given the time frames it will not be possible to conclude a treaty reform during the current mandate. But it's a question of maturity and responsibility to get it started.

Here is one last quote from Tony Blair's above-mentioned stage appearance: "I would say, look, work hard, play hard, right? That's a good rhythm, right? Then you've got a chance of success. But if you play hard, work hard. No, that's going to fail completely. And the political equivalent, in my view is this: policy first, politics second. The single most important thing, if you're in government, is to work out what the right answer is. And part of the trouble with modern politics is that it's still quite driven by what I think are essentially 20th century ideologies of left and right, and people don't just sit down and work up, well, what is the answer?" I believe that Manfred Weber presents the answer: "Content, content, content".

These persuasive and even wise words qualify not only as a note to myself, but they would also be my recommendation to my colleagues of all political groups in the EP, and they define my wish for the further legislative procedures:

I have tried to describe the political environment through numerous examples, especially the one of the votes on the trilogue mandate for the first Omnibus package via a secret ballot. I very much hope for stable majorities via the "platform"-Groups. At the same time, I can only urge my Socialists and Democrats Group (S&D) and ECR-Group (European Conservatives and Reformists) colleagues who care more for the right answers than for ideologies of whatever kind to—when needed for the sake of Europe's future—sit down with the EPP- and the Renew-Group in order to find proper solutions. Of course, also among the Green Group are members who would probably agree with such an approach.

5 Conclusion

Europe stands once again at a crossroad. The strength of our Union lies not in the absence of disagreement, but in our ability to resolve conflict through constructive negotiations and sound compromise. This is what makes the European project unique in history; and what must continue to guide us in the years ahead.

The EP has proven time and again that it can act when the moment calls for it. Yet, the recurring tests of confidence and the growing populist exploitation of parliamentary tools remind us that democracy is not self-sustaining. It must be practised, defended, and constantly renewed. The "Platform" cooperation between the main political groups remains the most viable way forward, provided that it focuses on content rather than tactics, on the needs of European citizens rather than small political wins.

Ursula von der Leyen's second mandate (2024-2029) offers an opportunity to steer Europe towards a brighter future: strengthening prosperity, deepening integration, and safeguarding stability in a turbulent world. Policy must come before politics; substance must come before symbolism. The European Union can deliver for citizens. The task of the European Parliament is to make this happen: to ensure that democracy not only survives but succeeds.

References

Cokelaere, H., & Griera, M. (2025, September 18). Does the EPP really vote with the far right? 5 things we learned from the data. *Politico*. Retrieved: 30 October 2025 https://www.politico.eu/article/epp-far-right-data-socialists-democrats-policy-eu-politics-centrist/

Milken Institute, & Blair, T. A. (2025). Conversation with Former Prime Minister of the United Kingdom Tony Blair (N. Kristof, Interviewer). In *Milken Institute* (1–3). Retrieved 10 November 2025 https://milkeninstitute.org/sites/default/files/2025-05/GlobalOverviewFormerPrimeMinisterUKTonyBlair_Transcript_GC25.pdf

Reagan Foundation. (1989). *"Since this is the last speech that I will give as President, I think it's fitting to leave one final thought..."* 19 January. [Online] Retrieved 10 November 2025: https://www.reaganfoundation.org/ronald-reagan/quotes/since-this-is-the-last-speech-that-i-will-give-as-president-i-think-it-s-fitting

Von der Leyen, U. (2025, September 10). '*State of the Union (debate)*', European Parliament debates, 10 September.

Weber, M. (2025, September 10). '*State of the Union (debate)*', European Parliament debates.

Lukas Mandl has been a Member of the European Parliament since 2017. He was re-elected in 2019 and in 2024. Today he is the longest-serving Austrian Member in the European People's Party's Group (EPP), whom he represents as chair in the Development Committee (DEVE). Mandl focuses on geopolitics, security, economy, and regions. In 2025 he was elected President of the Assembly of European Regions (AER). Serving in the Committees on Civil Liberties (LIBE) and Justice (JURI) during the current mandate (2024-2029) he has been negotiating, among other topics, on different "Omnibus" packages.

(Inter)institutional Bargaining and Interaction

Managed Compromise: Trilogues and the Technopolitical Logic of EU Legislation

Bernhard Zeilinger

Abstract Trilogues are informal tripartite meetings between the European Parliament, the Council of the EU and the Commission, aimed at reaching early agreements under the Ordinary Legislative Procedure. Although not mentioned in the EU Treaties, trilogues have become a de facto standard in EU lawmaking. This chapter examines the transformation of trilogues from an informal coordination mechanism into a structured and routinised instrument of EU lawmaking, governed by internal procedures and interinstitutional agreements. Particular attention is devoted to the sequential phases of trilogue negotiations, including preparatory coordination, interinstitutional technical meetings and high-level political bargaining. The chapter concludes with a critical assessment of how the institutionalisation of trilogue practices has reshaped power relations within the EU's legislative framework and highlights ongoing concerns regarding transparency, accountability and democratic legitimacy.

Keywords Trilogue procedure · Conciliation procedure · Fast-Track Legislation · Technocratic–Executive Nexus · Technopolitical Governance · Informal coordination mechanism · Interinstitutional agreements

1 Introduction

In recent decades, the European Union has developed into a multifaceted legislative system, where most EU legislation is adopted within the Ordinary Legislative Procedure (OLP). Since the European Parliament (EP) received co-legislating

B. Zeilinger (✉)
University of Applied Sciences BFI Vienna, Vienna, Austria
e-mail: bernhard.zeilinger@fh-vie.ac.at

G. Füricht-Fiegl et al. (eds.), *Handbook on EU Law-making*, Professional Practice in Governance and Public Organizations, https://doi.org/10.1007/978-3-032-16559-6_16

powers with the Treaty of Maastricht 1993, the demand for coordination and information exchange between the EP and the Council as well as the Commission became crucial for effective lawmaking. Since then, the following treaty reforms with Amsterdam 1999 and Lisbon 2009 led to an exponential growth in the EU's legislative workload from 165 legislative in 15 policy areas in the parliamentary term 1994–1999 to 495 legislative files in 85 policy areas in the parliamentary term 2009–2014 (Maurer, 2003, p.229; European Parliament, 2024a, p.10; 2024b, p. 17). Furthermore, the increasing number of Member States from 13 in 1993 to 28 Member States in 2013 has increased the complexity in EU's multilevel governance system. Both have necessitated procedural streamlining and further incentivised informal bargaining formats.

Originally conceived as an exceptional tool to bridge institutional disagreements during conciliation after the third reading, trilogues have since evolved into an essential tool to elaborate on compromises already early in the legislative procedure. Compared to the previous legislative periods, the first-reading agreements increased since the Amsterdam Treaty from 28% of 405 OLP files in the fifth term from 1999 to 2004 to 86% of 415 OLP files in the ninth period from 2019 to 2024 (see Fig. 1) and, subsequently, placed growing institutional pressure on trilogue negotiations as a means of ensuring timely decision-making. Out of a total of 973 trilogue meetings in the ninth legislative term 164 trilogues are allocated to the Committees on Civil Liberties, Justice and Home Affairs, 119 to Environment, Public Health and Food Safety, 101 to Industry, Research and Energy and 91 to Economic and Monetary Affairs (ibid., 14).

This chapter provides a systematic yet practice-oriented overview of the rationale and procedural logic underpinning trilogue negotiations as a core feature of contemporary EU lawmaking. It begins by outlining their historical emergence and

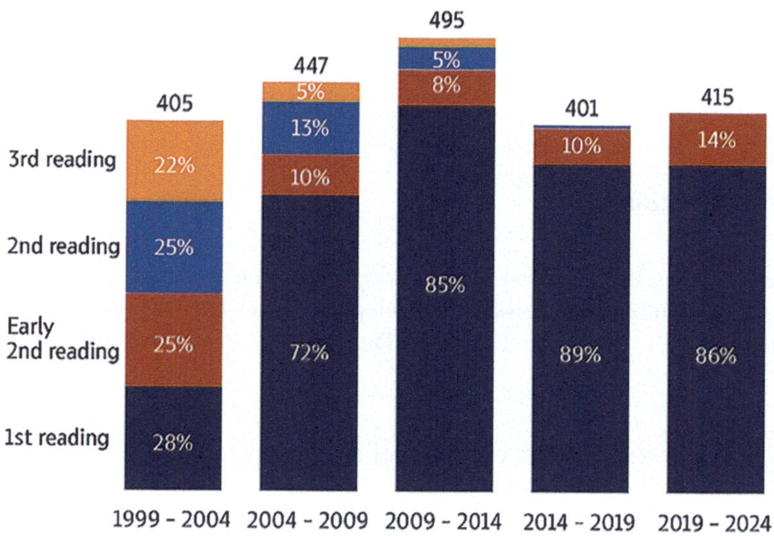

Fig. 1 Stage of adoption of OLP files (European Parliament, 2024b, p. 24)

institutional rationale, explains the roles of key actors involved from all three institutions and describes the inter- and intra-coordination mechanisms that underpin successful negotiation outcomes. The chapter concludes with discussing some of the critics on the procedures' informal nature such as a lack of public access to documents and negotiations, reduced parliamentary scrutiny and shifting power to technocrats.

2 Tracing the Origins of Trilogue: How Informal Talks Became Institutional Norm

Over the past three decades, trilogues have developed from an informal, ad hoc coordination tool into an essential element of the OLP. Originally conceived in the early 1990s as a pragmatic response to institutional gridlock between EP and Council, the gradual transformation into a more structured and routinised instrument of EU lawmaking was shaped by a series of legal and procedural milestones. Trilogues emerged in the wake of the Maastricht Treaty, which introduced the co--decision procedure and granted the EP significant co-legislative powers.[1] In this new institutional setting, informal tripartite meetings between the EP, the Council and the Commission were used to pre-empt conflicts and facilitate compromise—initially outside any formal procedural framework and largely behind closed doors.

Paragraph 56 of the Amsterdam Treaty marked a turning point by amending Art. 228, allowing co-decision to be concluded at any stage of the legislative process (EUR-Lex 11997D002/P56). This reform significantly increased the frequency of early legislative agreements and created fertile ground for the routine use of trilogues. The trilogue negotiations in the first- and second-reading phase are, yet, not legally defined in the treaties and, thus, are informal in nature. Instead, the EP and the Council systematised the structure of trilogues by interinstitutional agreements and through internal rules such as Rule 72–75 and Annex XX of the Rules of Procedure (RoP) for the EP (European Parliament, 2025) and Annex 5 of the RoP for the Council of the EU (Council of the EU, 2009). The current form of the trilateral procedure was first institutionalised with the Interinstitutional Agreement (IIAs) of 7 November 2002 and based on the 'Joint Declaration on Practical Arrangements for the Co-decision Procedure' (Art. 251 EC-Treaty).[2] The IIA of 2002 and its revision in 2010 established shared procedural rules aiming to facilitate a more structured and increasingly transparent negotiation format. These included requirements for written negotiation mandates, reporting obligations like summary records of meetings and the use of four-column documents as consolidated negotiating texts.

[1] See also Sect. 2.1 of this handbook.

[2] See also Sect. 2.3 of this handbook.

Another major step was the 'IIA on Better Law-Making' of 13 April 2016, which clarified the conduct of trilogues and emphasised transparency, accountability and accessibility of trilogue documentation by introducing extended provisions regarding disclosure, the content of negotiating mandates and reporting obligations (European Commission, European Parliament, Council of the European Union, 2016, title VI). Although trilogues remain informal and are not publicly announced, mandates and meeting dates must be uploaded to the EP's internal trilogue portal and the General Secretariat of the Council's electronic record-keeping and coordination service called 'Greffe'. These corresponding intranet systems allow for central documentation of mandates, agendas and short summaries or internal notes of the meetings and consolidated texts, such as the so-called four-column document.

3 The Trilogue Explained: From Technical Drafting to Political Agreement

Tripartite meetings take place at various stages of the OLP, involving different institutional actors and serving distinct purposes depending on the phase of negotiation. The trilogue serves to facilitate early consensus-building, resolve technical ambiguities and maintain legislative momentum across institutional boundaries. Negotiations in the trilogue are mandate-based and conducted within an informal but structured and routinised framework, despite being embedded within the formal stages of the OLP.

The trilogue process unfolds into a pre-legislation phase, including the adoption of the negotiation mandate in the EP and the Council and the trilogue negotiations, ranging from technical-level consultations in interinstitutional technical meetings (ITMs) to high-level political negotiation rounds (see Fig. 2). Understanding this division of labour is essential for assessing institutional influence and accountability within the EU's legislative process.

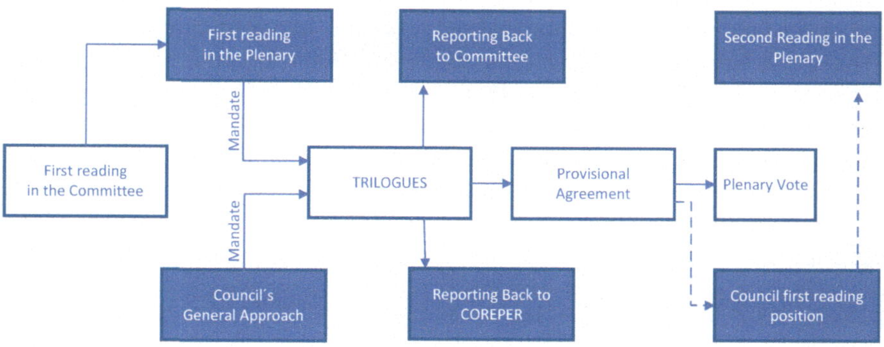

Fig. 2 Different steps leading to a first-reading agreement (own drawing, European Parliament, 2024a, p. 51)

Each phase plays a specific role fulfilling distinct functions and exhibiting varying degrees of influence over the final legislative outcome—ensuring both technical precision and political consensus in the legislative process. Although political trilogues retain formal authority over final compromises, the technical level exercises significant de facto decision-making power, especially on less controversial or highly technical files.

Understanding the interaction between both levels is essential for a full account of legislative power in the EU. Each institution, in accordance with its internal rules, designates its participants for meetings in distinct phases (see Fig. 3).

As the initiator of legislative proposals, the Commission maintains a continuous and strategically adaptive presence throughout all phases of trilogue negotiations. Serving as an indispensable procedural actor, it exerts influence through its informal

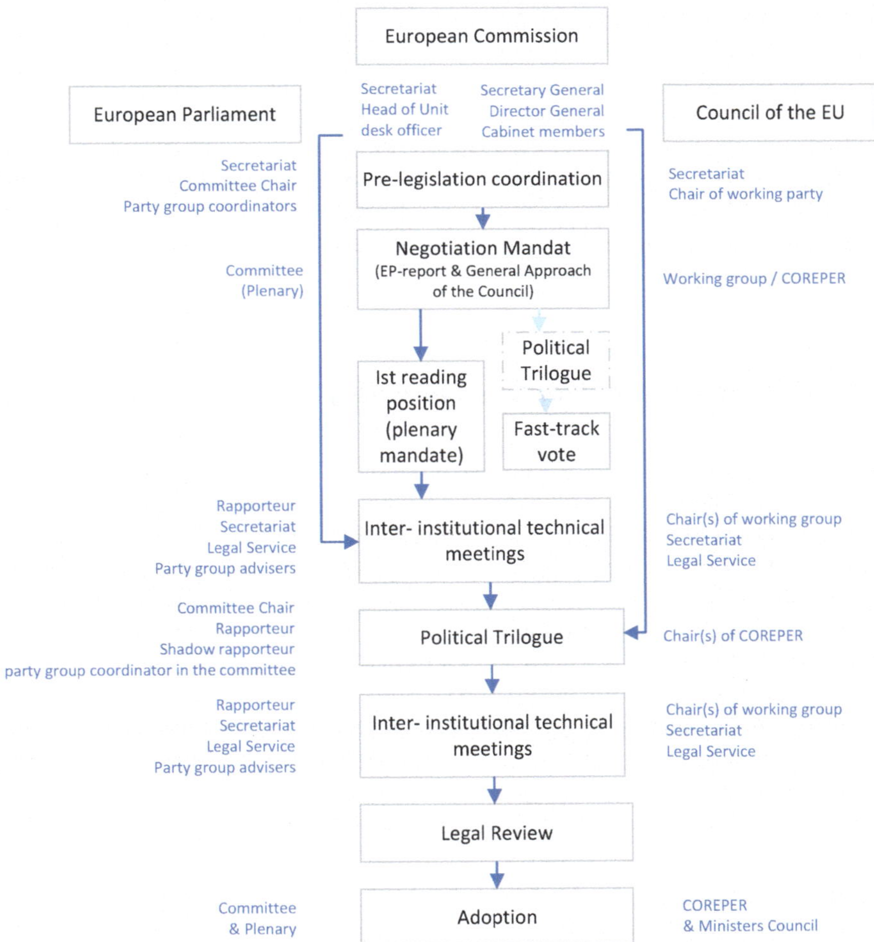

Fig. 3 Actors of the trilogue procedure (own drawing)

authority, legal expertise and drafting competence. Within ITMs, the Commission acts as a legal-technical coordinator. Its active presence helps ensure that the final legislative act is not only politically viable, but also legally sound, technically feasible and strategically aligned with the Union's broader objectives. The Commission often takes the lead in formulating compromise proposals or revising legal language to bridge gaps between the co-legislators. Its contributions carry weight not only because of its legal and policy expertise, but also because it is generally regarded as a neutral broker. The Commission's delegation in trilogue meetings typically includes technical staff from the lead DG, often accompanied by representatives from the Legal Service and the Secretariat-General (SECGEN), especially in cases involving cross-cutting political issues or interinstitutional sensitivities. The SECGEN ensures that the Commission speaks with one voice by preparing internal briefings. It does so by aligning with the various DGs through internal 'synchronisation meetings' as part of the Inter-Service Consultation (ISC), which serves to harmonise institutional positions and prepare the Commission's input for the upcoming trilogue sessions.[3] Moreover, the SECGEN acts as a critical interface with the cabinets of Commissioners, channelling political guidance into the technical preparation (European Commission, 2024; Brandsma et al., 2021, p. 4).

This chapter provides a detailed analysis of the four phases of the trilogue process as a core yet informal mechanism within the EU's legislative architecture. By focusing on the interplay between institutional actors and their respective mandates, the chapter elucidates how coordination practices and procedural adaptations shape legislative outcomes.

3.1 The Pre-trilogue Mandate Formation

Following the submission of a legislative proposal by the Commission, both the EP and the Council appoint their respective negotiating teams and formally adopt negotiation mandates to provide political legitimacy and institutional coherence during the trilogue process. These mandates guide negotiators while discussing and negotiation policy proposals at interinstitutional talks by defining each institution's political priorities and outlining red lines and areas of flexibility. According to Rule 72 of the EP's RoP, a committee must adopt a formal mandate before entering trilogue negotiations (European Parliament, 2025).

On the parliamentary side, it is the so-called EP report,[4] adopted at the first reading, which serves as the substantive mandate authorising the rapporteur and the negotiation teams to seek a compromise with the Council within the agreed positions (European Parliament, 2025, Rule 60/4 and 61). The mandate includes a draft

[3] See also Chap. 17 of this handbook.

[4] Database on EP-reports (last accessed 21. July 2025): https://www.europarl.europa.eu/committees/en/documents/interinstitutional-negotiations.

legislative resolution on whether the legislative proposal may be accepted, rejected or amended. This comes with an explanatory statement by the rapporteur. If the committee responsible decides to propose amendments (AMD) and the plenary adopts them, the report will also include the amended proposal. AMDs express specific changes to legislative wording, such as adding, deleting or replacing clauses or articles. While AMDs are often very precise textual proposals, the mandate frequently allows for interpretive flexibility. It provides, for instance, 'room for manoeuvre' when compromises are necessary. Nonetheless, politically sensitive or majority-approved AMDs are typically considered red lines.

It is the rapporteur's team who proposes the text of the mandate, which integrates input from shadow rapporteurs and party group coordinators. The proposed mandate is usually issued by the parliamentary committee responsible. This decision must be announced at the start of the next plenary session. Members or political groups representing at least the medium threshold or any committee that has submitted an opinion under Rule 56 may request an additional plenary vote (Rule 61) though such challenges are rarely successful. Between 2019 and 2024, 187 mandates were adopted at committee level, 20 were challenged in plenary (none successfully) and 93 mandates were approved directly by plenary vote, bypassing the committee (European Parliament, 2024a, p. 23). For politically sensitive files, additional approval is required from either the Conference of Committee Chairs or the Conference of Presidents.

The Council's negotiation mandate is developed through a tiered process: technical working groups draft initial proposals, which are then consolidated by COREPER into the so-called General Approach of the Council.[5] The General Approach serves as a basis for the Council position, though mandates may also derive from informal consensus among Member States (Council of the EU, 2025, para 3). This mandate outlines the Council's red lines, areas of flexibility and specific instructions for the rotating presidency. Although the presidency leads negotiations, it remains at any time accountable to COREPER, which must approve any major shift in position and determine whether talks proceed or require recalibration.

3.2 *Interinstitutional Technical Meetings*

The Interinstitutional Technical Meetings (ITMs) mark a pivotal yet often understated role in the OLP, as defined by Art. 289 and 294 of the TFEU. They play a preparatory and supportive role within the broader legislative negotiation process. Meetings may occur weekly during intensive negotiation phases, often concentrating on particular sections of a legislative proposal. These expert-level coordination and negotiations are primarily concerned with legal clarity, linguistic alignment and reconciling discrepancies across the institutions by drafting compromise

[5] See also Chap. 17 of this handbook.

amendments. These compromise texts include the widely used four-column format, annexes and tracked text revisions. The four-column document juxtaposes the original Commission proposal and the AMDs by the EP and the Council and includes any provisionally agreed compromise texts.

The nomination of the negotiation team of the EP falls under the authority of the relevant Committee Chair. First and foremost, it will be the rapporteur of the file to represent the EP's position in the negotiations in close coordination and support with policy advisers from relevant political groups. The shadow rapporteurs and committee chairs attend occasionally. During the trilogue, they get administrative assistance from the EP's Legal Service and from the Secretariat, particularly the Conciliation and Co-decision Unit (CODE) and the Coordination of legislation unit (CORDLEG) (EP's RoP, Rule 71; Greenwood & Roederer-Rynning, 2019). The Secretariat prepares position documents, manages deadlines and facilitates legal and procedural coordination. After each trilogue, the team reports back to the committee and political group coordinators. Internal coordination is maintained through regular 'shadow meetings', where political parties align on strategies and compromise options.

The negotiation team of the Council is led by the attaché of the rotating presidency who chairs the relevant Council working group and includes legal advisers and technical staff from the Directorate for Interinstitutional Relations of the General Secretariat of the Council (European Union, 2016, p. 20; Council of the EU, 2025, Annex V). These officials serve as the primary technical negotiators, defending national positions on specific provisions, revising text line by line and regularly reporting back to their national liaison officers in their ministry.

During ITMs, the Commission serves as a bridge between the EP and the Council, especially when it comes to legally or technically intricate matters. As the originator of the legislative proposal, the Commission acts as both a facilitator and technical authority, helping the co-legislators reconcile their differing positions and find workable compromises on complex and often sensitive issues. It provides expert interpretation of the initial proposal and is regularly asked by both institutions to clarify intentions and contextual meanings or to substantiate legal coherence. The Commission is primarily represented by the head of unit and legal experts from the relevant DGs, who have been responsible for drafting the legislative proposal. In case of sensitive files, the Commission's team may also include representatives of the SECGEN and the cabinet of Commissioners. It is the so-called Interinstitutional Relations Group (GRI) which prepares the position of the Commission on files being negotiated (European Parliament, 2024a, p. 52).

Although these actors operate under institutional mandates, they enjoy limited discretion and often defer unresolved items to the political level. It is their primary responsibility to align legislative drafts on technocratic or less contentious issues, ensuring terminological coherence and preparing ground for political decision-making by resolving basic discrepancies (European Union, 2016, pp. 22–23). The influence of ITMs extends beyond mere technical adjustments. They precede or accompany political trilogues and are often iterative. By resolving complex legal and linguistic issues early in the legislative process, they effectively shape the scope and content of the compromise text. While it can significantly frame the options available for political decision-making, no actor at this level has the authority to formally conclude an agreement. All outcomes remain provisional and subject to endorsement by the political trilogue. As stated in Rule 75 of the EP's RoP, after each negotiation round, the head of the parliamentary delegation and the assigned rapporteur are obliged to inform the competent committee or its coordinators on the state of interinstitutional talks and elaborated compromises. In this way, ITMs enhance the efficiency and quality of the legislative process, ensuring that political decision-makers can focus on core strategic choices, supported by a legally coherent and operationally sound foundation. Standard legislative files may entail approximately 10–15 negotiation meetings; most of them are conducted at the technical level. Although in the early years most coordination occurred at the political level, today an estimated 70% of the final compromise text is already settled during the ITMs while the political trilogue remains decisive for core compromises (Roederer-Rynning & Greenwood, 2015, p. 1154).

3.3 *Political Trilogue*

The political trilogue meets less often than the ITMs but carries decisive authority to resolve competing policy priorities that cannot be resolved through technical reasoning alone. As such, political trilogues exert a significantly greater influence on the final content of legislative acts, frequently determining the overall direction and brokering on compromises and/or trade-offs.[6] The topics addressed in the political trilogue go beyond a legal-technical clarification and touch on fundamental questions regarding the scope of the regulations and details of their implementation. Especially in case of directives, intense political negotiations are required, as the respective files need to be transposed into diverse domestic legal systems. This transposition imperative leads to greater political sensitivity in negotiations and a broader range of contested issues. Consequently, national ministry experts are more actively involved in shaping directive-related compromises, given their responsibility for domestic implementation. EP negotiators, however, focus more in detail on legal constraints and enforcement mechanisms.

In contrast to ITMs, political trilogues involve high-ranking representatives from the Council and EP, who are formally mandated to negotiate binding compromises. The negotiation teams are typically led by COREPER I from the current Council team presidency and the rapporteur from the EP. Both guide discussions within their institutions and seek to broker compromises among Member States within the Council and among various party groups and particular national party group delegations within the EP.

The EP is represented by a structured team of about 20 to 30 political actors, each playing a distinct role in shaping the institution's negotiation stance (Roederer-Rynning & Greenwood, 2015, p. 1155). The negotiation team is led by the

[6] See also Chap. 17 of this handbook.

rapporteur of the file, who is appointed by the committee members. As the main architect of the EP's position, the rapporteur drafts and defends the EP report, and holds very high influence—particularly when backed by broad political group support. Shadow rapporteurs from other political groups are also key players. They play a pivotal role in forging internal compromises within parliamentary committees and political groups prior to interinstitutional negotiations, thereby laying the groundwork for a cohesive majority position. The negotiation team is supported by its accredited assistants and policy advisors from the political groups and assisted by an 'administrative project team' including the secretariat of the committee and the legal service (European Parliament, 2017, para 4). Throughout the process, EP's negotiators regularly update the committee and political groups to ensure that the agreed direction remains within the mandate (European Parliament, 2024a, p. 84). Political group coordinators and advisers work behind the scenes to align negotiation strategies with their party group positions. Their medium to high influence depends on the political complexity of the file and the level of ideological divergence among groups. Together, these actors ensure that the EP's position is both politically robust and strategically coherent. The committee chair oversees the procedural aspects and may intervene when strategic or institutional concerns arise. While less central to the detailed negotiations, their influence is moderate but can increase in politically sensitive files. Once a tentative compromise text with the Council has been concluded, it has to be presented to the committee responsible which finally needs to endorse the provisional agreement (European Parliament, 2025, Rule 74).

On the side of the Council, the negotiation team is completed by a coordinated network of one to ten actors with varying degrees of authority and influence (Roederer-Rynning & Greenwood, 2015, p. 1155). Representatives from the rotating presidency of the Council conduct trilogue discussions and serve as political brokers both within the Council and in interinstitutional dialogues. After each trilogue, results must be communicated by the negotiation teams to the COREPER and, subsequently, Member State's administration. COREPER closely monitors the negotiations, validating major decisions or adjusting the presidency's mandate if needed. Given the complexity of the files, the negotiation team is supported by the chair of the relevant working group and by the Council secretariat and its legal service.

The Commission is represented by approximately ten members, consisting of directors or deputy directors and head of unit from the relevant DGs. Furthermore, cabinet members and representatives from the SECGEN are often involved in high-profile or politically sensitive files, particularly those requiring coordination across multiple DGs (Roederer-Rynning & Greenwood, 2015, p. 1155). Their role is to ensure coherence with the Commission's overall political strategy and to convey political signals when needed. At times, when negotiations between EP and Council reach an impasse, the Commission may step in to help broker a solution. In such moments, the responsible Commissioner or Vice-President may engage directly, leveraging their political authority to facilitate a breakthrough.

Within the trilogue, decisions are made entirely by consensus, without any formal voting procedures or records of votes. Instead, approval is typically signalled discreetly, often orally or through a simple hand gesture in small negotiation settings. If objections are raised, discussions continue or are deferred to future meetings. If the negotiators manage to agree on a compromise text, this interinstitutional consensus needs to be transformed into politically sustainable outcomes by being delegated back once more to the ITMs for final linguistic and legal refinement (see Fig. 3). Finally, the agreement—tentative, yet technically robust compromise texts—is then forwarded to the political level for endorsement before becoming law across the 27 Member States.

3.4 Adoption of Trilogue Agreements

Once a provisional agreement is reached in trilogue by unanimous consensus, the final step is its formal adoption by the EP and Council. First, it is the chair of the COREPER, who transmits the Council's conditional readiness to endorse the compromise to the chair of the responsible parliamentary committee via a formal letter. A copy of this correspondence is simultaneously sent to the coordinator in the lead DG of the Commission. This communication outlines the substance of the agreement, typically presented as amendments to the Commission's original proposal—documented in a four-column document. The rapporteur in the EP adjusts their draft report accordingly. Within the EP, it is the lead committee and within the Council it is the COREPER, where the compromise text awaits to be endorsed through a vote. These votes ensure that formal bodies retain control over the process, while the actual content is shaped informally through consensual negotiations during the trilogues. Finally, after alignment in both institutions, the Commission ensures legal-technical finalisation.

3.5 Conciliation Procedure

If no agreement is reached even after the second reading, the process enters its most formalised phase in the third reading: the *conciliation procedure* (Art. 251/24–38 TFEU). The Commission is expected to deliver its formal opinion on the EP's second-reading amendments within 3 weeks after the negative vote and may propose compromise texts to facilitate convergence between the institutions' positions.

Unlike informal trilogues, conciliation meetings follow a more structured process, with formal agendas and some degree of minute-taking. This adds transparency and makes institutional roles easier to track. Although the meetings are not fully public, certain documents—such as progress reports or summaries—are included in the official legislative file. Each institution selects its 27 representatives for the Conciliation Committee based on its internal procedures and defines a clear negotiation mandate. The EP delegation is typically chaired by the Vice-President of the EP responsible for conciliation and accompanied by committee chairs, rapporteurs and a proportional number of Members of Parliament (MEPs) reflecting the political composition in the plenary. The Council is represented by the COREPER from each Member State, chaired by the Council presidency.

If a joint text is agreed, it undergoes legal-linguistic finalisation and is formally approved either during a meeting or via an exchange of letters between the co-chairs. The final joint text is then transmitted to the presidents of the EP and the presidency of the Council for adoption. A conciliation agreement is adopted only if both institutions endorse a brokered compromise within 6 weeks (extendable to eight). If no agreement is reached, the act fails. Whereas conciliation once functioned as the final institutional stage for resolving interinstitutional disagreements, its practical significance has diminished considerably. Third-reading procedures, which involved the formal convening of the Conciliation Committee, accounted for approximately 28% of legislative acts during the fifth parliamentary term. This share dropped to around 5% in the sixth term and fell below 2% in the seventh term and almost none in the eighth and ninth term (see Fig. 1).

4 Summary and Outlook

Over the past three decades, trilogues have undergone a profound transformation from an ad hoc coordination mechanism into a routinised and structurally embedded practice within the OLP. Despite their lack of formal codification in the treaties, trilogues have become indispensable in mitigating legislative gridlock, enhance procedural efficiency and foster interinstitutional cohesion. This convergence of expertise and executive decision-making has proven effective in advancing early agreements—today achieved in approximately 86% of legislative files during the first reading (see Fig. 1).

However, the efficiency gain has weakened institutional accountability and contributes to a marginalisation of plenary deliberation (Brandsma, 2019; Brandsma et al., 2021; Burns, 2013; Rasmussen & Reh, 2013; Reh et al., 2013; Kulger Dionigi & Koop, 2017). Especially legislative actors from smaller states and smaller party delegations face a limited ability to shape decision-making in the trilogue procedure. It is the management of legislative texts and informational asymmetries that serve as a critical source of intra-institutional power, reinforcing the strategic role and institutional primacy of technocrats as well as rapporteurs and the Council presidency during the trilogue. The influence of technocrats has substantially grown in both scope and importance, as they are now responsible for settling an estimated 70% of the final legislative text in ITMs prior to political-level negotiations (Roederer-Rynning & Greenwood, 2015). These sessions are often dominated by policy advisers, legal services and secretariat staff who operate with high degrees of specialisation and continuity but without public visibility. The influence of rapporteurs and the Council presidency is manifested merely in their control over drafting, agenda-setting and the timing of compromises, often without broader deliberative input or plenary scrutiny (Roederer-Rynning & Greenwood, 2015; Brandsma et al., 2021).

The informal structure of trilogues further raises concerns about the lack of transparency and traceability of EU lawmaking due to behind-the-door negotiations which insulates decision-makers from external oversight. A central challenge lies in rebalancing the increasing consolidation of legislative authority within a technocratic-executive nexus—a structure where legal and policy experts closely collaborate with a narrow circle of politically empowered negotiators, particularly rapporteurs in the EP, COREPER representatives in the Council and senior Commission officials. Several initiatives since the IIA of 2010 and its revision with the IIA on Better Law-Making of 2016 (Title IV) and a General Court ruling of 2018 (Case T-540/15, 2018)[7] have enhanced access to consolidated documents and increased reporting obligations, many meetings still remain unannounced, mandates are only published selectively and negotiation records are still informal or internal. ITMs, as highlighted by Jérémie Zeitoun in this handbook,[8] do not fall under this publicity and reporting obligation and remain beyond any scrutiny despite being responsible for about 70% of the final text.

In conclusion, the legitimacy of trilogue negotiations hinges on their procedural recalibration. Reforms should aim to render trilogues more transparent, inclusive and accountable to the citizens in whose name EU legislation is made. This includes codifying clearer standards for document disclosure—such as the systematic publication of four-column documents, agendas and legislative calendars—and strengthening committee-level oversight. Only through such institutional adjustments can trilogues better align with democratic principles while maintaining their role as a core instrument of efficient EU lawmaking.

References

Brandsma, G. J. (2019). Transparency of EU informal trilogues through public feedback in the European Parliament: Promise unfulfilled. *Journal of European Public Policy, 26*(10), 1464–1483.

Brandsma, G. J., Greenwood, J., Ripoll Servent, A., & Roederer-Rynning, C. (2021). Inside the black box of trilogues. *Journal of European Public Policy, 28*(1), 1–9.

Burns, C. (2013). Consensus and compromise become ordinary but at what cost? A critical analysis of the impact of the changing norms of codecision upon European Parliament committees. *Journal of European Public Policy, 20*(7), 988–1005.

Council of the EU. (2025). *Rules of Procedure*. Council Decision 2009/937/EU. https://eur-lex.europa.eu/legal-content/EN/TXT/?uri=celex:32009D0937

[7] A General Court ruling of 2018 (Case T-540/15, 2018) affirmed the applicability of Regulation 1049/2001—regarding public access to EP, Council and Commission documents—to trilogue documents.

[8] See also Chap. 17 of this handbook.

European Commission. (2024). *Rules of Procedure of the Commission*. Consolidated version of 06.12.2024. https://eur-lex.europa.eu/eli/proc_rules/2000/3614/oj/eng

European Commission, European Parliament, Council of the European Union. (2016, April 13). *Interinstitutional Agreement on Better Law-Making (2016/L 213/1). Official Journal of the European Union, L 123/1*. https://eur-lex.europa.eu/eli/agree_interinstit/2016/512/oj/eng, last accessed 2025/04/19.

European Parliament. (2017). *Code of Conduct for negotiating in the context of the ordinary legislative procedures. Conference of Presidents on 28*. September 2017. https://www.europarl.europa.eu/cmsdata/214480/C2_EN.pdf

European Parliament. (2024a). *Handbook on the Ordinary Legislative Procedure. A guide to how the European Parliament co-legislates. Directorate-General for Internal Policies*. https://www.europarl.europa.eu/cmsdata/293152/Handbook%20on%20the%20Ordinary%20legislative%20procedure_January%202025.pdf

European Parliament. (2024b). *Activity Report: Developments and Trends in the Ordinary Legislative Procedure, 9th Parliamentary Term (2019–2024). Directorate for Legislative and Committee Coordination*. https://www.europarl.europa.eu/cmsdata/289662/1305846_EN.pdf

European Parliament. (2025). *Rules of Procedure of the European Parliament. 10th Parliamentary Term*. https://www.europarl.europa.eu/rules/rules20240716/Rules20240716_EN.pdf

European Union. (2016). *Guide to the Ordinary Legislative Procedure. Public Information Service of the General Secretariat of the Council*. https://op.europa.eu/en/publication-detail/-/publication/fccde0b0-23cc-11e6-86d0-01aa75ed71a1/

Greenwood, J., & Roederer-Rynning, C. (2019). Taming Trilogues the EU'S lawmaking process in a comparative perspective. In O. Costa (Ed.), *The European Parliament in times of EU crisis. European administrative governance*. Palgrave Macmillan. https://doi.org/10.1007/978-3-319-97391-3_6

Kulger Dionigi, M., & Koop, C. (2017, July). *Investigation of informal trilogue negotiations since the Lisbon Treaty—Added value, lack of transparency and possible democratic deficit, Study for the European Economic and Social Committee*. Retrieved April 13, 2025, from https://www.eesc.europa.eu/sites/default/files/files/qe-01-17-783-en-n.pdf

Maurer, A. (2003). The Legislative Powers and Impact of the European Parliament. *Journal of Common Market Studies, 41(2), 227–247.*

Rasmussen, A., & Reh, C. (2013). The consequences of concluding codecision early: Trilogues and intra-institutional bargaining success. *Journal of European Public Policy, 20*(7), 1006–1024.

Reh, C., Héritier, A., Bressanelli, E., & Koop, C. (2013). The informal politics of legislation: Explaining secluded decision making in the European Union. *Comparative Political Studies, 46*(9), 1112–1142.

Roederer-Rynning, C., & Greenwood, J. (2015). The culture of trilogues. *Journal of European Public Policy, 22*(8), 1148–1165.

Bernhard Zeilinger is Head of the Department of Political Science at the University of Applied Sciences BFI Vienna. He also lectures at several renowned institutions, including the University of Vienna and the Vienna University of Economics and Business. Zeilinger's scholarly work is situated at the intersection of political theory and European studies, with recent research addressing the transformation of statehood and democratic governance in the context of European integration.

Bargaining and Practical Perspective in Trilogues: Power Behind the Scenes

Jérémie Zeitoun

Abstract Trilogues have become the new normal of EU lawmaking. The limited formalisation of these interinstitutional contacts during trilogues opens the door to flexible and innovative working arrangements. These, in turn, are marked by power plays inherent to the transactional nature of trilogues. This chapter deciphers how different negotiation techniques are mobilised throughout trilogues. It outlines how informal talks are influenced by factors such as institutional loyalty, institutional pride and personal links, leading to agreements not always balanced but in which co-legislators should recognise themselves. Power games between institutions and within them can be witnessed all along the process, until the very last provision is agreed.

Keywords Trilogues · EU Lawmaking · Interinstitutional technical meetings · Compromise making · Power games · Rapporteur · Interinstitutional contacts

1 Introduction

Some 415 files, i.e. an average of 83 per year, have been adopted in compliance with the Ordinary Legislative Procedure (OLP) over the 5 years of the previous parliamentary term 2019–2024 (European Parliament, 2025)—86% of them via a first reading agreement, outlining the importance of the trilogue phase. These informal

J. Zeitoun (✉)
Attaché at the Permanent Representation of Luxembourg to the EU, Brussels, Belgium
e-mail: Jeremie.zeitoun@mae.etat.lu

G. Füricht-Fiegl et al. (eds.), *Handbook on EU Law-making*, Professional Practice in Governance and Public Organizations, https://doi.org/10.1007/978-3-032-16559-6_17

talks are not codified by the EU Treaties, yet they emerged as the standard way of EU law-marking and became the institutional norm.[1]

Trilogues are described in a vague interinstitutional agreement, using undefined terms, suggesting appropriate contacts between institutions to clear the way for the adoption of the act concerned at an early stage of the procedure (European Commission, Parliament, & Council, 2007). Institutions praise the trilogue procedure for demonstrating its vitality and flexibility. The numbers mentioned above do confirm the vitality of the process. When it comes to its flexibility, the trilogue system is largely into the hands of the institutions' leadership. Concrete means of running appropriate contacts are left to the discretion of EU institutions.

In this chapter, we will discuss how the wide margin of interpretation given to policymakers in a trilogue process leaves the door open to innovative ways of interinstitutional interactions, to power plays and bargaining strategies.

2 Getting Ready to Bargain

Power games apply in the very early phase of trilogues. We will discuss the strategic importance to define a negotiation agenda and to operate a distinction between technical and political matters.

2.1 Negotiation Boxes

Submitting a proposal for the trilogue agenda is a prerogative of the inviting institution that should therefore make a strategic decision as to the topics and the order in which it proposes to include them on the draft agenda. The inviting party may consider that an issue is not mature enough to be discussed in trilogues. That can be the case when an issue is not so important for the EP but bears essential political priority for the Council: in such a case, the rapporteur may be inclined to keep this bargaining asset in its sleeve for a later trilogue. On the contrary, rapporteurs may decide to include on the agenda an issue they intend to close as soon as possible, to avoid internal pressure coming from other political groups within the EP delegation, leaving them little time to get organised and build a coalition against them. Setting the agenda is a delicate exercise: One may want to include some elements on which a provisional agreement could be reached, giving the impression that negotiations are moving on, while keeping the most sensitive issues for the final deal.

The running order is also an indication of power plays. The rapporteur may suggest placing last on the agenda a topic that bears the most importance for them, so that EP concessions made on all previous elements would pay back when discussing

[1] See also Chap. 16 in this handbook.

this very last agenda item. This strategy can also be followed to discreetly add specific provisions at the very end of a long meeting, when exhaustion kicks in and when negotiators do not want secondary issues to form an obstacle to the agreement within reach (Turmes, 2017, p. 32).

2.2 *Technical or Political?*

Trilogue meetings are held at senior level to negotiate political issues, while technical provisions are left to interinstitutional technical meetings (ITMs). However, the distinction between political and technical aspects is not always clear-cut (Del Monte, 2025). It may even be very controversial and does not necessarily reflect the importance of things. Elements considered political are rather those considered the easiest to decide on for non-expert policymakers. That is typically the case for numbers, for example targets and dates. In most cases, an agreement is reached at ITM level on a very broad majority of the legislative provisions discussed during sessions aimed at pre-cooking a maximum number of agreements (Egendal, 2025). Therefore, ITMs represent a fundamental, yet largely unknown, element of trilogues. In practice, they constitute the place where most of the detailed negotiations take place, and where the main drafting is done, playing an increasingly pivotal role in the legislative process.[2] Since ITMs are not trilogue meetings as strictly defined, rules related to publicity, distribution of documents, mandate formation and reporting do not apply. It is difficult to know where and when the meetings take place, who takes part and what is being discussed, elements deemed indispensable for stakeholders to participate in the decision-making process (Cabral, 2020). ITMs rather recreate a situation of closed door, secluded scene, away from the public pressure of journalists and stakeholders. While trilogues can be attended by about a hundred participants, ITMs gather way fewer negotiators, allowing for more open discussions. Therefore, labelling an element as technical rather than political is a way to conduct discussion in an even less formal format than trilogue meetings.

3 The Transactional Nature of Trilogues in Practice

Trilogues are an iterative process, involving constant give and take. It is illustrated by the following mantra, *nothing is agreed until everything is agreed*, heard dozens of times throughout trilogues whenever an institution is about to make a concession. Indeed, trilogues largely follow a transactional approach. We will see in this section how the substantive value of arguments is sometimes secondary to the discussions guided by the dynamics of the negotiation.

[2] See also Chap. 16 in this handbook.

3.1 Institutional Loyalty

The overall objective of the trilogue is to make some concessions and to push the other institution to also concede on some elements on an allegedly equal value, obtaining a balanced deal. Therefore, the most important part of the power play is to assess which elements are of value for the other institution, while keeping yours unknown to the other party.

On the Council side, the presidency may decide on its own to initiate interinstitutional negotiations at any stage of the procedure. In most cases, the presidency does so after obtaining a general approach in a Council meeting (or a partial general approach on a block of articles of the draft legislation) that equals a mandate to start trilogues. Between trilogues, the presidency may also seek a revised mandate but is not bound to do so. The presidency may consider that it has a clear enough vision of the balance of powers and where flexibility of the Member States lies, making it unnecessary to seek a revised mandate. In most cases though, the presidency comes back to COREPER to seek a revised mandate from the delegations. Like for a general approach, there is no formal vote on the mandate neither in COREPER nor in the Council. The presidency must *feel the room* and consider that guidance given during the exchange of views is solid enough to constitute a mandate. Therefore, there is little public indication on whether the mandate is weak or strong. Individual Member States can be tempted not to be loyal to the general approach and push their own national positions towards like-minded Members of the European Parliament (MEPs), therefore increasing pressure on the Council presidency to deviate from their mandate. This approach is sometimes fully transparent: the moment a general approach is reached in COREPER or in the Council, some Member States may issue a declaration stating they do not oppose the general approach for the sake of compromise but will deploy efforts to correct flaws during trilogues (see an example in the box below).

Member States Statement Ahead of Trilogues

Statement from Belgium, France, Germany, Ireland, Luxembourg, the Netherlands annexed to the minutes of the meeting of the Council on the October 25, 2022.

Today the Council adopted, at a qualified majority and after numerous rounds of negotiations, a compromise position on the proposal for a directive on [...].

Belgium, France, Germany, Ireland, Luxembourg, The Netherlands, underline that the ambition [...] still need to be substantially increased in the further steps to come. [...].

We call the co-legislator to follow this principle during the trilogue in the follow-up of the negotiations and we stand ready to pursue the negotiations with a view to improve the ambition of the directive.

Such efforts may also be less transparent and lead to a fragilisation of the Council mandate. Individual Member States may side with the EP to obtain a result more favourable to their position. They may also try to break the EP negotiation team on a national basis, attempting to convince MEPs that an issue is of national interest and requires a deviation from the line of their political group. For a Member State, this strategy is easier to implement with MEPs from the same political colour as the government in place. Also, the way the mandate was given in the EP plays a major role. Where the mandate was approved by a plenary vote in the EP and where amendments were put to vote, the analysis of roll-call votes delivers precious indications on which MEPs are more likely to break institutional loyalty. It also helps assessing the strength of the mandate. A large majority with strong voting cohesion within parliamentary groups reinforces the rapporteur's position during trilogues. Conversely, a slim majority and weak voting cohesion within parliamentary groups demonstrate institutional divide, allowing Member States to play national delegations against each other within parliamentary groups and create extra pressure on the rapporteur during trilogues.

The objective of the EP negotiation team is to understand the dynamics within the Council and see which national interests are at stake and how strong the Council mandate is. MEPs and political groups can also mobilise external forces to increase pressure on the Council. This strategy implies to establish trusted relations with journalists, civil society organisations and businesses and elaborate a common strategy of influence. For a greater chance of success, these alliances can be declined on a national basis: a government will always be more sensitive to a national press campaign than to a Brussels-based event.

Overall, it is easier for a Member State to shift the position of an individual MEP than the opposite. Since the ability to break institutional loyalty is asymmetrical, the balance of power tends to be more favourable to the Council.

3.2 Institutional Pride

Reaching an agreement is not always enough to trigger institutional pride by itself but the agreement should be balanced and each institution should be able to recognise its influence on it. Giving the impression that a negotiation was lengthy, exhausting and took the whole night makes it more likely that the result will be accepted and considered as the only possible outcome. Some trilogues may even be artificially prolonged to reinforce this impression.

One way to reach an agreement that is either balanced or at least perceived as such is to focus on items that can easily be divided in two, such as figures and dates. In those cases, the numerical concessions made by each institution may look similar, allowing both the EP and the Council to show institutional pride. In a trilogue held in 2022, the mandate of the Council was to set a 40% binding target on a given policy objective for 2030. The EP mandate was to set the target at 45%. During the last trilogue sessions, institutions agreed on a 42.5% binding target, hereby applying a simple mathematical operation to reach the average, leaving the impression that a fair compromise is located precisely on the middle of the way. This binding target was complemented by a 45% aspirational target.

A similar approach can be followed to agree on dates of entry into force, where the EP tends to claim reduced periods of time while the Council's objective is to leave more time for public administrations to be compliant. Another way of saving face is to give the allegedly losing side a compensation that looks ambitious—but sometimes is not. One means is to enshrine a review clause in the legislation. Another one is to add a recital that suggests that the narrative borne by one institution is embedded in the legislation. A third one is to annex a Commission statement to the legislation. However, neither a review clause or a recital nor a Commission statement has the same legal effects as a text included in the operative provisions of the legislation. A recital has a declarative value only. A review clause is conditioned to the good will of the Commission to exercise its prerogative of legislative initiative. And a Commission statement is a mere declaration of intent, equally conditioned to the good will of the Commission with an even lower impact since it is annexed to the legislation and not included in it. Despite these considerations, all three instruments send a political signal, create hooks to hold Commission accountable at a later stage and are instrumental to unlock negotiations. They tend to work better to gain support of the EP than to gain support of the Council since, among co-legislators, the EP is the most politicised and least technical one, more prone to be satisfied with a good narrative easily translatable into general messaging.

Another demonstration of the institutional pride lies with the rotating nature of the Council presidency. A six-month period is relatively short in the scale of EU lawmaking. Therefore, the presidency tends to deploy its best efforts to conclude negotiations on the largest possible number of files to extend their merit. The rotating nature of the Council presidency is a powerful factor to bring negotiations to a swift close. It can be easier to close a file with a presidency for which the subject matter is important rather than the contrary. Having a friendly presidency in charge can represent a happy coincidence for a rapporteur (Turmes, 2017, p. 48). The magnitude of the pride of EU diplomats chairing trilogues, in general Permanent Representatives or their deputies (DPRs), tends to correlate with the number of trilogues they held and the number of agreements they brokered. Although this factor may play in favour of the EP, an institution that should in principle not be subject to time pressure, the reality shows that at the end of a presidency, trilogues are not necessarily more favourable to the EP and that the EP is equally pushed to make large concessions. Some EU diplomats went as far as to hold several trilogues at the same time, walking in and out different rooms, running parallel negotiations on different topics. The most blatant example is the one of a DPR chairing up to five trilogues on the same day.

Negotiation Agenda—November 2023

List of trilogues chaired by the DPR—November 2023—As communicated by the Presidency on 6 November 2023 and updated on 14 November (Mertens notes).

6 November SoHo.
7 November Ecodesign.
7 November Hydrogen and Gas (Regulation).
8 November Population and housing statistics.
8 November CRA.
8 November eIDas.
9 November Platform Work Directive.
9 November Nature Restoration Law.
13 November CRMA.
13 November IEA.
14 November Lead and Diisocyanates.
14 November TEN-T.
14 November Methane.
15 November Short-term rentals.
15 November Industrial Designs.
16 November SES2+.
16 November EMD.
16 November REMIT (tbc).
16 November Waste shipments.
21 November 883 (tbc).
21 November Urban Wastewater Treatment.
21 November WEEE.
22 November Due Diligence.
23 November Multiple vote shared structures.
27 November Hydrogen and Gas Package (Regulation and Directive).
28 November Platform Work Directive.
28 November SoHo.
28 November Equality bodies.
28 November Industrial Emissions.
28 November Carbon Removal Certification.
29 November SMEI.
29 November EMFA.
30 November CSA+.
30 November CRA.

(Acronyms are not expanded since they are not relevant but rather here to illustrate the organisation of the negotiation agenda and the variety of the topics covered)

3.3 The Commission as Honest Broker

The Commission's mandate in trilogues is to preserve the integrity of its original proposal and to facilitate an agreement between co-legislators[3] and describes how their influence is high, stemming from their drafting authority, subject-matter expertise and the Commission's institutional role as initiator and guardian of the treaties. Commission is often described in the trilogue process as an honest broker. However, it is not rare to see the Commission openly siding with one of the co-legislators. For years, the Commission was perceived as the strongest ally of the EP during trilogues, allegedly teaming up in favour of stronger European integration and greater harmonisation to oppose the approach of the Council more protective of the capacity for Member States to adopt national decisions better fitting their specific national circumstances. This pattern has become decreasingly obvious over time, with the EP hosting an ever-greater share of Eurosceptic MEPs more prone to defend approaches based on national sovereignty.

In addition, the Commission is not a monolithic institution either. Internal power plays have an impact on how the trilogue is run. It is not rare to hear different directorate generals (DGs) expressing different opinions on a given legislation. Although trilogues are run by the lead DG, other DGs may also intervene and side with one of or both co-legislators to undermine the original Commission proposal on some critical elements. For example, tensions may frequently be observed between operational DGs designing a policy where competence is shared between the EU and the Member States, and the DG in charge of competition, keen to preserve their exclusive EU competence of state aid control, directly deriving from the treaty. Similarly, views from DGs in charge of the internal market and industrial policy such as DG GROW may critically diverge from those from DGs in charge of international trade (DG TRADE) exercising an exclusive EU competence.

3.4 Personal Links Matter

Working relationships between individuals involved in trilogues can have a substantial influence on the negotiation dynamics. Individuals working close to each other for hours along a lengthy trilogue process dragging over months end up developing personal relationships that favour or hinder deal making. These links can also stem from political affiliation, language or nationality. For example, that was the case for the trilogue related to a text negotiated in 2018, where the rapporteur was a Spaniard, with limited English proficiency.[4] It happened that Commission officials in charge of the file were either Spaniards or Spanish-speaking officials. The Commissioner in charge was Spanish. The EP official in charge of the file at the committee secretariat was Spanish. That combination created a personal proximity and a relationship of trust.

---

[3] See also Chap. 16 in this handbook.

[4] https://oeil.secure.europarl.europa.eu/oeil/en/procedure-file?reference=2016/0382(COD).

It can also happen that, in view of facilitating an agreement, in the middle of the night of the final trilogue, a small group of people gather in a separate room, possibly even in a location outside institutional premises like a restaurant, to hold discussions and make a deal, sidelining the rest of the negotiation team. Another example is related to trilogues held in 2025: the fact that the lead negotiator on the EP side was Polish and that the Council was led by the Polish presidency, both of them with the same political affiliation, helped a swift conclusion. It could also be the case that, on grounds of political affiliation, a Committee Chair and a rapporteur from the same political group deliberately prolong a final trilogue to obtain a result possibly more favourable to their own political force, although a comprehensive deal is within reach with a great likelihood to obtain a sufficient majority both in the EP and in the Council.

4 Success and Misfortunes of a Provisional Agreement

Due to the asymmetrical level of trilogue representation from the EP and Council side, a provisional agreement always entails a risk that it will not be approved by the respective chamber. In this section, we will see how negotiators can reduce this risk to the lowest possible level and discuss possible ways out.

4.1 Structural Uncertainty

The EP and the Council are not on an equal footing when it comes to measuring the acceptability of an agreement by a majority within their respective institution. Thanks to a comprehensive delegation composed of representatives of each parliamentary group, the EP can be reactive and agile during trilogue sessions and during ITMs. It is common practice that the chief EP negotiator asks for a break-out session and convenes a short meeting for the exclusive attendance of the members of the EP negotiation team to decide on the spot whether they can make a concession or accept a Council proposal. Although it is not an absolute guarantee of acceptability given the limited representativeness of shadow rapporteurs compared to their political group as a whole and given the very relative voting discipline in the EP, the risk of a future rejection is small.

In the Council, Member States representatives are not present during trilogues and the negotiating mandate granted by COREPER to the presidency ahead of the trilogue cannot be modified on the spot. Thus, the subtle art of closing a trilogue relates to the ability of a presidency to limit to its lowest possible level the degree of uncertainty that a qualified majority of Member States will be able to support the agreement. For that purpose, they regularly take stock of progress at COREPER level. However, these formal debriefings are not helpful on that matter and purely formal steps, usually made of generic statements (see example in the box below).

COREPER Debriefing from a Trilogue

Debriefing on 12 October 2023 (sent in writing by the Mertens channel and orally at a following COREPER).

'The third trilogue on the Directive [...] took place this morning at the premises of the Parliament in Brussels in a constructive atmosphere.

The co-legislators validated the progress made so far at the technical level. The institutions exchanged views and outlined their positions on the following elements of the trilogue, namely: [factual list of issues].

Negotiators moved closer to each other and potential avenues forward could be discerned on the points discussed during the trilogue. The technical level was tasked to further work on them in order to identify possible areas of compromise.

The next political trilogue will take place on 27 November.'

Therefore, the presidency usually tries to find means to keep national delegations very closely informed of the developments in trilogues and ITMs. When time allows, this is done through meetings of the Working Parties where Member States delegates are informed of trilogues progress, or through bilateral meetings. Most of the time however, especially during final open-end trilogues, that is done via informal phone calls, text messages and pictures of parts of printed documents shared via instant messaging applications. Some may argue that such uncertainty weakens the position of the Council compared to an agile parliamentary delegation. On the contrary, we can sustain this setting gives all latitude to the presidency to be inflexible and to reject any significant concession requested by the EP under the reason that their mandate cannot be changed.

4.2 A Deal Is a Deal?

Perceptions lead to believe that a negotiation is closed once a deal has been made in the early hours of the morning after a lengthy open-end trilogues and once senior policymakers reunite on a picture posted on social networks with a victory caption. However, the trilogue result clearly indicates that co-legislators reached what is called at this stage a provisional agreement. The nature of this provisional agreement tends to be blurry and even sometimes difficult to decipher. Indeed, fatigue can play a role and allow for factual mistakes, or for unintended concessions. It is not uncommon to see trilogue results in the form of handwritten notes on a piece of paper subsequently pictured by participants to keep track of it or handwritten annotations to the margins of a printed document. These notes may be approximate or even worse, ambiguous.

ITMs are convened, sometimes very shortly after the trilogue ended, to translate these notes into a consolidated legal text. When institutions have a different understanding of what has been agreed, it may lead to a sort of trilogue after the trilogue, where co-legislators fight to get their own interpretation of the agreement in the legal text. Powers games are still vivid during this period that may be very fast or drag over several weeks.

Based on the provisional agreement, the presidency reverts to COREPER under an agenda item entitled *Analysis of a compromise in view of an agreement.* This agenda point is generally purely formal, very brief and limited to counting which delegations cannot support the agreement. Only at this moment can national delegations and MEPs see the detailed provisions. The presidency inscribes such an item on the agenda when it is reasonably sure a qualified majority is reached. In case of doubts, the presidency usually withdraws the item from the COREPER agenda, even on a very short notice, to hold bilateral discussions and possibly, but very rarely, ask the EP to convene a new trilogue and reopen the provisional agreement.

On at least two recent occasions, one could witness attempts from the two largest Member States, Germany and France respectively, to rally support of other Member States for a blocking minority to oppose the adoption of the provisional agreement in COREPER and reverse a deal. On these two occasions, the adoption of the legislative act was delayed by several months. No new trilogue was formally convened but substantial changes to the provisional agreement were discretely introduced to satisfy those delegations. Power plays happen until the very last minute.

5 Conclusions

From several perspectives, trilogues are perceived as opaque and non-democratic. Some authors consider them at odds with standard norms of democratic practice and targets for public anxiety or easy targets for euro-sceptical narratives (Greenwood & Roederer-Rynning, 2019). However, these arrangements are effective, and their effectiveness is due to the wide flexibility given to lawmakers in organising their contacts. They lead to power games between institutions and within them all along the process, until the very last provision is agreed. Power games apply at all levels, both the political and the technical ones, with ITMs being an important element of the trilogue process. Institutions are not necessarily cohesive, and negotiators try to break institutional loyalty at any time. The transactional nature of the trilogue process does not necessarily lead to a balanced deal, but to a deal giving the impression of being balanced and in which both co-legislators can recognise themselves. Given the institutional structure, we can also state that the result is, in most cases, closer to the Council's mandate than to that of the EP. One could summarise the power plays and bargaining dynamics during trilogues by paraphrasing Gary Lineker, a legend of football: *Trilogues are a simple game. Two institutions chase an agreement for the whole night and at the end, the Council always wins.*

References

Egendal, W. (2025). The Corridors of Power in Brussels: Interinstitutional Negotiations and Informal Governance in EU Law-Making. PhD thesis, University of Copenhagen.

Cabral, T. S. (2020). A short guide to the legislative procedure in the European Union. *UNIO - EU Law Journal, 6*(1), 161–180.

Del Monte, M. (2025). *Understanding trilogue Parliament's rules and practices for reaching provisional agreement on legislation*. European Parliamentary Research Service (EPRS).

European Commission, European Parliament & Council of the European Union. (2007). *Joint Declaration on Practical Arrangements for the Codecision (2007/C 145/02)*.

European Parliament. (2025). *Handbook on the Ordinary Legislative Procedure. A guide to how the European Parliament co-legislates*.

Greenwood, J., & Roederer-Rynning. (2019). Taming trilogues: The EU'S law-making process in a comparative perspective. In O. Costa (Ed.), *The European Parliament in times of EU crisis: Dynamics and transformations* (pp. 121–141). Palgrave Macmillan. https://doi.org/10.1007/978-3-319-97391-3

Turmes, C. (2017). *Energy transformation: An opportunity for Europe*. Biteback Publishing.

Jérémie Zeitoun has been an attaché at the Permanent Representation of Luxembourg to the EU for five years. Beforehand, he held positions in the European Commission and the European Parliament and took part in numerous trilogues. This 2-decade-long institutional experience provides him with insiders' views on the EU decision-making process from different perspectives. He is also an occasional lecturer in several higher education establishments.

The European Council: Defining the Political Guidelines

Edgar Lenski

Abstract The European Council (EUCO), although explicitly barred from exercising legislative functions, nevertheless can and does play a key role in legislative procedures. As a political body composed of the Heads of State or Government of the Member States, the European Council gives the political guidelines for the EU. These guidelines are on the one hand laid down in the so-called Strategic Agenda; on the other hand, they are contained in the European Council Conclusions that are adopted at each meeting. And these conclusions can be quite concrete and specifically concern legislative dossiers that are being deliberated by the Council and European Parliament (EP)—with a substantive impact on these deliberations.

Keywords EU Law · European Council · EUCO · Heads of state or government · Political guidelines · General political directions · Impetus · Strategic Agenda conclusions

1 Introduction

The European Council[1] and its functioning are well-known to Brussels insiders. However, outside the Brussels bubble its role in EU lawmaking is rather little known, notably since it does not have a *formal* role in the legislative process.

[1] The usual abbreviation for the European Council in 'Eurospeak' is EUCO—derived from the abbreviation on the documents of the General Secretariat of the Council.

E. Lenski (✉)
Deputy Director General for EU Affairs of the German Federal Chancellery, Fellow at the Walter Hallstein-Institute for European Constitutional Law, Humboldt-University Berlin, Berlin, Germany
e-mail: edgar.lenski@gmx.de

G. Füricht-Fiegl et al. (eds.), *Handbook on EU Law-making*, Professional Practice in Governance and Public Organizations, https://doi.org/10.1007/978-3-032-16559-6_18

The origins of the European Council date back to the summits of the 1960s and 1970s. It came formally into life with the Paris Summit of December 1974[2] and has been an EU institution since the Lisbon Treaty (Art. 15 TEU).

In the European Council, the Heads of State or Government of the Member States, the Commission President and the President of the European Council meet at least four times a year, in March, June, October and December. But in case it is politically necessary the President of the European Council convenes extraordinary meetings.[3] Notably since the COVID pandemic video conferences of the European Council are also a possible way of convening the European Council if necessary (Van Middelaar, 2021a, b, p. 133).[4] Additionally, informal meetings of the European Council (usually in the Member State holding the rotation Council presidency) are held—often dedicated to a specific topic. So, in practice the EU Heads of State or Government meet very regularly.

All these features (leaders only, deliberations behind closed doors, no vertical representation, regular meetings) lead to the European Council having a special spirit. The leaders know each other very well. They know their respective political positions and discuss very frankly with each other. The atmosphere in the European Council differs considerably from an international meeting where leaders read out official statements. It is much more a true deliberating body.

In this context, one important feature of decision-making in the European Council is the principle of consensus for conclusions. Except for some enumerated formal decisions, the conclusions of the European Council, the main output of this body, have to be agreed upon by consensus.[5]

In substance, the European Council deals with the 'big issues' of European politics. But this does not mean that the European Council only debates about the general approach to European integration in general or Europe's role in the world. Quite the opposite, very often the European Council extensively discusses 'normal' topics which are, of course, politically relevant in daily EU politics. Here, the European Council plays its role in EU legislation. Formally, however, the European Council

[2] French President Valéry Giscard d'Estaing declared in his press release on the occasion of the meeting of the Heads of State or Government in Paris on 10 December 1974: 'Le Sommet européen est mort; vive le conseil européen!' ('The European summit is dead; long live the European Council!').

[3] Extraordinary meetings do not substantially differ from ordinary meetings.

[4] Some of these meetings have been convened at very short notice and at high frequency. Notably at the beginning of the COVID-19 pandemic, the Heads of State or Government took far-reaching political decisions via videoconference, including the decision to work on a recovery fund in response to the economic consequences of the pandemic, cf. the videoconferences of 10, 17 and 26 March and of 23 April 2020. Political agreement on the 'Next Generation EU' (NGEU) proposal was then reached—after another videoconference in June 2020—at the longest European Council meeting to date (17–21 July 2020) which took place in Brussels under pandemic conditions.

[5] N.B. Consensus is not unanimity; it is an agreement where nobody objects, even if some might be not happy with the result, whereas unanimity requires consent by all Member States (abstentions do not prevent the adoption of an act which requires unanimity, Art. 238 TFEU).

does not legislate. The treaties explicitly exclude the European Council from any legislative work (Art. 15(1) TEU).

2 Composition

The European Council is the body of the European Union where the Heads of State or Government of the Member States, the Commission President and the President of the European Council meet. They meet, unlike Council meetings, in a very restricted format; i.e. no advisers or civil servants are in the room. And since 2009 the Foreign Ministers are also excluded from the meetings, which leads to a significant decrease in participants. Only the Secretary General of the Council, the Secretary General of the Commission, the Head of Cabinet of the President of the European Council and the Permanent Representative of the Council Presidency as well as a handful of staff members of the General Secretariat of the Council are in the room. There is no listening room but only an indirect, oral reporting by the General Secretariat to the Member States' Anticis[6] (i.e. the close collaborators of the Permanent Representatives of the 27 Member States) whose task is then to debrief the delegations.

Again, unlike in Council meetings, the members of the European Council cannot be represented by deputies, ministers, state secretaries or the Permanent Representatives. If a member of the European Council is not able to attend, he or she can only give his or her right to vote to another member of the European Council. This rule strengthens the level of attendance quite considerably and boosts the team spirit among the members of the European Council.

The Treaty of Lisbon added a new actor to the institutional framework with the creation of the permanent President of the European Council (PEC). However, the President of the European Council is neither an independent body nor institution nor the 'President of the EU'. The office of the PEC serves primarily to ensure the efficiency and continuity of the EUCO's work, and to facilitate discussions and consensus among the members of the European Council (Wessels & Traguth, 2010, p. 297). The role of the PEC is positioned between that of a chairperson and that of a moderator.

3 Tasks of the European Council

As a political body without any formal legislative role, the European Council is the key steering body of the European Union setting the broad political lines directly by the Heads of State or Government jointly with the Commission President (Calliess,

[6] See also article 3.2 of this handbook

2022, para. 6, 8). According to Art. 15 TEU, the European Council shall provide the EU with the necessary impetus for its development and shall define the general political directions and priorities thereof. The Treaty explicitly states that the European Council shall not exercise legislative functions. Even though this is, of course, true in a formal sense, informally the European Council can and does play a decisive role notably in politically controversial legislative files. As the European Council is not part of the institutional triangle composed of the Commission, the European Parliament (EP) and the Council of the EU where the legislative work is concentrated within the European Union it can play its role 'only' by adopting (1) its Strategic Agenda and (2) conclusions at its meetings.

The Strategic Agenda sets out the broad guidelines for each 5-year institutional cycle ahead of the election of the new Commission president (European Council, 2017, 2019, 2025a). It defines the priorities for all essential policy areas—at least for those which are deemed to be essential at the time of adoption. On that basis—at least in theory—the Commission President will draw up its political programme. In practice, however, the Strategic Agenda rather contains general positions which the Commission President will take into account.

More relevant for the legislative process, however, are the European Council Conclusions on specific legislative files. The European Council regularly calls upon the two co-legislators to speedily conclude individual legislative projects (under the ordinary legislative procedure)—with clear, sometimes very detailed specifications regarding content. These conclusions have no legal force but a strong political impact since all Heads of State or Government adopt them by consensus together with the Commission President. Consequently, two 'sides' of the institutional triangle are at least politically bound by this: The representatives of the Member States in the Council will not contradict their Head of State or Government, and the Commission services will neither do so with regard to the Commission President.

Building on this, the European Council regularly (even though not outspoken) reclaims the role of motor of integration, a role traditionally foreseen for the European Commission. Even before the Treaty of Lisbon entered into force, it was noticeable that the European Council Presidency conclusions regularly 'requested' or 'invited' the Commission to submit proposals or reports. This has not changed since then. In addition, the European Council—especially under President Van Rompuy (2009–2014)—occasionally relied on ad hoc working structures led by the European Council President himself elaborating concrete proposals.[7] Moreover, the European Commission regularly will counter such proposals with its own proposals.[8] Accordingly, the relationship between the European Council and the European Commission (and the EP) is not without tension and is characterised by certain

[7] Cf. the so-called Van Rompuy Task Force as set up by the European Council of 25/26 March 2010 and the so-called Quadriga-Report of 2012.

[8] Cf. the Commission legislative package on economic governance of 29 September 2010, or the Commission Communication on institutional reforms of 14 February 2018, COM(2018) 95.

rivalries, even though the Commission President is a member of the European Council.[9]

4 Conclusions of the European Council

The European Council's predominant mode of action has always been the adoption of so-called conclusions. Before the Lisbon Treaty these were Conclusions of the Presidency. Since then, the conclusions have been formally agreed upon by the European Council. The conclusions are political decisions which, according to the general rule in Art. 15(4) TEU, are agreed upon by consensus and constitute an instrument to exercise leadership (Puetter, 2014a, b, p. 133).

As already described, the conclusions are not drawn up during the course of the European Council meeting, but are largely coordinated beforehand, so that only contentious passages are negotiated at the highest level of the Heads of State or Government. Already in 2002, the European Council agreed to keep its conclusions as concise as possible, after they had previously sometimes comprised several dozen pages. A further streamlining of the conclusions was achieved under the new regime of the Treaty of Lisbon and the chairmanship of the President of the European Council. The conclusions are no legislative texts neither in their language nor in their content. Naturally, European Council conclusions cannot alter or override the regular voting quorum in the Council, i.e. qualified majority, even though political attempts are made in individual cases to achieve a veto over the European Council (Calliess, 2025, p. 137). This means that a debate in the European Council does not override the qualified majority voting on a regulation or a directive in the Council. But sometimes conclusions of the European Council are held 'hostage' by individual Member States: They threaten to veto the conclusions if their position is not reflected both in the conclusions and in the concrete legislative texts decided upon by the Council. This practice—which also exists for files in the Council which require unanimity—is, however, not very sustainable. It does necessitate a considerable amount of political capital by that Member State. And sometimes the political costs go far beyond the respective dossier.

In recent years, sometimes consensus could not be found on parts of the conclusions. In such a case, there is now an established practice that a 'consensus minus one' is put into a separate conclusion (European Council, 2025b). And in some (very rare) cases even after the entry into force of the Treaty of Lisbon, it was necessary to resort (in full or in part) to conclusions of the European Council President because a consensus could not be reached due to the resistance of one or two Member States (European Council, 2014, 2017, 2023).

[9] The cooperation between President of the European Council and Commission President depends to a large extent on the personal relationship of the two incumbents—as can be seen in the respective design of the relationship of Van Rompuy and Barroso, Tusk and Juncker, Michel and von der Leyen and Costa and von der Leyen.

5 Preparation of Conclusions

The Treaty stipulates that the meetings of the European Council are prepared by the General Affairs Council (i.e. the foreign or European affairs ministers) together with the Presidents of the European Council and of the Commission. In practice, however, a key role lies with the President of the European Council, who coordinates closely with the President of the Commission and the Heads of State or Government. To this end, the PEC usually defines key topics for the meetings well in advance. But these plans can be overridden by day-to-day business or by current political necessities. The PEC submits his draft of an annotated agenda to the General Affairs Council no later than 4 weeks before each ordinary European Council meeting, after consulting with the Head of State or Government of the current Council Presidency and with the President of the Commission. The former practice of each Council configuration submitting a contribution to the European Council has been discontinued. Rather, the President of the European Council, i.e. technically the General Secretariat of the Council, drafts the conclusions. These are then discussed further in the 2 weeks preceding the European Council meeting, primarily within the Permanent Representatives Committee, and further coordinated among the EU Sherpas of the European Council members. The General Affairs Council discusses the provisional agenda and the draft conclusions before the European Council meeting. However, the final negotiations on the text of the conclusions are made by the Permanent Representatives in an informal meeting directly before the meetings of the European Council.[10]

6 Meetings and Working Methods

In contrast to the work of the Council, which has long been criticised for a lack of coordination, this has not been the case for the European Council. One of the European Council's strengths lies in its uniform composition and the coherence-enhancing effect of its President—together with the President of the Commission.

In practice, finding consensus is sometimes quite difficult. And it is the main task of the President of the European Council to reach this goal—with the support of his cabinet and the General Secretariat of the Council as well as, usually, some (not only large) Member States who function as 'facilitators' (even though they are often also 'demandeurs').

The conduct of negotiations, and thus also voting or the determination of a consensus, is the responsibility of the President of the European Council. According to

[10] This practice was established despite Art. 3(3) of the Rules of Procedure of the European Council because of the frequently short-term developments before the European Council and the operational relevance of the Committee of Permanent Representatives as the key preparatory body for the European Council conclusions.

Art. 235(1), subpara. 2 TFEU, he himself—like the President of the Commission—does not vote. The standard procedure for voting or reaching consensus is the oral procedure during European Council meetings. Art. 6 of the Rules of Procedure stipulates that a quorum of two-thirds of the voting members of the European Council is required for a vote to be valid. Usually, the President of the European Council concludes after the debate of a subject that there is consensus on this part of the conclusions. Art. 7 of the Rules of Procedure also allows for a written procedure, which can be used in urgent matters on the proposal of the President of the European Council and with the (de facto simultaneous with the vote) consent of all Heads of State and Government.

7 Beyond Conclusions: Decisions of the European Council

Since the Treaty of Lisbon, the European Council can also adopt legally binding decisions in addition to conclusions. The need for formal European Council decisions arose, not least, from the abolition of the configuration of the 'Council in the composition of Heads of State or Government' whose powers were largely transferred to the European Council. These decisions are legal acts within the meaning of Art. 288(4) TFEU and are adopted partly as decisions addressed to individual addressees and partly as decisions without a specific addressee. These decisions are generally taken by consensus, in accordance with Art. 15(4) TEU. Unanimity is required, in particular, for decisions short of treaty amendments. Qualified majority voting is possible, especially for appointments, organisational measures and the Strategic Guidelines for the Area of Freedom, Security and Justice (Article 68 TFEU). Also, for these legally binding decisions, consensus is generally sought, but qualified majority voting is used if necessary (as was the case with the nomination for the President of the Commission in 2014,[11] the re-election of Donald Tusk as PEC in 2017[12] and the nomination for the President of the Commission in 2019 and 2024[13]). The procedural rules regarding voting by unanimity and qualified majority correspond to the rules for the Council and are further specified in Art. 235(2) TFEU and Art. 238(2) TFEU.

[11] The European Council of 26/27 June 2014 nominated Jean-Claude Juncker, but the United Kingdom (Prime Minister Cameron) and Hungary (Prime Minister Orbán) voted against.

[12] The re-election of Donald Tusk as PEC on 9 March 2017 was done against the vote of the Polish Prime Minister Szydło.

[13] Germany (Chancellor Merkel) had to abstain for internal coalition political reasons at the European Council Decision of 2 July 2019 to nominate Ursula von der Leyen as Commission President. Her re-nomination by the European Council on 28 June 2024 was not unanimous either (Hungary's Prime Minister Orbán voted against her, Italy's Prime Minister Meloni abstained).

8 Relationship with the European Parliament

The EP is not involved in the adoption of European Council conclusions. Their democratic legitimacy—in the sense of input legitimacy—consequently derives from the national governments (Art. 10(2) subpara 2 TEU), but not from the EP.

Moreover, the relationship between the EP and the European Council is characterised by institutional mistrust. The President of the EP is not a member of the European Council. He or she only has the opportunity to exchange views with the members of the European Council at the beginning of each session but does not participate in the deliberations. Furthermore, the information provided to the EP by the President of the European Council after each session, while usually timely, is merely a report. Thus, while the European Council listens to and informs the EP, it does not involve the EP in its actual work.

This also means that the EP mostly does not perceive itself as being bound by the Strategic Agenda let alone by the European Council conclusions. Nevertheless, in practice, these institutional tensions as such do not hamper the legislative process (Wessels, 2016a, b, p. 92), notably because of the practical cooperation among the Council, EP and Commission in the 'institutional triangle'.

9 Conclusion

The European Council is a key actor in EU decision-making, including in EU legislation. Regular exchanges among the Heads of State or Government are, on the one hand, essential for progress in EU integration, but also constitute, on the other hand, a considerable intergovernmental component within the EU—despite the participation of the President of the Commission in the European Council meetings. However, this set-up is much less a matter of intergovernmentalism per se than the expression of an intergovernmental *status quo* which still determines European integration. Both intergovernmental and supranational elements remain deeply anchored in the institutional structure and are apparently necessary for European integration. The European Council's role in the ordinary legislative procedure—even though indirect—is therefore only logical.

References

Calliess, C. (2022). Kommentierung des Art. 15 EUV. In C. Calliess & M. Ruffert (Eds.), *EUV AEUV* (6th ed.). C.H. Beck.

Calliess, C. (2025). 50 Jahre Europäischer Rat. *Integration, 48*(2), 129–143.

European Council. (2014). *Strategic Agenda for the Union in Times of Change*. Retrieved October 20, 2025 from https://data.consilium.europa.eu/doc/document/ST-79-2014-INIT/en/pdf

European Council. (2017). *Conclusions of the President of 9 March 2017 (Polish blockade because of the re-election of Donald Tusk as PEC against the Polish governments will).* Retrieved October 25, 2025 from https://www.consilium.europa.eu/media/24113/09-conclusions-pec.pdf
European Council. (2019). *A new Strategic Agenda 2019–2024*. Retrieved October 20, 2025 from https://www.consilium.europa.eu/media/39914/a-new-strategic-agenda-2019-2024.pdf
European Council. (2023). *Conclusions of the President on the external dimension of migration of 29 and 30 June 2023 (Polish and Hungarian blockade because of migration policy).* Retrieved October 25, 2025 from https://www.consilium.europa.eu/en/press/press-releases/2023/06/30/conclusions-by-the-president-of-the-european-council-on-the-external-dimension-of-migration
European Council. (2025a). *Strategic Agenda 2024–2029*, Retrieved October 20, 2025 from https://www.consilium.europa.eu/media/yxrc05pz/sn02167en24_web.pdf
European Council. (2025b). *Conclusions on Ukraine of 23 October 2025.* Retrieved October 25, 2025 from https://www.consilium.europa.eu/media/zs3a30wp/20251023-text-ukraine-en.pdf
Puetter, U. (2014a). *The European council and the council.* Oxford University Press.
Van Middelaar, L. (2021a). *Pandemonium—Saving Europe*. Agenda Publishing.
Wessels, W. (2016a). *The European council.* Palgrave.
Wessels, W., & Traguth, T. (2010). Der hauptamtliche Präsident des Europäischen Rates: 'Herr' oder 'Diener' im Haus Europa? *Integration, 33*(4), 297–311.

Further Readings

Puetter, U. (2014b). *The European council and the council.* Oxford University Press.
Van Middelaar, L. (2021b). *Pandemonium—Saving Europe*. Agenda Publishing.
Von Bogdandy, A., & Rugge, G. (2025). Der Europäische Rat – Regieren in der europäischen Gesellschaft. In Bast, J. & von Bogdandy, A. (Eds.), *Unionsverfassungsrecht* (1st ed., 935–986). Nomos.
Wessels, W. (2016b). *The European council.* Palgrave.

Edgar Lenski is Deputy Director General for EU Affairs at the German Federal Chancellery. He deals with inter alia General EU Affairs, Enlargement, EU external relations, Common Foreign and Security Policy, Justice and Home Affairs and EU law. Prior to his current post he was Head of Unit for EU coordination and for the preparation of the European Council meetings for the Federal Chancellor. Edgar Lenski lectures EU law among others at the Centre Internationale de Formation Européenne (CIFE) and is a fellow at the Walter Hallstein-Institute for European Constitutional Law at Humboldt-University Berlin. The views in this chapter are personal and cannot be attributed to the Federal Chancellery.

Advisory Bodies with Institutional Ambitions: The European Economic and Social Committee and the European Committee of the Regions

Doris Dialer

Abstract What role do the European Economic and Social Committee (EESC) and the Committee of the Regions (CoR) play in EU decision-making, including the Ordinary Legislative Procedure (OLP)? To answer this question, we conceptualise both advisory bodies as highly active institutional actors although they do not possess formal legislative power. Based on a comparative approach the central message is that they successfully have been extending their role beyond their Lisbon Treaty mandate. As rational side actors within the EU institutional framework who strive to maximise their power, they have done so in three ways: first, by a creative use of their respective Rules of Procedure (RoP) reflecting their right of self-organisation. Second, by establishing an in-depth interinstitutional and external network. Third, by smartly spreading the news. Against this background, the analysis confirms that both bodies still have limited legislative influence through their non-binding opinions under co-decision. However, their proactive advisory role via initiative opinions, innovative agenda-setting and intensive interinstitutional cooperation contributes to a constant upgrading within the institutional set-up beyond treaty change.

Keywords Committee of the Regions · European Economic and Social Committee · Advisory bodies · Consultative bodies · Consultation · Interest representation

---

D. Dialer (✉)
Consumer Affairs Attaché, Permanent Representation of Austria to the EU, Brussels, Belgium

Innsbruck Center for European Research (ICER), Innsbruck, Austria
e-mail: doris.dialer@hochschule-burgenland.at

G. Füricht-Fiegl et al. (eds.), *Handbook on EU Law-making*, Professional Practice in Governance and Public Organizations, https://doi.org/10.1007/978-3-032-16559-6_19

1 Introduction

In the Treaty of the European Union (Art. 13, TEU)[1] seven institutions of the European Union are listed. Neither the European Economic and Social Committee (EESC) nor the European Committee of the Regions (CoR)[2] is among them, but they are nevertheless mentioned in the same article as acting in 'an advisory capacity'.

Within the EU's institutional framework, the EESC and the CoR are the most comparable bodies. They share the common legal bases in the TEU and the Treaty on the Functioning of the European Union (TFEU) and are both the 'Union's advisory bodies, exercising advisory functions'. Both consist of 329 members plus the same number of alternates[3] and for both bodies the seats per Member State are allocated as follows: Germany, France and Italy (24), Spain and Poland (21), Romania (15), Greece, Czechia, Belgium, Hungary, Portugal, Sweden, Bulgaria and Austria (12), Slovakia, Denmark, Finland, Ireland, Croatia and Lithuania (9), Latvia, Slovenia, Estonia (7), Cyprus and Luxembourg (6) and Malta (5). Despite these similarities, they are two distinct EU bodies. As Art. 300 (4) TEU states, CoR and EESC members 'shall be completely independent in the performance of their duties (…)'. Members do not receive a salary and most of them are not Brussels-based. Both bodies are supported by around 700 staff.

However, their composition is very different: Art. 300 (2) TFEU declares that the EESC 'shall consist of representatives of organizations of employers, of the employed and of other parties, representatives of civil society, notably in socio-economic, civic, professional and cultural areas', while in contrast, CoR Art. 300 (3) TFEU states, 'shall consist of regional and local bodies who either hold a regional or local authority electoral mandate or are political accountable to an elected assembly'. Thus, from a political point of view the EESC is considered rather apolitical while the CoR is seen as political due to its members' party affiliation. In contrast to the EESC, international cooperation of the CoR is much weaker. Nevertheless, external networking has been increased, particularly with regard to EU enlargement candidate countries (Dialer et al., 2025).

The CoR was established by the Maastricht Treaty around 1992, which means 35 years after the EESC. The latter was already 'born' by the 1957 Treaty of Rome. However, since the EESC covers all economic and social areas, advisory competences remain considerably broader than those of the CoR, which are focused primarily on the regional dimension.

---

[1] Pursuant to Art. 13 TEU, only the seven following bodies enjoy the status of the Union's institutions: European Parliament, European Council, Council, European Commission, Court of Justice of the European Union, European Central Bank and Court of Auditors.

[2] In 2015, the CoR was renamed the European Committee of the Regions, and for the first time, its political programme was instead of 4 years for the full five-year term, in step with the Commission and the EP.

[3] Overall, the size of the committees was reduced from 350 to 329 members with effect from 1 February 2020 (following the United Kingdom's withdrawal from the EU).

Mandatory consultation in the framework of the OLP is regulated in the following TFEU articles for the CoR and the EESC: Transport (91, 100), Employment (148, 149), Social Policy (153), European Social Fund (164), Education, Vocational Training, Youth and Sport (165–6), Public Health (168), Consumer Protection (169), Trans-European Networks (172), Economic, Social and Territorial Cohesion (175, 177, 178), Environment (192), and Energy (194). The CoR is also involved in Culture (167). The EESC is additionally involved in Agriculture (43), Free Movement of Persons and Services (46, 50, 59), Transport (94), Tax Provision (113), Social Policy (156, 157, 159) and Industry (173), as well as Research (182, 188). Besides mandatory referrals, EESC and CoR may also be consulted voluntarily by Parliament, the Commission or the Council on *any* other matter. In addition, they can file their own-initiative opinions.

In the case of referrals, the lawmaking institutions may set a time limit (of at least one month) after which the absence of an opinion cannot prevent them from taking any decision (Art. 304 TFEU). In order to have influence concerning the OLP, both advisory bodies must deliver their opinions as early as possible. However, timing is a particular difficulty, as they receive legislative proposals at the same time as the EP and the Council (Hönnige & Panke, 2016).

Since the creation of the CoR in the early 1990s, the two bodies tended to be seen as rivals, but they do rather co-exist amicably, even sharing the same premises. Since June 2004 they have been jointly using the 'Delors building' in the European Quarter. An agreement on administrative cooperation was first signed in 2007, updated in 2015 and revised lately in 2021 to further increase the scope of the joint activities (Westlake, 2016, p. 99; Dialer, 2020, p. 443; EESC, 2025).

The CoR and especially the EESC are underrepresented in academic literature when compared to the EU institutions. Of research dedicated to both advisory bodies, most attention has been paid to functional analysis and their legislative influence (Abels, 2022; Hönnige & Panke, 2013; McCarthy, 1997; Smismans, 2000) and how they try pushing the boundaries of their consultative mandate (Schönlau, 2017). Meanwhile, interinstitutional and external networking has so far received surprisingly little attention (e.g. Walli, 2020).

This chapter attempts to contribute to filling this research gap. Based on a comparative approach the central message is that consultative bodies, while not having legislative power, provide valuable expertise and guidance regarding the OLP. In addition, they both have enhanced their treaty-based role via formal and informal cooperation within and beyond the institutional set-up.

To carry out its consultative mission successfully, the committees established Rules of Procedure (RoP) in accordance with Art. 303 (2) TFEU for the EESC and Art. 306 (2) TFEU for the CoR. Against this background, this chapter suggests that a reform of the mandates of the EESC and CoR would be necessary to develop their role from advisory bodies to institutions with legislative impact. However, an expansion of the treaty-based powers seems to be out of sight. The committees have therefore evolved organically through successive re-drafts of their RoP, insofar as the creative use of the latter together with fostered interinstitutional collaboration and communication strategies reflects the desire to become a real player within the OLP.

To this end, the central analytical categories such as actors (members) are to be examined. We will then discuss the power (mandate) and consultative procedures. As a second step, we shed light on the interinstitutional cooperation agreements. Finally, we underline that the EESC and the CoR are bodies in constant evolution seeking for legislative power. This is particularly relevant in an institutional set-up where continuous changes in competencies are shaped by actors exploiting loopholes to enhance their powers.

2 European Economic and Social Committee

The EESC was set up by the Rome Treaties 1957 in order to involve economic and social interest groups in the establishment of the common market. Thus, it acts as an intermediary between organised civil society and the EU institutions. The committee's expertise and debating culture improve the quality and credibility of the EU decision-making process, insofar as they make it more transparent, comprehensible and acceptable for Europe's citizens (Preamble, RoP, 2022).[4]

However, the EESC has so far received very limited scholarly attention. Research has analysed the EESC from a deliberative democracy perspective (Smismans, 2000; Uhlin & Arvidson, 2023; Westlake, 2016), described the inner functioning (e.g. Johansson et al., 2022), examined its impact on the EU's legislative process (Hönnige & Panke, 2016; Panke, 2019; Westlake, 2016), explored the committee as a promoter of participatory democracy (Organ & Vogiatzis, 2023) and analysed its formal and informal networks (Walli, 2020).

Even if the formal political influence of the EESC as a consultative body might be limited (Hönnige & Panke, 2016; Panke, 2019; Dialer, 2014a, 2015, 2016, 2017, 2018), the access and linkage its members have to the lawmaking EU institutions and Member States' capitals, regions and civil society counts. The preamble and Rule 30 'Relations with external organizations' of the RoP (2022) underlines that 'the Committee helps to strengthen (democracy), including the promotion of relations between the EU and socio-economic groupings in third countries'.

2.1 *Members and Leadership*

The EESC currently consists of 329 members. The number and national allocation of seats are determined by Art. 301 TFEU. Members are nominated by national governments and appointed by the Council for a renewable five-year term of office (Art. 302 TFEU).

[4] Rules of Procedure and Code of Conduct for Members of the European Economic and Social Committee (May 2022), OJ of the EU, L 149/2022. Retrieved from: https://eur-lex.europa.eu/legal-content/EN/TXT/HTML/?uri=OJ:L:2022:149:FULL.

Members belong to one of the three groups: Employers Group (Group I), Workers' Group (Group II) or Civil Society Organizations' Group (Group III). The conflict between employers (capital) and workers (labour) constitutes a major structural tension which relates to their recognition as social partners at EU level. National delegations may, however, provide a common social arena and a source of socialisation into the culture of the EESC (Johansson et al., 2022).

The EESC's work is organised into six sections specialised in different policy areas: Economic and Monetary Union, Economic and Social Cohesion (ECO), Single Market, Production and Consumption (INT), Agriculture, Rural Development and Environment (NAT), External Relations (REX), Employment, Social Affairs and Citizenship (SOC), Transport, Energy, Infrastructure and the Information Society (TEN). Members belong to one or more of these sections depending on their areas of expertise and it is here that the EESC's opinions are drafted and discussed. The Committee also has a Consultative Commission on Industrial Change (CCMI) and three specialist observatories—on the Digital Transition and the Single Market (DSMO), the Labour Market (LMO) and Sustainable Development (SDO). It also has a group focused on the European Semester (ESG), a group on Fundamental Rights and the Rule of Law (FRRL) and a Liaison Group (LG) promoting civil dialogue and participatory democracy (EESC, 2023).

Every two-and-a-half year, the EESC elects a bureau made up of the EESC president and two vice-presidents ('the presidency'), the presidents of the three groups, the presidents of the sections and of the CCMI (Consultative Commission on Industrial Change) and a varying number of members, in total no more than the number of Member States (Rule 11, RoP, 2022). The bureau's main task is to organise and coordinate the work and to lay down policy guidelines (Johansson et al., 2022).

2.2 *Powers and Procedures*

In the framework of the OLP it is determined in the respective TFEU provisions that consultation with the EESC is required. Thus, the Committee advises on various EU policies, especially those impacting economic, social and employment issues, representing employers, workers and civil society groups.

Opinions—adopted by simple majority in plenary—are drafted by study groups with members from all three groups and are led by a rapporteur from one of the groups. Opinions are either issued at the request of the three lawmaking EU institutions (mandatory/optional) or on their own initiative. In addition, the body performs its consultative duty by drawing up evaluation reports, information reports or resolutions on current topics. Mandatory consultation is requested for in 10 policy areas. These non-binding opinions boost the EESC's role in influencing legislative decisions since gaining the ability to independently adopt reports and opinions in 1972.

All in all, the EESC issues between 160 and 190 opinions and information reports a year. 70% are mandatory or optional referrals by the Council, Commission and EP. 21% are its own initiative opinions and information reports, while 9% are exploratory opinions generally requested by the country holding the Council presidency. In 2024, the EESC adopted all in all 142 opinions and reports. This number is composed as follows: 64 referral-based opinions, 53 own-initiative opinions, 22 exploratory opinions and three other opinions and reports (EESC, 2025, p. 20).

The plenary assembly, which brings together the 329 EESC members six times a year, is the supreme decision-making body. The EESC sees itself as a bridge to organised civil society (Art. 300, para. 1, TFEU), which is why EESC plenary debates fulfil an important publicity function, especially as representatives of civil society are very often invited (Dialer & Walli, 2019).

2.3 Cooperation Agreements

Cooperation between the EESC and the Commission, the Council and the EP is regulated in Art. 13 (4) TEU and Art. 304 TFEU. Since 1989, a member of the "College" has been responsible for relations with the EESC and the Commission has voluntarily informed the EESC on a quarterly basis about the consideration of its opinions in the subsequent legislative process. The first cooperation agreement with the Commission dates back to 2001 (renewed in 2005, amended in 2007 and 2012). The last revision took place in 2022. It includes a chapter that offers broadened possibilities for optional consultation and initiative reports.

The kick-start of the EESC's cooperation attempts with the Council dates back to 1974. Since 1987, the President of the Council has presented his work programme to the EESC plenary. The EESC's opinions have been attached to the Council's working documents since the end of 1988. More recently, the EESC as well as the CoR has deepened its working relationship with the Council presidency by aligning its activities with the Council presidency's priorities. However, up to now the committee's attempts (starting in the early 2000s) to enter into a cooperation agreement with the Council have failed.

Official cooperation between the EESC and EP has only been possible since the Treaty of Amsterdam (1997) but has recently been intensified. In addition to the previous annual attendance of the President of the EP at EESC plenary sessions, the number of contacts between the rapporteurs of both institutions and their reciprocal participation in meetings has increased. The first agreement with the EP dates back to 2014 and was renewed in May 2024.

3 European Committee of the Regions

In 2024, the CoR celebrated its 30th anniversary. The CoR was created by the Treaty of Maastricht in 1991–93, following a period when regional and local interests had been demanding greater involvement in the EU decision-making process (Cîrlig,

2021).[5] Indeed, the CoR's real power lies in its capacity to influence the Commission's regional policy formulation and decision-taking.

As an advisory body it has been studied from a functional perspective mainly with a focus on how and to what extent it can exercise influence on EU decision-making (Warleigh, 1999; Christiansen, 1996; Christiansen & Lintner, 2005; Hönnige & Panke, 2013). The CoR has also been examined in the context of 'shaping EU policy from below' in a multi-level system (Carroll, 2011; Piattoni & Schönlau, 2015; Schönlau, 2017; Dialer & Eppler, 2020) and regional interest representation (Hooghe & Marks, 1996; Stahl, 2014; Trobbiani, 2019).

A special feature of the CoR is that, as a consultative legislative body, it bridges all four levels of the EU system, the municipal, regional, national and European, and thus has the potential to bring together the various democratic systems of European multi-level democracy (Dialer & Eppler, 2020). Other analytical approaches focus on its historical evolution (Wasserberg, 2020). Recent studies cover both the application of the internal rules and mechanisms and the external links, cooperation and networking to consolidate and expand its role (Blavoukos & Oikonomou, 2023; Dialer et al., 2025).

3.1 Members and Leadership

The 329 members of the CoR and the same number of alternates are appointed for five years. The CoR (as well as the EESC) thus works in the same periodic rhythm as the Commission and the EP which ensures better interinstitutional cooperation. Under Union law, only the Member State has the right to nominate members. The regions therefore have no direct right of nomination. Each EU Member State has its own procedure for nominating candidates. The Council decides on the proposals by qualified majority (Art. 16 (3) 3 TEU). The appointment is published in the Official Journal of the EU.

Since the entry into force of the Treaty of Nice in 2003, only members of a democratically elected assembly of a regional or local authority or persons who are politically accountable to such an assembly can be appointed as members. In the Treaty of Lisbon (2009), this condition was further strengthened in Art. 300 (3) 3 TFEU. This restriction to elected representatives leads to a stronger legitimisation of the CoR in comparison to the EESC. CoR members are not bound by any instructions (Art. 300 (4) 4 TFEU) and are *de jure* independent of their regional or local authorities.

[5] In the 'architecture' of the EU, the regions have only been formally recognised since the Maastricht Treaty, not least due to the massive pressure exerted by federally constitutedMember States like Germany. This recognition was expressed in the principle of subsidiarity (Art. 5 TEU), the possibility for an EU state to be represented in the Council by a representative of one of its regions (Art. 16 (2) TEU) and, last but not least, the introduction of the CoR (Dialer & Eppler, 2020).

CoR members are grouped into national delegations (made up by mandataries from the same Member State) as well as according to their political affiliation into six different political groups: European People's Party (EPP), Party of European Socialists (PES), Renew Europe, European Conservatives and Reformists Group (ECR), European Alliance (EA) and The Greens. Members can also be non-attached.

The legislative work is organised into six Commissions: Citizenship, Governance, Institutional and External Affairs (CIVEX), Territorial Cohesion Policy and EU Budget (COTER), Economic Policy (ECON), Environment, Climate Change and Energy (ENVE), Natural Resources (NAT) and Social Policy, Education, Employment, Research and Culture (SEDEC) (Cîrlig, 2021).

As a result of the mandatory right to be consulted, the CoR adapted its thematic Commissions to European Commission portfolios,, Councilformations and preparatory bodies, and EP committees. Cooperation between the CoR political groups and the EP political groups intensified over the years. In spring of 2000, the first meeting of EP and CoR political group leaders took place. This increasing politicisation can be seen as a strengthening of the CoR's quality as a political actor in terms of influencing European decision-making (Dialer et al., 2025).

In accordance with Art. 306 TFEU, the CoR's political governing body is the Bureau. The CoR Bureau consists of the president, the first vice-president, one vice-president per Member State, 26 other members and the chairs of the political groups. This makes a total of 61 Bureau members. The Conference of Presidents (CoP) consists of the president, the first vice-president and the political group leaders. The governing body is primarily concerned with reaching consensus at a political level, thereby facilitating decision-making in plenary (Rules 47–48, RoP, 2024).

3.2 *Powers and Procedures*

The treaty gives the CoR an exclusively advisory role in the EU legislative process. The CoR is doing so via issuing opinions. Art. 307 TFEU distinguishes between four cases of opinions. These are opinions on mandatory consultations, on optional consultations, on accessory consultations and on the right of self-referral. The CoR is also informed when the EU institutions request an opinion from the EESC, so that it may adopt an opinion on the same issue if it believes regional interests are involved. In practice, consultation can take place at any stage of the legislative process, i.e. from the preparation of a legal act to its final adoption. In particular, the Lisbon Treaty granted the CoR a right to go before the Court of Justice for infringements of the principle of subsidiarity in the fields of mandatory consultation or in the event of a breach of CoR prerogatives (Westlake, 2016, p. 6; Cîrlig, 2021).

Since 2002, the Commission has involved the CoR in selected projects at an early stage by means of exploratory opinions or forward-looking reports if the legal dossier concerns regional issues. It also does this for reports on the success of certain Union measures. By being involved at a very early stage in the preparation of legal acts, the CoR is usually able to exert much greater legislative influence.

The impact of CoR opinions is assessed in terms of achievements in the EU legislative process and in general European debates (impact on preparatory or final legal texts) and visibility for local and regional authorities in the setting of the EU's agenda. In 2024, the CoR adopted 53 opinions and four resolutions, which is a slightly lower figure than in previous years (68 in 2021, 63 in 2022 and 59 in 2023), but higher than in 2019, which is comparable to 2024 from the EU interinstitutional cycle perspective (CoR, 2025a).

Art. 306 TFEU (which is identical to Art. 303 TFEU) regulates the organisation of the CoR, insofar as this is not left to the Rules of Procedure (RoP, 2024).[6] The treaty largely leaves it to the CoR to organise its institutional structure and procedures. Since the Treaty of Amsterdam (1996), the CoR no longer has to submit its RoP to the Council for approval. Indeed, the CoR has revised its RoP several times with a view to strengthening its position towards the lawmaking institutions. However, its longstanding ambition to be recognised as an institution in the form of a third legislative chamber (senate) with consent power over territorial cohesion matters has yet to materialise (Cîrlig, 2021; Dialer et al., 2025).

3.3 Cooperation Agreements

CoR relations with the representatives of the legislative institutions are further structured by so-called cooperation agreements. These agreements highlight the territorial dimension of the EU and the importance of multi-level governance and amplify the voice and influence of regions and cities in the EU decision-making process (CoR, 2025a).

In 2001, the Commission and CoR signed a first cooperation agreement. This initial agreement was revised in 2005, 2007, 2012 and recently in 2024.[7] The latter is structured as follows: I. Cooperation as regards legislative procedures and planning (Commission work programme, consultation planning, procedures throughout the legislative process), II. Thematic cooperation as regards activities (European Semester, cross-border cooperation and European Grouping of Territorial Cooperation), III. Implementation of subsidiarity and proportionality and multilevel governance and better regulation, IV. External dimension of EU policies, V. Information and communication policy and VI. Administrative matters.

Despite some initial distrust, the EP and CoR have achieved to build a strong partnership, materialised particularly by the intense working relations of Parliament's Committee on Regional Development (REGI) with the CoR (Dialer, 2014b).

---

[6] Rules of Procedure of the Committee of the Regions (2024/2142), OJ of the EU, 14 August 2024, ELI: https://data.europa.eu/ei/proc_rules/2024/2142/oj.

[7] Protocol on cooperation between the European Commission and the European Committee of the Regions (C/2024/2478), OJ of the EU, 4 April 2024, ELI: http://data.europa.eu/eli/C/2024/2478/oj.

According to Decoster et al. (2018), the relationship has steadily evolved and matured—most recently by the conclusion of a strengthened cooperation agreement before the tenth EP Elections in May 2024 (revised version of the 2014 agreement).

The CoR has established privileged relationships with the Council and in particular with its rotating Council presidencies. The consultative body works with them via dedicated referrals and ordinary legislative work, the participation in high level meetings and events organised by the presidencies. CoR representatives may also be invited to Council working parties and informal ministerial meetings in legislative areas with a clear local or regional dimension.[8]

4 Conclusion

In the course of this analysis, it was claimed that CoR and EESC members contribute significantly to the expansion of the respective advisory bodies' competences, influence and public perception. This finding is based on two premises anchored in active institutionalism (Schönlau, 2017). Both advisory bodies have indeed been actively seeking to consolidate and expand both its formal standing and its informal tools to enhance its impact within the OLP. Firstly, the EESC and CoR are using loopholes (e.g. RoP) to enlarge their treaty-given role. In this context, both consultative bodies follow the role model of the EP's successful 'creative' application of the RoP (Roos, 2017; Cherneva-Mollova, 2014). Secondly, they try to 'institutionalise' and broaden their impact via formalised cooperation agreements with the Commission and the EP. The EESC and CoR have established formal cooperation agreements with the Commission since 2001 and the EP since 2014. Against this background, cooperation with the Council is rather informal and not based on an agreement. The Council argues that according to Art. 295 TFEU binding interinstitutional agreements are limited to the Council, EP and Commission (Westlake, 2016, p. 98). However, both committees insist on being integrated in trilogues and meetings of the Council's preparatory bodies.

In the framework of the OLP it is determined in the respective TFEU provisions that consultations with both consultative bodies are required. The EESC's involvement in the EU decision-making process has expanded continuously since 1958. The treaties have gradually increased the number of EU policy areas where the opinion of the EESC is required. In 1958, the EEC Treaty provided for the mandatory consultation of the EESC in 10 areas. Currently, there are 14 areas where consultation is mandatory.

As well as the EESC, with the various treaty changes, the CoR has managed to increase the number of policy areas where the Council and Commission (and since 1999, the EP as well) have an obligation to consult the CoR during the OLP. Currently, there are 10 areas where consultation is mandatory. Significantly, the Lisbon Treaty

[8] https://cor.europa.eu/en/cooperation-eu-institutions-and-agreements.

gave the CoR the right to bring proceedings before the EU Court of Justice for infringements of the principle of subsidiarity. The CoR has become a hub for the aggregation of subnational interests and their translation into political input at EU level (Cîrlig, 2021).

Optional consultation of both bodies is also possible. Furthermore, the EP, the Council presidency or the Commission may request exploratory opinions before legislation is proposed. However, the steadily increasing number of initiative opinions shows that both bodies want to become legislative actors within the OLP.

However, consultative bodies tend to play a marginal role, being kind of supporting actors in the legislative process, especially since their opinions do not have to be taken into account. A closer look at the CoR's and EESC's current competences and rights reveals that the 'advisory bodies' are still a long way from becoming institutions with semi-legislative powers. However, its increasing professionalisation puts them in a position to deserve a more comprehensive integration in the OLP over time.

Thus, this chapter attempted to contribute to a more sophisticated understanding of the multi-faceted potential and re-positioning of the two advisory bodies within the EU institutional setting. However, the chance of being eventually recognised 'officially' by the 'Masters of the Treaties' as an EU 'institution' or not—a demand which has consistently been made by both committees—is rather low.

References

Abels, G. (2022). The European economic and social committee and the Committee of the Regions: Consultative institutions in a multichannel democracy. In D. Hodson, U. Puetter, S. Saurugger, & J. Peterson (Eds.), *The institutions of the European Union* (5th ed., pp. 369–390). Oxford University Press.

Blavoukos, S., & Oikonomou, G. (2023). Newcomers in EU foreign policy: The Committee of the Regions as an EU para-diplomatic actor. *Journal of European Integration, 46*(1), 107–125.

Carroll, W. (2011). The Committee of the Regions: A functional analysis of the CoR's institutional capacity. *Regional and Federal Studies, 21*(3), 341–354.

Cherneva-Mollova, D. (2014). *The EP's Rules of Procedure and their Implications for the EU institutional Balance*, SOG Working Papers 13.

Christiansen, T. (1996). Second thoughts on Europe's "third level": The European Union's Committee of the Regions. *Publius: The Journal of Federalism, 26*(1), 93–114.

Christiansen, T. & Lintner, P. (2005). The Committee of the Regions after 10 Years: Lessons from the Past and Challenges for the Future, *Eipascope* 2005/1.

Cîrlig, C. C. (2021). *Understanding the European Committee of the Regions (CoR)*, European Parliamentary Research Service. Retrieved from https://www.europarl.europa.eu/RegData/etudes/BRIE/2021/689377/EPRS_BRI(2021)689377_EN.pdf

CoR. (2025a). *Impact of CoR Opinions. 2024 Impact Report*. Retrieved from https://cor.europa.eu/en/our-work/opinions/impact-cor-work-eu-legislation#toc-highlights-of-the-2024-annual-impact-report

Decoster, F., Delhomme, V., & Rousselle, J. (2018). The Committee of the Regions and the European Parliament: An evolving relationship? In *The European Parliament in times of EU crisis: Dynamics and transformations* (pp. 99–118). Springer International Publishing.

Dialer, D. (2014a, 2015, 2016, 2017, 2018). Europäischer Wirtschafts- und Sozialausschuss. In: Weidenfeld, W., & Wessels, W. (Eds.). *Jahrbuch der Europäischen Integration*, Baden-Baden.

Dialer, D. (2014b). The regional policy power of the EU parliament after the European elections 2014. In G. M. Grabher & U. Mathis-Moser (Eds.), *Regionalism(s). A variety of perspectives from Europe and the Americas* (pp. 89–106). Schriftenreihe des Instituts für Föderalismus, (119). New Academic Press (NAP).

Dialer, D. (2020). Peter Straub und Michael Schneider: Deutsche Christliche Demokraten im Ausschuss der Regionen. In M. Borchard (Ed.), *Deutsche Christliche Demokraten in Europa* (pp. 431–452). Mit uns für Europa, Konrad Adenauer Stiftung.

Dialer, D., & Eppler, A. (2020). Der Ausschuss der Regionen. Brücke zwischen vier politischen EU-Ebenen. In A. T. Hermann, D. Ingruber, F. Perlot, K. Praprotnik, & C. Hainzl (Eds.), *Regional.national.föderal. Zur Beziehung politischer Ebenen in Österreich* (pp. 221–235). Facultas.

Dialer, D. & Walli, T. (2019, 2020, 2021, 2022, 2023, 2024, 2025). Europäischer Wirtschafts- und Sozialausschuss. In Weidenfeld, W., & Wessels, W. (Eds.), *Jahrbuch der Europäischen Integration*, Baden-Baden.

Dialer, D., Eppler, A., & Obermüller, A. (2025). Der Ausschuss der Regionen. Vorbemerkung und Kommentierung zu Art. 305 bis 307 AEUV. In J. Schwarze, A. Hatje, & J. P. Terhechte (Eds.), *Von der Groeben—Kommentar zum Europäischen Unionsrecht, Vertrag über die Europäische Union—Vertrag über die Arbeitsweise der Europäischen (8. Aufl., 4 Bde)*. Nomos.

EESC. (2023). *2022 - European Economic and Social Committee. A Year in Review*. Retrieved from https://www.eesc.europa.eu/sites/default/files/files/qe-am-23-001-en-n.pdf

EESC. (2025). *Annual Activity Report 2024*. Retrieved from https://www.europarl.europa.eu/cmsdata/296670/Annual%20Activity%20Report%202024.pdf

Hönnige, C., & Panke, D. (2013). The Committee of the Regions and the European economic and social committee: How influential are consultative committees in the European Union? *Journal of Common Market Studies, 51*(3), 452–471.

Hönnige, C., & Panke, D. (2016). Is anybody listening? The Committee of the Regions and the European economic and social committee and their quest for awareness. *Journal of European Public Policy, 23*(4), 624–642.

Hooghe, L., & Marks, G. (1996). Europe with the regions: Channels of interest representation in the European union. *Publius: The Journal of Federalism, 26*(1), 73–91.

Johansson, H., Uhlin, A., & Arvidson, M. (2022). Capital and closure in the EU field. Advancement in the European economic and social committee. *JCMS: Journal of Common Market Studies, 60*(4), 1069–1085.

McCarthy, R. E. (1997). The Committee of the Regions: An advisory body's tortuous path to influence. *Journal for European Public Policy, 4*(3).

Organ, J., & Vogiatzis, N. (2023). The Role of the European Economic and Social Committee in Improving EU Citizen Participation. *The Changing Role of Citizens in EU Democratic Governance, 251-270.*

Panke, D. (2019). The European economic and social committee (EESC) and the Committee of the Regions (CoR). In W. R. Thompson (Ed.), *Oxford research encyclopedia* (pp. 1–13). Oxford University Press.

Piattoni, S., & Schönlau, J. (2015). *Shaping EU policy from below: EU democracy and the Committee of the Regions*. Edward Elgar.

Roos, M. (2017). Far beyond the treaties' clauses: The European Parliament's gain in power, 1952-1979. *Journal of Contemporary European Research.*

Schönlau, J. (2017). Beyond mere 'consultation': Expanding the European Committee of the Regions' role. *Journal of Contemporary European Research, 13*(2), 1166–1184.

Smismans, S. (2000). The European economic and social committee: Towards deliberative democracy via a functional assembly. *European Integration Online Papers (EIoP), 4*(12), 1–21.

Stahl, G. (2014). Der Ausschuss der Regionen: Politische Vertretung und Lobbyist für Städte und Regionen. In D. Dialer & M. Richter (Eds.), *Lobbying in der Europäischen Union: zwischen Professionalisierung und Regulierung* (pp. 127–140). Springer VS.

Trobbiani, R. (2019). European regions and their interests. In D. Dialer & M. Richter (Eds.), *Lobbying in the European Union* (pp. 185–203). Springer.
Uhlin, A., & Arvidson, M. (2023). A European civil society elite? Analysing capital and drama at the European economic and social committee. *European Societies, 25*(1), 87–106.
Walli, T. (2020). *Die Strategie der Vernetzung. Die interinstitutionellen und externen Beziehungen des Europäischen Wirtschafts- und Sozialausschusses*, Baden-Baden/Innsbruck 2020.
Warleigh, A. (1999). *The Committee of the Regions—Institutionalising multi-level governance*. Sage.
Wasserberg, B. (2020). *The History of the Committee of the Regions. 25 years of cities and regions furthering European integration*, Brussels.
Westlake, M. (2016). *The European economic and social committee: The house of European organised civil society*. John Harper Publishing.

Doris Dialer is an Attachée for Consumer Affairs at the Permanent Representation of Austria to the EU. She has over 20 years of EU professional experience. From 2006 to 2019, she worked at the European Parliament. During the COVID pandemic, she was a policy adviser on EU, WHO and International Affairs to the Austrian Federal Minister for Social Affairs, Health, Care and Consumer. She has a strong academic angle, and lectures and publishes intensely on EU lawmaking, policies, institutions and lobbying. Doris holds an MA and PhD in Political Science from the University of Innsbruck.

Empowered by Lisbon: National Parliaments and Their Role in the Multi-Level Governance

Deniz Alkan and Eike Hortsch

Abstract The significance and the role of national parliaments in EU decision-making have changed dramatically since the Treaty of Maastricht in the early 1990s. While the EU remained oblivious regarding the regional level within its Member States for many decades, in the last 30 years the role and influence of national parliaments has been broadened by the introduction of various new procedures and avenues to invite their participation, most prominently by the subsidiarity early warning mechanism introduced by the Treaty of Lisbon. This chapter seeks to outline these changes and the ways in which national parliaments can make their voices heard today. A particular focus will be laid on the aforementioned early warning mechanism as well as the underlying principles of subsidiarity and proportionality. As a case study, the coordination of European Affairs in Germany and within its federal bicameral system will be explained in more detail to illustrate the options parliamentary chambers have to exert influence vis-à-vis their own governments or European institutions.

Keywords Early warning mechanism · National parliaments · Multi-level governance · Principle of subsidiarity · Principle of proportionality · Germany · Federalism · COSAC · Bundestag · Bundesrat

---

D. Alkan (✉)
Director for European and International Affairs at the State Chancellery of Saarland, Saarbrücken, Germany
e-mail: D.alkan@europa.saarland.de

E. Hortsch (✉)
Head of Division for Europe, Finance and Science at the Saarland State Representation in Berlin, Berlin, Germany
e-mail: E.Hortsch@lv.saarland.de

G. Füricht-Fiegl et al. (eds.), *Handbook on EU Law-making*, Professional Practice in Governance and Public Organizations, https://doi.org/10.1007/978-3-032-16559-6_20

1 Introduction: Bridging the National and European Divide

7 February 1992, the day the Treaty on European Union (TEU) was signed in Maastricht, marked a turning point in the role of national parliaments within the process of European integration. During the IGC (Intergovernmental Conference) preceding the treaty in 1990/1991 and even more substantially through national reforms stipulated by the founding of the EU in 1992/1993, national parliaments gained a more prominent role in the Union's system of multi-level governance and its legislative procedures. In the early days of European integration, the decision-making process produced supranational law mainly involving the European Commission and the Council.

Although the European Parliament (EP) gained influence in the legislative process already in the 1970s, national parliaments remained quasi-sidelined until much later. Today domestic democratic institutions are seen as one of the many pillars essential to help ensure democratic accountability and legitimacy within the EU. The evolution towards a stronger role for national parliaments culminated in the Treaty of Lisbon (entered into force 2009), in which formal legal rights to scrutinise EU legislation, primarily through the principles of subsidiarity and proportionality, were given to national parliaments. The Lisbon Treaty transformed the former co-decision procedure into the so-called Ordinary Legislative Procedure (OLP), which today constitutes the main process by which the EU passes laws. The co-legislation of the EP and the Council, which share equal power in adopting legislative acts, is complemented by instruments such as the Early Warning System (EWS) and encouraged direct political dialogue of national parliamentary chambers with EU institutions. These mechanisms seek to involve national legislative bodies more directly in supranational lawmaking.

Furthermore, the principle of subsidiarity (Art. 5 (3) TEU) prescribes those decisions should be taken at the most immediate level of governance. Although the effectiveness of the so-called subsidiarity mechanism remains obscure, some authors argue that national parliaments still serve as guardians of the principle itself (Jaroszyński, 2020, p. 96). This argument is even stronger in countries where a federal constitutional order is combined with a bicameral parliamentary system, like Germany, Spain or Austria.

By increasing information rights, consultation procedures and a deepened inter-parliamentary cooperation through structures like the Conference of Parliamentary Committees for Union Affairs (COSAC), national parliaments are gradually bridging the institutional divide between the national and EU levels. The willingness and ability of individual parliaments to make strategic use of these rights and instruments differs as well as their influence (Auel et al., 2015; Buzogány & Stuchlik, 2012).

2 Empowered by Lisbon: Rights and Duties of National Parliaments

The Treaty of Lisbon granted the national parliaments of the Member States a formal position within the legal framework of the European Union (EU). For the first time in the EU the national parliaments became part of the legal process, and they also got mechanisms to intervene. These new rights for the national parliaments should somehow compensate for their losses in sovereignty due to new competences of the European Union (Buzogány & Stuchlik, 2012, p. 341).

The division of competence areas of the EU arises from Art. 3, 4 and 6 of the Treaty on the Functioning of the European Union (TFEU). The EU has exclusive competence in the customs union, the establishment of competition rules, monetary policy for the countries of the Eurozone, the conservation of marine biological resources under the Common Fisheries Policy and the common commercial policy (Art. 3 TFEU).

The much larger parts of competences fall into the category of shared competences. In this field, the EU as well as the Member States can legislate and adopt legally binding acts. Member States may exercise their competence in areas where the EU has not acted or has chosen not to act. Examples of these areas are internal market, social policy (but only for specified aspects), economic, social and territorial cohesion, agriculture and fisheries, environment, consumer protection, transport, trans-European networks, energy, area of freedom, security and justice, common safety concerns in public health matters (limited to the aspects defined in the TFEU), research, technological development and space, development cooperation and humanitarian aid.

The third and last field of competences is the supporting competences (Art. 6 TFEU). In these supporting competences, the EU can only intervene to support, coordinate or complement the action of its Member States. These competences cover health protection, industry, culture, tourism, education, vocational training, youth and sport, civil protection and administrative cooperation.

Because of the division of competences in the TFEU 3, 4 and 6 most areas for regulation are outside of an exclusive competence of the EU and therefore part of a process in which the national governments and national parliaments can intervene.

The principle of subsidiarity, defined in Art. 5 (3) TEU, ensures decisions are made as close to citizens as possible and checks if EU-level action is justified compared to national, regional or local levels.

It states that the EU only acts when more effective than lower levels, except in areas within its exclusive jurisdiction. It is closely linked to the principle of proportionality, which requires that the EU's actions are necessary for treaty aims. The principle of conferral maintains that areas not agreed upon in treaties remain under Member States' control.

Nevertheless, there is no common standard or shared understanding of the principle of subsidiarity. As Buzogány and Stuchlik (2012) rightly point out we can find different understandings of the principle of subsidiarity and therefore different ways of using it.

To enact their role as guardians of subsidiarity Member State parliaments have different instruments.

2.1 The Early Warning System (EWS): Monitoring Subsidiarity

The establishment of the Early Warning System (EWS) with the Treaty of Lisbon involves national parliaments in the legislative process at an early stage. Art. 5 (3) and Art. 12 (b) TEU form the legal basis for the role of the national parliaments. They have the right to send a reasoned opinion to the Presidents of the EP, of the Council and of the Commission setting out why a draft does not comply with the principle of subsidiarity. These opinions must be submitted within eight weeks of the transmission of the draft legislative act (Huysmans & van Gruisen, 2022, p. 420).

In practice, the European Commission (2024) received 22 reasoned opinions in 2023. Nine of them were issued by the Italian parliament and five by the Swedish Riksdag. In total, just 9 of the 39 parliaments and chambers submitted reasoned opinions (European Commission, 2024, p. 10).

These numbers are in line with former empirical findings that reasoned opinions are relatively rare (Huysmans & van Gruisen, 2022, p. 421). In the literature, various reasons for the small number of resolutions and their very uneven distribution across parliaments are discussed. These are covered in more detail in Sect. 5.

2.2 Reasoned Opinions and the 'Yellow Card' Procedure

If at least one-third of the national parliaments[1] submit reasoned opinions, a draft must be reviewed by the originator. This procedure is called the 'yellow card' and is laid down in Protocol 2 of the TFEU. Bearing in mind that the Commission received just 22 reasoned opinions in 2023, the prescribed one-third threshold for a yellow card is a relevant hurdle for the national parliaments. In the past, this procedure has only been triggered three times.[2] In one case, the Commission withdrew its proposal.

---

[1] Bicameral parliaments have one vote per chamber. Unicameral parliaments have two votes. Therefore, parliaments need 13 reasoned opinions out of 39 national parliaments to trigger a 'yellow card'.

[2] In 2012: Proposal for a COUNCIL REGULATION on the exercise of the right to take collective action within the context of the freedom of establishment and the freedom to provide services. In 2013: Proposal for a COUNCIL REGULATION on the establishment of the European Public Prosecutor's Office. In 2016: Proposal for a DIRECTIVE OF THE EUROPEAN PARLIAMENT AND OF THE COUNCIL amending Directive 96/71/EC of the European Parliament and of the Council of 16 December 1996 concerning the posting of workers in the framework of the provision of services.

In two cases, the Commission submitted an opinion in which it laid out why these cases are not falling under the subsidiarity rule.

2.3 *The 'Orange Card': A Stronger Stance*

If, under the Ordinary Legislative Procedure, at least a simple majority of the votes of all national parliaments contest the compliance of a legislative proposal with the principle of subsidiarity and the Commission decides to maintain its proposal, it is submitted to the two legislative bodies (EP and Council), which deliver their opinion at first reading. If the two legislative bodies consider that the legislative proposal does not comply with the principle of subsidiarity, they can reject it by a majority of 55% of the members of the Council or a majority of the votes cast in the EP. In this case, we would speak of an 'orange card'. So far, there has not occurred any issuing of an 'Orange Card'.

2.4 *Beyond Subsidiarity: The Political Dialogue*

Even before these formal instruments and legal rights came into effect with the Treaty of Lisbon, the Barroso Commission introduced in 2006 the political dialogue between the Commission and the national parliaments. This dialogue ensures that the national parliaments receive all relevant information (all draft legislative proposals, consultation documents (Green and White Papers)) directly from the Commission and that they can submit their opinions directly to the Commission (which means that they can bypass the national government).

In 2023, the Commission received 380 written opinions, which relate to legislative proposals (70%) as well as to non-legislative initiatives (30%) (European Commission, 2024, p. 16). The numbers show that the political dialogue is much more often used than the early warning mechanism, even if we also see in the numbers that 80% of all issued opinions are raised by ten different parliaments (European Commission, 2024, p. 17).

Besides the written dialogue, there is also an oral dialogue between the Commission and the parliaments of the Member States. The oral dialogue consists of different forms of interaction (visits by members of the Commission to national parliaments and of delegations from national parliaments to the Commission; Commission participation in interparliamentary (committee) meetings and conferences). In 2023, the Commission conducted 127 visits to national parliaments (European Commission, 2024, p. 23).

As a result, we see that national parliaments have a wide range of formal rights to intervene in legislation at the European level. The few cases of yellow cards also show that the formal process does work and lead to active decisions of the Commission. Nevertheless, the most common interaction between the national parliaments and European legislation is through the more informal political dialogue with the Commission.

Reasons for these outcomes will be discussed in Sect. 5 of this article.

Principle of subsidiarity	This principle aims to ensure that decisions are made by those most affected and who are closest to the problem, promoting efficiency and accountability
Principle of proportionality	This principle requires that any action taken should be balanced and least intrusive in relation to its intended objective
Principle of conferral	This principle dictates that the European Union (EU) can only act within the powers granted to it by its member states in the EU treaties

3 Interparliamentary Cooperation: A Collective Voice

Besides the bilateral interaction between national parliaments and the Commission there is also a collective dialogue between the Committees for Union Affairs of Parliaments of the European Union and the European Union. The Conference of Parliamentary Committees for Union Affairs of Parliaments of the European Union (COSAC) serves as the collective voice of national parliaments in EU affairs.

COSAC was established in 1989 way before the Lisbon Treaty, but it is named in Protocol Nr. 1 (Art. 10) as an institution that '[..] submit any contribution it deems appropriate for the attention of the EP, the Council and the Commission.' COSAC plenary meetings are held twice a year, typically in the capital of the EU presidency country. Each Member State parliament is represented by six members; candidate countries are invited to attend with individually three observers (COSAC, 2025).

COSAC's practices have been criticised in many ways, both regarding its structure and its focus (House of Lords, 2014). As a result, COSAC is more of a forum for exchange among parliamentarians, rather than a place for coordinated action with regard to European legislation.

Besides COSAC there are also other interparliamentary forums at the EU level. These forums have a more thematic focus on Common Foreign and Security Policy/ Common Security and Defence Policy (CSDP) or on Economics (Fromage, 2016).

4 Challenges and Limitations to Effective Influence

As we could see, the national parliaments have a variety of instruments to act during the legislative process in the EU. Nevertheless, there are practical and theoretical limitations to their effective influence.

Primarily, the time constraints of the Early Warning System are a practical barrier to more effective use of the subsidiarity control. If national parliaments want to make use of the 'yellow card' mechanism they need one-third of them to issue a reasoned opinion within 8 weeks. This is a tough barrier not just because you have different meeting weeks of the different parliaments but also because there is no common structure for coordination between the parliaments.

At the same time, we can see varying levels of resources and expertise among national parliaments. Parliaments with more formal rights for information in EU affairs as well as their own infrastructure to deal with EU affairs seem to be more engaged in the formal processes of the subsidiarity control (Auel et al., 2015). In addition to varying levels of resources and expertise, the literature also observes different political or policy motivations in EU affairs (Gattermann & Hefftler, 2015).

Further limitations arise from informal practices in the EU decision-making process, the so-called trilogues. These informal meetings between the EP, the Council and the Commission take place before the EP and the Council have adopted their positions. They serve to accelerate the legislative process and reach a compromise between the EU institutions. If they then reach an informal compromise, they can act in concert at first and second readings. National parliaments are not part of these informal processes that often bypass regular legislative procedures. Due to the informality, national parliaments have little opportunity to influence the debate. Furthermore, the formal legislative process can be drastically shortened, rendering the possibility of a resolution by the parliaments ineffective.

5 National Perspectives: The Case of the German Bundestag and Bundesrat

Germany represents a highly institutionalised case of national parliamentary involvement in EU affairs. Both chambers, the Bundestag and the Bundesrat, are granted extensive rights to scrutinise EU legislation. These rights and the requirement of the Federal Government to take the reasoned opinions of the parliamentary actors into account are outlined in Art. 23 of the Basic Law (Grundgesetz) for the Federal Republic of Germany (Abels, 2021).

With an integration process increasingly affecting the competences of the federal states, the so-called Länder, and the Maastricht Treaty looming, in the early 1990s German federal actors called for more influence on the European legislative procedures and in the European Communities' central decision-making body at the time, the Council of Ministers. In the Munich Declaration passed in 1990 and the adoption of a 'European article' in the Basic Law, the participation of the federal states in German European policy was fundamentally strengthened (Bierling, 2005, p. 25). Today the influence of the Länder is the strongest, where their exclusive competencies are affected. This includes the areas of media, culture and education, where the federal states can even be entrusted with leading negotiations in the Council (in coordination with the Federal Government). The Bundestag followed in the footsteps of the Länder and demanded to be heard in European matters.

The exact channels of participation can be found in the so-called EUZBLG, the Act on Cooperation between the Federal Government and the Länder in European Union Affairs and the EUZBBG, the Act on Cooperation between the Federal Government and the German Bundestag in matters concerning the European Union as well as the Federal-Länder-Agreement (BLV) and the Integration Responsibility Act (with the Bundestag).

The participation of the Bundestag and Bundesrat is not only procedural but also political. The Bundestag and the Bundesrat may issue a formal opinion on EU proposals, influencing Germany's negotiation stance at the EU level in a legal but more importantly a political way. To that end, both chambers receive draft legislative proposals, positions from the Federal Government and Commission communications.

In the Bundestag the Committee on European Affairs deals with EU topics. Its position is legally provided for in the Basic Law (Art. 45 GG). Nevertheless, advancing European integration has led to a situation in which European policy is now increasingly being discussed in the specialist committees within the Bundestag. Nevertheless, statements and reasoned opinions by the Bundestag on proposals from the European Union are rare. This can be explained, among other things, by the fact that the majority in the Bundestag is aligned with the interests of the Federal Government (Sterzing & Tidow, 2001, p. 280).

In the Bundesrat, the responsible EU Committee discusses numerous EU proposals before the plenary session takes place. The EU Committee generally relies on the recommendations of the specialist committees. Regularly this reasoned opinion addresses the Federal Government. For some opinions, the EU Committee recommends that the plenary session forwards them directly to the EU Commission. This also applies to opinions that are to be submitted expressly as part of the early warning mechanism on subsidiarity. The Bundesrat is therefore responsible for the majority of all opinions submitted from Germany to the Commission. Nevertheless, reasoned opinions on subsidiarity are also in the Bundesrat rarely adopted. This is because it remains controversial in the political arena whether subsidiarity control should be used as a political or European legal instrument.

Other instruments of state participation include the Conference of Minister Presidents and European Affairs Ministers and the conferences of specialist ministers, in which European policy positions are defined and conveyed, e.g. currently on the upcoming MFF, the Union's Multiannual Financial Framework 2028–2034 and the future of cohesion policy.

Despite these institutional strengths, German parliamentary actors face challenges which curb their influence, particularly informal EU legislative procedures like trilogues. These closed-door negotiations limit transparency and the ability of national parliaments to intervene timely. A key obstacle therefore remains the complexity and pace of EU lawmaking. Still, Germany's case shows how structural capacity, legal avenues and political commitment can enhance parliamentary influence in a multi-level governance system (cf. Gattermann & Hefftler, 2015; Hrbek, 2017).

6 Conclusion: National Parliaments—Essential Partners or Peripheral Players?

National parliaments yield different resources and expertise and operate within different political frameworks. Some parliaments have developed sophisticated systems of EU scrutiny, while others remain under-equipped or politically disinterested. These disparities affect the overall impact of parliamentary engagement at the EU level.

Nevertheless, national parliaments are an indispensable pillar of the multifaceted legitimacy and democratic accountability of the EU. The German case illustrates how institutional reforms, judicial reinforcement and active use of new instruments can elevate the role of national legislatures. For parliaments to move from peripheral players to essential partners in EU governance, ongoing political commitment and institutional learning are crucial (cf. Auel & Benz, 2006; Fabbrini & Granat, 2013; Goldoni, 2014).

References

Abels, G. (2021). Die Rolle des Bundestages in der deutschen Europapolitik aus politologischer Perspektive. In *Handbuch zur deutschen Europapolitik 2021* (pp. 114–129). Nomos.

Auel, K., & Benz, A. (2006). *The Europeanisation of parliamentary democracy*. Routledge.

Auel, K., Rozenberg, O., & Tacea, A. (2015). To scrutinise or not to scrutinise? Explaining variation in EU-related activities in National Parliaments. *West European Politics, 38*(2), 282–304. https://doi.org/10.1080/01402382.2014.990695

Bierling, S. (2005). *Die Außenpolitik der Bundesrepublik Deutschland*. Oldenbourg.

Buzogány, A., & Stuchlik, A. (2012). Subsidiarität und Mitsprache. Nationale Parlamente nach Lissabon. *ZParl, 43*(2), 340–361. https://doi.org/10.5771/0340-1758-2012-2-340

COSAC. (2025). *Conference of parliamentary committees for Union Affairs of Parliaments of the European Union (COSAC)*. COSAC. Retrieved: 6 August 2025 from: https://ipex.eu/IPEXL-WEB/conferences/cosac/home

European Commission. (2024). Annual Report 2023. On The Application of the principles of subsidiarity and on the proportionality and on relations with national parliaments.

Fabbrini, F., & Granat, K. (2013). 'Yellow card, but no foul': The role of the national parliaments under the subsidiarity protocol and the commission proposal for an EU regulation on the right to strike. *Common Market Law Review, 50*(1), 115–144.

Fromage, D. (2016). Increasing inter-parliamentary cooperation in the European Union: Current trends and challenges. *European Public Law, 22*(4), 749–772.

Gattermann, K., & Hefftler, C. (2015). Beyond institutional capacity: Political motivation and parliamentary behaviour in the early warning system. *West European Politics, 38*(2), 305–334. https://doi.org/10.1080/01402382.2014.990696

Goldoni, M. (2014). The early warning system and the Monti II regulation: The case for a political interpretation. *European Constitutional Law Review, 10*(1), 90–114.

House of Lords: The Role of National Parliaments in the European Union. 9th Report of Session 2013–2014. Hg. v. European Union Committee. Retrieved: 6 August 2025 from: https://publications.parliament.uk/pa/ld201314/ldselect/ldeucom/151/15102.htm.

Hrbek, R. (2017). Die Rolle der Länder und des Bundesrates in der deutschen Europapolitik. In K. Böttger & M. Jopp (Eds.), *(2021). Handbuch zur Deutschen Europapolitik*. Nomos.

Huysmans, M., & van Gruisen, P. (2022). Substance and subsidiarity: The economic dimension of conflict in the early warning system. *Journal of European Integration, 44*(3), 411–427. https://doi.org/10.1080/07036337.2020.1869956

Jaroszyński, T. (2020). National Parliaments' scrutiny of the principle of subsidiarity: Reasoned opinions 2014–2019. *European Constitutional Law Review, 16*(1), 91–119. https://doi.org/10.1017/S1574019620000048

Sterzing, C., & Tidow, S. (2001). Die Kontrolle der deutschen Europapolitik durch den EU-Ausschuss des Bundestags—Bilanz und Reformpotenziale. *Integration, 24 (3), 274–288.*

Deniz Alkan focused in his dissertation on the history of European law; he currently serves as the Director for European and International Affairs at the State Chancellery of Saarland. Until 2023 he held the position of Director for European and International Affairs at the State Chancellery of Rhineland-Palatinate and of Head of Unit for European Affairs at the State Chancellery of Nordrhein-Westfalen, where he served from 2004 to 2017.

Eike Hortsch serves as Head of Division for Europe, Finance and Science at the Saarland State Representation in Berlin since 2023. Previously, he worked in various positions for members of the German Bundestag in the European Affairs committee.

Influencing EU Law- and Decision Making: Strategies of Business and Civil Society

Lobbying in the European Union: Integrating Academic Approaches and Practitioner's Perspectives

Doris Dialer and Irina Michalowitz

Abstract After Washington D.C., Brussels is considered 'the' hotspot for lobbying in the European Union (EU). On the one hand, integration and enlargement dynamics have contributed to the growth, differentiation and professionalisation of the occupational area; on the other hand, in-transparent lobbying practices, structural imbalances and systemic legitimacy deficits are criticised. At the same time, exerting influence is a treaty-based (Art. 11 (1–2) TEU, Art. 13 TEU, Art. 57, 245, 295 TFEU) component of the EU law- and decision-making process. The chapter seeks to provide an exhaustive overview by focusing on the institutional, theoretical and practical factors framing EU lobbying strategies and their success.

Keywords Lobbying in the EU · Interest representation · Lobbying techniques · Lobbying strategies · Public affairs · Lobbyists · Lobbying targets

1 Introduction

This chapter offers a comprehensive assessment of academic approaches to EU lobbying and practitioners' perspectives on those findings. The authors' combined four decades of experience in this field—encompassing both scholarly research on interest representation and professional engagements in EU institutions and in public

D. Dialer (✉)
Consumer Affairs Attaché, Permanent Representation of Austria to the EU, Brussel, Belgium

Innsbruck Center for European Research (ICER), Innsbruck, Austria
e-mail: doris.dialer@hochschule-burgenland.at

I. Michalowitz (✉)
Vice President Public Policy & Government Relations, DeepL SE/Cologne, and Founding Director, IMConsult bv, Brussels, Belgium
e-mail: im@imconsult.eu

G. Füricht-Fiegl et al. (eds.), *Handbook on EU Law-making*, Professional Practice in Governance and Public Organizations, https://doi.org/10.1007/978-3-032-16559-6_21

affairs—allow a unique perspective on lobbying and advocacy in Brussels. The EU's multi-level governance system creates a complex environment for lobbyists, necessitating a deep understanding of decision-making processes and in particular the Ordinary Legislative Procedure (OLP), the roles of the various EU institutional actors and their interaction.

This chapter addresses the following core questions: How have theoretical approaches to EU lobbying evolved, and how do they contribute to understanding influence on policy- and lawmaking? What are the specific challenges and opportunities for interest representatives in targeting European lawmaking institutions such as the European Commission, the European Parliament (EP) and the Council of the EU, and what is successful lobbying? To answer these questions, we first provide an overview of the theoretical approaches conceptualising lobbying through an academic lens. Next, we identify the key actors and institutional stakeholders involved, followed by a discussion of techniques and strategies used to achieve lobbying success.

2 Academic Approaches

Academic literature on EU lobbying has grown significantly over the past two decades. A simple Google Scholar search reveals more than 3000 scholarly articles specifically on EU lobbying, with more than 300,000 when less restrictive search terms are used—a significant increase from only 142 publications detected prior to 2000, reflecting the escalating academic interest in this subject examined by numerous scientific disciplines (Bunea & Baumgartner, 2014). In terms of focus, a shift has taken place, starting from general research on interest groups (e.g. Mazey & Richardson, 1993) to more nuanced assessments of institutional access, strategies and influence (e.g. Bouwen, 2002; Coen & Richardson, 2009; Dialer & Richter, 2014, 2019; Michalowitz, 2002).

Early theoretical conceptualisations primarily adopted a macro-level view of stakeholder relations. Initial attempts to derive concepts from national observations—such as pluralism which viewed interest groups in an open competition with each other (Schmitter & Lehmbruch, 1979) or (neo)corporatism which focused on institutionalised negotiations between selected umbrella associations and the government (Streeck & Schmitter, 1985)—proved insufficient in adequately depicting the EU's evolving political system (Greenwood, 2007; Mazey & Richardson, 1993).

Rationalist variations of neo-institutionalism offered an alternative theoretical framework by illuminating how stakeholders strategically adapt to the conditions of the political system (March & Olsen, 1989).

However, those approaches still fell short of comprehensively capturing the unique character of EU's governance system. A significant theoretical development was the conceptualisation of the EU as a multi-level governance system, significantly shaped by Marks (1993) and later applied to interest representation by scholars like Kohler-Koch and Eising (1999).

In a multi-level governance system, political decisions are interpreted as contingent upon the interaction of various public and private stakeholders, thereby extending beyond the narrow circle of policymakers with a political mandate. This approach helped to conceptually place private actors into a theoretical framework of EU decision-making processes. Around the turn of the millennium, an 'informational theory of lobbying' gained prominence, interpreting lobbying as primarily an exchange of information. It was informed by a range of broader theoretical concepts, such as exchange theory, institutional theory, access theory or policy network theory (e.g. Hall & Deardorff, 2006).

This perspective initially led to predominantly descriptive assessments across various policy sectors, with the underlying assumption that lobbying influence depends on the quality and relevance of information provided, and the ability of lobbyists to match their offerings with the specific needs of policymakers. Building on this approach, Bouwen (2002, 2004) developed a 'logic of access', and Michalowitz (2004, 2007) explored lobbying as a triangle between principals (private stakeholders such as companies or national public interest organisations), their agents (lobbyists) and EU institutions. Bouwen argued that the Commission grants access to interest groups primarily based on their capacity to provide relevant policy information and expertise. Michalowitz maintained that the informational exchange between policymakers and private actors is led by self-interests of all actors involved.

More recently, scholars expanded on this work by examining in greater detail how transparency and accountability influence EU lobbying (e.g. Coen & Richardson, 2009). Integrity of EU Institutions has been often called into question, especially in the wake of major cash-for-influence scandals (Dialer & Richter, 2013, 2014). Thus, policymakers have been considering regulatory options (e.g. transparency rules, codes of conducts, financial disclosure commitments) to minimise undue influence and conflicts of interests in particular.

In this context, Chari (2024) distinguishes broadly between two generations of research on lobbying regulation. The first generation consists of single country analyses (e.g. Dialer & Opitz, 2011), comparative approaches and analysis of the strength of national lobbying laws in terms of promoting transparency and accountability. Building on this, the second generation of lobbying regulation research that started mostly after 2009 expands investigation on several themes, including the need for reform; the international dimensions of regulating foreign lobbyists; how lobbying transparency can be linked to other transparency policies; the impact of lobbying (soft) laws on lobbyists; how data from transparency registers can be used to understand lobbying behaviour; and whether or not having rules increases public trust.

During this period, quantitative empirical methods have gained high popularity (e.g. Kritzinger & Michalowitz, 2005). The focus has also shifted to understanding the relevance of financial resources (Baumgartner et al., 2009) and refining the assessment of lobbying influence, often with a more specific focus on influence exertion within specific sectors or by particular stakeholders (Coen et al., 2024; Coen & Richardson, 2009).

Indeed, interest group density and diversity vary significantly across policy areas. Generally, there is greater business interest mobilisation in policy areas that are primarily regulatory in nature, such as finance, technology and transport. Policymakers in these fields require technical expertise provided by the business interests they impact. Conversely, we tend to observe diverse interest mobilisation, such as civil society and NGOs, in policy areas that can be understood broadly as (re-)distributive, for example employment, youth and migration (Coen & Katsaitis, 2024, p. 3).

While the scope of this chapter is limited and cannot fully encompass the vast literature on EU interest representation and lobbying, the authors try to draw a differentiated and practical picture of EU lobbying as the 'art' of influencing EU decision- and lawmaking.

3 Key Actors

EU Treaties lay down the principle of open Union decision-making which should be carried out 'as closely as possible to the citizen' (Art. 10 (3) TEU) and prescribe that both citizens and representative associations should be given the opportunity to 'make known and publicly exchange their views in all areas of Union action' (Art. 11 (1) TEU).

Against this background, scholarly accounts of key actors in lobbying vary in their focus, typically concentrating on decision-makers labelled as holders of *de jure* power as lobbying targets on the one hand, and the lobbyists (interest representatives) without political legitimacy or executive power (e.g. Earnshaw & Judge, 2002; Marshall, 2010; Panke, 2012) on the other as well as the processes through which they interact (e.g. De Bruycker & Beyers, 2019; Stoilova, 2021), or broader principles uniting targets, lobbyists and processes.

From the practitioner's standpoint, it is particularly valuable to understand the respective interests of institutional decision-makers and lobbyists as engaging in an exchange of information for a limited level of influence in return for a limited level of information.

3.1 Lobbyists: Influencer's Sphere

EU institutions interact with a wide range of lobbyists representing specific interests. This is a legitimate part of the lawmaking process, ensuring EU policies reflect society's and business's real needs. Insofar as interest representation activities are carried out in return for remuneration, these, including those for third countries, constitute a service according to Art. 57 TFEU. The EU (COM(2006)194) defines lobbying as 'all activities carried out with the objective of influencing the policy formulation and decision-making processes of the EU institutions'.

Given the fact that there is no strict typology, interests can be differentiated in various ways, be it according to the number of cooperating members, the organisational form, the type of interests or the policy areas (e.g. security, health, energy, etc.). As of Feb. 2026 the European Union Transparency Register (EUTR)[1] counts around 16,850 lobbying organisations.

Those who engage in lobbying activities are predominantly private stakeholders, representing a broad spectrum of civil society interests, ranging from corporate entities to NGOs. Companies typically aim to avoid new regulation or identify new business opportunities, while NGOs tend to focus on overarching goals such as the protection of fundamental rights or climate change (see Coen & Richardson, 2009; Greenwood, 2007).

Although there is no universally recognised, comprehensive typology of Brussels lobbyists, five major categories can be distinguished—whose members are trying to influence European policy and lawmaking processes in slightly different ways.

3.1.1 Associations (Businesses, Trade Unions, Professionals)

Associations are the most common way of interest representation in Brussels. The EUTR provides a fairly accurate account of lobbying interests, at the time of writing counting over 10,000 associations of various types, out of a total of 16,850 entries (see EUTR, February 2026).[2] Associations act as a broad radar for monitoring important policies and are particularly important where representativity matters. They manage both priority and non-priority issues for their members and represent the strength of the sector to policymakers—if they manage to align their members' views. Associations representing sectors with strong competition between members are often forced to rely on the lowest common denominator, which pushes some members to divert to other lobbying channels.

3.1.2 Companies (In-House Lobbyists)

Many larger organisations maintain internal teams dedicated to analysing public policy initiatives and engaging with policymakers. In-house lobbyists provide organisation-specific knowledge. They often focus on priority cases, with a particular strength in engaging with national Members of European Parliament (MEPs) and their organisation's EU member countries in the Council. They also provide a control mechanism and security net if other interest representation methods fail. Their main advantage is in their ability to lobby the specific interests of their organisation, without needing to align those interests with others. This advantage is at the

[1] An open database (www.transparency-register.eu) with up-to-date information about EU interest representation activities.

[2] Professional lobbyists have a powerful incentive to join the register, as this is a prerequisite for regular meetings with MEPs and for receiving an entry badge to the European Parliament building.

same time their main disadvantage: views from a single company are of interest to policymakers to understand the concrete impact of legislation, but can be perceived as too narrow (Michalowitz, 2002). Broad coalitions are necessary to identify broader economic or societal issues and to achieve policy changes.

3.1.3 Non-Governmental Organisations (NGOs)

There is a dense landscape of NGOs advocating at EU level for virtually every imaginable cause relying on a universalist approach to legitimacy, drawing on EU funding and grants from independent foundations and utilising to the full various resource sharing and coalition building models. As economic interests dominate, the Commission attempts to compensate for the inferiority of weakly organised civil society interest organisations through financial support. However, the lack of financial independence diminishes their credibility. In addition, research has demonstrated that EU funds have also instigated a growth process among NGOs, especially humanitarian ones, transforming them into large entities with substantial budgets, enabling them to effectively engage in advocacy activities. Hence the disclosure of the lobbying budgets of NGOs in the EUTR and the use of EU funds for lobbying purposes has been the subject of controversy and discussion (Dialer, 2025).

3.1.4 Public Affairs Consultancies, Law Firms and Think Tanks

External consultancies provide specialised public affairs expertise, often working on a retainer or project basis for various clients who may lack in-house capacity, a network of relevant contacts, or require supplementary services. Consultancy support ranges from establishing lobbying offices, developing lobbying strategies, organising meetings and taking on outsourced tasks. They typically have an especially good expertise regarding appropriate points of contact on their clients' policy issues. At the same time, they are costly, and they cannot perform interest representation themselves because they are regarded a hired service that cannot credibly speak on behalf of a client. Their credibility is sometimes questioned regarding their transparency and 'revolving door' practices where former EU officials switch into lobbying roles (Michalowitz, 2007).

A sub-set of consultancy services is the category of law firms and think tanks. International law firms often offer public affairs as an adjacent service to their legal expertise, especially in highly technical and regulated fields. The difficulties in distinguishing clearly when certain services provided by law firms are classified as legal services or when they instead touch the realm of lobbying raise major issues in terms of registration of law firms in the EUTR (Korkea-Aho, 2021). Brussels think tanks are generally not seen as lobbyists. However, if they are financed mainly by business via membership fees their autonomy and credibility is likely to be questioned (Dialer & Füricht-Fiegl, 2014; Dialer & Kelstrup, 2019).

3.1.5 Regions and Third States

The main goals behind regional presence in Brussels can be described as lobbying, accessing EU funds, gathering and providing information and cooperating with other regions. Stronger regions from high-devolution countries are making active efforts to influence EU policymaking, while weaker regions from centralised Member States rather concentrate on seeking EU funding. Most European regions and local authorities started to formally establish liaison offices in Brussels in the 1980s, in a rising wave which can be attributed to multiple factors, like the expansion of the European Community legislative fields and the reform of structural and cohesion policies. With the creation of the Committee of the Regions[3] territorial interests were accommodated within the institutional framework (Dialer & Mast, 2012; Greenwood, 2014; Rodriguez-Pose & Courty, 2018).

Third states or foreign lobbying have not figured prominently in the study of European lawmaking. However, lobbying of other countries' political and legal elites has emerged as a security risk globally (Lavenex & Öberg, 2023). The EU regulates foreign lobbying through its general transparency tool, the EUTR which also applies to foreign governments, foreign entities and non-profits based abroad. This means that professional consulting (both EU and non-EU) firms need to disclose their third country governments as clients. The change reflects the growing role of intermediaries, such as public affairs consultants, at the inter-state level and the growing proportion of foreign governments as clients for lobbying services (Korkea-aho, 2023).

3.2 Targets: Lawmakers' Sphere

The EU's complex multi-level system offers lobbyists a large number of contact points. Art. 13 TEU lists a total of seven institutions that safeguard the interests of citizens. Nevertheless, lobbying in the narrower sense is concentrated on the Council of the EU, the European Parliament (EP) and the Commission, with the latter being the focus due to its right of initiative. The EP can shape or weaken a legislative proposal through amendments. The Council basically represents the interests of the Member States.

3.2.1 European Commission

The Commission serves as the initial and crucial entry point for lobbyists, as it holds the exclusive right to initiate legislation, even though Member States prepare guidance, and the EP attempts to influence its agenda. Commission officials are keen to

---

[3] See Chap. 22 Consultative Bodies of this handbook.

balance their need for stakeholder input to understand the practical challenges of proposed legislation with their independent role as lawmakers.

A key strategic consideration for lobbyists is whether to engage at the 'bottom' (administrative services level) or the 'top' (cabinet level) of the Commission's internal hierarchy. Engagement at earlier stages of the legislative process offers greater opportunities for advocating alternative options, as officials' positions are less entrenched (see Coen & Richardson, 2009; Greenwood, 2019). Once the responsible unit has drafted a legislative proposal, the scope for influence narrows significantly, and meetings tend to focus on a limited number of contentious points and anticipated conflicts with the EP or Council (Michalowitz, 2007).

A legislative proposal first advances internally through the Directorates-General (DGs) hierarchy, followed by an 'inter-service' consultation involving a limited number of other DGs representatives who express their concerns or support. Finally, the proposal reaches the political level, specifically the responsible Commissioner's cabinet. The Commissioner then seeks support from their peers during weekly College of Commissioners meetings. Although the College could theoretically vote, consensus is the preferred decision-making method. Not all Commissioners hold equal standing: Executive Vice-Presidents, for instance, have higher seniority than ordinary Commissioners, each of whom is subordinate to an Executive Vice-President. Informally, certain sectors and nationalities may also carry more weight than others.

Influencing the political level demands political acumen, knowledge of political interests and contacts, often requiring the direct involvement of senior executives from the private stakeholder organisation. Depending on the politicisation of an issue, lobbyists might choose to engage directly with the political level, hoping to exert pressure on the service levels.

Academic discourse on lobbying the Commission emphasises its unique role as both legislator and executive branch of the EU's governance system, which makes it a particularly important target for lobbying actors (Michalowitz, 2007; Coen & Richardson, 2009). In line with informational theories of lobbying, where influence is largely considered an exchange of expertise and information, some authors, such as Michalowitz (2005), examined the conditions under which interest groups exert influence and found that while private actors contribute to decision-making, their overall influence on EU policymaking might be less strong than sometimes assumed.

3.2.2 Council of the European Union

The Council of the EU (Council of Ministers) brings together the governments of the EU's 27 Member States and is primarily known as co-legislator, coming to an agreement (in most cases under what is known as the ordinary or co-decision procedure) with the EP on Commission's legislative proposals. Often the Council takes a less progressive position than the EP—watering down good proposals or opposing EP's efforts to improve bad proposals.

Final decisions—generally based on 'qualified majority'—are ultimately agreed by the Council of Ministers in a series of 10 different configurations depending on the subject being discussed. Although EU ministers meet in public as required by Art. 15 (2) TFEU, the work of its preparatory bodies, notably the Committee of Permanent Representatives (COREPER) and the approximately 150 working parties, is still taking place in camera.

The Council is also a fertile territory for lobbyists: whether it is via Member State ministers and officials in their capitals; via the 27 Member States' permanent representations—the multi-lateral embassies to the EU—in Brussels; or via the General Secretariat (based in Brussels with around 3000 staff members) of the Council which supports the work of both the European Council and the Council (presidency).

Beyond the Council procedures, lobbyists can exert influence via states' membership of Commission expert groups; via 'comitology' committees which oversee the implementation of EU laws; and through informal routes, such as personal contacts with national stakeholders. The lobbying of Member States is far more indirect, subtle and harder to map because Council interests are primarily capital's interests, which lobbyists must address to gain a country's support in Council negotiations.

A distinctive feature of the Council is that it operates under rotating leadership which grants governments substantial agenda-setting power and influence over policy outcomes. As a result, presiding Member States as well as incoming presidencies are prime targets of lobbyists. The Council presidency rotates among the EU Member States, changing every six months. It organises and chairs meetings and draws up compromises to facilitate decision-making. Acting as a chair in all Council formats, the presidency is simultaneously responsible for different agendas, thus having the power to slow down or speed up compromise finding especially on priority files.

In this context, Van Gruisen (2025) underlines that for interest groups seeking to influence decision-makers in the presiding country, hiring a local lobbyist is common practice to get access. This fact highlights not only the key role of consultancies in the lobbying industry but also the necessity of effective national-level lobbying regulation.

3.2.3 European Parliament

The growth in EP's legislative power post-Lisbon Treaty concurred with an increase in lobbying and scholarly attention. Research comprises access to EP committees and MEPs (Binderkrantz & Pedersen, 2017; Marshall, 2010, 2015) and levels of lobbying success (Dionigi, 2017) as well as regulatory attempts (Dialer, 2025; Dialer & Richter, 2014).

Once a policy initiative enters the legislative process, it is subject to scrutiny and amendment by the Council and EP as well as the national parliaments. Especially the enormous highly technical workload MEPs have to deal with gives room for lobbyists to influence them directly or their personal staff, the Accredited Parliamentary Assistants (APA) (Dialer et al., 2015; Dialer & Richter, 2019, pp. 7–8).

According to the latest Transparency International report MEPs have published 32,971 meetings with lobbyists since the start of this mandate back in July 2024. This is an increase of 314% compared to a similar period in the last mandate. This tremendous development can be attributed largely to the EP's stricter transparency rules, which now require that all MEPs—not only rapporteurs, shadow rapporteurs and committee chairs—and their assistants must declare lobby meetings, including with both lobby organisations and representatives of third countries. Unsurprisingly, the types of organisations MEPs are meeting reflect the political divide between the left and the right (Engelbrecht-Bogdanov, 2025).

The 22 EP standing committees and two subcommittees constitute the EP's legislative backbone. This means that the EP's overall position is determined in the responsible committee ahead of plenary discussions and votes. The composition of the committees reflects the plenary assembly. This means that lobbying focuses on the committee stage. Although all MEPs can seek to influence a dossier under scrutiny, the greatest influence is wielded by rapporteurs, co-rapporteurs, shadow rapporteurs and coordinators. Committees consist of 25 to 90 full members and an equivalent number of substitutes. Committee debates and hearings are held in public and, in principle, can be followed via web streaming.

MEPs are accountable to their constituencies in their home countries and must build majorities within the EP. Consequently, they actively seek arguments from private stakeholders that resonate with voters and can facilitate consensus building with other party groups. In this respect, Ibenskas and Bunea (2021) argue that MEPs give recognition to those organisations that are instrumental for achieving key political goals: re-election, career-progression and policy influence. This argument acknowledges the importance of the broader context in which MEPs operate.

4 Techniques, Strategies and Lobbying Success

Defining lobbying success is complex and often ambiguous. Identifying a successful lobbying campaign is dubious, as those who claim victory might have merely benefited from aligning with existing political interests or freeriding on others' activities—and those who worked successfully behind the scenes may prefer not to be publicly associated with the outcome. Success thus highly depends on its definition.

Given that lobbyists do not hold a mandate in democratically run systems, their influence is inherently 'soft'. It is limited to providing compelling arguments, rather than coercing or bribing policymakers into decisions. Success must therefore be measured differently.

Academic literature identifies key success factors for lobbying, including the ability to create high-quality arguments (Bouwen, 2002; Michalowitz, 2007), introducing them at the appropriate moment within the legislative process (e.g. Bernhagen & Bräuninger, 2005; Hall & Deardorff, 2006), and the smart utilisation of sufficient financial resources (Almansa-Martínez & Castillo-Esparcia, 2022; Baumgartner et al., 2009; Serna-Ortega et al., 2025)—all of which require a deep understanding of the decision-making process and the ability to spot and reap opportunities to shape that process. From practical experience, the following three factors have proven critical:

'Smelling the Coffee': Anticipation of Future Political Developments An efficient lobbyist must be able to identify and correctly interpret political developments early enough to provide ample warning to their organisation. Lobbyists play a critical role in enabling their employers or clients to react proactively and integrate anticipated effects into internal organisational processes.

Many Adequate Contacts When Push Comes to Shove Lobbyists should function as an 'insurance policy', ensuring that political developments do not create unforeseen obstacles for their respective organisations or client. In the rare instances where situations escalate unfavourably, they must be capable of facilitating engagement with appropriate levels of decision-makers when necessary. This capacity demonstrates a lobbyist's diligence in cultivating relationships and building trust when not under immediate pressure.

Knowing Where It Hurts: Addressing Pain Points A key aspect of effective lobbying is that critical pain points are recognised in discussions and, ideally, addressed within policy proposals and co-legislators' amendments. This requires diligent execution of core lobbying duties, such as responding to public consultations, creating 'leave-behind' documents, active engagement in trade associations, conducting bilateral meetings and generally garnering for support across the board.

Overall, lobbying success depends significantly on recognising emerging windows of opportunity opening and swiftly seizing them—mainly through engaging with third parties than solely direct approaches. Subtle differences in approach exist between in-house lobbyists, who may adopt a more direct engagement style, and associations, which must first achieve alignment among their members.

5 Conclusion

Lobbying is one of the pillars of any twenty-first-century democracy. It helps decision-makers navigate various policy options and diversifies their sources of information, which in practice leads to better outcomes. In this chapter, we address the important question about the relationship between EU lawmakers (targets) and influencers (lobbyists). We showed why, when and how key actors interact in the framework of the OLP and beyond. When conducted ethically and transparent, lobbying serves as a crucial element of a functioning democracy. In theory as well as in political practice, lobbyists are often expected to provide technical expertise and important insights into the potential impact of legislative ideas that would otherwise not be considered, and to function as a 'transmission belt' to reduce the distance between citizens and decision-makers. A key challenge for the future will be for the EU to ensure accountability for policymakers and lobbyists alike, to prevent and deter corruption attempts and to provide fair opportunities for representation to all types of interest.

References

Almansa-Martínez, A., & Castillo-Esparcia, A. (2022). Lobbying and the nonprofit sector. In *The Routledge handbook of nonprofit communication* (pp. 203–214). Routledge.

Baumgartner, F. R., Berry, J. M., Hojnacki, M., Kimball, D. C., & Leech, B. L. (2009). *Lobbying and policy change: Who wins, who loses, and why*. University of Chicago Press.

Bernhagen, P., & Bräuninger, T. (2005). Structural power and public policy: A signaling model of business lobbying in democratic capitalism. *Political Studies, 53*(1), 43–64.

Binderkrantz, A., & Pedersen, H. H. (2017). What is access? A discussion of the definition and measurement of interest groups. *European Political Science, 16*(3), 306–321.

Bouwen, P. (2002). Corporate lobbying in the European Union: The logic of access. *Journal of European Public Policy, 9*(3), 365–390.

Bouwen, P. (2004). Exchanging access goods for access: A comparative study of business lobbying in the European Union institutions. *European Journal of Political Research, 43*(3), 337–369.

Bunea, A., & Baumgartner, F. R. (2014). The state of the discipline: Authorship, research designs, and citation patterns in studies of EU interest groups and lobbying. *Journal of European Public Policy, 21*(10), 1412–1434.

Chari, R. (2024). New perspectives on lobbying regulation and reform: Two generations of research. *Interest Groups Advocacy, 13*, 381–395. https://doi.org/10.1057/s41309-024-00227-5

Coen, D., & Katsaitis, A. (Eds.). (2024). *Handbook on lobbying and public policy*. Edward Elgar Publishing.

Coen, D., & Richardson, J. (Eds.). (2009). *Lobbying the European Union: Institutions, actors, and issues*. Oxford University Press.

Coen, D., Katsaitis, A., & Vannoni, M. (2024). Regulating government affairs: Integrating lobbying research and policy concerns. *Regulation and Governance, 18*(1), 73–80.

De Bruycker, I., & Beyers, J. (2019). Lobbying strategies and success: Inside and outside lobbying in European Union legislative politics. *European Political Science Review, 11*(1), 57–74.

Dialer, D. (2025). Lobbying und Interessenvertretung. In W. Weidenfeld, W. Wessels, & F. Tekin (Eds.), *Europa von A bis Z. Taschenbuch der Europäischen Integration* (16th ed.). Springer VS.

Dialer, D., & Füricht-Fiegl, G. (2014). EU think tanks in the Back seat? Perspectives for the 21st century. In Spindler, M. & Van der Zouwen, T. (Eds.). On the move: Patterns, power, politics. *COS (Challenging Organizations and Society) Journal, 3*(2), 561–569.

Dialer, D., & Kelstrup, J. D. (2019). EU think tank lobbying strategies: Between theoretical advice and practice. In D. Dialer & M. Richter (Eds.), *Lobbying in the European Union: Strategies, dynamics and trends* (pp. 445–459). Springer.

Dialer, D., & Mast, F. (2012). EU-Lobbying der Regionen am Beispiel der österreichischen Bundesländer. In P. Filzmaier, P. Plaikner, & K. A. Duffek (Eds.), *Bundesländer und Landtage. Föderalismus und politischer Wettbewerb, österreichische Besonderheiten und internationaler Vergleich* (pp. 74–90). Facultas.

Dialer, D., & Opitz, A. (2011). Vienna prepares tougher lobbying law than Brussels after MEP scandal. *Europe's World, 19*, 133.

Dialer, D., & Richter, M. (2013). Catch the lobbyist. Regulierung von lobbying auf EU-Ebene. In T. Feri (Ed.), *Politikberatung in Österreich. Herausforderungen - Strategien - Perspektiven* (2nd ed., pp. 267–272). Braumüller.

Dialer, D., & Richter, M. (2014). *Lobbying in der Europäischen Union. Zwischen Professionalisierung und Regulierung*. Springer VS.

Dialer, D., & Richter, M. (Eds.). (2019). *Lobbying in the European Union: Strategies, dynamics and trends*. Springer.

Dialer, D., Maurer, A., & Richter, M. (2015). *Handbuch zum Europäischen Parlament*. Nomos Verlag.

Dionigi, M. K. (2017). *Lobbying in the European Parliament. The battle for influence*. Palgrave Macmillan.

Earnshaw, D., & Judge, D. (2002). No simple dichotomies: Lobbyists and the European Parliament. *The Journal of Legislative Studies, 8*(4), 61–79.

Engelbrecht-Bogdanov, P. (2025). MEPs and their lobby meetings, one year in: new rules, more meetings, more cause for concern? *Transparency International Report*. https://transparency.eu/new-mep-meetings/

Greenwood, J. (2007). Organized civil society and democratic legitimacy in the European Union. *British Journal of Political Science, 37*(2), 333–357.

Greenwood, J. (2014). Actors of the common interest? The Brussels offices of the regions. In *Functional and territorial interest representation in the EU* (pp. 89–103). Routledge.

Greenwood, J. (2019). *Interest organizations and European Union politics*. Oxford University Press.

Hall, R. L., & Deardorff, A. V. (2006). Lobbying as legislative subsidy. *American Political Science Review, 100*(1), 69–84.

Ibenskas, R., & Bunea, A. (2021). Legislators, organizations and ties: Understanding interest group recognition in the European Parliament. *European Journal of Political Research, 60*(3), 560–582.

Kohler-Koch, B., & Eising, R. (Eds.). (1999). *The transformation of governance in the European Union* (Vol. 12). Psychology Press.

Korkea-aho, E. (2021). Legal lobbying: The evolving (but hidden) role of lawyers and law firms in the EU public affairs market. *German Law Journal, 22*(1), 65–84.

Korkea-aho, E. (2023). The end of an era for foreign lobbying? The emergence of foreign transparency Laws in Washington, Canberra and Brussels. *JCMS: Journal of Common Market Studies*, 1529–1546.

Kritzinger, S., & Michalowitz, I. (2005). Party position changes through EU membership? The (non-) Europeanisation of Austrian, finish and Swedish political parties. *Politique européenne, 16*(2), 19–51.

Lavenex, S., & Öberg, M.-L. (2023). Third country influence on EU law and policy-making: Setting the scene. *JCMS. Journal of Common Market Studies, 61*, 1435–1453.

March, J., & Olsen, J. (1989). P (1989) Rediscovering Institutions: The Organizational Basis of Politics. *New York–London*.

Marks, G. (1993). Structural policy and multilevel governance in the EC. *The State of the European Community, 2*, 391–410.

Marshall, D. (2010). Who to lobby and when: Institutional determinants of interest group strategies in European Parliament committees. *European Union Politics, 11*(4), 553–575.

Marshall, D. (2015). Explaining interest group interactions with party group members in the European Parliament: Dominant party groups and coalition formation. *Journal of Common Market Studies, 53*(2), 311–329.

Mazey, S., & Richardson, J. (1993, March). Policy-Making Styles in the European Community: Consultation of Groups and the Process of European Integration. In *International Studies Association 34th Annual Convention, Acapulco, Mexico* (pp. 23–27).

Michalowitz, I. (2002). EU business associations: Meeting the needs of Europe's service sectors? In *The effectiveness of EU business associations* (pp. 131–142). Palgrave Macmillan UK.

Michalowitz, I. (2004). *EU lobbying-principals, agents and targets: Strategic interest intermediation in EU policy-making*. LIT-Verlag.
Michalowitz, I. (2007). What determines influence? Assessing conditions for decision-making influence of interest groups in the EU. *Journal of European Public Policy, 14*(1), 132–151.
Panke, D. (2012). Lobbying institutional key players: How states seek to influence the European Commission, the council presidency and the European Parliament. *JCMS: Journal of Common Market Studies, 50*(1), 129–150.
Rodriguez-Pose, A., & Courty, J. (2018). Regional lobbying and structural funds: Do regional representation offices in Brussels deliver? *Regional & Federal Studies, 28*(2), 199–229. https://doi.org/10.1080/13597566.2018.1441828
Schmitter, P. C., & Lehmbruch, G. (Eds.). (1979). *Trends towards corporatist intermediation: Organizing interests in Western Europe*. Sage.
Serna-Ortega, Á., Almansa-Martínez, A., & Castillo-Esparcia, A. (2025). Influence of lobbying in EU policy process phases. *Frontiers in Political Science, 7*, 1511918.
Stoilova, V. (2021). The Role of Lobbying in the Decision-Making Process in the European Union. In *International Conference KNOWLEDGE-BASED ORGANIZATION* (Vol. 27, No. 2).
Streeck, W., & Schmitter, P. C. (1985). *Private interest government: Beyond market and state*. Cambridge University Press.
Van Gruisen, P. (2025). *Lobbying and rotating leadership*.

Doris Dialer is Attachée for Consumer Affairs at the Permanent Representation of Austria to the EU. She has over 20 years of EU professional experience. From 2006 to 2019, she was working at the European Parliament. During the COVID pandemic, she was a policy adviser on EU, WHO and International Affairs to the Austrian Federal Minister for Social Affairs, Health, Care and Consumer Protection. She has a strong academic angle, and lectures and publishes intensely on EU lawmaking, public policies, institutions and lobbying. Doris holds an MA and Ph.D. in Political Science from the University of Innsbruck.

Irina Michalowitz is Senior Director of Policy and Government Relations at Palo Alto Networks. She has over 25 years of experience in senior management positions in corporations, NGOs and associations at the intersection of technology, governance and policy as well as an academic and trainer background focused on EU policymaking and lobbying. She holds an MBA from WU Executive Academy and a Ph.D. in Political Science jointly from Robert-Schuman University and the University of Hamburg.

The Importance of the Right Tone: How to Shape Successful Stakeholder Communication in EU Advocacy

Sebastián Rodríguez Pérez

Abstract This chapter explores how external stakeholders—particularly businesses and civil society groups—use tone in their communication to influence EU lawmaking. It shows how adjusting messages to fit the audience and stage of policymaking can open doors or close them. Drawing on case studies and communication research, it explains how tone shapes credibility, builds engagement and helps campaigns align with EU institutions. The focus is on practical strategies: How to speak so you get heard in Brussels.

Keywords Advocacy · Campaigning · Civil society · Lobbying · Storytelling · Emotions · Messaging · Social media · Digital · Persuasion

1 Introduction

In EU policymaking, *how* you speak often matters as much as *what* you say. The Union's legal machinery is complex, involving the Commission, the European Parliament (EP), the Council, agencies and national governments. Messages pass across different cultures, languages and political expectations. A wrong tone can shut you out. A right one can shift a vote.

Advocates who succeed in Brussels adapt their tone to audience and timing. Research by Serna-Ortega et al. (2025) confirms: Civil society groups lead with values and public engagement early on; business actors come in later with detailed technical input. Both types of actors switch tone depending on whom they are speaking to, whether it is a policymaker, a journalist or the general public.

S. R. Pérez (✉)
Rollout Democracy, Córdoba, Spain
e-mail: sebastian@campaignplaybook.eu

G. Füricht-Fiegl et al. (eds.), *Handbook on EU Law-making*, Professional Practice in Governance and Public Organizations, https://doi.org/10.1007/978-3-032-16559-6_22

This chapter frames tone as a strategic tool, with sections on audience, storytelling, emotional vs. rational appeals, credibility, feedback and coalition-building. Real examples show how tone shaped EU campaigns, with guidance for both civil society and business actors.

2 Strategic Elements of Tone in EU Campaigning

2.1 *Know Your Audience*

Begin by mapping *who* you are speaking to. Effective communication in EU advocacy begins with a clear understanding of who the audience is. The EU legislative arena is shaped by a wide range of stakeholders—officials from the Commission and its Directorates-General (DG), Members of the European Parliament (MEPs), national ministers and their staff operating within the Council, journalists and commentators, peer organisations and EU citizens themselves. Each has distinct priorities and communication styles, so tone is a strategic choice, not an aesthetic one.

Commission officials tend to expect formal, evidence-based communication. They respond best to structured, neutral language and references to legal frameworks or technical data. By contrast, MEPs are often more responsive to ideological framing and the direct relevance of an issue to their constituencies. Their discourse allows for greater emotional range and political colour. National ministries are more cautious, typically weighing messages against national policy interests and internal political dynamics. Meanwhile, communication aimed at the public—whether through campaigns or citizen engagement tools—must prioritise clarity, accessibility and cultural relevance. Here, metaphor, imagery and emotional tone may carry more weight than procedural detail.

This segmentation has been confirmed by Serna-Ortega et al. (2025), who show that advocacy groups adopt different strategies according to the phase of policymaking and the actors involved. Social-interest organisations—such as environmental, human rights or consumer groups—tend to lead during early agenda-setting stages through grassroots mobilisation, media outreach and emotionally resonant messaging. Economic lobbies, including business and trade associations, often gain prominence in the later stages of legislative drafting and amendment, where they use technical documentation, targeted briefings and formal consultation processes to shape outcomes. Gorwa et al. (2024) further distinguish between direct and indirect channels of influence (see Table 1).

These dynamics are not abstract. The "End the Cage Age" European Citizens' Initiative relied on emotionally charged visual storytelling, using images of caged farm animals and protest scenes to evoke moral responsibility and empathy. It succeeded in mobilising over 1.4 million verified signatures across EU Member States, compelling the Commission to formally respond with a legislative proposal on animal welfare (European Commission, n.d.). Here, tone was not incidental—it was central to the campaign's success (Fig. 1).

Table 1 Typology of platform policy influence strategies

General type	Specific strategy	Goals
Direct—Targeted at policymakers	Access lobbying	Leverage access to policymakers at various levels to negotiate for/against certain policy positions
	Coalition-building	Build legitimacy and authority for firm policy positions; use coalitions to increase access to policymakers
Indirect—Targeted at other stakeholders	Mobilisation	Leverage access to consumers and/or complementors to persuade them to engage policymakers on a firm's behalf
	Public relations	Use mediated channels of communication to reach public or segments of the public to make rhetorical arguments about legitimacy and product value

Source: Gorwa et al. (2024)

Fig. 1 *Campaign imagery from the "End the Cage Age" ECI. Source:* End the Cage Age (2025)

By contrast, pharmaceutical lobbying during the 2023 reforms relied on detailed consultation responses, technical papers and regulatory modelling, using precise, formal tone aligned with institutional expectations (EFPIA, and Technopolis Group, 2023).

Tailored Tone Tips for CSOs and Businesses

Civil society organisations (CSOs):

- Identify the primary forum for your message (e.g. an EP committee, Council working party or public consultation).

(continued)

- Use inclusive, citizen-oriented language when addressing the public or citizen panels, and adopt formal EU terminology (e.g. directives, treaty articles) when addressing officials.
- Tailor metaphors and cultural references. Brussels officials are multilingual; consider translating key phrases into French or German when targeting Council audiences.

Business representatives:

- When engaging with Commission staff, emphasise regulatory compliance and innovation: how your sector supports EU objectives (e.g. green transition, digitalisation).
- When addressing MEPs or national representatives, highlight economic contributions: jobs, competitiveness and alignment with EU/global standards.
- Use formal address ('Commissioner', 'Vice-President', 'Honourable MEP') and adapt emphasis to the political group: for instance, Greens may prefer environmental framing, while conservatives may prioritise market or security angles.

2.2 *The Power of Storytelling*

Policy is abstract; stories make it tangible. Framing issues as narratives—with characters, stakes, conflict and resolution—helps both policymakers and the public grasp why a dossier matters.

The Narrative Policy Framework (NPF) (Jones et al., 2014) shows communication is stickier when it mirrors familiar story structures. Campaigns that cast citizens as protagonists and identify clear villains or obstacles are more memorable. Studies of successful ECIs (Tosun & Schaub, 2021) note a common 'devil shift': name the threat, show the victims, present the remedy.

These dynamics played out in the 2019 campaign against the EU's Copyright Directive. By translating legal risks into personal consequences (teachers, creators, Wikipedia users) and staging Wikipedia blackouts, advocates turned a technical file into a story about defending free expression—mobilising five million petition signatures and prompting street demonstrations in Europe's capitals and beyond. The resulting public pressure led to amendments in the directive text and high-profile corrections of MEP votes (Deutsche Welle, 2019; Politico Europe, 2019; Reda, 2019).

Business uses narrative too, in a different register. During the EU plastics strategy, the Circular Plastics Alliance foregrounded practical success stories—recyclable packaging, city pilots—to portray industry as a partner in the green transition and to align with EU targets, reinforcing the plausibility of the ten million tonnes recycling target by 2025 (European Commission, 2018; European Environment Agency, 2023).

In both cases—civil society and industry—the conclusion is the same: A well-crafted narrative cuts through noise, creates emotional stakes and allows technical detail to be understood as part of a wider human story. The key is authenticity.

2.3 Emotional vs. Rational Messaging

Evidence gives authority; emotion creates resonance. In Brussels, where decisions rest on law, politics and perception, effective advocacy combines both. Emotion draws attention—fear, hope, compassion, pride—while reason persuades those scrutinising law, budgets or technical detail. The craft lies in sequencing: emotion frames urgency; facts substantiate.

Research shows leading CSOs routinely blend the two (Sanchez Salgado, 2018). A press release might cite that 110 million Europeans face unsafe noise pollution and then add the story of children losing sleep and learning capacity. Data signals scale; narrative makes it relatable.

Climate politics illustrates this balance. Institutions rely on reports from the Intergovernmental Panel on Climate Change (IPCC) and Eurostat data, while campaigns use images—a polar bear on melting ice, a child with a placard—to translate numbers into urgency. Strong campaigns present robust data to policymakers and emotional stories to the public, ensuring both attention and trust.

What matters is not whether emotion or logic is used, but how they are combined. Messaging that is purely emotional may feel manipulative or vague. Messaging that is purely technical may be ignored or misunderstood. A well-calibrated mix creates space for both attention and trust. The goal is not to overwhelm, but to connect—first emotionally, then intellectually.

Balancing Emotional and Rational Messaging

1. *Tailor emotion vs. logic.*

When addressing the public or media, lead with emotion to highlight urgency:

'Imagine your neighbourhood flooded.'

When targeting policymakers or technical audiences, prioritise data and logic. Use emotion sparingly, only to reinforce your argument.

2. *Blend them.*

Combine human stories with supporting evidence.

'Maria fled war with nothing – and #EUAsylum saved her life. We must uphold human rights (Charter of Fundamental Rights, Article 18).'

– Example from business: A corporate LinkedIn post shares a 'user success story' alongside a link to an industry white paper.

(continued)

3. *Match your actor.*

Commission officials expect well-sourced reasoning and clear policy impact. They are unlikely to be persuaded by emotional appeals alone.

The general public, on the other hand, may disengage from data-heavy content. Combine visuals or quotes (emotion) with charts or key figures (reason) to maintain balance.

2.4 Avoid Credibility Pitfalls

In Brussels, credibility is currency—once lost, it is hard to recover. Advocacy is judged not only on arguments but on the reliability of claims and integrity of methods. Tone signals whether an actor is informed and trustworthy or reckless and opportunistic.

The main risk is overstatement. Fear-mongering and exaggerated claims may spark short-term attention but erode legitimacy, especially with institutions used to evidence-based reasoning (Sanchez Salgado, 2018).

Digital policy illustrates this dynamic. As large tech firms expanded lobbying through direct contacts, sponsored research and partnerships, watchdogs exposed opaque practices (Corporate Europe Observatory, and LobbyControl, 2021). Regulators responded with stricter disclosure rules and tougher scrutiny of policy input. Increased visibility brought increased accountability.

The implication: passion is not enough. Claims must be verifiable, sources disclosed and rhetoric proportionate. Accusations should be made cautiously, if at all. Even social media posts are scrutinised; one misstep can define a campaign's reputation.

2.5 Monitor and Adjust Tone Based on Feedback

No matter how well a message is prepared, it may be received differently than intended. In EU advocacy, where political dynamics shift quickly and policymaking unfolds in public, being able to adjust tone based on feedback is essential. Communication is not a one-off event—it is an ongoing process shaped by reaction, interpretation and response.

Campaigners must treat feedback not as an interruption but as data. This includes direct feedback—comments from policymakers, stakeholders or allies in meetings—but also indirect signals: press coverage, social media reactions and silence. A lack of engagement can be as telling as open disagreement. Monitoring how a message lands can help identify whether the tone was too aggressive, too technical, too vague or simply misaligned with the audience's priorities.

Digital platforms provide both risk and opportunity in this regard. On the one hand, they allow real-time public response. On the other hand, they amplify missteps. A poorly worded tweet, a misleading infographic or a speech clip taken out of context can spread quickly and shape perceptions beyond the intended audience. Campaigns need to monitor reactions closely and be ready to respond. In some cases, this may involve correcting an error or clarifying a position. In others, it may mean recalibrating the tone for the next round of engagement.

Feedback also helps uncover blind spots. A message that sounds persuasive within an organisation may sound defensive or opaque to an external audience. Trusted interlocutors—such as sympathetic MEPs, journalists or partner organisations—can provide informal but valuable cues. If they signal confusion or discomfort with the language used, that is a strong indication that the tone needs adjustment.

Monitoring Tone and Adjusting Messaging

Tips for civil society organisations (CSOs):

- Use tools like Google Alerts, EU-focused news platforms (e.g. Euractiv, Politico Europe) and social media listening tools to track how your messages are received.
- If media coverage misrepresents your stance, issue a prompt clarification—via a press release, a LinkedIn note or a tweet thread.
- Seek informal feedback from allies. A supportive MEP or journalist may alert you if your tone sounds too confrontational or unclear.
- Adjust future messaging based on that feedback—for instance, by adding context, clarifying policy impacts or softening language.

Tips for business representatives:

- After submitting consultation feedback or appearing at a hearing, observe policymakers' responses closely.
- If questions suggest scepticism, your next message should speak directly to those concerns—avoid heavy jargon and highlight practical solutions.
- Update slide decks, fact sheets and talking points regularly.
- Avoid appearing defensive or dismissive; the wrong tone can shut down a conversation. Stay responsive and adaptable.

3 Tone Across Channels and Institutions

3.1 Adapt Tone Per Social Media Platform

Advocacy in the EU today does not only happen in official consultations, stakeholder meetings or parliamentary briefings. It also takes place online. Social media platforms have become integral to shaping narratives, signalling alignment and building pressure. But each platform operates by its own informal rules. The tone that works on one may be ineffective—or counterproductive—on another. A campaign must therefore not only choose its words carefully but also select its medium and tone with equal attention.

The EP's communications strategy during the 2024 elections offers a clear example of this differentiation. On X (formerly Twitter), the institution relied on video clips, mentions and reposts to boost visibility and engagement. On threads, by contrast, the content was more static and informational, often presented through infographics and short explanatory texts (Velasco Molpeceres et al., 2025). The EP adjusted its tone to fit the platform: dynamic and conversational on the one hand and calm and instructive on the other.

This approach is not limited to institutions. Stakeholders of all types increasingly treat social media as a parallel stage for advocacy. Research by Gorwa et al. (2024) shows that large technology firms use social platforms as part of their mediated strategy to reach public audiences while relying on direct lobbying to engage policymakers behind closed doors. The same division applies to NGOs and business groups: social media content is crafted for reach and visibility, not for legal precision or policy nuance.

Ultimately, tone is not platform-neutral. Social media is not an accessory to advocacy—it is a domain where tone is tested in real time. Treating it as such is not only a communications choice; it is part of strategic positioning in the EU arena.

Tailoring Tone to Social Media Platforms

1. **Platform fit:**

- On X (formerly Twitter): Be concise and punchy. Use active voice, clear calls to action and visual elements (e.g. short videos or GIFs). Avoid long text—use threads for complex points.
- On LinkedIn: More space allows detailed posts. Share articles, policy PDFs or infographics. Tone should be *professional*. Use formal grammar.
- On Instagram/TikTok: Prioritise visual storytelling. Use a human tone, emotive or humorous visuals, relatable captions and relevant hashtags. NGOs, for example, may explain draft laws with cartoons or mini-interviews. Keep messages short and accessible.
- YouTube: Best for explainer videos, campaign documentaries and expert interviews. Favour clarity and structure. Long-form is acceptable—20–40 min—if the audience is policy-engaged. Consistency in posting matters more than frequency spikes.
- Podcasts: Ideal for deep dives, especially with subject-matter experts, policymakers or frontline voices. Use a calm, credible tone. Length should match audience attention (e.g. 15–20 mins for casual listeners, 40+ mins for policy audiences). Regular episodes build trust—establish a rhythm (weekly, fortnightly, etc.).

(continued)

2. **Tips for civil society organisations (CSOs):**

- Different causes perform better on different platforms. Environmental campaigns often succeed on Instagram or YouTube through visual content; human rights stories travel fast on X.
- Use analytics tools to track engagement and refine your tone accordingly.

3. **Tips for business representatives:**

- For policy news and industry positioning, LinkedIn and professional newsletters are most appropriate. Use a confident, informed tone.
- For live updates (e.g. "Council meeting adjourned with no consensus..."), X is useful. Keep the tone neutral and informative.
- When using public-facing platforms for official input (e.g. consultations or stakeholder forums), maintain consistent professionalism—even in social formats.

4. **Always respect platform norms:**

- Avoid slang or memes on LinkedIn.
- Light humour or a well-chosen GIF may work on X—if tone and brand align.

3.2 Strike a Tone That Builds Coalitions

Many of the most effective campaigns in the EU are collective. Rather than acting alone, organisations form coalitions that span across NGOs, industry associations, municipal governments, trade unions or cross-party groups of MEPs. These coalitions allow for broader reach, increased legitimacy and better access to decision-makers. But they also require a carefully balanced tone—one that accommodates ideological and sectoral differences without diluting the message.

Tone becomes a tool for cohesion. Where actors from different sectors or political families align around a shared goal, communication must be inclusive, measured and forward-looking. Overly combative, ideological or technical language can alienate potential partners or create internal tension. Campaigns that succeed in coalition settings often avoid blame and polarisation, instead foregrounding shared values and mutual benefits.

A useful example is the 'Antwerp Declaration for a European Industrial Deal', launched in 2024. Although initiated by the European Chemical Industry Council (Cefic), it was endorsed by over 70 companies across sectors—from chemicals and steel to renewable energy. The declaration did not rely on sectoral jargon or adversarial tone. Instead, it framed the need for an 'Industrial Deal' as complementary to the Green Deal, using accessible language centred on competitiveness, innovation and skilled employment. This allowed actors with different institutional profiles and reputational concerns to co-sign a common platform. The framing was persuasive not only because of its content, but because the tone was inclusive and constructive. The result was a broader political reception: the European Commission announced a Clean Industrial Deal in direct response (Cefic, 2024).

Tone in Cross-Sector Campaigns
Tips for civil society organisations (CSOs):

- When partnering with business groups, avoid overly partisan or ideological language.
- Focus on shared outcomes. For example:

  'Investing in solar panels will create jobs and reduce carbon emissions.'

- Stay clear of slogans that may alienate partners. A climate group should not use phrasing like 'stop capitalist exploitation' when addressing industry allies. Aim for a tone that builds common ground.

Tips for business representatives:

- In joint efforts with NGOs or consumer associations, adopt a balanced and inclusive tone.
- Example: electronics firms supporting the right to repair partnered with NGOs by using shared language like 'fair access and sustainability', avoiding overt commercial arguments.
- Frame regulatory requests as win-win scenarios. For example:

  'Harmonised EU rules will boost innovation and build public trust.'

- Demonstrating respect for your coalition partners strengthens long-term unity and credibility.

4 Conclusion

Tone is not peripheral in EU advocacy—it is central. It affects whether messages are heard, whether alliances hold and whether an actor is viewed as credible. This chapter demonstrates how tailored tone—emotional or rational, technical or narrative—can be used strategically across institutions, audiences and platforms. From grassroots mobilisation to regulatory submissions, tone is one of the few tools that all actors—regardless of size or sector—can shape deliberately.

Yet tone is not a substitute for access, evidence or influence. It cannot correct for weak policy content or fragmented coalitions. It does not resolve power imbalances built into the EU lobbying ecosystem, where large actors still dominate key spaces. In many cases, tone only matters once entry to the conversation has already been secured.

There are also clear gaps in this chapter. The analysis largely draws on visible, institution-facing campaigns that rely on conventional tools—press releases, consultation inputs, social media and public demonstrations. It does not account for more closed or emerging communication spaces. Much advocacy now happens through encrypted messaging apps, private Slack groups, WhatsApp networks or long-form formats like podcasts, livestreams and newsletters. These channels carry their own tonal norms, and little research exists on how tone operates in such informal or hybrid spaces.

Equally, disinformation and crisis communication remain underexplored. Tone behaves differently under pressure. In disinformation environments, where factual claims are disputed and actors face reputational attacks, tone must be defensive and corrective, yet still persuasive. In crises—whether reputational, political or humanitarian—tone must adjust in real time, often with incomplete information. Few advocacy organisations are equipped for that.

Further research should explore how tone operates under these newer conditions. How do digital-native campaigns maintain coherence across fragmented platforms? How can tone be used to inoculate against false claims, or to recover from communication failures?

References

Cefic. (2024, February 20). *Antwerp Declaration: For a European Industrial Deal*. https://cefic.org/news/antwerp-declaration-for-a-european-industrial-deal/

Corporate Europe Observatory, & LobbyControl. (2021). *The lobby network: Big Tech's web of influence in the EU*. https://www.lobbycontrol.de/wp-content/uploads/Study_en_LobbyNetwork_31.8.2021.pdf

Deutsche Welle. (2019, March 23). *EU copyright bill: Protests across Europe highlight rifts over reform plans*. https://www.dw.com/en/eu-copyright-bill-protests-across-europe-highlight-rifts-over-reform-plans/a-48037133

EFPIA, & Technopolis Group. (2023). *Revision of the general pharmaceutical legislation: Impact assessment of European Commission and EFPIA proposals*. European Federation of Pharmaceutical Industries and Associations. https://efpia.eu/media/cm2jbsjx/revision-of-the-general-pharmaceutical-legislation-impact-assessment-of-european-commission-and-efpia-proposals.pdf

End the Cage Age. (2025). https://www.endthecageage.eu/en/

European Commission. (2018). *A European strategy for plastics in a circular economy*. https://ec.europa.eu/environment/circular-economy/pdf/plastics-strategy-brochure.pdf

European Commission. (n.d.). *End the Cage Age European Citizens' Initiative (ECI)*. https://food.ec.europa.eu/animals/animal-welfare/eci/eci-end-cage-age_en

European Environment Agency. (2023). *Pathways towards circular plastics in Europe—Good practice and evidence since 2018*. https://www.eea.europa.eu/publications/pathways-towards-circular-plastics-in

Gorwa, R., Lechowski, G., & Schneiß, D. (2024). Platform lobbying: Policy influence strategies and the EU's Digital Services Act. *Internet Policy Review, 13(2)*. https://doi.org/10.14763/2024.2.1782

Jones, M. D., McBeth, M. K., & Shanahan, E. A. (2014). *The science of stories: Applications of the narrative policy framework in public policy analysis*. Palgrave Macmillan.

Politico Europe. (2019, March 18). *Germany's last-ditch drive to derail EU copyright deal*. https://www.politico.eu/article/germanys-last-ditch-drive-to-derail-eu-copyright-deal/
Reda, F. (2019, April 11). *EU copyright reform: Our fight was not in vain*. https://felixreda.eu/2019/04/not-in-vain/
Sanchez Salgado, R. (2018). The advocacy of feelings: Emotions in EU-based civil society organizations' strategies. *Politics and Governance, 6*(4), 83–93. https://doi.org/10.17645/pag.v6i4.1505
Serna-Ortega, Á., Almansa-Martínez, A., & Castillo-Esparcia, A. (2025). Influence of lobbying in EU policy process phases. *Frontiers in Political Science, 7*. https://doi.org/10.3389/fpos.2025.1511918
Tosun, J., & Schaub, S. (2021). Constructing policy narratives for transnational mobilization: Insights from European citizens' initiatives. *European Policy Analysis, 7*(2), 344–364. https://doi.org/10.1002/epa2.1125
Velasco Molpeceres, A., Miranda-Galbe, J., & Prieto Muñiz, M. (2025). Digital political communication in the European Parliament: A comparative analysis of threads and X during the 2024 elections. *Journalism and Media, 6*(1), 42. https://doi.org/10.3390/journalmedia6010042

Further Readings

Coen, D., Katsaitis, A., & Vannoni, M. (2024). Lobbying in the European Union: Multi-venue & multi-actor strategies in the European Union. In D. Coen & A. Katsaitis (Eds.), *Handbook on Lobbying and Public Policy* (pp. 271–285). Edward Elgar.
Heimans, J., & Timms, H. (2018). *New power: How power works in our hyperconnected world – and how to make it work for you*. Doubleday.

Sebastian Rodríguez Pérez is a political consultant specialising in digital and EU lobbying and advocacy. He has worked for European Union institutions, advised political parties in the European Parliament and currently runs a consultancy supporting NGOs and business associations on how to influence the EU legislative process.

Lobbying from an NGO Perspective

Céline Mias

Abstract This chapter explores the role of NGOs in influencing EU policy processes, both during the Ordinary Legislative Procedure (OLP) and beyond. It looks at the role of NGO lobbying as an essential component of a thriving civic space and democracy; what and how NGOs seek to influence at EU-level; the limitations, challenges, and opportunities afforded to them in the EU policy- and decision-making space; and the importance of NGO's use of evidence, legal and normative frameworks, and collective strength, while remaining grounded in core values and principles. Practical examples are provided, primarily from the perspective of NGOs working in humanitarian aid, development cooperation, and related policy areas.

Keywords NGOs · Civil society · Influence · EU policy · Lobbying · Advocacy · Democracy · Civic space · Values · Coalitions

1 Introduction: Role of NGOs in EU Democratic Processes

> *Civic space is the political, legislative, social and economic environment which enables citizens to come together…to influence and shape their societies. A vibrant and independent civil society, in an open civic space, is vital for a healthy democracy, strong social justice, and to safeguard the rule of law. A culture of active participation and citizenship is vital to democratise the EU and ensure that it delivers for the good of both people and the planet.*
> Civil Society Europe (2022)

Across the European Union and globally, independent, diverse civil society organizations or Non-Governmental Organizations (NGOs) play a critical role in building a democratic society that is based on fundamental rights and commitment to social and environmental justice. At EU level, a strong civil society voice and participation in EU policy processes are essential to upholding the fundamental values enshrined in

C. Mias (✉)
EU Director at the Danish Refugee Council, Brussels, Belgium
e-mail: celine.mias@drc.ngo; celine.mias@cantab.net

G. Füricht-Fiegl et al. (eds.), *Handbook on EU Law-making*, Professional Practice in Governance and Public Organizations, https://doi.org/10.1007/978-3-032-16559-6_23

the Treaty on European Union (TEU) Art. 2[1] (European Union, 2016), while Art. 11 TEU explicitly stresses the requirement for the EU to have an open, transparent, and regular dialogue with civil society organizations, for example, when preparing proposals for EU laws, in "all areas of Union action.[2]" (European Union, 2016).

In the context of this formally recognized role for NGOs in the EU policy space, this chapter will explore the specific role of NGOs as lobbyists towards EU Institutions, outlining in general terms what NGOs seek to achieve through their influencing efforts, and how they go about it. This chapter will also highlight some of the limitations, challenges, and opportunities afforded to NGOs in the EU policy- and decision-making space, as well as the importance of NGO's use of evidence, legal and normative frameworks, and collective strength, while remaining grounded in core values and principles. Some examples will be shared to illustrate the different types of lobbying and influencing efforts that NGOs undertake at different levels of decision-making during the OLP as well as in other contexts.

Caveat: The author of this chapter, at the time of writing (September 2025), has spent 19 years in senior roles with NGOs in Brussels, influencing EU policies in the fields of humanitarian aid and development cooperation; therefore, examples and perspectives are drawn from the author's experience in this sector. Many of the insights shared are applicable across different sectors and types of NGOs, but there may be distinct differences with other sectors, of which the author does not have adequate expertise. This chapter aims to be practical and illustrative, providing an introduction to the lobbying efforts of NGOs in Brussels from a humanitarian NGO perspective, rather than serving as a comprehensive guide for all NGOs lobbying and influencing in Brussels.

What Are NGOs?

Nongovernmental organizations (NGOs) are mission- and value-driven civil society entities, which operate on a not-for-profit basis, independent from government control, focusing primarily on social, humanitarian, and environmental issues. NGOs are often characterized by their roles in meeting local or global challenges, and by their private citizen support bases; namely NGOs often rely on citizen activists and private financial supporters to meet their objectives. However, NGOs may also obtain support from Governments, foundations, and other types of donors, while maintaining their independence and right of initiative.

[1]Art. 2: *"The Union is founded on the values of respect for human dignity, freedom, democracy, equality, the rule of law and respect for human rights, including the rights of persons belonging to minorities. These values are common to the Member States in a society in which pluralism, non-discrimination, tolerance, justice, solidarity and equality between women and men prevail."* (European Union, 2016)

[2]Art. 11: *"The institutions shall, by appropriate means, give citizens and representative associations the opportunity to make known and publicly exchange their views in all areas of Union action. The institutions shall maintain an open, transparent and regular dialogue with representative associations and civil society."* (European Union, 2016)

2 What Do NGOs Seek to Influence in Brussels?

NGOs—with their strong values-based agendas, often involving visions for the future of society, Europe, and the world at large—seek to influence the EU on multiple levels and via both formal and informal processes in order to effect impact in the short-, medium-, and longer terms by:

- Influencing the development and adoption of EU Policies: Similar to other lobbyists, NGOs would like to see their interests and key messages reflected in relevant EU policies. NGOs seek to influence the development of new EU policies and frameworks—before and during OLPs—to influence scope, detailed language of policy texts, and concrete EU commitments.
- Influencing policy implementation: NGOs are also interested in influencing the implementation of key EU legislation. This could include influencing EU funding allocations or specific programming documents or seeking to influence Commission and EU Member State initiatives to implement policy commitments such as the development of action plans, and guidelines, or influencing messaging in relevant policy dialogues.
- Holding the EU to account: Another key role of NGOs is to hold the EU to account for its policy commitments. This is not just about influencing the process of policy implementation, but about monitoring implementation of what the EU committed to do, taking stock of what has happened, identifying successes and gaps and putting forth recommendations or calling out poor implementation.
- Setting agendas: NGOs do not only seek to work passively, in reaction to policy processes and their implementation, but they also aim to drive the agenda of EU policymaking, seeking to influence the prevalent political narrative and discourse to effect transformational change. This could be, for instance, through influencing political party platforms during European elections, influencing candidate Commissioners' questions or responses during hearings, or leading agenda-setting citizen initiatives or mass public mobilization. NGOs often seek to contribute visions and concrete approaches for the betterment of Europe, society, and the world. While much more challenging than influencing specific legislative files or policy implementation, this type of transformational change objective is often at the very core of NGO missions and *raison-d'être*.

3 How Do NGOs Influence?

Similar to other types of lobbyists, NGOs seeking to influence the EU take a multi-faceted approach in order to reach the different actors involved in the OLP, policy implementation, or agenda-setting. Concretely, this means that NGOs seek to influence all key stakeholders at Brussels-level: the Commission, European Parliament (EP), Council working parties and bodies; as well as at EU Member State capital-level. NGOs also try to influence stakeholders that can in turn influence key decision-makers, such as the media, think tanks, celebrities, champions, other civil society actors, and potential supporters.

NGOs generally work by developing deliberate advocacy strategies to influence or effect change on a specific file or policy initiative, or on a longer-term agenda. A starting point for any NGO influencing strategy is necessarily to identify the change they wish to make and the key messages they will convey in doing so. There are many different analytical tools that NGOs can employ to support the development of an overall influencing strategy[3] and these will not be explored in depth in this article. But it should be noted that as part of their influencing strategies, NGOs typically employ a combination of tools and tactics, depending on the policy or process they aim to influence. These tactics include (but are not limited to):

- Power analysis: NGOs use analytical tools[4] to map out and identify the most important targets to influence a specific OLP; to influence the specific allocation of funds or policy implementation; or to weigh in on the broader agenda. For instance, to influence an OLP, NGOs might identify particular staff in the Commission working on a Commission proposal; Commission leaders involved in setting the policy priorities; Members of the European Parliament (MEPs) involved as rapporteurs and shadow rapporteurs; coordinators of political parties and other key MEP supporters and/or those, who may still be on the fence or yet be convinced; staff involved in Council working parties; decision-makers at capital-level; champions or actors, who could influence the decision-makers; media widely read by policymakers, etc. The power analysis can thus identify a wide range of relevant actors who can wield influence on a policy or agenda allowing NGOs to focus their strategies on critical targets.
- Working in coalitions, networks, or informal alliances: In order to maximize their impact and voice, NGOs often work in formal or informal coalitions and networks to amplify their power and messages. This can be via membership of formal networks or confederations, which can offer NGOs direct and indirect access to a wider range of relevant policymakers and often allow NGOs to contribute to a wider influencing and transformational agenda. Formal networks, alliances, and confederations can be slower to agree on messages and take action due to their size, but they carry weight as they can represent hundreds if not thousands of NGO actors (especially if networks join to build coalitions of networks). Alternatively, coalition working can take the form of ad hoc alliances among two or more like-minded organizations seeking to influence a specific policy file at a specific point in time. These informal alliances can often be nimbler and can carry bolder messages when the group is strongly aligned on

[3] There are many different tools and approaches available to support the development of an NGO advocacy strategy; most big NGOs have their own tools, and many can be found in open sources on the Internet. Some examples are Lewin, K. (1951); Save the Children and The Open University training session. (n.d.)

[4] There are also numerous types of power mapping and analysis tools, from a simple xy axis as described in: Collinson, H. (2022); to more complex models such as PowerCube (n.d.).

approach or mission. Joining in alliances to influence EU policy processes is a critical tactic employed by civil society and a key success factor in NGO influencing as it allows a stronger, collective voice to convey key messages.

- Using evidence and legal frameworks to make the case: While most NGOs are driven by principles and values, the majority recognizes that a moral argument is insufficient to sway policymakers. Influencing is more effective when NGOs bring forward facts, figures, and expertise directly derived from their programmes or research. An NGO influencing tactic is therefore to invest in developing analytical, evidence-based policy papers and reports, either to document good practice, to evaluate the implementation of EU policies, or to shine a light on difficult issues (for instance, human rights abuses). Similarly, a powerful approach NGOs use is to bring local partners, community members, or project participants to Brussels or Member States to tell their stories or share their experiences with decision-makers directly. NGOs also draw consistently on existing EU policy frameworks and laws, international commitments and international law, and normative frameworks to make a case, for example, calling out violations of international humanitarian law or international human rights law. NGOs may also seek recourse to justice or draw on legal cases to convince policymakers via use of legal precedent, for instance, drawing on cases at the European Court of Justice or the International Court of Justice to compel policymakers to take action.
- Public influencing: NGOs may engage in public forms of advocacy, which can help raise awareness of an issue or perspective and sway political influencing targets via media and public opinion. This kind of influencing may take the form of publishing opinion editorials (Op-Eds) or public letters of support or opposition for a policy issue in the media. It could also entail hosting events with expert speakers and/or speaking in conferences or parliamentary hearings or promoting evidence/research findings/reports widely via traditional or social media outlets. NGOs may also engage in stunts for the media and decision-makers in front of European institution buildings, or they may develop broader public campaigns, drawing on support from their constituencies and the general public; for instance, engaging with their supporters to take action via petitions, participate in marches, write letters to key decision-makers, etc. This public engagement can also inspire activists and wider groups of citizens in the general public, creating informal influencing moments and movements with even greater impact.[5]
- Private influencing: NGOs, particularly those working on highly sensitive matters such as human rights defenders or humanitarian NGOs operating in conflict-affected contexts, often seek to influence in a more private manner. This can be in the form of developing and sharing unbranded policy briefs and recommendations, engaging in private meetings with key policymakers and /or roundtables

[5] Examples of such movements, which began as small-scale efforts (NGOs writing public letters and articles in the press) and grew exponentially with impact on EU policies are the climate marches that took place across the EU around 2018–2019, which influenced the EU in development of its Green Deal and pro-Gaza marches in 2025, which led a critical mass of Member States to request a review of Art. 2 of the EU-Israel Association Agreement in May 2025.

under Chatham House rules, pushing out messages under the umbrella of wider coalitions (where individual NGO members are not identified). These private approaches can be very effective, when coupled with strong evidence or concrete experiences.

4 NGO Influencing in Practice

4.1 Influencing EU Humanitarian Policy

In 2021, the Commission undertook to issue a new overarching policy for European Humanitarian action. Titled "the EU's humanitarian action: new challenges, same principles" (European Commission, 2021), the policy emphasized some of the EU's existing, fundamental commitments to humanitarian principles and humanitarian law, while also adopting commitments in new areas of importance to the humanitarian sector.

At the time, the author worked for CARE International (CARE), an NGO that aimed to see more formal EU commitment to disaster preparedness, environmental measures, gender equality in emergencies, and localization (the shifting of power to local NGOs in countries affected by crisis), and proactively sought to influence the Commission's Communication, the EP's Report, and the Council Conclusions on the new policy.

CARE learned of the planned new policy in autumn 2020 and quickly sought to identify who was involved in the drafting of the Communication, who was driving the strategy behind the document, and where the entry points for influence were. The Communication was developed in a rather tight timeframe, so there was insufficient time to produce any research report to support CARE's effort. Instead, CARE developed a set of clear, concise messages and recommendations for the policy based on its existing operational experience and shared them with relevant high-level Commission leaders, as well as with the drafting team itself. CARE also found out which consulting firm was involved in informing the development of the policy and provided a key informant interview, as well as contributing to a formal public online survey. In addition, CARE contributed to the drafting of joint NGO messages shared with the Commission on behalf of a formal NGO network. Once the Communication was published, CARE produced and shared an analysis of it with Member State representatives of the Council Working Party on Humanitarian Aid and Food Aid (COHAFA), stressing strengths and what could be improved in the Council Conclusions. In parallel, CARE shared its analysis with relevant MEPs and worked with the team of the MEP humanitarian rapporteur, other MEPs, and political groups to influence the EP report produced and adopted.

In the end, the Communication covered CARE's key advocacy points, while the EP report (European Parliament Committee on Development, 2021) and the Council Conclusions (Council of the European Union, 2021) adopted even stronger commitments. In particular, CARE saw specific language it had suggested included in both the EP and the Council documents. While CARE did not achieve this result on its own, it certainly played a role via its proactive efforts to provide evidence and analysis to relevant pen holders and decision-makers.

4.2 EU Gender Action Plan for External Action 2020–2027 (GAP III)

This was a long-term NGO influencing effort, involving years of advocacy towards Member States, MEPs, and the Commission. NGOs sought to see firm EU commitments and budget allocations for gender equality in EU external action, linking humanitarian, development cooperation, trade, and foreign policy areas under a single policy framework. As its name suggests, GAP III was the third Gender Action Plan of the EU and it was the strongest one adopted at EU level—adopting a transformational, intersectional approach to gender equality in the EU's external action, with associated commitments for funding and concrete implementation. NGOs had been involved in lobbying the EU prior to the adoption of the first GAP in 2010 and the ambition reached in GAP III was a real achievement for the sector.

NGOs working in both formal coalitions and informal alliances had influenced the GAP III by:

- Identifying key actors involved in the file including at the Commission (both supporters and those, who needed to be convinced); MEPs (rapporteurs, political party coordinators); and Member States, in particular representatives of relevant working parties as well as gender experts and officials at Member State capital level.
- Producing research on GAP II implementation to identify what was required for a stronger GAP III.
- Presenting the research and key recommendations at events, hearings in the parliament, and Council working parties.
- Participating in formal consultation processes on the GAP III and formal evaluations of GAP II commissioned by the Commission.
- Maintaining on-going dialogue with the Commission, MEPs, Member States, and EUDs.

This multi-year effort led to adoption of the GAP III in November 2020, the strongest ever Gender Action Plan, by the Commission and European External Action Services as a Joint Communication to guide all EU external action (European Commission, 2020). Many NGOs asks were specifically taken on board by the Commission and featured in the GAP III. Subsequently, in December 2020, 24 Member States committed to the GAP III via German presidency Conclusions (though sadly, not Council Conclusions due to opposition from three Member States) (Council of the European Union, 2020). NGOs collectively played an important role in maintaining pressure on the Commission and Member States to adopt an ambitious approach.

5 NGO Power: Limitations and Challenges in Influencing EU Policy

NGOs can and do have influence on relevant EU policy processes and collectively are able to wield some power. However, it is increasingly challenging for NGOs to do this, as space for civil society and NGO influencing has been increasingly shrinking over the past decade or so. Some of the important challenges that NGOs face:

- NGOs/CSOs have fewer resources than other lobbyists: As such, they can organize fewer events and hire fewer staff or outsourced support to conduct analyses, produce policy papers, and walk the corridors to influence MEPs, Commission staff, and Member States.
- NGOs have less access to policymakers than other actors: They are often not viewed as having relevance and are often deprioritized and taken less seriously than other stakeholders by policymakers. In practical terms, NGOs often find their meeting requests refused and they have limited access to the most critical discussions relevant to their files. In recent years, for instance, the Commission has regularly convened private sector advisory groups on international development cooperation files, but NGOs have rarely had similar, meaningful opportunities. This is compounded by the fact that at EU-level, NGOs rarely if ever have the opportunity to meet with the highest representatives, for example, the current President of the Commission. Having worked as an NGO lobbyist in Brussels for nearly two decades, the author certainly observes a trend of fewer opportunities for direct NGO engagement with policymaking and decision-makers in comparison with the past.
- Official Commission consultations offer limited opportunities to influence: They are often organized after policy documents or proposals have already been drafted, as an afterthought to meet requirements, thereby offering little opportunity to influence new policies. In the past, NGOs would more readily receive draft policy documents with opportunities to provide inputs/recommendations. Some good practice in this regard was observed when the Directorate-General for European Civil Protection and Humanitarian Operations (DG ECHO) developed environmental guidelines, it organized numerous consultations with partners, to ensure multiple opportunities for exchange on the concept and drafts prior to publication. The guidance, which became mandatory for NGO partners, was developed with strong inputs based on field experience.
- Anti-NGO sentiment: Perceptions of NGOs either as corrupt and seeking to play the system, or as small, irrelevant do-gooders, can also be harmful and affect NGO lobbying efforts. In truth, there is a great variety among NGOs and civil society actors—there is no one size fits all. More damaging are the narratives of

NGOs as fraudulent, corrupt actors, deriving from the scandal of *Qatargate*[6] and the poor behaviour of a small number of NGOs, which has affected perceptions and the space to act of a vast and diverse sector. The targeting of NGOs by political actors—deemed by the Corporate Europe Observatory as the "European right-wing on a mission to silence NGOs" (Corporate Europe Observatory, 2025)—is both an affront to democracy and severely limiting NGOs' ability to engage in lobbying and seek support for their activities;[7] this is despite the reality that NGOs, especially those receiving EU funding or on the EU transparency register for EU lobbyists, are highly scrutinized, regulated, and audited.
- Achieving impact in current political climate: In the current climate of anti-NGO sentiment (highlighted above), and populism, where there is more focus on political narratives and transactional approaches than on evidence and expertise, NGOs can struggle to see any impact of their lobbying efforts. When policy files become wholly political, to the extent that technical arguments are no longer taken into account by decision-makers, NGOs have fewer impactful tools at their disposal. For NGOs, this limited influence can be of serious concern, as some of the most political files can have devastating impact. For instance, far-right political narratives on migration have now become mainstream and normalized, raising the potential for the EU not only to renege on commitments to global conventions and human rights norms, but even to seek to re-open global frameworks; the EU's commitment to the Geneva Convention on Refugees and its principle of non-refoulement, as well as the overall global refugee protection system, is currently being put into question by some key political groups and policy makers. It is difficult, in this context, for NGOs to influence as the evidence and even the fundamental legal frameworks are no longer deemed relevant to decision-makers.

6 Conclusion—NGO Power

Despite the challenges, NGOs have power. NGOs have a critical role to play in EU policy influencing as well as having significant opportunities to grasp and tools at their disposal. They can rely on strong legal frameworks, both EU and global commitments, and the TEU, which enshrines civil society's role in policymaking. NGOs also have a lot of supporters for their missions, including support from EU citizens,

[6] *Qatargate* was a political scandal that made the headlines in December 2022 involving allegations that the Government of Qatar cash to MEPs to influence voting at the European Parliament in favour of Qatar. Bribes were allegedly channelled via an NGO founded by one of the MEPs called Fight Impunity. It is still under investigation at the time of writing.

[7] There are numerous anti-NGO efforts, from the Pieper Report in 2017 (Tamina, 2017), to the Commission defunding NGO lobbying activities in 2024 (Van Schuren & Haar, 2024), and a highly publicized narrative on an ECA report citing lack of NGO transparency (with little evidence but damaging media coverage) (European Court of Auditors, 2025; Kergueno, 2025).

MEPs, and Member States as well as from committed civil servants and Commissioner cabinet staff.

As highlighted above, NGOs can draw on the evidence they gather through research and documenting experiences from their community-level programmes. This is extremely powerful, as NGOs reach communities and constituencies, which EU policymakers and political decision-makers can rarely access directly. NGOs are a great source of information as well as of inspiration.

But to wield their power, NGOs must be self-aware, cognizant of the potential pitfalls they face. Where NGOs are struggling to influence the populist political narratives, there is a real danger of NGOs compromising on their values and principles. Seeking to find convincing narratives for politicians could lead NGOs to concede too far and instrumentalize the principled work they do. NGOs also risk becoming complacent, not listening or innovating enough, or no longer seeking to drive the overall policy agenda for longer-term change; this can result in some NGOs repeating the same messages for years, at times lacking nuance and ability to adapt to context, thereby limiting their influence and impact.

NGOs must therefore maintain a laser focus on their values, principles, and missions, which are their core strengths. NGOs must seek to change unhelpful political narratives and drive forward an agenda focused on people, environment, and rights by continuing to engage with their supporters and aligning with and supporting where helpful other movements and alliances, to help shape the EU and the world that the millions of citizens that support them would like to have. Finally, NGOs need to listen, adapt, and evolve, continuing to find new ways to make their voices heard by EU policymakers and decision-makers.

References

Civil Society Europe. (2022). The future of Europe is ours: A view from civil society: Recommendations from civil society organisations for the Conference on the Future of Europe. https://civilsocietyEurope.eu/wp-content/uploads/2023/12/The-Future-of-Europe-is-Ours_CSOCoFoE_report.pdf

Collinson, H. (2022). INTRAC Advocacy toolkit for small charities: Advocacy Tool Power and Stakeholder Analysis. https://www.intrac.org/app/uploads/2022/06/Advocacy-Tool-Power-and-stakeholder-analysis-mapping.pdf

Corporate Europe Observatory. (2025, January 28). European right-wing on a mission to silence NGOs. https://corporateeurope.org/en/2025/01/european-right-wing-mission-silence-ngos

Council of the European Union. (2020, December 16). Presidency Conclusions on the Gender Action Plan (GAP) III 2021–2025 – An ambitious agenda for gender equality and women's empowerment in EU external action. 13947/20. https://data.consilium.europa.eu/doc/document/ST-13947-2020-INIT/en/pdf

Council of the European Union. (2021, May 20). Council Conclusions on the Communication from the Commission to the European Parliament and the Council on the EU's humanitarian action: new challenges, same principles. 8966/21. https://data.consilium.europa.eu/doc/document/ST-8966-2021-INIT/en/pdf

European Commission. (2020, November 25). Joint Communication to the European Parliament and the Council, EU Gender Action Plan (GAP) III—An ambitious agenda for gender equality

and women's empowerment in EU External Action. JOIN (2020) 17 final eur-lex.europa.eu/legal-content/EN/TXT/PDF/?uri=CELEX:52020JC0017.
European Commission. (2021, March 10). Communication from the Commission to the European Parliament and the Council on the EU's humanitarian action: new challenges, same principles. COM (2021) 110 eur-lex.europa.eu/legal-content/EN/TXT/PDF/?uri=CELEX:52021DC0110.
European Court of Auditors. (2025). Special report: Transparency of EU funding granted to NGOs: Despite progress, the overview is still not reliable. 11/2025. https://www.eca.europa.eu/ECAPublications/SR-2025-11/SR-2025-11_EN.pdf
European Parliament, Committee on Development. (2021, November 19). Report on new orientations for the EU's humanitarian action. 2021/2163(INI). https://oeil.secure.europarl.europa.eu/oeil/popups/ficheprocedure.do?lang=en&reference=2021/2163(INI)
European Union. (2016, June 7). Consolidated versions of the Treaty on European Union and the Treaty on the Functioning of the European Union. *Official Journal of the European Union*, 59, 2016/C 202/01. eur-lex.europa.eu/legal-content/EN/TXT/PDF/?uri=OJ:C:2016:202:FULL.
Kergueno, R. (2025, May 13). Setting the record straight: Addressing the Opaque Scope of the ECA Report on NGO Funding. Transparency International EU. https://transparency.eu/setting-the-record-straight-addressing-the-opaque-scope-of-the-eca-report-on-ngo-funding/
Lewin, K. (1951). *Field theory in social science*. Harper & Row.
Power Cube. http://www.powercube.net
Save the Children and The Open University training session. Advocacy and Campaigning: Understanding Policy and Power, from https://www.open.edu/openlearncreate/mod/resource/view.php?id=53740
Tamina, P. (2017, September 21). Who is behind the EPP's latest attempt to tighten rules for NGOs? Euractiv. https://www.euractiv.com/section/politics/news/who-is-behind-the-epps-latest-attempt-to-tighten-rules-for-ngos/
Van Schuren, H., & Haar, K. (2024, December 13). Defunding NGOs that lobby the EU will be profoundly undemocratic. EUobserver. https://euobserver.com/*/arb285b91d

Further Reading

Civil Society Europe (2024). Entrust: Introduction to Civil Dialogue Training Manuel. https://civilsocietyeurope.eu/wp-content/uploads/2024/06/EnTrust_Introduction_Civil_DialogueTraining_Manual_EN_2024.pdf
Organ, J., & Alemanno, A. (Eds.). (2021). *Citizen participation in democratic Europe: What next for the EU?* ECPR Press.

Céline Mias has spent over 28 years leading NGO programmes in Europe, Africa, and Asia. She is currently the EU Director at the Danish Refugee Council in Brussels, spent over a decade as the EU Representative & Director at CARE International and served two terms as the Vice President of CONCORD Europe. Previously, Céline spent over 15 years working globally with international humanitarian NGOs. Céline holds a Master's degree in Development Studies from the University of Cambridge and a Bachelor's degree in History and Russian from McGill University.

Transparency in the European Union: Legal Framework, Lobbying Regulation, and Recent Developments

Oliver Drewes

Abstract Transparency is a constitutional principle of the European Union (EU), central to its democratic governance, accountability, and legitimacy. Enshrined in the Treaties (TEU, TFEU) and elaborated through secondary legislation such as Regulation (EC) No 1049/2001, it ensures openness, public access to documents, and scrutiny of decision-making. Over time, scandals and crises—from the resignation of the Santer Commission to recent affairs like "Qatargate" and "Pfizergate"—have reinforced the importance of transparency but also fostered an increasingly legalistic and bureaucratic approach.

While transparency promotes trust, prevents corruption, and enhances citizen participation, excessive formalism can hinder dialogue, stifle innovation, and alienate stakeholders. The balance between openness and effective governance remains delicate, especially in legislative processes and lobbying regulation. Instruments and instances such as the EU Transparency Register, the European Ombudsman, and the European Court of Justice (ECJ) play critical oversight roles. Nevertheless, challenges persist in managing access to documents, lobbying practices, and trilogue negotiations.

Recent controversies highlight risks of "activist" lawmaking without broad consultation, contributing to perceptions of overregulation, loss of competitiveness, and weakened legitimacy. The EU must recalibrate transparency: not merely as compliance or exclusion, but as a constructive partnership with citizens, industry, and civil society. Properly applied, transparency strengthens democratic legitimacy and supports innovation and prosperity. Misapplied, it risks bureaucratic paralysis, ineffective legislation, and growing Euroscepticism.

Keywords European Commission · Commission working methods · Decision-making · Democratic legitimacy · EU institutions · EU Transparency register · Transparency

---

O. Drewes (✉)
Managing Partner Pantarhei Europe, Brussels, Belgium
e-mail: Oliver.Drewes@pantarhei.com

G. Füricht-Fiegl et al. (eds.), *Handbook on EU Law-making*, Professional Practice in Governance and Public Organizations, https://doi.org/10.1007/978-3-032-16559-6_24

1 Introduction

Transparency is a cornerstone of democratic governance and a fundamental condition for the functioning of the European Union (EU) as a democratic organization based on the rule of law. It facilitates accountability, prevents corruption, and enhances the trust of EU citizens in the institutions that govern them. Legislation, as a public good, should be produced in a process for everyone to see and verify. It should be drafted and adopted by the parties designated in the legislative procedure to do so, and this should be verifiable.

The EU has its own approach to transparency, and it speaks for itself that this consists of more than the combined experiences and practices of the traditions in the Member States as it has its own legal base in the treaties. The principle plays a central role in the political and wider "Brussels bubble" debate.

This contribution will explore the multifaceted aspects of transparency in the EU, including the legal underpinnings, the regulation of lobbying, and recent initiatives aimed at strengthening open governance. It advocates for a constructive vision on transparency, one that not only aims at abuse prevention through bureaucratized procedures with a legalistic mindset aiming at keeping everyone at the same equidistance out of the debate, but an approach that focuses on the material inclusion of the legitimate voices which should be heard as well as one that fosters the best and most innovative ideas around what is best for society to move forward. It promotes a culture of strategic partnerships with relevant stakeholders and societal actors, aimed at fostering innovation, enhancing competitiveness, and securing long-term prosperity, through legislation that faithfully serves its primary objectives while ensuring compliance with procedural safeguards, including transparency obligations.

2 Legal Foundations of Transparency in the EU

The Treaty on European Union (TEU) and the Treaty on the Functioning of the European Union (TFEU) enshrine transparency as a guiding principle. Art. 10 (3) TEU emphasizes that decisions should be taken as openly and as closely as possible to the citizen. Art. 15 TFEU provides the legal basis for good governance, openness, and access to documents relating to the legislative procedures. But there is also secondary (implementing) legislation. Known is, for example, Regulation (EC) No 1049/2001 regarding public access to European Parliament (EP), Council, and Commission documents. It is not the aim of this contribution to engage in an all--encompassing analysis of legal aspects and jurisprudence around transparency. But it is important to note that transparency is not just a fashionable administrative tool, but a principle with constitutional status enshrined in the treaties and elaborated upon in implementing legislation and jurisprudence.

3 The Role of Transparency in EU Governance

Transparency plays an essential and determining role in the operations of the EU in general and within the legislative process specifically. Apart from being a legal principle, it became a guiding imperative in the debate around access to influence and combat and prevention of corruption and fraud. Transparency ensures that the decision-making processes of the EU are open to scrutiny by the public and all stakeholders. It supports informed participation by citizens and civil society.

More importantly, transparency should not be seen merely as a compliance requirement, but as a means of enabling greater involvement of those who are experts on issues being regulated, those who benefit from them, and those who are affected by them. Only proper involvement prevents the creation of asymmetrical legislation that does neither work nor deliver. Proper involvement should not be mixed up with undue influence. Because involving a party does not mean that one "buys" all its arguments. But not knowing the relevant contexts nor the arguments could mean that legislators are tapping unknowingly into the dark when they are, with the best intentions, regulating a certain area. If we read the press or look for information about the EU on social media and the Internet, then this is one of the biggest criticisms to be found: Too much bureaucracy and red tape delivering legislation that is out of touch with reality.[1] One wonders if this is really the case and how this is possible. Was there a mix-up between the concept of true transparency and undue influence? Were the relevant parties just not properly consulted? Did the rules and practices around transparency play a role here at all?

Over the past decades, transparency has assumed an increasingly prominent role in the European legislative process. However, this emphasis has often triggered reactive "this-should-not-happen-again" lawmaking, whereby isolated cases of misconduct lead to broad, prohibitive rules. While well-intentioned, this approach may help explain why many EU-related procedures have become burdened with red tape, requiring extensive form-filling and compliance exercises even for the most straightforward applications or grants.[2]

A big leap for transparency was the appointment in 1995 of Jacob Söderman as the first European Ombudsman, a position first created by the 1992 Maastricht Treaty. Jacob Söderman and all his successors made it their task to ensure transparency in governance and legislation at the EU level and around the EU institutions.

Another key defining moment was the "incidental scandal" around the dentist of French Commissioner Édith Cresson (Commissioner between 1995 and 1999) being hired as her scientific advisor. Leaving the details out for the sake of brevity,

---

[1] An FT-View editorial arguing that excessive bureaucracy in Europe—including at the EU level—is stifling competitiveness and that regulatory simplification should be prioritized. (Financial Times, 2025, January 2)

[2] A proposed transparency / lobbying registration law is criticized by civil society orgs who say it will impose additional administrative burdens and liability risks—even on small NGOs with limited capacity. (Delors Centre, 2025)

the incident led to the resignation of the whole Commission in March 1999 (Jacques Santer was president at the time). A committee of independent experts concluded a general lack of responsibility and accountability within the Commission. This was a key moment and a development leading to more powers for the EP and an essential step establishing more structured and verifiable governance and transparency rulemaking over the decades to come till today. But it also resulted in very formal professionalized processes with little space for individual voices to make themselves heard. The risk of this has been touched upon earlier.

More recent incidents and scandals show that finding the right balance in transparency is an ever-evolving process. For example, the ongoing "Qatargate scandal" at the EP (status: September 2025) involves allegations that Members of the EP (MEP) and their staff have been paid by foreign governments through environmental and human rights NGOs. This was allegedly done to create a friendly atmosphere towards these foreign countries within the EP and to ensure a voting behaviour in their favour. It is under investigation why the involved NGOs were not scrutinized by the transparency rules and procedures.

We can say that transparency not only has a strong legal footing in the EU but also plays a strong role in the everyday reality of the EU, its institutions and surrounding spheres of influence. This comes against the background of 27 Member States with sometimes completely differing cultures and practices on transparency. Over recent decades, transparency has rightly gained greater importance within the EU legislative process. At times, however, this has led to reactive lawmaking, where isolated cases of misconduct have prompted the introduction of broad preventive rules.[3] How this has contributed to the democratic legitimacy of the EU will be discussed under the following heading.

4 Transparency and Democratic Legitimacy

A transparent EU governance structure reinforces democratic legitimacy by allowing citizens to see how decisions are made and who is influencing them.

Transparency can help bridge the gap between EU institutions and the public. It also enhances confidence among private sector stakeholders, making it easier to build stable, long-term policy partnerships that serve both the public interest and Europe's competitiveness. This creates legal certainty based on stable rules, creating an atmosphere of trust, as a necessary precondition for investments to prosper and for citizens to go about their daily lives in confidence.

As mentioned earlier, transparency is most meaningful when it helps deliver outcomes that reflect both the letter and the spirit of rulemaking in democratic societies. When taken too far or misapplied, however, it can unintentionally distance

[3] See further a publication of the European Economic and Social Committee, which notes that complex EU rules can generate disproportionate administrative obligations and calls for simplification. (European Economic and Social Committee, 2022)

stakeholders, limit genuine dialogue, discourage innovation, and lead to legislation that falls short of its full potential. Transparency must be an equal-play promoter that keeps public institutions grounded in the realities of a dynamic society and economy. If the burden of participating in the process becomes too difficult and expensive, relevant participants will retract and their voices are lost.

5 Access to Documents and Public Information

The right of access to documents is a critical component of transparency. It is regulated through Regulation (EC) No 1049/2001 regarding public access to EP, Council, and Commission documents (European Commission, 2001).

It is also one of the principles often scrutinized through numerous procedures and a very politicized matter. The haggling is often about what should be covered? What type of access should be given? What is confidential? Does it only cover proper legislative texts or also contents of emails of officials, as well as their calendars? Or—to take an example from the recent past: Are President Ursula von der Leyen's SMS messages publicly accessible?

In the "Pfizergate" saga, the General Court (14 May 2025) annulled the Commission's refusal to release von der Leyen's texts with Pfizer's CEO, holding that the Commission failed to justify why it did not possess the requested messages and breached principles of good administration. The ruling confirms such messages can be within the access regime, but it did not itself release any text.

The interest in the matter was also kept alive just to keep pressure on the president for other political gains. On 10 July 2025, she won a vote of no confidence in the EP, which was also based on the "Pfizergate" allegations. But she came out weakened and it was portrayed as her "absolute last chance" (Politico, 2025). As seen from the author's perspective, this case also shows that the call for transparency can be an abusive one, even if in the example possibly justified. Sometimes the institutions receive requests that cost a lot of manpower to handle and seemingly are just there to grind the process.

Furthermore, legislators may adopt a more reserved stance if informal exchanges are perceived as potentially detrimental to their reputation. This dynamic can lead to fewer interactions and a reluctance to engage openly. Such tendencies raise the question of whether they are conducive to fostering constructive and transparent information exchange.

The EU is also in other fields being hampered by too much transparency. When negotiating, for example, trade or other deals with non-member states, the mandate of the Commission (acting on behalf of the EU) is often widely known in advance, as Member States and EP are involved, as well as general rules of transparency which must be respected. This means that the opposing party knows the EU's negotiating position easily in advance, giving the EU negotiators little leeway to truly negotiate for the benefit of the EU, as all their cards are on the table even before the talks start.

6 Transparency in the Legislative Processes

Transparency in the legislative process is a legal obligation as described above. Citizens and interested parties should be able to understand what is going on, who proposes what and why in the different stages of the legislative process. It is also linked to participation in the process, as those who have no access or information do not know what is going on, or understand how they should anticipate, follow up upon, or seek change of legislation. This is an imperative coming directly out of the treaties and a pillar of transparency, as Art. 10 (3) TFEU reads in full: "Every citizen shall have the right to participate in the democratic life of the Union. Decisions shall be taken as openly and closely to the citizen as possible". This is a clear reference to the principle of subsidiarity delivering on decisions at the lowest possible administrative level, the right to be informed and the right to be a shaper in the process. This is of interest as the EU has only powers explicitly given to it, while the Treaties remind the EU level also that a centralized power-grabbing exercise is against the letter and spirit of the Treaties. If something can be done better or equally good at the national, decentralized, or local level, it should be done there and not at the EU level.[4]

Even if the current Commission is lip-reading to better regulation[5] principles and for less red tape (see box below), one can wonder if its president is de facto following up on these principles. Why is there a commissioner for housing, for example? This is a national and, in some Member States, even a regional competence. For better isolation policies to save the climate some argue. Possibly true. But this issue could be dealt with by a Commissioner for environment, an area in which the EU has obvious competences. It can be made clear and transparent to citizens why we need better isolation, as saving of energy is a common concern for all. But the Commissioner for housing, going out there to tell the city councils of Stockholm, Paris, Prague, and Athens how they should organize their housing policy? It could reinforce the image of an over-eager central bureaucracy, intervening in people's lives at a micromanagement level.

Red Tape

Denotes excessive or unnecessarily complex administrative rules and procedures, which may hinder efficiency and delay decision-making processes. The term originates from the historical practice of binding official documents with red ribbon in European administrations, particularly in the sixteenth-century Spain and later in Britain.

[4] See also Chap. 2 of this handbook.

[5] See Chap. 9.1 of this handbook on better regulation.

Transparency should be seen in the light of its time. We had classically a very distinct Commission playing its role as the "*guardian of the treaties*" for the sake of the common European interest and as a sort of referee among the Member States as the members of the club. A minimal legalistic approach to transparency was the mantra of the day. But this changed over time. President Jacques Delors (1985–1994) started in the nineties more interventionist policies, flanked with more subsidies for all sorts of things all over Europe.

President Jacques Santer (1995–1999) got in directly after him with a "do less but better approach" (Politico, 15 November 1995) but ultimately failed through an unrelated scandal as described above. President Jean-Claude Juncker (2014–2019), much later, went even further by calling his College of Commissioners the "Political Commission", implying that from now onwards the Commission could intervene on whatever, whenever, if it served the goals it believed in. President Ursula von der Leyen (since 2019) took over this mantra with a drive to regulate quickly everything necessary to make the world a better place in her perception. Activists, like Ms. Thunberg on 4 March 2020, were invited to attend the official College of Commissioners meetings for all the world to see, as if she was a by the EP elected Commissioner. Others got no access to even the lower levels of the Berlaymont building,[6] and were sent into the transparency procedural processes.

Is all this important for the topic? Yes, because at the same time the EU and its institutions, primarily the Commission as the drafter of new legislation, did set up an even more highly systematized system to manage the transparency requirements coming out of the treaty. The system involves stakeholder hearings and various preliminary and more formalized engagement moments, before the final version is adopted by the College of Commissioners and sent to the co-legislators, EP, and Council of the EU.[7] Some stakeholders have expressed the view that transparency obligations were applied unevenly, with the perception that actors less favoured by the institutions were subject to more stringent procedural demands. In this sense, transparency requirements risk being perceived not only as a tool for openness but also as a mechanism that may constrain or marginalize unwelcome voices.[8]

Another critical moment is the final stage of lawmaking, through trilogue negotiations,[9] conducted behind closed doors involving EP, Council, and Commission. At this final stage of the Ordinary Legislative Procedure (OLP), often deals are being made, sometimes only understood by the negotiators present in the room. Enhancing transparency in these legislative areas should aim not to create antagonism but to build trust and co-creation with relevant actors across Europe.

[6] The Berlaymont building is the headquarter of the European Commission in Brussels.

[7] See Chap. 3. of this handbook.

[8] Bruch et al. analysed many submissions in public consultations on EU governance regulation and found out that certain types of stakeholders (industry, think-tanks, associations) dominate contributions. This suggests an imbalance in who can engage effectively. (Bruch, et al., 2024)

[9] See Chaps. 16 and 17 of this handbook.

It was Otto von Bismark who allegedly said that: "Laws are like sausages. It is best not to seem them being made".[10] Maybe this applies to the trilogue negotiations stage in the EU, as often perhaps no compromise could be reached if there would be no room for confidential conversation among the representatives of the three institutions. Total openness here could perhaps lead to a political stalemate and legislative inability.

7 Regulation of Lobbying in the EU

Lobbying is a legitimate part of the democratic process, but it must be transparent to avoid undue influence. The EU has established rules to regulate lobbying activities, aiming to ensure that policymaking is not skewed by powerful interests. Ethical guidelines and transparency rules apply to EU officials and lobbyists alike. A balanced transparency regime should recognize the constructive role that well-regulated lobbying can play in contributing expertise and grounding policies in real economic needs. In the meantime, public affairs became an established profession in Brussels, including representative organizations like the European Public Affairs Consultancies Association (EPACA) and the Society of European Affairs Professionals (SEAP). These organizations "defend and promote ethical, transparent lobbying with all relevant stakeholders, including the media" (EPACA, 2025).

Its operations being based on self-binding codes of conduct, their aim is to establish professional standards, also through regular dialogues with the EU institutions to further an all-integrated approach and practice throughout the EU ecosystem in Brussels.

8 The EU Transparency Register

The EU Transparency register is a database governed by a system of rules developed commonly by EP, Council, and Commission. It seeks to create a transparent overview of who is trying to influence policymaking in Brussels.

It is best explained in its own words: "The rules and principles governing the register are set out in an interinstitutional agreement between the EP, Council and Commission. The Transparency register is a database listing 'interest representatives' (organisations, associations, groups and self-employed individuals) who carry out *activities to influence the EU policy and decision-making process*. It is designed to show the public which interests are being represented at EU level, by whom and

[10] The quotation is widely attributed to Otto von Bismarck, though there is no contemporaneous evidence he said it. The earliest documented version appears in connection with the American poet John Godfrey Saxe (1816–1887). (Shapiro, 2006, 684); also: O'Toole, 2010)

on whose behalf—as well as the resources devoted to these activities (including financial support, donations, sponsorship, etc.).

The register has the following key features:

- A public website where interest representatives register up to date information about their activities at EU level.
- A code of conduct governing how interest representatives should interact with the EU institutions.
- A complaints mechanism to enable anyone to trigger an administrative inquiry into alleged cases where registered interest representatives have failed to observe the code" (Transparency register, 2025).

The register is in full operation now, while there are arguments to say that it covers too little or too much.

If it becomes too expensive or burdensome, bureaucratic or difficult to engage with the EU, some parties might just leave it or not understand how to do it. If you must publish key core and sometimes even confidential business information on websites or in published meeting reports you had with EU officials, while the desired results of such meetings are questionable as they might not deliver any change, you might as well leave it altogether.

And EU officials become increasingly risk averse and fearful: rather speak to no one directly you are regulating than running the risk to be under scrutiny by your hierarchy, the media or having to spend time on writing meeting reports on meetings with "outsiders", who do not contribute to your ranking in the internal performance measurement systems.

Professional lobbyists in Brussels could be seen as criticizing such registers, while praising them at the same time. But in the end, they could profit most from such a register. If even organizing a simple conversation with the EU becomes as difficult as going to the High Court, only specialist professionals can organize it in such a way that it is done in line with the transparency rules and in a way that it does not haunt you at a later stage.

9 Enforcement and Oversight Mechanisms

Enforcement of transparency obligations is essential for credibility. The European Ombudsman and the European Court of Justice (ECJ) are key actors in this domain. The Ombudsman investigates complaints about maladministration, including transparency violations, while the ECJ provides judicial oversight.

However, transparency enforcement should not be framed solely in adversarial or punitive terms. More emphasis should be placed on dialogue, guidance, and cooperative improvement with stakeholders. The complaints mechanism under the Transparency register must be mentioned here as a fast-moving effective tool, if applied in a comprehensive, transparent, and verifiable manner.

10 Recent Developments and Challenges

"One of the more surprising sights of 2025 has been watching Ursula von der Leyen devote so much energy in her second term as European Commission President to dismantle the success of her first" Simon Naxon wrote in the Financial Times on 8 August 2025 (Naxon, 2025).

He is referring to the fact that she is putting key legislation up for complete review without some of it ever having been in place or even worked out completely before now being up for scrapping again. The reviews are done through the so-called omnibus packages, as they put whole series of legislation up for review at the same time. Most of this legislation is around the so-called Green Deal package aimed at addressing the climate change challenges. But the approach is meanwhile extended to other areas. For the EU this is a somewhat unusual way of going about things, as classically it takes quite some time before legislation is produced in an all-inclusive consensual manner, producing a long-term robust package of legislation endorsed by most.

Why is this development important for our topic? In this context, the key issue is not so much the substantive content of the legislation, but the process through which it was produced. The Von der Leyen Commission was at times criticized for presenting major legislative packages with limited consultation and for relying heavily on a relatively narrow circle of preferred stakeholders. Critics argued that this style of lawmaking was highly activist and focused on delivering results quickly, sometimes at the expense of broader inclusiveness and transparency. This dynamic raised questions about the balance of participation and the consistency of the Commission's transparency practices (Kelemen & Follesdal, 2022). The politics around this were continued through the summer and autumn of 2025, flanked by a constant threat of a censure motion by the EP to sack the whole Commission. Normally a last resort instrument, seldomly used.

This is clearly the impression conveyed by several observers. Some argue that the Commission's legislative style appears highly ambitious and sometimes activist, driven by a coalition of supportive actors aiming to accelerate Europe's green transition. Whether this perception reflects political spin or reality, it nonetheless carried weight: Questions about inclusiveness and transparency in lawmaking became salient in the 2024 European Parliament elections, where concerns over competitiveness and regulatory burden contributed to a noticeable shift towards right-leaning parties. Critics contend that such an approach risks undermining legal certainty and the perceived legitimacy of the EU and may add to regulatory fragmentation if rapid revisions are not accompanied by comprehensive and systematic policy design. These debates underscore the importance of adhering to principles of good governance, stakeholder consultation, and transparency to sustain both the effectiveness and the acceptance of European policymaking (Kelemen & Follesdal, 2022; European Court of Auditors, 2019; Gravey & Jordan, 2022).

It is important to dedicate the necessary time and effort to the right conduct of the legislative process in terms of its legal base and ethical transparency requirements.

Nevertheless, legislation is there for a purpose, not only for the sake of the beauty of its production process. Legislating is not an objective for its own sake, but an instrument to organize society to deliver outcomes based on commonly agreed rules. If we concentrate only on the "purity of the process" while not addressing societal concerns, we have a problem. If the people believe that the laws are neither made for them nor serve their purposes, but for a small group of ideologists, we also have a problem. That is also of deep concern in a functioning democracy.

Legislation is not there for the transparency's sake of its production process only. Good lawmaking should produce legislation that works, legislation that enables progress. Not legislation that grinds economies, stifles innovation and creates but red tape while it addresses imaginary out of context solutions. To achieve this, there should be intensive contact with those concerned, as mostly only they know how things work in practice.

Transparency is in Brussels sometimes associated with orchestrated stakeholder processes. The more interests are outsourced into these processes, the better it looks for policymakers as they stay transparently "above and beyond", without risking their reputation by talking to unwelcome interests directly.

They are encouraged to have as little contact with the outside world as possible. Ivory tower politics as a principle and working methodology at the same time. A principle because contact with any interests is sometimes seen as breaching transparency rules. A methodology because it became so cumbersome for some legislators or policymakers to meet interest representatives that they sometimes rather meet no one than running the risk of getting into trouble. To be allowed to meet someone, they must fill explicatory forms and need to ask consent from their hierarchy. And if they have the courage to conduct a meeting with "outsiders", they must write evaluation reports and publish online whom they met and why. Then there is always the risk of being ex post exposed to public scrutiny. Transparency as a vibe and as a hype.

Transparency is not only a legal obligation, but a key principle. The author's concern is that we have gone somehow out of balance, running the risk of putting the whole EU under scrutiny. Lawmakers should actively engage with relevant parties when legislating to give these parties legal certainty and a foundation to grow. If transparency is only about keeping parties out while maintaining an ivory tower "we know best" attitude to citizens, economic participants, and other third parties, there is a huge risk that we get dysfunctional legislation, consisting of contradictory obligations and disproportionate costs for parties involved. The risk of such legislation is that it does not work, enhances Euroscepticism, stimulates extremist parties getting more power, and pushes companies into bankruptcy or out of the EU. As this contribution goes to print, we look back at some fundamental debates around the above during the tenure of the Von der Leyen Commission II. Just look at the many "omnibus" proposals to revisit by the Von der Leyen Commission I or the sudden withdrawal of the so-called Green Claims Directive in the summer of 2025.

When in the past speaking the US lawmakers for example, they often admired the well-founded EU legislation. It took a bit longer to produce but took aboard relevant concerns, providing workable solutions for all. The "Brussels effect" was setting global standards for consumer protection rules, for example. Currently Brussels is often associated with over-prescriptive rule-making, often not checked against what it achieves, while creating red tape and stifling economic progress. At the same time, all the "good rules" on transparency in the legislative process have been more precisely followed than ever, to the letter of the rules. At least for some.

11 Conclusion

Transparency in the EU is a dynamic and evolving field. While significant progress has been made, much work remains to ensure that all EU institutions operate openly and accountably. Strengthening legal frameworks, expanding the Transparency Register, increasing access to documents, and ensuring oversight will be key to maintaining and enhancing democratic legitimacy in the EU. Crucially, the EU must move beyond a solely punitive or litigious interpretation of transparency and embrace it as a tool for partnership. By fostering inclusive engagement with industry, civil society, and innovators, the EU can build a resilient and prosperous future grounded in trust, participation, and shared goals. If well-calibrated, transparency will deliver results in line with the spirit and structure of our democratic institutions. If misapplied or weaponized, it risks turning governance into a bureaucratic theatre disconnected from Europe's needs and aspirations.

Transparency is at the heart of a system that functions. But it is only one of the tools to deliver better legislation, not the only one. There will always remain a trade-off between a too legalistic and mechanical process-oriented view on transparency and an all-embracing inclusive one with the aim of creating better legislation for innovative societies. Is it about keeping everyone effectively and in a non-discriminatory way at bay? Or is it about actively including all the voices you need to improve legislation? I do not agree with Bismarck that only results count when it comes to legislation, similarly as to sausage production, as he allegedly said. But the opposite is not true either. If we only look at the production process of legislation, we get legislation that does not deliver, and that is the least desirable outcome.

References

Bruch, N., Knodt, M., & Ringel, M. (2024). Advocating harder soft governance for the European green Deal: Stakeholder perspectives on the revision of the EU governance regulation. *Energy Policy, 192*(2024), 113–126.

EPACA. (2025). Mission statement. https://epaca.org/

European Commission. (2001). Regulation (EC) No 1049/2001 of the European Parliament and of the Council of 30 May 2001 regarding public access to European Parliament, Council and Commission documents (OJ L 145, 31.5.2001, 43–48).

European Court of Auditors. (2019). Have Your Say! Commission's Public Consultations Engaged Citizens, but Impact Could Be Made Clearer, Special Report 14/2019.

European Economic and Social Committee. (2022). Cutting red tape: Assessing regulation impact and regulatory overreach, Brussels.
Financial Times. (2025, January 2). Europe need to tackle its red tape problem. https://www.ft.com/content/90a4f5f2-af31-46cd-a3f5-0ce42f71dfa7
Gravey, V., & Jordan, A. (2022). Does the European Union have a 'Legitimacy Crisis'? Reflections on EU Governance and the European Green Deal. *Politics and Governance, 10*(3), 224–234.
Jacques Delors Center. (2025, July 11), The EU's defence of Democracy Dilemma: The example of third country lobbying. https://www.delorscentre.eu/en/publications/detail/publication/the-eus-defence-of-democracy-dilemma
Kelemen, D., & Follesdal, A. (2022). Europe's green moment? The European Green Deal, legitimacy and multi-level governance. *Journal of European Public Policy, 29*(8), 1230–1245.
Naxon, S. (2025, August 8). In Financial Times, 2025.
O'Toole, G. (2010, August 12). Laws, like sausages, cease to inspire respect in proportion as we know how they are made. In: Quote Investigator.
Politico. (1995, November 15). https://www.politico.eu/article/santer-lives-up-to-pledge-to-do-less-but-better/
Politico. (2025, July 10). Von der Leyen wins vote of no-confidence but warned this is her 'absolute last chance'. www.politico.eu/article/eu-commission-president-ursula-von-der-leyen-wins-vote-no-confidence-european-parliament/
Shapiro, F. R. (2006). *The Yale book of quotations*. Yale University Press.
Transparency Register. (2025). https://transparency-register.europa.eu/index_en

Oliver Drewes is a Managing Partner at Pantarhei Corporate Advisors with over 25 years of experience, including 20 years in the European institutions. He served, for example, as European Commission spokesperson for Internal Market and Services and as a member of several Commissioners' cabinets, contributing to EU policy development. He holds degrees in law and governance, an LL.M. in European Legal Studies, and is fluent in German, Dutch, English, and French. He was a member of the Management Committee of EPACA, most recently in an advisory capacity.

Selected Policy Fields Under Debate

The EU's Digital Policy

Irina Michalowitz

Abstract The EU's digital policy evolved over the past decade, mainly through the procedural instrument of the Ordinary Legislative Procedure (OLP) and aims to balance the protection of the European citizen's fundamental right to data protection and privacy with digital innovation dependent on data, while also seeking to reduce dependence on non-EU companies and extending its regulatory influence globally. This chapter analyses how the EU manages these competing goals through its major digital regulations, from the General Data Protection Regulation (GDPR) to data governance, competition policy and cybersecurity to the recent Artificial Intelligence Act (AI Act), highlighting efforts to balance fundamental rights protection with innovation needs, while aiming to extend its influence beyond European borders. Particular emphasis is given to the GDPR as the foundational legislation, which creates principles like data minimization and consent and has achieved global influence. This approach creates a tension with the more recent increase of data-intensive needs of emerging technologies like AI or cybersecurity. New legislation, such as the EU's Data Act, attempts to reconcile these tensions by shifting the ownership of data from the data-collecting business to the individual and to mandate the sharing of data under strict conditions. The AI Act receives particular attention, as the most recent and most powerful example of these tensions, while also demonstrating the EU's difficulties in enforcing its regulations, notably given its ambitions to create a regulatory framework that will be adopted globally.

Keywords Digital policy · Data protection · Privacy · Cybersecurity · Artificial Intelligence · Data governance · AI Act · Brussels effect · Fundamental rights · Digital sovereignty · Extraterritoriality · GDPR · Digital Markets Act

I. Michalowitz (✉)
Vice President Public Policy & Government Relations, DeepL SE/Cologne, and Founding Director, IMConsult bv, Brussels, Belgium
e-mail: im@imconsult.eu

G. Füricht-Fiegl et al. (eds.), *Handbook on EU Law-making*, Professional Practice in Governance and Public Organizations, https://doi.org/10.1007/978-3-032-16559-6_25

1 Introduction

Digital technologies have profoundly transformed society, leading the EU to introduce a comprehensive regulatory framework of technology policy law for the digital economy. The OLP is the primary mechanism for this regulatory framework, ensuring that digital regulations are shaped by all three key EU institutions: the European Commission, the European Parliament (EP), and the Council of the EU. The digital policy framework encompasses topics such as data protection, data governance, content moderation, digital competition, cybersecurity, and artificial intelligence (Marcus et al., 2024).

These initiatives are unified by two central tensions: protecting fundamental rights—particularly privacy and data protection—while fostering innovation dependent on data, reducing dependence on non-EU technology companies, with the aim of promoting EU regulatory standards globally. An element of this goal is the attempt to ensure those companies adopt practices in compliance with EU regulation, with the side effect that those practices may become global standards because multinational companies prefer global solutions.

Understanding EU digital policy requires understanding how those tensions materialize throughout legislation. This chapter analyses how the EU manages these competing goals through its major digital regulations, from the General Data Protection Regulation (GDPR) to data governance, competition policy and cybersecurity to the recent Artificial Intelligence Act (AI Act), highlighting efforts to balance fundamental rights protection with innovation needs, whilst aiming to extend its influence beyond European borders.

2 The GDPR as the Foundation of the EU's Digital Policy

The GDPR, adopted in 2016 and implemented in 2018, established the foundation for what became the EU's digital policy. Understanding the GDPR is crucial because it serves as the cornerstone of the digital policy architecture, from which the tensions originate.

The GDPR was designed to safeguard EU citizens' fundamental right to data protection, established as a fundamental right in the EU Charter of Fundamental Rights (Art. 8 CFR), unlike other jurisdictions where it is often regarded as a commercial or consumer rights issue (Brkan, 2019; Fuster, 2014).

The GDPR's core principles reflect this approach. Data minimization, for instance, means that only data strictly necessary for a specific purpose can be collected (Art. 5c GDPR). For data processing, consent is required—data processing must rely on "freely given, specific, informed consent" (Art. 4 GDPR) or other lawful bases such as legitimate interest.[1] This conflict manifests in multiple ways. The

[1] Those legal bases are narrowly defined in Art. 6 GDPR.

principle of purpose limitation forces organizations to define the scope for which they request consent to data processing, and for which they can then use those data. Together with a series of explicit rights, such as data portability (Art. 20 GDPR) or the "right to be forgotten" (Art. 17 GDPR), those principles help the individual user gain a certain extent of control over their personal data.

The GDPR is one of the first EU legislations gaining global influence, demonstrating how an EU regulation can extend beyond its territorial borders due to its market attractiveness rather than coercive power (Jarlebring, 2022). It applies to any organization processing personal data of EU residents, irrespectively of the location of that organization and it requires non-EU organizations with business ties to the EU to nominate a Data Protection Officer (DPO) who can be held accountable on behalf of the organization (Art. 37 GDPR). The significant fines of up to 4% of global annual revenue can be considered a strong incentive for compliance and are actively enforced (Art. 83 GDPR, CMS, 2025).

Many companies opted to adopt their GDPR-compliance measures globally rather than maintaining separate practices for EU and non-EU markets. Bradford (2020) named this development the "Brussels Effect", describing a situation where EU standards are adopted globally because companies prefer to adopt the highest requirements across all markets they operate in rather than tailoring approaches for different regulatory regimes. However, questions remain whether this influence translated into meaningful behavioural change, given that the EU struggles to enforce the GDPR beyond its borders (Czerniawski, 2024).

While the GDPR can be considered a success in terms of establishing strong data protection rules across the EU, it also created tensions with consequences for subsequent laws. Particularly the strong emphasis on consent requirements and data minimization is at odds with the extensive need for data in the field of emerging technologies such as AI or with the need for information sharing in cybersecurity, as will be explained in more detail later in this chapter.

3 Data Governance: Attempting Reconciliation

The GDPR's restrictive approach soon showed potential negative implications for innovation in a data-hungry technology space. The European Data Strategy (2020) and subsequent Data Governance Act (DGA) (2021) and Data Act (2023) represent the EU's attempt to respond to this need and allow controlled data sharing while maintaining privacy protection.

The first instrument of this kind, the DGA, establishes the so-called Data Spaces for key economic sectors, which are virtual marketplaces with vetted participants and a common set of rules, for key economic sectors (see Recital 2 & 3 DGA). The Commission's main idea of this legislation is to provide European businesses, notably Small and Medium Enterprises (SMEs) the opportunity to access data shared voluntarily and in certified compliance with the GDPR within this closed group of data space participants (European Commission, 2025d). For example, the Healthcare

Data Space, which has been adopted in 2025, can help share medical data across EU Member States while protecting patient data.

The Data Act takes a more direct approach to the data protection versus innovation tension by mandating data sharing in specific circumstances. Unlike the voluntary mechanisms in the DGA, the Data Act creates legal requirements for businesses to share data generated by connected products and services with other businesses if the user desires this. This is a fundamental change of the perspective on data ownership. Previously, data were considered as belonging to the collecting entity—generally a business offering a product or service an individual seeks to use, who then generates data through this use. The Data Act moves the ownership to the individual, who can now mandate the data collector to share the data with third parties. For instance, a car manufacturer would previously have owned data generated by the vehicle, whereas the car owner is now in control and can request access or request the sharing with other companies and thereby even monetize the data.

Both the DGA and Data Act include provisions on international data transfers that go beyond the GDPR's provisions, thus amplifying the GDPR's extraterritorial reach and reflecting the growing concern about data sovereignty and foreign governments' access to data since the establishment of the GDPR. While the GDPR allows data transfers of personal data in the presence of adequate privacy protection laws in the country to which the data is transferred or with adequate safeguards (Chapter V GDPR), the DGA and the Data Act, which predominantly but not only cover non-personal data, include language that allows prohibition of data transfers even if this is the case (Recital 21, Art. 30 DGA; Art. 32 Data Act). Considering that most technology companies are US-based, data sharing from the EU to the US is an important aspect. The provisions can be interpreted as learnings from the European Court of Justice (CJEU)'s "Schrems II" decision, which invalidated the EU-US Privacy Shield due to overly broad US government surveillance powers (CJEU, 2020; Christakis, 2024).

4 The Digital Markets Act: Ex Ante Competition Regulation

In 2021, the EU adopted another two legislative frameworks aimed at governing aspects of the digital economy: The Digital Markets Act (DMA) and the Digital Services Act (DSA). While the DSA focuses on control over online content, the Digital Markets Act (DMA) represents the EU's most direct attempt to regulate non-EU technology dominance. Traditional competition law imposes most of its measures *ex post*—competition authorities investigate potential market failures or suspicions of unlawful behaviour after they occur, such as the creation of cartels or price-fixing, and impose fines and obligations to remedy the damage on businesses found at fault. As a supplement to the *ex post* mechanisms of European competition policy, the DMA aims to *ex ante* address the perceived negative consequences that may arise from certain behaviours by the largest digital companies. This shift demonstrates the EU's concern that *ex post* measures are insufficient to address the dominance and resulting market power achieved by the largest multinational technology companies.

The DMA applies to companies identified as "gatekeepers", i.e. companies that are able, due to their significant market power, their entrenched position, and strong intermediation position, to impose their conditions on the market and on competitors (Recital 2 DMA). Companies are designated as "gatekeepers" based on quantitative and qualitative criteria[2] or following a case-by-case assessment during a market investigation (Art. 3 DMA). They are required to comply with specific requirements and restrictions, some of which intersect with the GDPR, demonstrating the growing importance of data protection and privacy law in the economic space. Key obligations include ensuring interoperability with third-party services, allowing users to uninstall pre-installed applications, transparency about advertising performance, and a prohibition to prioritize own services in online rankings (Art. 5–7 DMA).

The DMA also has direct implications for the EU's ability to reduce its dependence on non-EU companies and has a strong extraterritorial dimension. The Commission has so far designated seven companies as gatekeepers, of which five are US-headquartered, one is Chinese, and only one is a European business (European Commission, 2023). In anticipation of this selection, the DMA was met with international criticism, notably from US policymakers, who argue the law constitutes an abuse of competition law to constrain US companies (Chu, 2023). Indeed, certain dynamics of the legislative process leading to the DMA created the impression that discrimination might be intentional. At least two prominent Members of the EP alluded to the law's intention to constrain US companies, one of them even calling for limiting the law's effect to non-EU companies (Hufbauer & Hogan, 2022).

Some scholars therefore view the DMA as part of a larger strategy, considering it an unhelpful element of digital sovereignty aspirations. They view the US–EU conflict over its effects as part of a broader struggle for opinion leadership concerning governance principles for a global digital economy (Hadebe, 2022). In this context, the broader question revolves around designing globally effective instruments that protect competition while simultaneously considering data subjects' privacy rights—a question the Commission appears to have sought to address through the extraterritorial effect of its regulation but whose global value remains to be proven.

5 Cybersecurity

The EU's cybersecurity framework is an example of how the tension between data protection and other policy objectives manifests. Cybersecurity professionals consider data sharing a necessary means to advancing cybersecurity but face a conflict

[2] Annual turnover, market capitalization, number of users in the so-called core platform service, namely online search engines, social networks, video sharing platforms, messaging services, cloud computing service, operating systems, web browsers, virtual assistants, online advertising services.

with data protection rights, particularly with the principles of data minimization and consent, where personal data is included.

Four key laws present the core of the EU's cybersecurity framework: the Cyber Security Act (CSA), the Network and Information Security Directive (NIS2), the Cyber Resilience Act (CRA), and the Digital and Operational Resilience Act (DORA). These instruments establish an order of criticality and legal granularity, addressing different aspects of cybersecurity across various sectors and stakeholders (European Commission, 2020a, 2020b).

A new trend is the strengthening of cybersecurity in defence policy, as exemplified in the Cyber Solidarity Act (2025), the Blueprint (Council, 2025), the development of a European Cybersecurity Shield, and the Preparedness Union Strategy (European Commission, 2025c). Furthermore, sectoral policies are emerging, such as the European action plan on the cybersecurity of hospitals and healthcare providers (European Commission, 2025a) or the planned revision of the Medical Devices Regulation (see European Commission, 2025b).

Significant implementation challenges are likely to arise from these initiatives due to overlapping requirements, varying implementation timelines and sometimes different enforcement agencies. NIS2, as a directive, allows some flexibility in transposition by EU Member States, whereas the CRA and DORA are directly applicable regulations. This creates complexity for organizations that must comply with a variety of those laws. Additionally, the EU's technology sovereignty aspirations begin to infiltrate previously strictly technical cybersecurity discussions, demanding data localization in the EU and potentially even a majority ownership within the EU.[3]

In terms of the tension between data protection and innovation, cybersecurity faces specific challenges because it requires collecting, analysing large amounts of data, potentially including personal or even sensitive personal data, for threat intelligence and sharing them within the cybersecurity community. NIS2, for instance, requires critical infrastructure service providers to establish cybersecurity risk management measures, but they risk a breach with the GDPR because they cannot rule out the collection of sensitive data or automated decision-making when doing so. Providers often rely on the GDPR's legal base of "legitimate interest" for data processing, but uncertainty remains about the extent to which cybersecurity interests override individual data protection rights (Kun, 2025). With AI, the challenge becomes even more pertinent, because the accuracy of cybersecurity-related AI tools necessitates the collection of vast amounts of data, some of which may contain

[3] The inclusion of non-technical "sovereign requirements" applying to the highest assurance levels is currently discussed in the context of an EU cybersecurity certification scheme for cloud services (EUCS). Especially smaller Member States fear a limitation of choice among cybersecurity providers, while larger countries can rely on a certain number of national cybersecurity providers (Roure, 2024). Given that larger countries are more likely than smaller ones to host a certain ecosystem of cybersecurity companies, it cannot be excluded that commercial interests, namely, to help those providers broaden their European footprint, also play a role.

personal information. This poses additional challenges of data classification and data minimization for cybersecurity providers that integrate AI into their products.

6 The AI Act: Challenging Traditional Data Protection Principles

The AI Act, adopted in 2024, represents the first comprehensive regulation on AI by a major regulator and establishes a common framework of requirements for the use and supply of AI systems within the EU. It stands more than any other recent EU technology regulation for the attempt to bridge innovation interests with the protection of fundamental rights, in its attempt to provide guardrails for an emerging technology. Simultaneously and due to the global trend of AI development, the AI Act has global implications with potential to trigger the "Brussels effect".

It was originally drafted due to growing concerns regarding the algorithmic capabilities and their potential to have a consequential impact on individuals in areas such as credit scoring, coupled with increasing awareness of AI systems' flaws, especially regarding bias or inappropriate use. The EU chose a horizontal, risk-based approach rather than sector-specific legislation. Consequently, the AI Act applies to all sectors in the same way but distinguishes between risk levels associated with particular applications, thereby attempting to limit the curbing of innovation to the extent deemed necessary (European Commission, 2020a).

The legislation establishes five risk categories:

- **Unacceptable risks:** These are prohibited practices and include subliminal manipulation techniques, the exploitation of vulnerabilities, social scoring systems, untargeted scraping of facial images, emotion recognition in workplace/education contexts, biometric categorization using sensitive characteristics, or real-time biometric identification in public spaces (with limited exceptions) (Art. 5 AI Act).
- **High-risk applications** of AI, determined as AI systems used in critical infrastructure, educational and vocational systems, employment and worker management systems, systems providing essential services, law enforcement applications or remote biometric identification systems, which pose a potential physical or fundamental rights risk to individuals, are subject to particular oversight (Chapter III AI Act).[4]
- **General-purpose AI (GPAI):** This category was included after the launch of ChatGPT. Basic obligations for all GPAI models include technical documentation and copyright compliance. Additional obligations are imposed on GPAI models with "systemic risk", encompassing evaluation, risk assessment, incident reporting, and cybersecurity measures. The precise meaning of these obligations

[4] High-risk applications are not prohibited but subject to strict conditions, scrutiny, and transparency. (Chapter III and in particular Art. 14 AI Act).

has been detailed in a non-binding Code of Practice for GPAI models, which was published in July 2025 (Chapter V AI Act).
- **Limited or low risk:** Examples include chatbots or deepfakes, which must adhere to transparency obligations (Art. 50 AI Act).
- **No or minimal risk:** Examples include spam filters, which also have transparency obligations (Art. 50 AI Act).

Those provisions apply to the entire AI supply chain, including providers, deployers, importers, distributors, product manufacturers, authorized representatives of providers from outside the EU and affected individuals within the EU,[5] in line with their level of control over a particular AI system.

The interpretation of the AI Act's rules is still in flux at the time of writing this paper. The legislation is currently being reopened with a proposal for simplifying its rules - the so-called "Digital Omnibus". The proposal foresees to push the entry into force of the provisions by another year or at least until AI standards have been produced. The staggered implementation over a period of 2 years will thus likely see the bulk of the provisions entering into force in 2027 instead of 2026, and some critical rules especially on data protection are already strongly questioned by MEPs and NGOs. Also, further guidance on compliance with high-risk AI systems' requirements and other aspects is still being developed.

While the political approval process appears chaotic at best, the fact that the AI Act is the first regulation of AI worldwide gives it great potential to establish the global standard of AI governance or at least inform other regulations across the world. The extraterritorial effect is crucial for ensuring a level-playing field for EU and non-EU developers because currently, successful AI foundation model providers are primarily from outside the EU. Without an interest to comply with the AI Act, EU startups that have higher compliance burdens than their non-EU counterparts are potentially disadvantaged. Siegmann and Anderljung (2022) expect that companies will either apply the same standards as in the EU to their AI systems globally or they may provide different products in the EU and outside of it. The jury is still out if this would lead to qualitatively worse or better products for European consumers and the differentiation remains unlikely for large multinational companies due to the EU's market size.

The concrete consequences of the regulation on AI companies and the services they offer only begin to become apparent (Tarafder & Vadlamani, 2025). Furthermore, the EU has yet to prove that it is able to enforce the AI Act. Šonková (2024) maintains that a de jure Brussels effect hinges upon the actual enforcement and the issuance of fines—a factor that has previously significantly bolstered the GDPR's impact but has not been consistently applied in the case of other legislation. For the AI Act, there is reason for concern: AI-skilled personnel are scarce and

[5] With partial exemptions where rules are already in place, and total exemptions for national security, military, defence, national security purposes, law enforcement in international cooperation, scientific research and development, purely personal non-professional activities and free and open-source licenses.

highly compensated; businesses already struggle to attract such talent, and similar difficulties can be anticipated for the European Commission, which seeks to hire approximately 100 additional staff members for this task (Kroet, 2024).

7 Conclusions and Future Challenges

The EU's digital policy framework is a comprehensive attempt to address technological change through the procedural instrument of the OLP. This chapter examined the success of this approach by focusing on two central tensions that run through the different legislative initiatives forming the framework: (1) protecting EU citizens' data while fostering innovation and (2) achieving an extraterritorial effect of its regulation.

Following the previously presented arguments, the EU's ability to balance data protection with innovation needs shows mixed results. The GDPR successfully established data protection as a global norm and allowed individuals to exert greater control over the use of their personal data. However, it also created costly and complex compliance burdens that can hinder innovation, particularly for SMEs and emerging technologies and is at odds with other digital legislation—cybersecurity legislation mandates information sharing among cybersecurity stakeholders, while the Data Governance Act and the Data Act establish a legal basis for large-scale data sharing. The contradiction between data protection, on the one hand, and information sharing interests and needs of technologies such as AI or cybersecurity, on the other hand, remains challenging where the sharing of data is crucial to advance the products and services individuals desire.

As for the goal to achieve extraterritorial governance, the geopolitical landscape for the EU has fundamentally shifted from the Von der Leyen I to the Von der Leyen II Commission, leading to a determination of European policymakers to significantly enhance its defence capabilities and increase its economic independence from non-EU actors, particularly the US. Given that most significant technology companies are headquartered in the US, this trend, if it continues, will have substantial implications for both consumers and businesses.

Finally, a new technological advancement is already on the horizon and will test the EU's ability to achieve its goals again: quantum computing. A breakthrough could potentially occur during the Von der Leyen II Commission's mandate, leading to yet another radical transformation with enormous risks and opportunities. EU legislation is beginning to anticipate those changes, yet again with little technological knowledge and uncertainty as to whether the applied legal principles can appropriately balance the protection of individuals with the promotion of innovative powers.

The success of the EU's future technology regulation will depend on policymakers' ability to defend the EU's values while eliminating the contradictions in its legislative approach and limiting the compliance burden to ensure Europe remains competitive.

References

Bradford, A. (2020). *The Brussels effect: How the European Union rules the world.* Oxford University Press.

Brkan, M. (2019). The essence of the fundamental rights to privacy and data protection: Finding the way through the maze of the CJEU's constitutional reasoning. *German Law Journal, 20*(6), 864–883.

Christakis, T. (2024). *The "zero risk" fallacy: International data transfers, foreign governments' access to data and the need for a risk-based approach.* Information Policy Centre.

Chu, K. (2023). Wyden and Crapo call on Biden administration to fight EU digital trade policies that discriminate against U.S. Workers and employers. United States Senate Committee on Finance, Chairman's News, March 9.

CJEU. (2020). Case C-311/18 data protection commissioner v Facebook Ireland limited and Maximillian Schrems ("Schrems II").

CMS. (2025). `CMS.law GDPR Enforcement Tracker´. Accessed December 6, 2024, from https://dataprivacymanager.net/5-biggest-gdpr-fines-so-far-2020/#:~:text=1.,on%20US%20tech%20giant%20Meta

Council of the EU. (2025). EU adopts blueprint to better manage European cyber crises and incidents. Press release, 6 June 2025.

Czerniawski, M. (2024). On digital sovereignty, extraterritoriality and EU digital Laws—GDPR case study. The Digital Constitutionalist. https://digi-con.org/on-digital-sovereignty-extraterritoriality-and-eu-digital-laws-gdpr-case-study/.

European Commission. (2020a). White Paper on Artificial Intelligence—A European approach to excellence and trust. COM Brussels 19.2.2020, COM(2020)65 final.

European Commission. (2020b). Joint communication to the European Parliament and the council. The EU's Cybersecurity strategy for the digital decade. Brussels 16.12.2020, JOIN(2020)18 final.

European Commission. (2023). Gatekeepers. https://digital-markets-act.ec.europa.eu/gatekeepers_en

European Commission. (2025a). Communication from the Commission to the European Parliament, the Council, the European Economic and Social Committee and the Committee of the Regions. European action plan on the cybersecurity for hospitals and healthcare providers, Brussels, 15.1.2025, COM (2025) 10 final.

European Commission. (2025b). Communication from the Commission to the European Parliament, the Council, the European Economic and Social Committee and the Committee of the Regions. Commission work programme 2025. Moving forward together: A Bolder, Simpler, Faster Union. Strasbourg, 11.2.2025, COM (2025) 45 final.

European Commission. (2025c). Joint Communication to the European Parliament, the European Council, the Council, the European Economic and Social Committee and the Committee of the Regions on the European Preparedness Union Strategy. Brussels, 26.3.2025, JOIN (2025) 130 final.

European Commission. (2025d). Data Governance Act explained. https://digital-strategy.ec.europa.eu/en/policies/data-governance-act-explained

Fuster, G. G. (2014). *The emergence of personal data protection as a fundamental right of the EU* (Vol. 16). Springer Science & Business.

Hadebe, S. (2022). Digital sovereignty and tight regulation in the EU: Analysing the motivation behind the digital markets act. Available at SSRN 4785054.

Hufbauer, G. C., & Hogan, M. (2022). The European Union renews its offensive against US technology firms (No. PB22-2).

Jarlebring, J. (2022). 'Regime vetting': A technique to exercise EU market power. *Journal of European Public Policy, 29*(4), 530–549.

Kroet, C. (2024). Commission's staffing and financing of AI office raises eyebrows in capitals. Euronews. 1 February 2024. https://www.euronews.com/next/2024/02/01/commissions-staffing-and-financing-of-ai-office-raises-eyebrows-in-capitals

Kun, E. (2025). Searching for the appropriate legal basis for personal data processing for cybersecurity purposes under the NIS 2 directive: Legal obligation and/or legitimate interest? *Computer Law & Security Review, 56*, 106098.

Marcus, J. S., Sekut K., & Zenner, K. (2024). A dataset on EU legislation for the digital world. Bruegel. https://www.bruegel.org/dataset/dataset-eu-legislation-digital-world

Regulation (EU) 2016/679 of the European Parliament and of the Council of 27 April 2016 on the protection of natural persons with regard to the processing of personal data and on the free movement of such data, and repealing Directive 95/46/EC (General Data Protection Regulation).

Regulation (EU) 2019/881 of the European Parliament and of the Council of 17 April 2019 on ENISA (the European Union Agency for Cybersecurity) and on information and communications technology cybersecurity certification and repealing Regulation (EU) No 526/2013 (Cybersecurity Act).

Regulation (EU) 2022a/868 of the European Parliament and of the Council of 30 May 2022 on European data governance and amending Regulation (EU) 2018/1724 (Data Governance Act).

Regulation (EU) 2022b/2554 of the European Parliament and of the Council of 14 December 2022 on digital operational resilience for the financial sector and amending Regulations (EC) No 1060/2009, (EU) No 648/2012, (EU) No 600/2014, (EU) No 909/2014 and (EU) 2016/1011 (Text with EEA relevance)Regulation (EU) 2022/2065 of the European Parliament and of the Council of 19 October 2022 on a Single Market For Digital Services and amending Directive 2000/31/EC (Digital Services Act).

Regulation (EU) 2023/2854 of the European Parliament and of the Council of 13 December 2023 on harmonised rules on fair access to and use of data and amending Regulation (EU) 2017/2394 and Directive (EU) 2020/1828 (Data Act).

Regulation (EU) 2025/38 of the European Parliament and of the Council of 19 December 2024 laying down measures to strengthen solidarity and capacities in the Union to detect, prepare for and respond to cyber threats and incidents and amending Regulation (EU) 2021/694 (Cyber Solidarity Act).Regulation (EU) 2024/1689 of the European Parliament and of the Council of 13 June 2024 laying down harmonised rules on artificial intelligence and amending Regulations (EC) No 300/2008, (EU) No 167/2013, (EU) No 168/2013, (EU) 2018/858, (EU) 2018/1139 and (EU) 2019/2144 and Directives 2014/90/EU, (EU) 2016/797 and (EU) 2020/1828 (Artificial Intelligence Act).

Roure, A. (2024). The EUCS Saga: Europe cannot afford to further delay its Cybersecurity framework. CCIA Disruptive Competition Project, 22 October 2024. https://project-disco.org/european-union/europe-cannot-delay-its-cybersecurity-framework/

Siegmann, C., & Anderljung, M. (2022). The Brussels effect and artificial intelligence: How EU regulation will impact the global AI market. arXiv preprint arXiv:2208.12645.

Šonková, M. (2024). *Brussels effect reloaded? The European Union's Digital Services Act and the Artificial Intelligence Act*. College of Europe.

Tarafder, A., & Vadlamani, A. (2025). Will the EU AI regulations give rise to another 'Brussels effect'? Lessons from the GDPR. *Journal of Development Policy and Practice, 10*(1), 45–60.

Further Reading

Baum, K., Bryson, J., Dignum, F., Dignum, V., Grobelnik, M., Hoos, H., & Vinuesa, R. (2023). From fear to action: AI governance and opportunities for all. *Frontiers in Computer Science, 5*, 1210421.

Fry, H. (2018). *Hello world: How to be human in the age of the machine*. Random House.
Stengg, W. (2024). *Digital policy in the EU: Towards a human-centred digital transformation*. Edward Elgar Publishing.
Werner Marcus, J. S., Sekut, K., & Zenner, K. (2024). A dataset on EU legislation for the digital world. Bruegel. https://www.bruegel.org/dataset/dataset-eu-legislation-digital-world

Irina Michalowitz is Vice President Global Government Relations & Public Policy at DeepL, and Founder and Advisory Director at IMConsult. She has over 25 years of experience in senior management positions in corporations, NGOs, and associations at the intersection of technology, governance, and policy as well as an academic and trainer background focused on EU policy-making and lobbying. She holds an MBA from WU Executive Academy and a Ph.D. in Political Science jointly from Robert-Schuman University and the University of Hamburg.

Disinformation as Evolving Policy Challenge: Legal Responses Taken by the European Union

Marina Jovanovic and Julia Kreyler-Valsky

Abstract In the digital age, disinformation has become a significant threat to democratic societies, as particularly evidenced during the US election campaign (2016) and the Brexit referendum (2016). The European Union (EU) has responded with a "whole-of-society" approach, combining regulatory and awareness-raising measures. The following article outlines this response framework, beginning with the establishment of the East StratCom Task Force (ESTF) in 2015 and concluding with the AI Act of 2024. Our objective is to provide a comprehensive overview, showcasing the development of a multi-layered and gradually more binding policy approach to combat disinformation, strengthen societal resilience, and safeguard democratic integrity across the EU.

Keywords Disinformation · Influence operations · Foreign interference · Rapid Alert System · Digital Services Act · AI Act · Action Plan against Disinformation

1 Introduction

In an age where information flows instantaneously, the intentional spread of disinformation has become an acute challenge for democratic societies, carrying profound political, societal, and security consequences. While the phenomenon of disinformation is not new, rapid advances in communication and digitalisation have rendered its reach and impact unprecedented.

M. Jovanovic
International Institute for Applied Systems Analysis (IIASA), Laxenburg, Austria
e-mail: jovanovic@iiasa.ac.at

J. Kreyler-Valsky (✉)
University of Applied Sciences Burgenland, Eisenstadt, Austria
e-mail: julia.kreyler-valsky@hochschule-burgenland.at

G. Füricht-Fiegl et al. (eds.), *Handbook on EU Law-making*, Professional Practice in Governance and Public Organizations, https://doi.org/10.1007/978-3-032-16559-6_26

Gradually, news media have shifted from a *modus operandi* of "gatekeeping", where journalists and editors prepare and distribute news, to one of "gate-watching", where participation in news production is open to anyone interested, from individual news bloggers to citizen journalism communities (Bruns, 2008; Bruns, 2014). These gate-watching environments provide fertile ground for the dissemination of falsehoods, as content can be created and shared among users without editorial oversight or significant fact-checking (Allcott & Gentzkow, 2017, 211).

The logics of social media further add to the rise of disinformation. Algorithms prompt users to follow people that mirror their own views, giving rise to the so-called echo chambers, where individuals are rarely exposed to opposing perspectives and often react defensively when they are (Sunstein, 2001; Terren & Borge, 2021; Allcott & Gentzkow, 2017). In the so-called filter bubbles, users receive contents based on their past activities, which further limits the novelty and diversity of what they see, thereby fuelling polarisation and clustering of like-minded individuals (Pariser, 2011; Terren & Borge, 2021; Allcott & Gentzkow, 2017). The conformity found within such closed environments is a perfect setting for disinformation to thrive (Journell, 2021).

Malicious actors seek to exacerbate these political and social divisions, with the objective to erode public trust in democratic institutions, elected officials, and the media, inflame political tensions, and influence democratic processes such as elections (Watts, 2017; Cizik, 2017; Chivvis, 2017). They employ a range of tactics, including bots, trolls, and coordinated "hack and leak" operations to seize control over social media and orchestrate waves of disinformation (SafeGuard Cyber, 2019; Council of the European Union, 2019, 2).

Recognising the danger posed by disinformation campaigns, EU institutions responded with a range of initiatives and measures, which we will explore in this chapter. While the Ordinary Legislative Procedure (OLP) is not typically used for disinformation-specific policies, it has been employed in the development of broader legislative frameworks that include provisions related to disinformation, notably the Digital Services Act (DSA) and the AI Act. This recourse to the OLP only in the context of more recent legal instruments mirrors a gradual shift by European policymakers, most notably the European Commission, in tackling disinformation; a shift from relying primarily on strategic communication and voluntary measures to adopting legally binding obligations, demonstrating an increased recognition of disinformation as a systemic threat to democratic processes and societal cohesion.

2 The EU's Regulatory and Institutional Response to Disinformation

The EU defines disinformation as "false or misleading content that is spread with an intention to deceive or secure economic or political gain and which may cause public harm" (European Commission, 2020, 18). In light of growing concerns over

Russian disinformation campaigns, the European Council underscored in March 2015 the need for an action plan in this matter (European Council, 2015; EEAS, 2022; Bentzen, 2017). As an initial step, the East StratCom Task Force (ESTF) was established that same year within the European External Action Service (EEAS)[1] to tackle Russia's disinformation and influence operations. The ESTF conducts strategic communication activities to explain and promote EU policies and values in the Eastern Partnership countries and Central Asia Regions. In cooperation with EU institutions and Member States, the ESTF team developed the Action Plan on Strategic Communication to support measures aimed at increasing public awareness of disinformation activities and enhancing the EU's capacity to address them (EEAS, 2015). The main products of the ESTF are the weekly updated Disinformation Review and the website EUvsDisinfo (EEAS, 2017).

Drawing on lessons from international democratic processes such as the UK vote on Brexit in 2016 and the US presidential election campaign in 2016, the EU gradually intensified its efforts to combat disinformation, particularly in the lead-up to the May 2019 European Parliament (EP) elections (Bentzen, 2019). In 2017, the Commission launched a public consultation on fake news and online disinformation (European Commission, 2018), alongside a Eurobarometer survey to gather citizens' perceptions and concerns around the topic (European Union, 2018; European Commission, 2018a). It also established a High-Level Expert Group to "advise on policy initiatives to counter fake news and disinformation spread online" (HLEG, 2018).

Building on the findings of the public consultation, the Eurobarometer survey, and the recommendations of the HLEG's final report (HLEG, 2018), the Commission published its Communication on Tackling online disinformation: A European approach in 2018, which was a significant starting point for developing a coordinated European response (European Commission, 2018b).

2.1 Tackling Online Disinformation: A European Approach

The Communication recognised disinformation as a major challenge for democracies across Europe and laid the foundation for a comprehensive EU approach to countering disinformation threats. It outlined key principles and objectives to guide future action, including enhancing the transparency, diversity, and credibility of information, as well as promoting inclusive solutions through awareness raising, education, and media literacy.

Emphasising the importance of a multi-stakeholder response, the Communication called for cooperation among public authorities, online platforms, advertisers, fact-checkers, journalists, and media organisations (European Commission, 2018b). In a

[1] The European External Action Service (EEAS) is the EU's diplomatic service. The EEAS carries out the EU's foreign and security policy.

move to bolster the role and responsibilities of online platforms in tackling disinformation, it also encouraged an EU-wide voluntary Code of Practice on Disinformation, which was presented in September 2018 (European Commission, 2022).

2.2 From the Code of Practice to the Code of Conduct on Disinformation

The 2018 EU Code of Practice on Disinformation represented an important milestone as the first global self-regulatory framework that brought together online platforms such as Facebook, Twitter, Google, and Mozilla, along with advertising industry and leading tech companies, in a joint effort to combat the spread of online disinformation via voluntary commitments.

Although self-regulation has been widely regarded as a necessary first step to encourage stakeholder commitment to the code, assessments highlighted inconsistent implementation across platforms and Member States, as well as a lack of oversight and enforcement mechanisms (European Commission, 2020a; European Commission, 2019). To address these shortcomings, the Commission issued Guidance on Strengthening the Code of Practice on Disinformation, which recommended measures to enhance the code's effectiveness, including the addition of new signatories, more tailored commitments, and improved efforts to demonetise disinformation. It also emphasised empowering users by increasing their understanding of how online services function and by promoting tools that help detect or report false and misleading content (European Commission, 2021).

As a result, the 2018 code was revised into the Strengthened Code of Practice in 2022 (European Commission, 2022). Notably, the revised code was developed with the objective of becoming a Code of Conduct under the DSA (see 2.5), marking a shift towards a co-regulatory framework in which the code's voluntary measures are embedded in a broader regulatory framework of the DSA (European Commission, 2022a; European Commission, 2022b; European Commission, 2025).

2.3 Action Plan Against Disinformation and Rapid Alert System (RAS)

Another initiative from 2018 was the Commission's Action Plan against Disinformation, launched in direct response to the European Council's call for measures to "protect the Union's democratic systems and combat disinformation" ahead of the 2019 EP elections (European Commission, 2018c, 1; European Council, 2018). The Action Plan aimed to operationalise the objective of establishing close cooperation among EU institutions, Member States, civil society, and the private sector, especially online platforms. To this end, it set out four main pillars as a basis for a coordinated response to disinformation.

Under the first pillar, the Action Plan encouraged an increase in resources needed to improve the detection, analysis, and exposure to disinformation. As part of the second pillar, the Rapid Alert System (RAS) was launched in March 2019, serving as a platform between the EU institutions and Member States, enabling real-time information sharing, joint assessments, and swift coordination of responses to disinformation threats (EEAS, 2019). Through the third pillar, the Action Plan called on all signatories of the 2018 Code of Practice (see 2.2) to promptly and effectively implement the identified actions and procedures, with a focus on measures that were critical for ensuring the integrity of the EP elections in 2019. The fourth pillar emphasised the need to raise public awareness about disinformation and improve societal resilience (European Commission, 2018c).

In the aftermath of the EP elections in 2019, the EU further advanced its commitment to empowering citizens and fortifying democratic resilience across its Member States. Acknowledging the evolving challenges to democracy, including the persistent threat of disinformation, the Commission introduced the European Democracy Action Plan (EDAP) in 2020, followed by the Defence of Democracy package in 2023 (European Commission, n.d.-a; European Commission, 2020; European Commission, 2023).

2.4 European Democracy Action Plan and Defence of Democracy Package

The EDAP outlined measures to (1) promote free and fair elections, (2) strengthen media freedom, and (3) counter disinformation. In addressing disinformation, it highlighted the necessity for even closer cooperation within the EU and the refinement of the existing toolbox to counter foreign interference. It also underscored the Commission's efforts to increase obligations and accountability for online platforms through the transformation of the Code of Practice on Disinformation (see 2.2) into a co-regulatory framework under the DSA (see 2.5) (European Commission, 2020).

The complementary Defence of Democracy package encompasses a legislative proposal aimed at setting common transparency and accountability standards for persons representing interests of third country governments in the EU. A key element of this proposal is the introduction of mandatory registration requirements for such entities, alongside the establishment of national transparency registers (European Commission, 2023; European Commission, 2023a). Furthermore, the Defence of Democracy package includes recommendations on promoting free, fair, and resilient elections (European Commission, 2023b) and on enhancing the participation of civil society in policymaking (European Commission, 2023c). The former recommendation encourages measures to protect election-related information from manipulation and disinformation, such as proactive publication of credible information on election processes and rapid de-bunking of false narratives. It also addresses emerging challenges associated with content generated by artificial intelligence (AI) and the need to enhance the EU's efforts in this regard (see 2.6).

2.5 Digital Services Act (DSA)

The DSA was proposed by the Commission in 2020 with the aim of preventing illegal and harmful online activities through stronger oversight, accountability, and transparency. It introduced a structured framework of layered responsibilities aimed at various types of services, i.e. intermediary services, hosting services, online platforms, very large online platforms (VLOPs) and very large online search engines (VLOSEs). Due to the significant risks their services may pose to society, the so-called VLOPs and VLOSEs with more than 45 million users per month in the EU are subject to stricter rules under the DSA. These include obligations to identify, assess, and mitigate systemic risks that their services may pose, such as the spread of disinformation (European Commission, n.d.-a; European Union, 2022; European Parliament, 2025a).

The Commission is responsible for supervising VLOPs and VLOSEs, while national authorities oversee platforms established in their respective countries. For non-compliance, Commission and Member States may issue fines of up to 6% of a respective provider's annual worldwide turnover in the preceding financial year (European Commission, n.d.-a; European Union, 2022). In 2023, the Commission opened formal proceedings to assess whether the social media platform X (formerly Twitter) may have breached the DSA. The ongoing investigation focuses on several areas, including risk management, content moderation, dark patterns, advertising transparency, and data access for researchers (European Commission, 2023d).

With the conversion of the Code of Practice on Disinformation into the Code of Conduct as part of the co-regulatory framework under the DSA (see 2.2), effective and auditable as of July 2025, the code has become an important benchmark for assessing compliance with disinformation-related obligations for VLOPs and VLOSEs (European Commission, 2025). Although it remains a voluntary instrument, the code offers a structured framework with concrete measures that signatories can implement to address disinformation risks. Full adherence is regarded as an important risk mitigating measure under the DSA, thereby embedding the code within the broader regulatory framework as a robust basis for case-by-case assessment of VLOPs' and VLOSEs' compliance (European Commission, 2025a; Jahangir, 2025).

The DSA has emerged as a significant point of conflict between President Trump's administration and EU policymakers. Senior US officials have voiced strong opposition, arguing that the DSA imposes censorship on free speech and places financial burdens on US tech companies (Haeck, 2025; Pamuk, 2025). Additionally, major platforms, including Google, YouTube, and LinkedIn, have signalled their withdrawal from fact-checking commitments under the code, while Meta has announced that it will end its fact-checking programme in favour of a community notes model, which allows users to add textual notes to potentially misleading posts (EFCSN, 2025; Oxford, 2025). Meta's founder, Mark Zuckerberg, justified the move by citing bias among fact-checkers and emphasising the need to safeguard free speech (Oxford, 2025). The EU has dismissed allegations of censorship as unfounded (Haeck, 2025a; Pamuk, 2025).

2.6 AI Act[2]

The proliferation of generative AI tools has introduced new challenges in the fight against disinformation. Within seconds, anyone can create and spread large amounts of realistic images, videos, or voice clones that mimic real people, known as deepfakes (Bontridder & Poullet 2021; Feuerriegel et al., 2023). In the EU context, deepfakes are addressed by the DSA (see 2.5) and the AI Act, which impose transparency obligations requiring generated or manipulated content to be clearly labelled (European Union, 2022; European Union, 2024).[3]

2.7 Actions Taken by the European Parliament

Apart from contributing to the DSA and the AI Act and supporting various EU-level initiatives, the EP adopted several resolutions aimed at strengthening the EU's response to disinformation (European Parliament, 2016; European Parliament, 2017; European Parliament, 2019; European Parliament, 2023). In 2020, the EP set up a special committee on foreign interference in all democratic processes in the EU, including disinformation (INGE), followed by its successor, INGE 2, 2 years later (European Parliament, 2020; European Parliament, 2022). These committees were tasked with compiling reports with recommendations on measures to counter foreign interference and disinformation, which highlighted concerns over inadequate response of major platforms, the absence of binding commitments under the Code of Practice, and gaps in public awareness. Among others, they also stressed the importance of involving traditional media and increasing funding for fact-checking and independent, pluralistic media outlets (European Parliament, 2023a).

In the 2024–2029 parliamentary term, MEPs established a special committee whose work will contribute to the Commission's upcoming European Democracy Shield initiative, aimed at addressing severe threats to EU democracy and building

---

[2] See also Chap. 29 of this handbook.

[3] Chapter 29 of this handbook provides a detailed analysis of the AI Act.

on the EDAP and the Defence of Democracy Package (see 2.4) (European Parliament, 2025; European Commission, n.d.-b).

3 Awareness Raising and Resilience Building

The EU's response to disinformation extends beyond policy instruments, adopting a "whole-of-society" approach that engages a range of stakeholders in a collaborative effort to build societal resilience against disinformation. A diverse set of resources has been made available to raise awareness, help citizens recognise false narratives, and better understand the mechanisms of today's media systems. Educators are supported with tools and materials to promote digital and media literacy from an early age (European Commission, n.d.-c), including the Guidelines for Teachers and educators on tackling disinformation and promoting digital literacy through education and training (European Commission, 2022c), developed under the Digital Education Action Plan (2021–2027) (European Commission, 2020b).

Restoring public trust in the media is also at the heart of this approach. The EU fosters partnerships with quality media and fact-checkers to promote access to verified and reliable information. Key initiatives include the establishment of the European Digital Media Observatory (EDMO) (EDMO, n.d.) and the European Code of Standards for Independent Fact-Checking Organisations (EFCSN, n.d.), both of which aim to enhance the quality and coordination of fact-checking across Member States. Complementing these efforts, the EU has allocated funding through programmes such as Horizon Europe, Erasmus+, and Creative Europe to empower journalists, researchers, educators, and civil society actors to implement projects aimed at countering disinformation (European Commission, n.d.-d).

4 Discussion and Outlook

As a symptom of large societal divides and geopolitical changes, amplified by the rapid evolution of the digital information space, the issue of disinformation requires a holistic, "whole-of-society" response. The analysis of the EU's approach to this complex problem reveals a careful balance between the proactive adjustment of the regulatory framework, multi-stakeholder cooperation, and the cultivation of public awareness and resilience, leaving no room for a "Ministry of Truth". Rather than leaning on heavy-handed legislative action as a cure-all, the EU favours a layered approach, where legislation is complemented by the active involvement of diverse societal actors, aiming to safeguard democratic processes and equip citizens with the tools to navigate the information environment.

The EU responded early to the growing threat of disinformation with the establishment of the ESTF in 2015, the Action Plan against Disinformation, and the creation of the RAS. Its regulatory efforts began with a self-regulatory approach through the Code of Practice on Disinformation, which later evolved into a co-regulatory framework under the DSA. The DSA marked the first instance where the OLP was applied in this context, reflecting the EU's increasing commitment to addressing disinformation at a legal level. The AI Act was subsequently also adopted under the OLP.

While voluntary self-regulation was an important first step, it has proven insufficient in addressing the complex and evolving nature of disinformation. Technology companies, including online platforms, operate primarily based on commercial incentives rather than democratic stewardship, raising concerns about the effectiveness of voluntary commitments alone. Acknowledging these limitations, the EU's shift towards co-regulation under the DSA represents an important advancement. For the first time, platforms are not only held accountable for illegal content but also required to assess and mitigate risks arising from the potentially harmful use of their services. Nonetheless, the DSA faces significant implementation challenges due to push back from major tech companies and political pressure from the US.

Looking ahead, there is a clear need to consolidate existing regulatory instruments and maximise the impact of EU efforts against disinformation. Furthermore, as the information environment is reshaped by rapid advances in AI, new layers of complexity for democratic societies demand closer attention. Advances in commercially available AI tools made it increasingly difficult for online users and fact-checkers to tell authentic content from fabricated material. Recent evidence from at least 50 countries worldwide, including many in the EU, highlight how AI has already undermined democratic elections across the globe (Myers & Thompson, 2025).

At the same time, AI holds significant promise as part of the solution, with the potential to detect, analyse, and mitigate the spread of disinformation across platforms. To fully harness these opportunities, further research is needed to evaluate the strengths and limitations of AI-based solutions (Saeidnia et al., 2025). On the regulatory side, fostering cross-sectoral collaboration will be essential to leverage insights from diverse stakeholders and ensure the development of ethical and effective AI tools grounded in fundamental rights (Feuerriegel et al., 2023; Saeidnia et al., 2025).

References

Allcott, H., & Gentzkow, M. (2017). Social media and fake news in the 2016 election. *Journal of Economic Perspectives, 31*(2), 211–236. https://doi.org/10.1257/jep.31.2.211

Bentzen, N. (2017, November). *Disinformation, 'fake news' and the EU's response* (At a Glance, PE 608.805). European Parliamentary Research Service. https://www.europarl.europa.eu/RegData/etudes/ATAG/2017/608805/EPRS_ATA(2017)608805_EN.pdf

Bentzen, N. (2019, February). *Online disinformation and the EU's response* (At a Glance, PE 620.230). European Parliamentary Research Service. https://www.europarl.europa.eu/RegData/etudes/ATAG/2018/620230/EPRS_ATA(2018)620230_EN.pdf

Bontridder, N., & Poullet, Y. (2021). The role of artificial intelligence in disinformation. *Data & Policy, 3*, e32. https://doi.org/10.1017/dap.2021.20

Bruns, A. (2008). The active audience: Transforming journalism from gatekeeping to gatewatching. In D. Domingo & C. Paterson (Eds.), *Making online news: The ethnography of new media production* (pp. 171–184). Peter Lang Publishing.

Bruns, A. (2014). Gatekeeping, gatewatching, real-time feedback: New challenges for journalism. *Brazilian Journalism Research, 7*(2), 117–136. https://doi.org/10.25200/BJR.v7n2.2011.355

Chivvis, C. S. (2017). *Understanding Russian "hybrid warfare" and what can be done about it. [testimony presented before the committee on armed services]*. RAND Corporation. https://www.rand.org/content/dam/rand/pubs/testimonies/CT400/CT468/RAND_CT468.pdf

Cizik, T. (2017). *Information warfare—New security challenge for Europe*. Centre for European and North Atlantic Affairs (CENAA).

Council of the European Union. (2019). *Report of the Presidency to the European Council on 20–21 June 2019, on countering disinformation and the lessons learnt from the European elections* (10415/19). https://data.consilium.europa.eu/doc/document/ST-10415-2019-INIT/en/pdf

European Commission. (2018). *Synopsis report of the public consultation on fake news and online disinformation*. Retrieved June 18, 2025, from https://digital-strategy.ec.europa.eu/en/library/synopsis-report-public-consultation-fake-news-and-online-disinformation

European Commission. (2018a). *Final results of the Eurobarometer on fake news and online disinformation*. Retrieved June 18, 2025, from https://digital-strategy.ec.europa.eu/en/library/final-results-eurobarometer-fake-news-and-online-disinformation

European Commission. (2018b). *Communication from the Commission to the European Parliament, the Council, the European Economic and Social Committee and the Committee of the Regions. Tackling online disinformation: A European Approach* (COM(2018) 236 final). https://eur-lex.europa.eu/legal-content/EN/TXT/?uri=CELEX%3A52018DC0236#footnote15

European Commission. (2018c). *Joint Communication to the European Parliament, the European Council, the European Economic and Social Committee and the Committee of the Regions. Action Plan against Disinformation* (JOIN(2018) 36 final). https://eur-lex.europa.eu/legal-content/EN/TXT/?uri=celex:52018JC0036

European Commission. (2019). *Annual self-assessment reports of signatories to the Code of Practice on Disinformation 2019*. Retrieved June 18, 2025, from https://digital-strategy.ec.europa.eu/en/news/annual-self-assessment-reports-signatories-code-practice-disinformation-2019

European Commission. (2020). *Communication from the Commission to the European Parliament, the Council, the European Economic and Social Committee and the Committee of the Regions. On the European democracy action plan* (COM(2020) 790 final). https://eur-lex.europa.eu/legal-content/EN/TXT/PDF/?uri=CELEX:52020DC0790

European Commission. (2020a). *Assessment of the Code of Practice on Disinformation—Achievements and areas for further improvement*. Retrieved June 18, 2025, from https://digital-strategy.ec.europa.eu/en/library/assessment-code-practice-disinformation-achievements-and-areas-further-improvement

European Commission. (2020b). Communication from the Commission to the European Parliament, the Council, the European Economic and Social Committee and the Committee of the Regions. Digital Education Action Plan 2021–2027 (COM(2020) 624 final). https://eur-lex.europa.eu/legal-content/EN/TXT/?uri=celex:52020DC0624

European Commission. (2021). *Communication from the Commission to the European Parliament, the Council, the European Economic and Social Committee and the Committee of the Regions. European Commission Guidance on Strengthening the Code of Practice on Disinformation* (COM(2021) 262 final). https://eur-lex.europa.eu/legal-content/EN/TXT/?uri=celex:52021DC0262

European Commission. (2022). *2018 Code of Practice on Disinformation*. Retrieved June 18, 2025, from https://digital-strategy.ec.europa.eu/en/library/2018-code-practice-disinformation

European Commission. (2022a). *2022 Strengthened Code of Practice on Disinformation.* Retrieved June 18, 2025, from https://digital-strategy.ec.europa.eu/en/library/2022-strengthened-code-practice-disinformation

European Commission. (2022b). *Questions and Answers: Strengthened Code of Practice on Disinformation.* Retrieved June 18, 2025, from https://ec.europa.eu/commission/presscorner/detail/en/qanda_22_3665

European Commission. (2022c). *Guidelines for teachers and educators on tackling disinformation and promoting digital literacy through education and training*. Publications Office of the European Union. https://data.europa.eu/doi/10.2766/28248

European Commission. (2023). *Documents on Defence of Democracy.* Retrieved June 19, 2025, from https://commission.europa.eu/publications/documents-defence-democracy_en

European Commission. (2023a). *Defence of Democracy.* Retrieved June 19, 2025, from https://ec.europa.eu/commission/presscorner/api/files/attachment/877028/DoD_Factsheet.pdf

European Commission. (2023b). Commission recommendation (EU) 2023/2829 of 12 December 2023 on inclusive and resilient electoral processes in the Union and enhancing the European nature and efficient conduct of the elections to the European Parliament. https://eur-lex.europa.eu/eli/reco/2023/2829/oj/eng.

European Commission. (2023c). Commission recommendation (EU) 2023/2836 of 12 December 2023 on promoting the engagement and effective participation of citizens and civil society organisations in public policy-making processes. https://eur-lex.europa.eu/legal-content/EN/TXT/PDF/?uri=CELEX:32023H2836.

European Commission. (2023d). *Commission opens formal proceedings against X under the Digital Services Act.* Retrieved June 18, 2025, from https://ec.europa.eu/commission/presscorner/detail/en/ip_23_6709

European Commission. (2025). *The Code of Conduct on Disinformation.* Retrieved June 18, 2025, from https://digital-strategy.ec.europa.eu/en/library/code-conduct-disinformation

European Commission. (2025a). *Commission endorses the integration of the voluntary Code of Practice on Disinformation into the Digital Services Act.* Retrieved June 18, 2025, from https://ec.europa.eu/commission/presscorner/detail/en/ip_25_505

European Commission. (n.d.-a). *Protecting democracy.* Retrieved June 19, 2025, from https://commission.europa.eu/strategy-and-policy/priorities-2019-2024/new-push-european-democracy/protecting-democracy_en#countering-disinformation

European Commission. (n.d.-a). *The Digital Services Act package.* Retrieved June 19, 2025, from https://digital-strategy.ec.europa.eu/en/policies/digital-services-act-package

European Commission. (n.d.-b). *European democracy shield.* Retrieved June 19, 2025, from https://ec.europa.eu/info/law/better-regulation/have-your-say/initiatives/14587-European-Democracy-Shield_en

European Commission. (n.d.-c). *Building societal resilience against information manipulation.* Retrieved June 20, 2025, from https://commission.europa.eu/topics/countering-information-manipulation/building-societal-resilience-against-information-manipulation_en

European Commission. (n.d.-d). *Cooperating with fact-checkers, civil society, media and academia.* Retrieved June 20, 2025, from https://commission.europa.eu/topics/countering-information-manipulation/cooperating-fact-checkers-civil-society-media-and-academia_en

European Council. (2015). *European Council meeting (19 and 20 March 2015)—Conclusions* (EUCO 11/15). https://data.consilium.europa.eu/doc/document/ST-11-2015-INIT/en/pdf

European Council. (2018). *European Council conclusions, 18 October 2018.* https://www.consilium.europa.eu/en/press/press-releases/2018/10/18/20181018-european-council-conslusions/

European Digital Media Observatory (EDMO). (n.d.). *Homepage.* https://edmo.eu/

European External Action Service (EEAS). (2015, June). *Action Plan on Strategic Communication* (Ref. Ares(2015)2608242–22/06/2015). https://www.eeas.europa.eu/sites/default/files/action_plan_on_strategic_communication.docx_eeas_web.pdf

European External Action Service (EEAS). (2017, September). *Don't be deceived: EU acts against fake news and disinformation.* Retrieved June 18, 2025, from https://www.eeas.europa.eu/node/32408_en

European External Action Service (EEAS). (2019, March). *Rapid Alert System.* https://www.eeas.europa.eu/sites/default/files/ras_factsheet_march_2019_0.pdf

European External Action Service (EEAS). (2022, March). Disinformation: Speech by High Representative/Vice-President Josep Borrell at the EP debate. https://www.eeas.europa.eu/eeas/disinformation-speech-high-representativevice-president-josep-borrell-ep-debate_en

European Fact-Checking Standards Network (EFCSN). (2025, January 22). *EFCSN statement on platforms' reduced commitments to the code of practice on disinformation.* Retrieved June 18, 2025, from https://efcsn.com/news/2025-01-22_efcsn-statement-on-platforms-reduced-commitments-to-the-code-of-practice-on-disinformation/

European Fact-Checking Standards Network (EFCSN). (n.d.). *Homepage.* https://efcsn.com/

European Parliament. (2016). European Parliament resolution of 23 November 2016 on EU strategic communication to counteract propaganda against it by third parties (2016/2030(INI)) (2018/C 224/08). https://eur-lex.europa.eu/legal-content/EN/TXT/?uri=oj:JOC_2018_224_R_0009.

European Parliament. (2017). *European Parliament resolution of 15 June 2017 on online platforms and the digital single market (2016/2276(INI))* (2018/C 331/19). https://eur-lex.europa.eu/legal-content/EN/TXT/?uri=oj:JOC_2018_331_R_0020.

European Parliament. (2019). *European Parliament resolution of 10 October 2019 on foreign electoral interference and disinformation in national and European democratic processes (2019/2810(RSP))* (2021/C 202/06). https://eur-lex.europa.eu/legal-content/EN/TXT/?uri=CELEX%3A52019IP0031%2801%29

European Parliament. (2020). *European Parliament decision of 18 June 2020 on setting up a special committee on foreign interference in all democratic processes in the European Union, including disinformation, and defining its responsibilities, numerical strength and term of office (2020/2683(RSO))* (2021/C 362/41). https://eur-lex.europa.eu/legal-content/EN/TXT/?uri=CELEX:52020DP0161

European Parliament. (2022). *European Parliament decision of 10 March 2022 on setting up a special committee on foreign interference in all democratic processes in the European Union, including disinformation (INGE 2), and defining its responsibilities, numerical strength and term of office (2022/2585(RSO))* (2022/C 347/28). https://eur-lex.europa.eu/legal-content/EN/TXT/?uri=oj:JOC_2022_347_R_0029

European Parliament. (2023). *European Parliament resolution of 1 June 2023 on foreign interference in all democratic processes in the European Union, including disinformation (2022/2075(INI))* (C/2023/1226). https://eur-lex.europa.eu/eli/C/2023/1226/oj/eng

European Parliament. (2023a). *REPORT on foreign interference in all democratic processes in the European Union, including disinformation.* Retrieved June 19, 2025, from https://www.europarl.europa.eu/doceo/document/A-9-2023-0187_EN.html

European Parliament. (2025, January). *Composition of Parliament's new committees released.* Retrieved June 19, 2025, from https://www.europarl.europa.eu/news/en/press-room/20250116IPR26333/composition-of-parliament-s-new-committees-released

European Parliament. (2025a, May). *Proposal for a regulation of the European Parliament and of the Council on a single market for digital services (digital services act) and amending Directive 2000/31/EC.* Retrieved June 18, 2025, from https://www.europarl.europa.eu/legislative-train/theme-a-europe-fit-for-the-digital-age/file-digital-services-act

European Union. (2018). *Fake news and disinformation online.* Retrieved June 18, 2025, from https://europa.eu/eurobarometer/surveys/detail/2183

European Union. (2022). *Regulation (EU) 2022/2065 of the European Parliament and of the Council of 19 October 2022 on a Single Market For digital services and amending Directive 2000/31/EC (Digital Services Act)* (L277/1). https://eur-lex.europa.eu/legal-content/EN/TXT/?uri=CELEX%3A32022R2065&qid=1666857835014.

European Union. (2024). Regulation (EU) 2024/1689 of the European Parliament and of the Council of 13 June 2024 laying down harmonised rules on artificial intelligence and amending Regulations (EC) No 300/2008, (EU) No 167/2013, (EU) No 168/2013, (EU) 2018/858, (EU) 2018/1139 and (EU) 2019/2144 and Directives 2014/90/EU, (EU) 2016/797 and (EU) 2020/1828 (Artificial Intelligence Act). https://eur-lex.europa.eu/eli/reg/2024/1689/oj/eng

Feuerriegel, S., DiResta, R., Goldstein, J. A., Kumar, S., Lorenz-Spreen, P., Tomz, M., & Pröllochs, N. (2023). Research can help to tackle AI-generated disinformation. *Nature Human Behaviour, 7*(11), 1818–1821. https://doi.org/10.1038/s41562-023-01726-2

Haeck, P. (2025, January 31). US presses Brussels for answers over EU social media law. Politico. https://www.politico.eu/article/jim-jordan-presses-european-commission-for-answers-over-eu-social-media-law-henna-virkkunen-digital-services-act/

Haeck, P. (2025a, March 10). EU social media law isn't censorship, tech chief tells US critic. *Politico*. https://www.politico.eu/article/social-media-law-does-not-regulate-speech-eu-tech-chief-tells-us-lawmaker-henna-virkkunen/

High Level Expert Group on Fake News (HLEG). (2018). *Final report of the high level expert group on fake news and online disinformation*. Publications Office of the European Union. https://digital-strategy.ec.europa.eu/en/library/final-report-high-level-expert-group-fake-news-and-online-disinformation

Jahangir, R. (2025, February 25). The EU's code of practice on disinformation is now part of the digital services act. What does it mean?. *Tech Policy Press*. https://www.techpolicy.press/the-eus-code-of-practice-on-disinformation-is-now-part-of-the-digital-services-act-what-does-it-mean/

Journell, W. (2021). Exacerbating existing divides: Fake news, desire, and partisanship. In T. L. Heafner, L. K. Handler, & T. C. Rock (Eds.), *The divide within: Intersections of realities, facts, theories, and practices* (pp. 1–24). IAP-Information Age Publishing, Inc.

Myers, S. L., & Thompson, S. A. (2025, June 26). A.I. Is starting to wear down democracy. *The New York Times*. https://www.nytimes.com/2025/06/26/technology/ai-elections-democracy.html

Oxford, D. (2025, January 10). Meta, Facebook to drop fact-checkers: What does this mean for social media?. *Al Jazeera*. https://www.aljazeera.com/news/2025/1/10/meta-facebook-to-drop-fact-checkers-what-does-this-mean-for-social-media

Pamuk, H. (2025, August 7). Exclusive: Rubio orders US diplomats to launch lobbying blitz against Europe's tech law. *Reuters*. https://www.reuters.com/sustainability/society-equity/rubio-orders-us-diplomats-launch-lobbying-blitz-against-europes-tech-law-2025-08-07/

Pariser, E. (2011). *The filter bubble: What the internet is hiding from you*. Penguin Books.

Saeidnia, H. R., Hosseini, E., Lund, B., Tehrani, M. A., Zaker, S., & Molaei, S. (2025). Artificial intelligence in the battle against disinformation and misinformation: A systematic review of challenges and approaches. *Knowledge and Information Systems, 67*, 3139–3158. https://doi.org/10.1007/s10115-024-02337-7

SafeGuard Cyber. (2019). Contactless actions against the enemy: How Russia is deploying misinformation on social media to influence European parliamentary elections. https://cdn2.hubspot.net/hubfs/3918364/SafeGuardCyber_November2017/New%20White%20Papers/SafeGuardCyber_Contactless%20Actions%20Against%20the%20Enemy%20-%20EU%20Elections_May2019%20(1).pdf

Sunstein, C. R. (2001). *Echo chambers: Bush v. Gore, impeachment, and beyond*. Princeton University Press.

Terren, L., & Borge, R. (2021). Echo chambers on social media: A systematic review of the literature. *Review of Communication Research, 9*, 99–118. https://doi.org/10.12840/issn.2255-4165.028

Watts, C. (2017). *Disinformation: A primer in Russian active measures and influence campaigns* [statement prepared for the U.S. senate select committee on intelligence hearing]. United States senate select committee on intelligence. https://www.intelligence.senate.gov/wp-content/uploads/2024/08/sites-default-files-documents-os-cwatts-033017.pdf

Marina Jovanovic is a project officer at the International Institute for Applied Systems Analysis (IIASA) and a lecturer at the University of Applied Sciences Burgenland. She holds a PhD in Social Sciences/Communication (University of Vienna), an MA in European Studies (UAS Burgenland), and an MA in Marketing (Webster University Vienna). She gained professional experience in UN organisations in Vienna and is a member of the European Association of Political Consultants (EAPC) and the Foreign Policy and United Nations Association of Austria (UNA-Austria). Any views expressed in this article are those of the author and do not represent IIASA.

Julia Kreyler-Valsky is a lecturer at the University of Applied Sciences Burgenland and an expert in equal opportunities. She has held positions with the Austrian Minister for Women's Affairs, the OECD, and the financial sector in Central and Eastern Europe. Her research focuses on inclusive institutional structures and the effectiveness of anti-discrimination policies. Julia holds a Master's in Public Administration (London School of Economics) and a PhD in Sociology (University of Vienna).

EU Social Policy: Balancing Between National Sovereignty and EU's Social Objectives

Birgül Tütün-Ince

Abstract Since the founding of the European Economic Community (EEC), the social policy has evolved significantly. What began as a peripheral field at the community level—initially focused on the coordination of social security rights for mobile workers—has gradually expanded into a substantial component of EU integration.

This chapter offers an analysis of the treaty-based legal foundations that define EU social policy today. A particular focus is placed on the regulatory dimension of EU social policy: the Ordinary Legislative Procedure (OLP) serves in limited specific fields as a central tool in shaping social policy areas where the EU may legislate, provided that the principles of subsidiarity and proportionality are respected.

In addition, the chapter gives particular attention to the autonomous role of the European social partners in shaping and negotiating EU social policy. This interconnection is of special interest, as it illustrates how social governance mechanisms can operate beyond the OLP—and, under certain conditions, even lead to legislative acts.

Keywords European Semester · European Pillar of Social Rights (EPSR) · Passerelle clause · Open Method of Coordination (OMC) · Sectoral Social Dialogue · Social Scoreboard · European social partner

B. Tütün-Ince (✉)
Austrian Federal Railways (ÖBB), Vienna, Austria

University of Applied Sciences BFI Vienna, Vienna, Austria
e-mail: birguel.tuetuen-ince@fh-vie.ac.at

G. Füricht-Fiegl et al. (eds.), *Handbook on EU Law-making*, Professional Practice in Governance and Public Organizations, https://doi.org/10.1007/978-3-032-16559-6_27

1 Legal Foundations of European Social Policy

1.1 Treaty Basis for Social Policy

The social policy dimension of the European Union is deeply embedded in the Union's fundamental values and objectives. Art. 2 of the Treaty on European Union (TEU) defines key values such as "*human dignity, freedom, democracy, equality, the rule of law,* and *respect for human rights, including the rights of persons belonging to minorities*" (European Union, 2012a). These principles create the fundamental normative foundation for shaping social policy at the EU level.

Moreover, the Union's objective of protecting the well-being of EU citizens is clearly anchored in Art. 3(1) TEU. This reflects the Union's broader commitment to peace, prosperity, and the rule of law. While the internal market remains a central pillar of European integration, Art. 3 also points to a strong connection with the EU's social objectives: social policy is not separate, but part of the internal market's overarching purpose. This includes aiming for "full employment, advancing social progress, and combating social exclusion and discrimination" (Art. 3(1) TEU).

This interdependence is further underlined by Art. 3(3) TEU, which explicitly commits the Union to "social justice and protection, gender equality, solidarity between generations, and the rights of the child". Taken together, these provisions convey a central message of the EU's constitutional framework: economic integration and social progress are not in opposition but are designed to evolve in parallel and reinforce one another (Art. 3(3) TEU).

Art. 9 of the Treaty on the Functioning of the European Union (TFEU) serves as a significant article in embedding considerations within the broader EU policy framework (European Union, 2012b). With this provision, a horizontal social clause obliges the EU to take account of social objectives across all its policymaking fields. This means that EU institutions must integrate concerns such as "social protection, the prevention of unemployment, the fight against social exclusion, and improved access to education, training, and healthcare" into both the formulation and the implementation of Union policies (Art. 9 TFEU).

The EU's social agenda has gained additional legal weight through the Charter of Fundamental Rights (European Union, n.d.). Since the Lisbon Treaty came into effect, the CFR EU has been legally binding on the EU institutions and Member States, but only insofar as they legislate within the scope of Union law (Art. 6(1) TEU). The CFR EU is therefore not merely a political declaration. It is a legally enforceable text with direct implications for both EU legislation and policymaking.

Title IV of the CFR EU, entitled "Solidarity", sets out a range of rights with strong social relevance. These include "the right to fair and just working conditions (Art. 31), protection against unjust dismissal" (Art. 30), "the rights to collective bargaining and collective action" (Art. 27–28), and "the right to social security and assistance" (Art. 34) (Art. 27–28, 30, 31, 34 CFR).

While the practical effect of these rights may vary—depending on national implementation and the legal form of the act concerned—they nonetheless express key social values embedded in the EU's legal order. They reflect a deeper normative commitment that goes beyond economic integration and affirms the importance of shared social values.

The treaties and the Charter of Fundamental Rights together provide the legal and value-driven foundation for EU social policy: one rooted in the EU's constitutional framework; the other in its binding commitment to fundamental rights and social justice as part of the EU's fundamental values. As such, EU social policy is not merely a functional or economic complement to market integration—it is legally grounded in social norms and principles that are recognized as integral to the Union's constitutional identity.

Against this background, it is essential to clarify the precise legal competences that enable the EU to take legislative action in the field of social policy. Building on these normative foundations, the legislative competences are laid down in the TFEU, which defines both the scope and the limits of EU action in this domain.

1.2 Legislative Mechanisms in EU Social Policy: The Central Role of the OLP

European social policy has only been partially integrated at the supranational level. This is largely due to the deep national anchoring of key policy fields—such as wage-setting, pension systems, and labour law—which remain closely tied to national institutions and political cultures. These policy fields reflect not only long-standing institutional arrangements but also a strong sense of national sovereignty, which continues to shape how much influence the EU can exert. Against this background, the enduring differences between the welfare state structures of EU Member States become more understandable. Esping-Andersen's classic typology of welfare regimes—distinguishing between the universalistic Scandinavian model, the contribution-based continental model, and the market-oriented liberal model—continues to serve as a helpful analytical framework (Esping-Andersen, 1990). While its ideal types no longer fully capture the reality of increasingly hybrid and reformed welfare systems, the typology remains a central point of reference for comparing social policy across Europe.

This diversity is also reflected in the EU's legal competences. While some areas of social policy remain an exclusive national responsibility, the EU shares legislative competence in others. This chapter examines in which specific areas of EU social policy the OLP is used.

Both—the EU and its Member States—are entitled to adopt legislation and binding measures in the field of social policy. However, national action is limited where the Union has already exercised its competence (Art. 4(2)(b) TFEU). Against this background, the principles of subsidiarity and proportionality are of particular importance as they are jointly intended to make sure that EU action in the social field is only taken where it is necessary and justified.

The principle of subsidiarity holds that the Union should only intervene when the aims of a proposed initiative cannot be sufficiently fulfilled by the Member States on their own and where the EU-level action would be more appropriate or effective given the nature or impact of the issue at stake (Art. 5(3) TEU). The principle of proportionality also requires that the EU only acts to the extent needed to fulfil the objectives of the Treaties (Art. 5(4) TEU). To summarize: the principles of subsidiarity and proportionality aim to ensure that the Union intervenes in the social field only when necessary and appropriate. This highlights a structural tension at the centre of EU social policy: the balance between national sovereignty and the EU's ability to act where joint solutions are needed.

The core legal framework for EU social policy is set out in Art. 151 to 161 TFEU. These articles constitute the core legal framework of the Union's social policy area and lay down the EU's social objectives, delineate its competences, and specify the procedures through which it can take legislative action in the social field.

Article 151 TFEU lays down the overarching aims that guide EU social policy. These include the "improvement of living and working conditions, the promotion of high employment, adequate social protection, support for social dialogue, and the fight against social exclusion" (Art. 151 TFEU).

Although Article 151 does not itself give the Union the power to legislate, it plays a key role in shaping the direction and priorities of EU social policy.It reflects a shared understanding among the Member States that social progress is a core dimension of European integration and serves as a normative foundation for all EU-level initiatives in the social field.

In the areas covered by Art. 153(1) TFEU, the EU can adopt directives that set minimum standards in the areas of: "health and safety at work, working conditions, social protection, employment termination, consultation and representation of workers and employers, employment rights of third-country nationals, labour market integration, gender equality, and fighting exclusion" (Art. 153(1) TFEU). Most of these areas fall under the OLP[1] (Art. 153(2)(a), Art. 294 TFEU). In essence, Article 153 serves as the central link between the Union's social goals and its legal instruments. It defines both the scope of EU action and the procedures required while also highlighting the role of the social partners. As such, Art. 153 TFEU is the key instrument for operationalizing the Union's social policy agenda through legislative means.

Some sensitive areas—such as social security, protection in case of dismissal, codetermination, and the employment rights of third-country nationals—remain subject to a special legislative procedure. In these cases, the Council must act unanimously, with the prior consultation of the EP and the relevant committees (Art. 153(2) (b) TFEU).

[1] In 2024, two regulations and seven directives in the field of social policy were adopted under the OLP (European Union, 2024).

The final subparagraph of Article 153(2)(b) TFEU establishes a sector-specific passerelle clause which permits a shift from the special legislative procedure to the OLP in selected areas of social policy, subject to unanimous agreement in the Council on a proposal from the Commission and prior consultation of the EP.

Art. 153(2)(b) TFEU also makes clear that EU directives in the field of social policy can only set minimum requirements (Art. 153(2)(b) TFEU). Recent examples adopted under this legal basis include the Pay Transparency Directive (EU 2023/970) (European Union, 2023) and the Work–Life Balance Directive (EU 2019/1158), both of which were passed through the OLP.

Certain areas of social policy remain entirely outside the scope of EU legislative competence. Art. 153 (5) TFEU explicitly excludes provisions relating to "pay, the right of association, the right to strike, and the right to impose lockouts" from any form of harmonization at the Union level.

To complement this legislative framework, Art. 156 to 161 TFEU set out additional provisions that support coordination across Member States, encourage the exchange of best practices, and facilitate distributive social policy. In this context, instruments such as the European Social Fund Plus (ESF+), for instance, play a key role in promoting employment and reducing poverty (Zeitlin & Vanhercke, 2018).

Passerelle Clause in EU Social Policy (Article 153(2) TFEU)
This clause allows the Council, acting unanimously on a proposal from the Commission and after obtaning the consent of the European Parliament, to apply the OLP to certain sensitive areas of social policy.

1.3 Social Dialogue and Sectoral Social Dialogue

Employer and worker organizations—commonly referred to as the European social partners—play a treaty-based role in shaping EU labour and social policy. The legal framework for structured consultation and, where applicable, autonomous negotiations at the EU level are grounded in Art. 152 to 155 TFEU.

Art. 152 TFEU recognizes social dialogue as a cornerstone of the Union's social dimension. It obliges the EU to support social dialogue between employers and workers, while ensuring the independence of the social partners. This article also provides the creation of the Tripartite Social Summit, where EU institutions, employers, and trade unions come together—reflecting the Union's focus on inclusive and representative policymaking. At this point, a clear distinction should be made between bipartite and tripartite social dialogue: Bipartite dialogues involve directly employers' associations (such as BusinessEurope) and trade unions (e.g. European Trade Union Confederation—ETUC), taking place at both intersectoral and currently 44 sectoral levels representing, e.g., railway sector, social services, and telecommunications (European Commission, 2023). These negotiations are independent of the EU institutions.

In contrast, tripartite dialogue involves European institutions—primarily the Commission—working together with the social partners. It provides a platform for joint discussions and helps shape policy through shared input.

In policy areas covered by Art. 153 TFEU, the Commission is obliged to engage social partners before proposing any legislation. The consultation happens in a two-stage process (Art. 154 TFEU): In the first stage, the Commission seeks the views of the social partners on potential EU action. In the second stage, the Commission asks the social partners whether they intend to start negotiations themselves.

Once negotiations begin, they have up to 9 months to finalize an agreement—extendable if both sides and the Commission agree. If the social partners reach an agreement, they can ask the Council to turn their agreement into a binding directive. The EP receives information in these cases, but it does not participate in the legislative process (Art. 155 (2) TFEU).

Not all negotiations lead to binding law. Many results take the form of autonomous agreements, joint texts, or non-binding opinions. Some may later be implemented through legislation, but many rely on voluntary application by the signatory parties.

1.3.1 Negotiation Versus Legislation: Competing Pathways in the Formation of EU Social Policy

In the late 1980s, the Commission presented a proposal on a directive to regulate cross-border information and consultation rights in multinational companies. The aim was to introduce a binding legal framework for European Works Councils (EWCs). However, the initiative failed several times—mainly due to opposition from some Member States, particularly the United Kingdom, at a time when Council decisions on social policy still required unanimity (Falkner, 1998, 1998b).

The Maastricht Treaty included a Protocol on Social Policy that introduced new instruments to strengthen EU-level social policy. The protocol applied to all Member States—except the UK—which opted out and offered two major avenues for action (European Union, 1992):

- Legislation based on qualified majority voting in the Council and
- Art. 3 of the Protocol on Social Policy provides collective negotiations between the European social partners.

The Commission initially sought to involve the social partners in negotiations for a framework agreement on EWC. However, talks failed due to strong opposition from UNICE (now BusinessEurope) and the Confederation of British Industry. In response, the Commission adopted a new strategy, basing its revised proposal on the internal market provision (Art. 100 EEC), rather than the Social Protocol. This allowed the directive to be adopted by qualified majority without the UK's support. While this procedure did not directly rely on the Social Protocol, the political signal was similar: it marked the first time that social legislation at the EU level was adopted against the will of a Member State. This demonstrated that the EU institutions could advance social regulation even without unanimity (Falkner, 1998, 1998b).

A successful example of the Social Protocol in action was the 1995 Framework Agreement on Parental Leave. Following a two-stage consultation by the Commission on reconciling work and family life, the European social partners reached an autonomous agreement, once again, without the participation of the UK (Falkner, 1998, 1998b). This marked the first full application of the Maastricht procedure—from consultation and negotiation to the adoption of Directive 96/34/EC.

2 Coordinative and Normative Instruments in EU Policy

Even though the OLP remains the main instrument through which the EU adopts binding social policy, achieving the Union's broader social objectives increasingly relies on a variety of non-legislative tools. These so-called soft governance instruments such as the Open Method of Coordination (OMC) and the European Semester—enable the EU to define common objectives, monitor progress, and align national strategies, even in areas where it lacks direct legislative competence.

A major impulse for strengthening the social dimension was the adoption of the European Pillar of Social Rights (EPSR) in 2017, which outlines 20 guiding principles related to equal opportunities, fair working conditions, and social protection. While not legally binding, it serves as a normative compass for EU institutions, national governments, and social partners. The 2021 EPSR Action Plan further translated these principles into concrete headline targets and monitoring indicators for 2030, reinforcing the link between shared goals and political follow-up.

Together, the EPSR, the European Semester—the EU's annual cycle of economic and social policy coordination—and the OMC create a structured framework for advancing social objectives across the EU. They identify policy gaps, generate political momentum, and help build consensus on national and European levels. In many cases, this soft governance process lays the groundwork for future legislation. Recent directives on adequate minimum wages, pay transparency, and platform work were all preceded by non-binding recommendations, scoreboards, and country-specific analyses shaped by these mechanisms. In this way, soft governance functions as an incubator for legislative action—transforming shared priorities into binding legal instruments through the OLP.

The table below summarizes a selection of key flagship initiatives, highlighting their legal form and the governance instruments involved (Table 1).

Table 1 Key EU social policy initiatives since 2019—legal instruments, EPSR principles, and (selected) governance frameworks

Initiative (European Union, 2024)	Year	Legal form/ procedure	EPSR principle(s)	Governance instrument
Work–Life Balance Directive	2019	Directive (OLP)	9: Work–life balance	EPSR, EPSR Action Plan, OMC (Joint Employment Reports (JER)), country-specific recommendations (CSRs), European Semester/ Social Scoreboard[a]
Adequate Minimum Wages Directive	2022	Directive (OLP)	6: Wages	EPSR, OMC (JER), European Semester/CSRs/ Social Scoreboard[b]
Pay Transparency Directive (2023/970)	2023	Directive (OLP)	2: Gender equality	EPSR, European Semester/ Social Scoreboard[c]
Platform Work Directive (2021/762)	2024	Directive (OLP)	5, 12: Secure and adaptable Employment, social protection	OMC (JER), EPSR, European Semester/CSRs/ Social Scoreboard[d]
Recommendation on Access to Social Protection	2019	Council Recommendation	12: Social protection	EPSR, OMC,[e] European Semester/CSRs
European Child Guarantee	2021	Council Recommendation	11: Childcare and support to children	EPSR, OMC (National Action Plans), European Semester/Social Scoreboard[f]
Council Recommendation on Minimum Income	2023	Council Recommendation	14: Minimum income	EPSR, OMC[g] (MINT), European Semester/CSRs/ Social Scoreboard[h]

[a]Children aged less than 3 years in formal childcare, employment rate
[b]In-work poverty
[c]Gender pay gap, Gender gap in part-time employment (Eurostat, n.d.)
[d]People at-risk-of-poverty or social exclusion (AROPE), in-work-at-risk-of poverty rate, self-reported unmet of medical care (Eurostat, n.d.)
[e]OMC through national plans, mutual learning workshops and monitoring framework (European Commission, n.d.)
[f]Social protection and inclusion: children aged less than 3 years in formal childcare (Eurostat, n.d.)
[g]Minimum Income Network
[h]Income quintiles share ratio, At-risk-of-poverty or social exclusion rate (AROPE)

3 Current Priorities and Outlook (2024–2029)

Between 2024 and 2029, the Commission is pursuing a strategy that connects industrial competitiveness with social fairness and sustainability. This approach builds on several key frameworks, including the Competitiveness Compass, the Union of Skills, and the Clean Industrial Deal responding to deep structural shifts—falling productivity, ageing populations, labour shortages, and the dual green and digital transitions.

The new legislative cycle begins with two flagship initiatives scheduled for the fourth quarter of 2025: the new EPSR Action Plan and the Quality Jobs Roadmap. Both seek to identify future fields for legislation and policy coordination. The roadmap, developed in cooperation with the social partners, focuses on improving job quality in light of a changing labour market.

Beyond this roadmap, the Commission aims to strengthen the implementation of the social policy principles set out in the EPSR. In this context, several legislative options are currently under discussion such as a proposal for a possible EU framework directive on minimum income schemes. It would set binding minimum standards for social assistance covering benefit levels, access, and scope. These standards would be linked to the economic situation of each Member State. The legal situation of live-in careers is also moving up on the policy agenda. A future directive could establish common rights and duties in this sector and introduce EU-wide minimum standards (EESC, 2025).

The forthcoming EPSR Action Plan is expected to include further proposals. Civil society and institutional actors have, among other things, called for a non-legislative initiative on psychosocial risks at work and a possible legal right to disconnect (ETUC, 2023; EESC, 2025).

The legislative process for these initiatives is shaped by the Commission's political agenda, the EP's position, and the results of consultations with the social partners as foreseen in Art. 154 TFEU.

4 Conclusion and Reflections

The development of EU social policy has long been shaped by the structural tension between market integration and social cohesion. A major breakthrough occurred under the Delors Commission (1985–1995), which is often remembered for a wave of legislation that significantly expanded the Union's social acquis. This progress was not only politically driven but also considered essential to balance the deepening of the internal market.

However, the ambition to reconcile a sustainable balance between economic freedoms and social rights has faced considerable challenges. The years that followed were marked by institutional stagnation. Even ambitious strategies—like the Lisbon Strategy (2000–2010)—failed to strengthen the EU's social dimension in a lasting way.

A cautious revival began only with the Lisbon Treaty in 2009 and the inclusion of the horizontal social clause in Art. 9 TFEU. This policy shift was further consolidated by the proclamation of the EPSRS in 2017. Important secondary legislation—such as the Pay Transparency Directive (2023/970) can be linked directly to the EPSR. Today, the EPSR serves as a normative compass for promoting upward social convergence across the Union.

In its current policy cycle (2024–2029), the Commission has committed to promoting fair working conditions, just transitions, and a sustainable transformation of work through initiatives such as the Quality Jobs Roadmap, the Clean Industrial Deal, and a new Action Plan on the EPSR.

However, this socially progressive agenda is increasingly confronted by competitiveness-oriented narratives. Recent communications, such as the Competitiveness Compass, explicitly urge Member States to avoid additional regulatory burdens. Likewise, the Omnibus Simplification Package proposes streamlined legal frameworks that may dilute existing social protections. Such initiatives reflect a broader discourse that prioritizes market efficiency and regulatory lightening over social harmonization—a discourse that complicates the use of the OLP for ambitious social legislation.

At the same time, a fundamental tension becomes visible: Although the OLP is the central instrument for adopting EU social legislation, its practical use is constrained by the heterogeneity of Member States' welfare regimes. This limits the scope and ambition of common standards. Therefore, whether the European Union can credibly pursue its goal of building a "Social Europe" will not depend on legislative proposals alone. The broader challenge lies in the dual function of the OLP—it must foster upward social convergence while respecting and accommodating national differences in policy design and social governance.

References

Esping-Andersen, G. (1990). **The three worlds of welfare capitalism**. Polity Press / Princeton University Press. Accessed July 4, 2025, from https://pagotto.wordpress.com/wp-content/uploads/2018/05/the-three-worlds-of-welfare-capitalism-1990.pdf

European Commission. (2023). Employment, social affairs and inclusion. Accessed June 10, 2025, from https://employment-social-affairs.ec.europa.eu/news/commission-decision-setting-european-social-dialogue-committee-social-services-2023-07-10_en

European Economic and Social Committee (EESC). (2025). Opinion on the future implementation of the EPSR. Accessed May 30, 2025, from https://www.eesc.europa.eu/en/our-work/opinions-information-reports/opinions/new-action-plan-implementation-european-pillar-social-rights

European Union. (1992, July 29). Treaty on European Union—Protocol on social policy. Official Journal of the European Communities, C 191. Accessed May 22, 2025, from https://eur-lex.europa.eu/legal-content/EN/TXT/?uri=OJ:C:1992:191:TOC

European Union. (2012a). Consolidated version of the Treaty on European Union. Official Journal of the European Union, C 326, 13–45. Accessed May 22, 2025, from https://eur-lex.europa.eu/legal-content/EN/TXT/?uri=CELEX%3A12012M%2FTXT

European Union. (2012b). Consolidated version of the treaty on the functioning of the European Union. Official Journal of the European Union, C 326, 47–390. Accessed May 22, 2025, from https://eur-lex.europa.eu/legal-content/EN/TXT/?uri=CELEX%3A12012E%2FTXT

European Union. (2024). EUR-Lex. Access to European Union Law. Accessed May 14, 2025, from https://eur-lex.europa.eu/search.html?lang=de&SUBDOM_INIT=LEGISLATION&DTS_DOM=EU_LAW&typeOfActStatus=REGULATION%2CDIRECTIVE&type=advanced&DTS_SUBDOM=LEGISLATION&whOJ=YEAR_OJ_OLD%3D2024&qid=1753048707463&DB_TYPE_OF_ACT=regulation%2Cdirective&whOJAba=YEAR_OJ_ABA%3D2024&CC_1_CODED=05&PROC_TYP=OLP

European Union. (n.d.). Charter of fundamental rights of the European Union. EUR-Lex. Accessed May 23, 2025, from https://eur-lex.europa.eu/en/legal-content/summary/charter-of-fundamental-rights-of-the-european-union.html

Falkner, G. (1998). *EU social policy in the 1990s: Towards a corporatist policy community*. Routledge. Accessed May 14, 2025, from https://ebookcentral.proquest.com/lib/fh-vie/reader.action?docID=165492&c=RVBVQg&ppg=1

Zeitlin, J., & Vanhercke, B. (2018). Socializing the European semester: EU social and economic policy co-ordination in crisis and beyond. *Journal of European Public Policy, 25*(2), 149–174. Accessed May 18, 2025, from. https://doi.org/10.1080/13501763.2017.1363269

Further Readings

European Commission: Directorate-General for Employment, Social Affairs and Inclusion, employment and social developments in Europe 2024, Publications Office of the European Union, 2024.

Falkner, G. (1998b). EU social policy in the 1990s: Towards a corporatist policy community.

Kennett, P., & Lacey, N. (Eds.). (2017). *Handbook of European social policy*. Edward Elgar Publishing.

Vandenbroucke, F., Barnard, C., & De Baere, G. (2017). A European social union after the crisis. Cambridge.

Vanhercke, B., Ghailani, D., Spasova, S., & Fronteddu, B. (Eds.). (2020). *Social policy in the European Union: State of play 2019. Facing the challenges*. European Trade Union Institute (ETUI).

Birgül Tütün-Ince is a lecturer in Political Science at the University of Applied Sciences BFI Vienna. She previously worked as a policy officer in the European Parliament with a focus on employment and social affairs. At ÖBB (Austrian Federal Railways), she represents the company in the Community of European Railway and Infrastructure Companies (CER) and serves as a member of the Sectoral Social Dialogue Committee for Railways. Her academic and professional expertise centres on EU employment and social affairs, social dialogue, and the interface between European policymaking and national implementation.

Competitiveness Compass: Cutting the Red Tape Off the Green Deal (and More)

Harald J. Jauk

Abstract The last European Commission's term was largely focused on "green" goals, whereas the current Commission's mandate put competitiveness in a central position. As one of its first key initiatives, the Competitiveness Compass was presented as an attempt to provide orientation for the diverse 2024–2029 competitiveness policies (June 2025). Apart from a general view on the competitiveness goal, this chapter offers an overview of the key action areas related to this goal and the planned modes to reach it. One of these modes being regulatory simplification, which includes a modification of already under the OLP concluded Green Deal legal acts and proposals, also the question if more than cutting red tape (but actually policies themselves) is dealt with.

Keywords Competitiveness · Competition · Green Deal · Clean Industrial Deal · Red tape · Regulatory simplification · Single Market · Trade

H. J. Jauk (✉)
University of Applied Sciences Wiener Neustadt, Wiener Neustadt, Austria

IMC University of Applied Sciences Krems, Krems an der Donau, Austria
e-mail: r203626@fhwn.ac.at

G. Füricht-Fiegl et al. (eds.), *Handbook on EU Law-making*, Professional Practice in Governance and Public Organizations, https://doi.org/10.1007/978-3-032-16559-6_28

1 Introduction

In her speech on the new European Commission's programme at the European Parliament (EP) end of November 2024,[1] Ursula von der Leyen mentioned the word *competitiveness* no less than 12 times in several of its variations: "competition", "competitors", "competitive", "competitiveness". In light of that, it already seemed evident that this is—among other core issues like *defence* (mentioned only 7 times)—what the 2024–2029 Commission would place its focus on.

At any cost? President von der Leyen clarified that this goal must be attained in a *green* (mentioned 3 times) and *clean* (mentioned 6 times) way. In other words, a *Green Deal* but with (more) competitive elements (and, actually, as we will see, more than that), giving way to a new key term: the *Clean Industrial Deal*. This Deal forms part of a larger concept providing orientation—the *Competitiveness Compass* we will have a look at in this chapter.

The majority of the policy areas and related legal acts covered by the Competitiveness Compass falls under the OLP (e.g. single market [Art. 114, 116 TFEU], environment [Art. 192 TFEU], industry [Art. 173 TFEU]), while some matters, e.g. the conclusion of international trade agreements (Art. 218 TFEU), follow a special legislative procedure.

2 Competitiveness as Key Agenda of the 2024–2029 European Commission

Not only the speech of the Commission's president, but also the Political Guidelines of the European Commission published after the EP elections 2024 place European competitiveness in a central position.

European Commission Political Guidelines
It has become a tradition that every time after the elections to the EP, the candidate for the European Commission President presents the Political Guidelines for the next European Commission. These guidelines are a document of merely political character of usually more than 20 and less than 50 pages (in its official published and lay outed version) that stresses the 5-year (planned) *priorities* of the respective European Commission. These political guidelines are detailed for each of these 5 years by the annual Commission Work Programme (see box below).

[1] This speech can be seen as of major importance due to the fact that in 2024, no "State of the (European) Union" address took place due to the reconstitution of the Commission following the 2024 elections to the EP. See European Commission (2024a).

The 2024–2029 Political Guidelines contain the seven priorities of the current Commission's mandate, the first one[2] of these referring to, again, *competitiveness*—"A new plan for Europe's sustainable prosperity and competitiveness".[3]

Capturing the essence of these seven priorities, we could come up with *three key elements*: 1. *Competitiveness* with green and social elements delivered, among other things, by digitalization,[4] 2. *Defence and security* and 3. *Democracy, rule of law and values* both internally considering the recent threats to the European values by certain Member States, and externally via partnerships with non-EU countries.

The competitiveness goal is described in a very broad manner by the Commission, covering diverse policy areas like

- The European Single Market and EU Competition Law (internal trade side).
- (Clean) International trade and investment agreements (external trade side)
- Climate neutrality and decarbonization (including energy and clean tech).[5]
- Research and innovation (specifically digitalization including AI and data access) and
- (Clean) Industrialization start-up and scale-up support and reducing red tape including a "stress-test [of] the entire [!] EU *aquis*" (European Commission, 2024b, 7).

Also some at first sight less related matters - of generally mainly supporting, coordinating and supplementing EU competence (Art. 6 TFEU) - like health ("European Health Union") and education ("Union of Skills") are part of the Commission's competitiveness priority appearing in its political guidelines. (European Commission, 2024b, 9, 12)

---

[2] According to the EU Competitiveness Compass, competitiveness even is "front and center of this [European Commission's] mandate" (European Commission, 2025c, 2).

[3] The others are "A new era for European Defence and Security", "Supporting people, strengthening our societies and our social model", "Sustaining our quality of life: Food security, water and nature", "Protecting our democracy, upholding our values", "A global Europe: Leveraging our power and partnerships", and "Delivering together and preparing our Union for the future". (European Commission, 2024b)

[4] See the chapters in this handbook focusing on *digital* and on *social policy*. The "green" elements are part of this chapter.

[5] "Clean industrialization" becoming a new key term of the current Commission.

In view of this large variety of policy areas mentioned, the Commission included in its Work Programme of the first year of its term (2025) the (non-legislative) initiative of the so-called Competitiveness Compass[6] to provide some orientation.

European Commission Annual Work Programme
The annual Commission Work Programme details the Commission's 5-year Political Guidelines (see box above) by specifying the upcoming legal and non-legal Commission proposals.[7] Formally it represents a Communication by the Commission to the EP, the Council, the European Economic and Social Committee and the Committee of the Regions presented early each year. Annex I of this Communication is of special practical relevance because it displays in a succinct table the names of the planned legislative and non-legislative initiatives of the Commission for this year and specifies in what quarter which of these initiatives is to expect.[8]

The 2025 Work Programme itself—similarly to the mentioned Political Guidelines—enlists some of the plans on fostering competitiveness and therefore, does not itself provide more clarity or orientation against the background of the diversity of policy areas covered. Nonetheless, it explicitly mentions the Competitiveness Compass (which the Political Guidelines did not), a political tool that "will steer our efforts throughout the mandate to enhance Europe's competitiveness, a top priority for this Commission" (European Commission, 2025a, 3). In other words, the Competitiveness Compass should provide guidance not only for the first year or so but for the entire term of the current Commission 2024–2029.

3 Competitiveness Compass—How It Aims to Provide Orientation

The Competitiveness Compass represents a 26-page Communication from the Commission to the EP, the European Council, the Council, the European Economic and Social Committee and the Committee of the Regions dated January 29, 2025, aimed at

---

[6] Not to be confused with the *Strategic* Compass (for Security and Defence) or the *Digital* Compass.

[7] Designated as "strategies", "deals", "(action) plans", "pacts", "roadmaps", etc., which are normally of non-legal orientation providing character, and "acts", "packages", regulations, directives, etc., being of legal character.

[8] As for the policy objective Competitiveness/Competitiveness and Decarbonization, the table of Annex 1 of the 2025 Work Programme, e.g., contains the non-legislatives initiatives of the Competitiveness Compass and the Clean Industrial Deal (both quarter 1). (European Commission, 2025b, Annex 1)

(a) Identifying necessary policy changes[9] and
(b) Better coordination of EU and EU Member States' (taxation, labour, industrial[10]) policies (European Commission, 2025c, 3).

In contrast to the Political Guidelines and the Work Programme, the Competitiveness Compass actually does give some orientation in the "jungle" of policy areas the Commission wants to tackle for fostering competitiveness.

Based on the *Draghi (Competitiveness) Report* (see box below), the Competitiveness Compass follows its division into *three "action areas"*: (1). innovation, (2). decarbonization and competitiveness jointly and (3). decreasing dependencies and increasing security (Draghi, 2025a, 6–7; European Commission, 2025c, 3).

Draghi Competitiveness Report

The former President of the European Central Bank, Mario Draghi, had been tasked by the Commission to produce a report on the future of European competitiveness. The outcome, the Draghi Report from September 2024, can be seen as a warning that Europe can no longer rely largely on a functioning global free trade (result also of a formerly high degree of geopolitical stability) but has to find its way to economic prosperity (more) on its own (Draghi, 2025a, 2025b). The results of the 2024 US presidential election and the subsequent trade-limiting actions of a highly protectionist second Donald J. Trump administration later confirmed Draghi's thinkings.[11]

According to the Competitiveness Compass, the three mentioned substantive goals ("action areas": innovation; decarbonization and competitiveness; less dependencies and more security) potentially leading to a stronger European competitiveness should be reached by action across all sectors (*five "horizontal enablers"* or "action modes") by

- *Simplifying the regulatory environment*, reducing burden and favouring speed and flexibility
- Fully exploiting benefits of scale offered by the *Single Market* by *removing barriers*
- Financing through a *Savings and Investments Union* and a refocused EU budget
- *Promoting skills* and quality jobs while ensuring social fairness

---

[9] E.g. excessively ambitious (or administratively exuberant) and competition-limiting legal acts part of the Green Deal (see below).

[10] Which are mainly policy areas of state (and not EU) competence.

[11] The COVID-19 pandemic and the Russia-Ukraine war (and the resulting energy supply issue) as well as China's monopoly on some raw materials are other examples for the truthfulness of this message of Draghi's report. In addition, the international trade system of the World Trade Organization has experienced a huge backlash due to the blockage of its Appellate Body since 2017 by the USA. (Jauk, 2024, 146)

Image 1 Competitiveness Compass. Source: European Commission (2025)

- Better *coordinating policies* at EU and national levels (European Commission, 2025c, 3, italics added).

In other words, we have *three cardinal points* of the compass (instead of *four* like in reality, which is why the compass metaphor falls short a bit) referring to substantive policy areas/goals and *five additional points* on the compass representing cross-sector action modes by which these policy goals should be reached (Image 1).

3.1 Competitiveness Compass Action Areas/Goals

A glance at the **three substantive action areas/goals**—innovation; decarbonization and competitiveness; and less dependencies and more security—shows as follows.

The first one, ***closing the innovation gap***, refers to policy areas such as *artificial intelligence* (AI), which has been regulated by the EU AI Act—a legal act that rather limits AI instead of seizing and promoting it (European Union, 2024a). New planned initiatives, by contrast, like "AI Gigafactories" and "Apply AI", are aimed at promoting it. Other policy areas this action goal covers are, for example, *research* and access of innovative companies to it (facilitated, e.g., by the upcoming European Innovation Act), *digital infrastructure* and *technologies* like "semiconductor and quantum technologies, advanced materials, biotechnologies, clean energy technologies, robotics, space technologies" (European Commission, 2025c, 5, 4–7).[12]

[12] For more information on this action goal, refer to the chapter on digital policy and AI.

The second action area/goal, ***a joint roadmap for decarbonization and competitiveness***, refers to policy areas such as *industry* (as part of the Clean Industrial Deal), *energy* (including the transition of energy-intensive sectors like metals and chemicals), *mobility and transport* and *agriculture and food* (European Commission, 2025c, 8–11).

Clean Industrial Deal

The Clean Industrial Deal, the new main "deal" for decarbonization of the European Union, was presented by the Commission in February 2025. It focuses on (a) energy-intensive industries (decarbonization and electrification, lowering energy costs), (b) clean tech and clean products (increased financing and investment as well as boosting demand, e.g., by reformed public procurement rules), (c) circularity (and better access to critical raw materials) and (d) clean international trade and investment agreements. (European Commission, 2025n)

The third action area/goal, ***reducing excessive dependencies and increasing security***, refers primarily to the *external trade* side, i.e. clean trade (and investment) agreements with non-EU countries.[13] However, it also covers internal policy areas such as *fair competition* (including a revision of the public procurement rules so strategic sectors and technologies can get an advantage), defence industry (reducing external supply dependence) and weather (e.g. improving resilience against extreme weather events and securing access to water) (European Commission, 2025c, 12–16).

3.2 *Competitiveness Compass Horizontal Enablers*

The **five horizontal action modes** (or "horizontal enablers") by which these three substantive action goals should be reached—(a) regulatory simplification; (b) removing single market barriers; (c) targeted financing; (d) better coordination between Member States and between these and the EU; and (e) promoting skills—will be illustrated by a few examples each. The first one, *regulatory simplification*, will be explained last and in more detail due to the by some feared "dismantling of the EU climate policy" by it.

Europe's Single Market has been the cornerstone of European integration and competitiveness. However, the share of the EU's GDP represented by trade between Member States has recently decreased both for goods and services (European Commission, 2025c, 19; European Commission, 2025h, 3).

[13] Thus overlapping partly with the Clean Industrial Deal.

For (b) ***removing barriers to the Single Market***, the Commission, as presented in its Single Market Strategy in May 2025, plans to tackle the "terrible ten":

1. Overly complex EU rules (overlapping with the action mode *regulatory simplification*)
2. Lack of Single Market ownership by Member States
3. Complicated business establishment and operations
4. (Limited) recognition of professional qualifications
5. Delays in standard-setting
6. Fragmented rules on packaging, labelling and waste
7. Outdated harmonized product rules and lack of product compliance
8. Restrictive and diverging national services regulation
9. Burdensome procedures for temporary posting of workers
10. Territorial supply constraints (European Commission, 2025i, 4–16)

As for (c) ***targeted financing***, the Commission, e.g., plans to increase the financing of innovative companies, which has been relying mainly on classic bank financing, (also) through other forms like equity (and other forms of risk capital) financing as part of the Savings and Investments Union Strategy. This strategy was presented in March 2025 and is more of a general roadmap lacking concrete proposals, most of which are expected in the second half of 2025 and in 2026 (European Commission, 2025c, 4, 5; European Commission, 2025j).

Industrial and research policies, among others, are fragmented between the EU and the Member States and focused often (only) on attaining national competitiveness while lacking coordination. (d) ***better cooperation*** between Member States and between these and the EU should be achieved primarily by the Competitiveness Coordination Tool (including a Competitiveness Fund). Aimed at "align[ing] industrial and research policies and investments at the EU and the national levels", the Competitiveness Coordination Tool will work together with the European Semester and a planned Steering Mechanism for reforms and investments at EU and national levels (European Commission, 2025c, 23, 24).

For (e) ***promoting skills*** *and quality jobs*, in March 2025, the Commission presented the Union of Skills Strategy. Education, being primarily competence of the Member States, the Commission, e.g., plans to support these at developing intervention schemes (e.g. early identification, monitoring, effective support, teacher training, cooperation) for achieving higher basic skills[14] among the European people (European Commission, 2025k, 6). Apart from that, the Union of Skills, e.g., covers attracting skilled people from non-EU countries[15] and easier recognition of qualifications across the EU (this contributing to the horizontal enabler *removing barriers to the Single Market*) (European Commission, 2025l).

---

[14] For this, the Commission also issued an *Action Plan on Basic Skills*.

[15] An initiative with this aim is, e.g., the investment of €1,25 billion for calls under the "Choose Europe for Science" initiative (European Commission, 2025m), which in light of the scientific restrictions realized in the USA by the Trump administration seems a wise choice.

3.2.1 Horizontal Enabler *Regulatory Simplification*—(Excessively?) Cutting Red Tape

The strong need for ***regulatory simplification*** (first horizontal enabler of the Competitiveness Compass) is already shown in the fact that, for the first time, there is a specifically dedicated Commissioner for *Implementation and Simplification*.[16] This simplification, e.g., finds its materialization in the planned Industrial Decarbonization Accelerator Act aimed at providing faster permitting to energy-intensive industries in transition (i.e. industries in process of decarbonization) (European Commission, 2025c, 17).

Another example is the famous *Omnibus package* presented in February 2025 targeted at cutting red tape especially for small and medium-sized companies regarding reporting and due diligence obligations in areas like finance, investment, taxonomy[17] and the Carbon Border Adjustment Mechanism[18] (European Commission, 2025c, 17, 2025d, 2025e).

Emission Trading System and "Carbon Border Tax"
The Carbon Border Adjustment Mechanism (CBAM), sometimes also referred to as "carbon border tax" represents the necessary *external* complement for a functioning *internal* Emission Trading System.

The *Emission Trading System* (ETS) can be seen as the most important instrument of the EU for lowering its CO2 emissions. Somewhat simplified, it establishes that a company covered by it must acquire an emission allowance for each ton of CO2[19] it emits. These allowances are limited in number and traded in an own market regulated by demand. If companies in Member States decide to emit lots of CO2, they need to buy lots of allowances which makes the allowances more expensive. The ETS covers the emissions from energy-intensive stationary industrial installations (oil, gas, metal, etc.), aviation, maritime transport and, as of 2027, also road transport (gas stations) and buildings (fuel suppliers) (European Union, 2003, 2023a).

[16] Currently the former MEP and former Vice-President of the Commission Valdis Dombrovskis.

[17] Taxonomy, in short, refers to the allowance to classify something as "green" (necessary to avoid greenwashing).

[18] In fact, the package from February 2025 consisted of two thematically intertwined "Omnibuses"—the Omnibus I package and the Omnibus II package. By the time of writing this chapter, two additional Omnibus packages (III on *agriculture* and IV on *SMEs*) have been presented by the Commission, the following Omnibuses to be expected on *defence* and *chemical industry*, respectively.

[19] Also other gases like N20 and PFCs are covered by the ETS.

The goal to be reached this way is, of course, the reduction of CO2 emissions (because companies [and, finally, consumers] want to save money and pay as few as possible for allowances). However, instead of reducing the CO2 levels of their installations, etc., in the EU, companies could opt for producing in third countries where CO2 emissions are cheaper and then import the cheaper high-emission-products to the EU.

This is where the CBAM comes into play: Put simply, the importing company must pay the difference between the lower CO2-price in the third country and the higher CO2-price in the EU in order to legally import its product (iron, steel, aluminium, cement, etc.). This way the so-called carbon leakage, i.e. the migration of EU industry to third countries, should be avoided.

Of course, this means also paperwork, e.g. importers having to investigate the CO2 emissions of third-country producers and to submit them to import a product (European Union, 2023b).

Apart from the planned reduced reporting obligations regarding the CBAM (thanks to Omnibus I these should take effect only for importers exceeding 50 tons of CO2 per year), the Commission has announced to modify several of its *Green Deal* legal acts.

The mentioned Omnibus I package, e.g., also notoriously proposes to drastically limit due diligence on human rights infringements and environmental pollution in the supply chain primarily to *direct* suppliers (and not also others down the supply chain).[20] Apart from that, it includes a postponement of both the due diligence requirements and the reporting obligations[21] (European Commission, 2025d, 2025e).

The Council position (Council negotiating mandate) did confirm this but went even further: It raised the threshold for the due diligence obligations of the Corporate Sustainability Due Diligence Directive from companies with more than 1000 employees to companies with more than 5000 employees and the turnover threshold from €450 million to €1.5 billion (European Union, 2024b, Art. 2; Council, 2025, 16).

Another act of reducing or flexibilizing formerly presented "green" goals that has caused some stir is the change in one of the key elements of the Green Deal, the *Fit for 55 package (55% less overall CO2 emissions by 2030, overall climate neutrality by 2050).*

[20] The affected Directive being the *Corporate Sustainability Due Diligence Directive* (2024/1760). Also the sustainability reporting requirements of the *Corporate Sustainability Reporting Directive* (2022/2464) were postponed and its scope reduced in the Omnibus I proposal.

[21] Of the *Corporate Sustainability Reporting Directive* (2022/2464), whose reporting obligation threshold was raised to companies with 1000 employees.

An essential part of this package is the amendment[22] of the CO2 Cars and Vans Emission Standards Regulation (2019/631) adopted in 2023 that set the CO2 emissions reduction goal for new **cars** at 55% by 2030 compared to 2021 levels and at 100% (climate neutrality) by 2035. Additionally, CO2 targets were fixed individually for each year until 2030.

Early 2024, the Commission issued a (non-binding) Communication recommending a mid-way goal between the 2030 and 2050 **overall** emission goals—a reduction of total CO2 emissions by 90% by 2040 (European Union, 2023c; European Commission, 2024c, 6).

As for cars and vans, bit more than 2 years after the regulation's amendment adoption, in April 2025, the Commission issued a formal legislative proposal on again amending the regulation. In this proposal, instead of the yearly CO2 targets for 2025, 2026 and 2027, a total target for all these years was established, giving automobile more flexibility but weakening the 2023 amendment of the regulation to some extent. Interestingly, the 2025 amendment proposal remains silent regarding the overall 2040 90% mid-way goal on total emissions recommended by the Commission in 2024 (European Commission, 2025f).

All these acts lead us to the question: Is the Commission just cutting the (unnecessary) red tape off the Green Deal with its first "horizontal enabler" (*regulatory simplification*) of the Competitiveness Compass? Or is it actually cutting down the Green Deal itself?

Some (and most) changes definitely do what the *Omnibuses* are officially aimed at, they cut unnecessary red tape. A prime example would be the aforementioned CBAM, which now will not cover products from all importers but only those from importers exceeding 50 tons of CO2 per year. This way, approximately 90% of importers are exempted from it (being mostly SMEs) but 99% (!) of all emissions are still covered (European Commission, 2025g).

On the other hand, amendments like the one regarding the cars' CO2 emission thresholds certainly exceed a mere regulatory *simplification*. In some cases, like in this one, allowing some pragmatism instead of a merciless maintaining of rules could bring more than it costs though:

Example: If the total CO2 emissions by new cars limit for three years is, let's say, *3*, it most likely is the same for the environment if the emissions are *1.5* in year 1, *1* in year 2, and *0.5* in year 3 or if they were *2* in year 1 and *0.5*, respectively, in years 2 and 3 (the total emissions are in both cases *3*).

While the outcome for the environment in both cases is the same, sticking strictly to the yearly limits (in our example *1.5 – 1 – 0.5*) might not lead to a faster reduction of CO2 levels, e.g. due to inevitable complications in complying with the limits for car manufacturers like a difficult economic situation and less demand for e-cars, but just to penalties manu-

[22] *Regulation 2023/851 amending Regulation 2019/631 as regards strengthening the CO2 emission performance standards for new passenger cars and new light commercial vehicles in line with the Union's increased climate ambition*, corresponding with the *European Climate Law* (Regulation 2021/1119).

facturers would have to pay. This wouldn't bring the environment much but only lead to dissatisfaction with EU policies (and possibly with the EU itself).

In other words, the Commission might partly have exceeded the mere administrative burden cutting in its new wave of amendment proposals of Green Deal (and other) legal acts, but in the cases it did (like the mentioned example) it has frequently acted with sensible pragmatism while maintaining key Green Deal goals.

Furthermore, the modification of Green Deal obligations has, until now, only affected some legal acts (especially those where public satisfaction was lacking) while maintaining most of them untouched. Let us not forget that the environmental efforts of the EU are not limited to supply chains and CO2 questions but go far beyond with legal acts on air pollution including other greenhouse gases, plastic and recycling, waste shipment, biodiversity including soils and deforestation, clean tech, animal and plant health and many more.

4 Conclusions and Outlook

Regaining competitiveness can be seen as the one primary goal of this Commission's mandate realized mainly via the OLP. This is clearly perceptible in the Commission's Political Guidelines and also in orientation-giving roadmaps like the Competitiveness Compass. While until now one of the main tools of this Compass for reaching its goals of *more innovation*, *competitiveness enhancing decarbonization* and *reducing dependencies* have been the scissors cutting red tape off existent legal acts and initiatives, it is, in fact, much more abundant: A functional deepening of the European Single Market and target-oriented trade agreements, strategic financing and investment, skilled workforce development as well as a better coordination between Member States and between these and the EU are to a similar extent (planned) key drivers for attaining more European competitiveness.

As for the question if these scissors cut more than red tape (but the Green Deal *itself*), a pragmatic middle course has been found that leaves the goals of the green transition untouched.

References

Council of the European Union. (2025). Proposal for a Directive of the European Parliament and the Council amending Directives 2006/43/EC, 2013/34/EU, (EU) 2022/2464 and (EU) 2024/1760 as regards certain corporate sustainability reporting and due diligence requirements – Mandate for negotiations with the European Parliament, 21.6.2025, Interinstitutional File 2025/0045(COD).

Draghi, M. (2025a). *The future of European competitiveness: Part A / A competitiveness strategy for Europe, September 2024*. Publications Office of the European Union.

Draghi, M. (2025b). *The future of European competitiveness: Part B / In-depth analysis and recommendations, September 2024*. Publications Office of the European Union.

European Commission. (2024a). Speech by President von der Leyen at the European Parliament Plenary on the new College of Commissioners and its programme. Accessed June 06, 2025, from https://ec.europa.eu/commission/presscorner/detail/en/speech_24_6084

European Commission. (2024b). Europe's choice—Political guidelines for the next European Commission 2024–2029, 18.07.2024, Strasbourg.

European Commission. (2024c). Communication from the Commission to the European Parliament, the Council, the European Economic and Social Committee and the Committee of the Regions: Securing our future – Europe's 2040 climate target and path to climate neutrality by 2050 building a sustainable, just and prosperous society, 6.2.2024, COM/2024/ 63 final.

European Commission. (2025a). Communication from the Commission to the European Parliament, the Council, the European Economic and Social Committee and the Committee of the Regions: Commission work programme 2025, 11.2.2025, COM/2025/45 final.

European Commission. (2025b). Annexes to the Communication from the Commission to the European Parliament, the Council, the European Economic and Social Committee and the Committee of the Regions: Commission work programme 2025, 11.2.2025, COM/2025/45 final.

European Commission. (2025c). Communication from the Commission to the European Parliament, the European Council, the Council, the European Economic and Social Committee and the Committee of the Regions: A Competitiveness Compass for the EU. 29.1.2025, COM/2025/30 final.

European Commission. (2025d). Proposal for a Directive of the European Parliament and the Council amending Directives 2006/43/EC, 2013/34/EU, (EU) 2022/2464 and (EU) 2024/1760 as regards certain corporate sustainability reporting and due diligence requirements (Omnibus 1), 26.2.2025, COM/2025/81 final.

European Commission. (2025e). Proposal for a Directive of the European Parliament and the Council amending Directives (EU) 2022/2464 and (EU) 2024/1760 as regards the dates from which Member States are to apply certain corporate sustainability reporting and due diligence requirements (Omnibus I), 26.2.2025, COM/2025/80 final.

European Commission. (2025f). Proposal for a of the European Parliament and the Council amending Regulation (EU) 2019/631 to include an additional flexibility as regards the calculation of manufacturers' compliance with CO2 emission performance standards for new passenger cars and new light commercial vehicles for the calendar years 2025 to 2027, 1.4.2025, COM/2025/136 final.

European Commission. (2025g). Commission simplifies rules on sustainability and EU investments, delivering over €6 billion in administrative relief, 26.2.2025, Press Release. Accessed June 30, 2025, from https://ec.europa.eu/commission/presscorner/detail/en/ip_25_614

European Commission. (2025h). Communication from the Commission to the European Parliament, the Council, the European Economic and Social Committee and the Committee of the Regions: The 2025 Annual Single Market and Competitiveness Report, 29.1.2025, COM/2025/26 final.

European Commission. (2025i). Communication from the Commission to the European Parliament, the Council, the European Economic and Social Committee and the Committee of the Regions: The Single Market: our European home market in an uncertain world – A Strategy for making the Single Market simple, seamless and strong, 21.5.2025, COM/2025/500 final.

European Commission. (2025j). Communication from the Commission to the European Parliament, the European Council, the Council, the European Economic and Social Committee and the Committee of the Regions: Savings and Investments Union – A Strategy to Foster Citizens' Wealth and Economic Competitiveness in the EU, 19.3.2025, COM/2025/124 final.

European Commission. (2025k). Communication from the Commission to the European Parliament, the Council, the European Economic and Social Committee and the Committee of the Regions on the Action Plan on Basic Skills, 5.3.2025, COM/2025/88 final.

European Commission. (2025l). Communication from the Commission to the European Parliament, the European Council, the Council, the European Economic and Social Committee and the Committee of the Region: The Union of Skills, 5.3.2025, COM/2025/90 final.
European Commission. (2025m). Commission invests €1.25 billion in researchers and invites them to 'Choose Europe for Science', Press Release. Accessed June 30, 2025.
European Commission. (2025n). Communication from the Commission to the European Parliament, the Council, the European Economic and Social Committee and the Committee of the Regions, The Clean Industrial Deal: A joint roadmap for competitiveness and decarbonisation, 26.2.2025, COM/2025/85 final.
European Union. (2003). Directive 2003/87/EC of the European Parliament and the Council of 13 October 2003 establishing a scheme for greenhouse gas emission allowance trading within the Community and amending Council Directive 96/61/EC, 25.10.2003, L275/32.
European Union. (2023a). Directive (EU) 2023/959 of the European Parliament and of the Council of 10 May 2023 amending Directive 2003/87/EC establishing a system for greenhouse gas emission allowance trading within the Union and Decision (EU) 2015/1814 concerning the establishment and operation of a market stability reserve for the Union greenhouse gas emission trading system, 16.5.2023, L130/134.
European Union. (2023b). Regulation (EU) 2023/956 of the European Parliament and of the Council of 10 May 2023 establishing a carbon border adjustment mechanism, 16.5.2023, L130/52.
European Union. (2023c). Regulation (EU) 2023/851 of the European Parliament and of the Council of 19 April 2023 amending Regulation (EU) 2019/631 as regards strengthening the CO2 emission performance standards for new passenger cars and new light commercial vehicles in line with the Union's increased climate ambition, 25.4.2023, L110/5.
European Union. (2024a). Regulation (EU) 2024/1689 of the European Parliament and of the Council of 13 June 2024 laying down harmonised rules on artificial intelligence and amending Regulations (EC) No 300/2008, (EU) No 167/2013, (EU) No 168/2013, (EU) 2018/858, (EU) 2018/1139 and (EU) 2019/2144 and Directives 2014/90/EU, (EU) 2016/797 and (EU) 2020/1828 (Artificial Intelligence Act), 12.7.2024, L.
European Union. (2024b). Directive (EU) 2024/1760 of the European Parliament and of the Council of 13 June 2024 on corporate sustainability due diligence and amending Directive (EU) 2019/1937 and Regulation (EU) 2023/2859.
Jauk, H. J. (2024/25). *Key Essentials of International Trade and Business Law*. BoD.

Further Readings

For a succinct summary on EU competition law, economic integration and international trade law (and other things): Jauk, H. J. (2024/25). Key Essentials of International Trade and Business Law. BoD.

For some insight into the complicated competitiveness situation of the EU and possible solutions (both documents available online for free): Draghi, M. (2025). The future of European competitiveness: Part A / A competitiveness strategy for Europe, September 2024, Publications Office of the European Union. Draghi, M. (2025). The future of European competitiveness: Part B / In-depth analysis and recommendations, September 2024, Publications Office of the European Union.

Harald J. Jauk teaches International Trade & Business Law and European Union Law at the Universities of Applied Sciences Wiener Neustadt and Krems (Austria) as well as the Austrian Federal Academy of Public Administration. After professional activities in international relations and at University of Vienna in the field of fundamental rights and in refugee law, he worked as Policy Advisor for Foreign Affairs and Social Matters for the former First Vice-President of the European Parliament, Othmar Karas.

The Evolving Landscape of EU Lawmaking

The Future of EU Lawmaking: Better Regulation

Antonina Cipollone

Abstract This article aims to provide the key elements to understand the European Commission's better regulation system, one of the most advanced systems in the Organisation for Economic Co-operation and Development (OECD), by explaining its tools and governance. Better regulation tools inform the Commission when preparing its initiatives; these are then negotiated and adopted by co-legislators. The article explains the link between better regulation and the overall competitiveness policy of the Commission and how the recently introduced changes relate to it. Finally, it provides elements of reflection on the challenges facing the system, called to respond at an increased high speed to complex interconnected problems with implementable solutions.

Keywords Better regulation · Impact assessment · Evaluation · Fitness check · Stakeholder's consultations · Substantial amendments · Gold-plating · Regulatory scrutiny board · Competitiveness and SME check · Subsidiarity

1 Introduction

An efficient regulatory framework is essential to address the twenty-first-century challenges, including climate change, digital transformation, geopolitical tensions, and economic inequalities. The European Commission's better regulation system is

A. Cipollone (✉)
European Commission, Head of Unit Better Regulation & Simplification, Brussels, Belgium
e-mail: antonina.cipollone@ec.europa.eu

G. Füricht-Fiegl et al. (eds.), *Handbook on EU Law-making*, Professional Practice in Governance and Public Organizations, https://doi.org/10.1007/978-3-032-16559-6_29

one of the most advanced, as recognized by the OECD (OECD, 2025) and aims to ensure that Commission's proposals are evidence-based, targeted, and inclusive, balancing the EU-level action with national flexibility. A good understanding of better regulation is therefore necessary to navigate the EU legal system, as it informs its preparation from the start. Better regulation is in fact the tool for evidence-based decision-making by Commissioners. The Interinstitutional Agreement on Better Law-Making of 2016 ensures a common and shared understanding of all Institutions about better regulation tools, procedures, and practices. This article comes at the end of the handbook to provide the essential elements of the Commission's system, its current application, and an outlook of strengths and challenges.

2 The Better Regulation System of the European Commission and Its Governance

2.1 The Place of Better Regulation in the Legislative Cycle

Better regulation is a system designed to ensure that decisions are taken with the best available evidence. It informs the College of Commissioners before it adopts its proposals at the start of the legislative process. The Interinstitutional Agreement on Better Law-Making signed by the European Parliament (EP), the Council, and the Commission in 2016 recognised that better lawmaking is a shared endeavour of the three institutions. It also contains a commitment from co-legislators to assess impacts of substantial amendments and recognises that the three institutions are free to organise their own better regulation procedures. Better regulation also fulfils an accountability purpose, particularly with evaluations of programmes and funds, by proving (or not) that proposals have efficiently reached their objectives and are fit for purpose. Finally, it guarantees that stakeholders' views are reflected in the proposals, fulfilling an important function of transparency and inclusiveness.

It should be noted that there is no common interinstitutional better regulation system as each institution is responsible for its own system. However, the Interinstitutional Agreement on Better Law-Making of 2016 sets out a common framework to which the three institutions agreed upon.

2.2 The Pillars of Better Regulation

The Commission's better regulation system is based on three pillars: ex ante analysis in impact assessments, ex post evaluation, and stakeholder consultation (Table 1).

Table 1 Pillars of better regulation

Ex ante analysis in impact assessments	Ex post evaluation	Stakeholder consultation
Impact assessments are ex ante assessments of new proposals or revisions of legislation to analyse different policy options and their expected significant impacts in a systematic manner	Evaluations and fitness checks assess the performance of existing legislation and programmes or funds and whether they are still relevant.	Consultations seek evidence and feedback from stakeholders at all stages of the policymaking process.

Source: own

The rules guiding the better regulation system in the Commission are included in better regulation guidelines and the toolbox, which includes more detailed guidance (European Commission, 2023).

2.2.1 Impact Assessments

Impact assessments are carried out for initiatives with significant impacts and where policy options exist. They consist of a comprehensive analysis describing in depth the problems to be tackled by the proposal, the objectives to pursue, and different policy options. These are compared against a baseline or 'no-policy/no policy change' scenario showing the most significant impacts, notably economic, social, and environmental. They present a cost–benefit analysis showing if benefits outweigh costs. Impacts on competitiveness and SMEs are also analysed. Impact assessments rely on different sources of information, including information provided by stakeholders and previous evaluations. Given the depth of the analysis and procedural requirements, it takes on average 1 year to carry out an impact assessment.

2.2.2 Evaluations

Evaluations look backward at the performance of existing laws or programmes. The analysis is based on five criteria: efficiency, effectiveness, coherence, relevance, and EU added value. These criteria help understand if the legislation is still necessary and is still adequate to respond to the problems originally identified, if it can be improved and if it can be simplified. Evaluations focus on individual pieces of legislation or programmes, while fitness checks assess a group of related pieces of legislation, usually in a certain policy area, to identify overlaps, inconsistencies, or synergies. In the Commission, a large part of the stock of legislation is subject to evaluation and review, and evaluation clauses are systematically inserted in legislation. The Commission applies the 'evaluate first' principle according to which before revising legislation, existing rules should be evaluated.

2.2.3 Stakeholders' Consultation

Both evaluations and impact assessments are informed by stakeholder consultations. The system of consultations in the Commission is based on essentially two types of consultations: targeted and public consultations. Targeted consultations are available for a set of specifically identified stakeholders and consist of surveys, interviews, or workshops. Public consultations are published on the website *Have your say* and are based on a document called *Call for Evidence*, translated in all EU languages. This document lays down the aim, the context, the problem to address, the objectives, and the potential impacts at the preliminary stage and seeks to collect as many contributions from as many stakeholders as possible. The 'calls for evidence' for initiatives that have an impact assessment are usually accompanied by questionnaires, published for 12 weeks. Public consultations provide the opportunity to all stakeholders to provide input. Moreover, the Commission publishes for feedback the proposals adopted by the College and the draft delegated and implementing acts. A complete analysis of the consultation activities is presented both in impact assessments and evaluations in the so-called synopsis report and informs the preparation of initiatives by the Commission at the start of the legislative process.

2.3 Governance and Oversight

The better regulation system is decentralised, meaning that the preparation of impact assessments and evaluations (with the associated consultations) is the responsibility of the directorate in the Commission responsible for the initiative. This ensures that policymaking is informed by the necessary specific and technical knowledge. Nonetheless there is a system of checks and balances put in place within the Commission to ensure objectivity and impartiality of the analysis.

2.3.1 Inter-Service Groups

An inter-service group is composed of different Commission's directorates affected by the initiative that work together to contribute to the analysis from the very beginning, i.e. the problem definition. The Joint Research Centre, the Commission scientific department, also supports this analysis. For key proposals, the Secretariat General of the Commission chairs the groups, ensuring overall coordination. While the responsible department leads the initiative and retains the overall responsibility, the work within the inter-service group makes it possible to collect all expertise and points of views within the Commission.

2.3.2 The Regulatory Scrutiny Board

The Regulatory Scrutiny Board (RSB) is an independent body within the Commission tasked to scrutinise the quality of draft impact assessments, selected evaluations, and fitness checks. The board consists of nine members who serve three-year mandates—four members are recruited externally and four from within the Commission, plus the chair. It reports on its activities to the President of the Commission and to the Commissioner responsible for implementation and simplification.

Its role is to provide quality assurance, based on the better regulation guidance and toolbox, enabling the College to take decisions based on best available evidence and stakeholders' views. This is why all impact assessments, all fitness checks, and selected evaluations are subject to scrutiny. It issues three types of opinions: positive, positive with reservations, and negative. Normally, a positive opinion on the impact assessments is required to move the proposal forward. In case of a negative opinion, the draft impact assessment must therefore be resubmitted to the board before the proposal can be tabled for adoption. When the board has given a negative opinion twice, the Commissioner responsible for implementation and simplification may submit the initiative for the College of Commissioners to decide whether to go ahead. This power is very significant, and it is normally not typical for other similar oversight bodies in Europe. In case of evaluations, the resubmission is not compulsory, but Commission departments must address recommendations of the board before publishing the evaluation. While the board has a critical oversight role on the quality of the analysis, it plays no political role in the decision-making process (Regulatory Scrutiny Board annual reports).

2.3.3 Inter-Service Consultation

After a positive opinion from the board on the impact assessment, the initiative is subject also to an inter-service consultation, to ensure that there is a comprehensive and informed decision before the College of Commissioners adopts the proposals. If there is a negative opinion from one service, the initiative needs to be further discussed to iron out divergent views. This is done first at service level and then among cabinets for final adoption during College meetings.

Decentralised Responsibility

Commission's Directorates lead their files but must collaborate.

Checks and balances:

Inter-service groups ensure multidisciplinary input.

RSB acts as an independent quality gatekeeper.

Inter-service consultation ensures comprehensive input before final approval.

The College of Commissioners adopts the proposal.

3 A Renewed Focus on Simplification and Implementation

3.1 Simplification Within Better Regulation

Simplification and burden reduction are well-established components of better regulation. The Regulatory Fitness and Performance (REFIT) programme was established in 2012 to make EU law simpler and to reduce unnecessary costs of regulation while still achieving their objectives (European Commission, 2013). It is based on the idea to actively look for simplification potential when revising legislation or evaluating it. The programme was further reinforced with the application of the 'one in, one out' approach. The latter concerns costs (not proposals) (European Commission, 2021). It provides that adjustment costs (i.e. investment costs) are transparently presented and compensated to the greatest extent, while administrative costs for businesses and citizens are offset by reducing existing burdens in the same policy area. The approach is fully implemented as of 2022 and has allowed to offset all new administrative costs.

3.2 A Closer Link with Competitiveness

Despite the positive results, a more comprehensive and ambitious focus on regulatory simplification was considered necessary to support EU growth (Draghi, M. 2025), tackle the accumulation of EU rules over time at different levels, their increased complexity and challenges in implementation. The Communication 'a simpler and faster Europe' (European Commission, 2025) spells out how better regulation will ensure easier implementation of EU rules, cut burdens, and avoid building up new ones, thus boosting competitiveness.

3.2.1 Focus on the Stock of Legislation

A key element of the new approach is to ensure that the existing laws (the 'stock' of legislation or EU acquis) are properly implemented and that unnecessary obligations are removed. To do so, each Commissioner has in its mandate to stress-test the acquis, i.e. to screen existing EU legislation to identify ways to simplify it, codify, and consolidate it. It is the first time that an exercise with such broad scope is launched in the Commission, under the coordination of the Commissioner responsible for implementation and simplification. The screening covers also secondary legislation (delegated and implementing acts). These are also subject to impact assessments when they entail policy options, significant impacts, and when the impact analysis was not done for the basic act. When this is not the case a costs benefits analysis is prepared when significant impacts are expected, even if there are no policy options to choose from.

3.2.2 A New Target

The screening of EU acquis is geared to simplify and reduce burdens. A new target to cut burdens by at least 25% and at least 35% for small and medium-sized enterprises (SMEs) is expected to result in removing recurring administrative costs by EUR 37.5 billion by the end of the current mandate (2024–2029).

Omnibus Proposals
The systematic screening of the EU stock of legislation might lead to the identification of targeted amendments of various legal acts rather than the full overhaul of a single one. Omnibus proposals, which are legal acts modifying several pieces of legislation with a compatible legal basis are thus useful to maximise impacts and ensure coherence.

3.2.3 New Tools

Two new consultations tools have been designed to facilitate stakeholders' engagement, adding up to existing ones: implementation dialogues and reality checks. Implementation dialogues identify issues of poor implementation and uncover opportunities for simplification and harmonisation. They are held by Commissioners and thus are broad and political.

Reality checks, on the other hand, seek to identify and solve practical issues through a direct dialogue with practitioners. They are carried out by Commission's departments and look concretely at issues of implementation of EU law to identify simplification opportunities.

Given the focus on competitiveness, the new approach includes new SME- and competitiveness-checks in impact assessments. This will help deepen the analysis and consider those specific impacts more systematically. In particular, competitiveness checks will have a strong sectoral focus while the impacts on SME will be detailed in the SME check.

4 Outlook and Challenges Ahead

4.1 The Role of Subsidiarity and Proportionality

Looking ahead, there are a number of challenges to the better regulation approach. There is a growing perception that the regulatory landscape has become too complex and that the EU intervenes in matters of national competence with strict and rigid solutions. The respect of subsidiarity and proportionality, which are core principles of better regulation, is therefore critical. The Union can only act in areas where the treaties confer competence to it. In areas not falling under its exclusive competence, the Union should only act where the principle of subsidiarity is respected (see box below). It is necessary therefore to conduct a thorough analysis on whether there is a value in acting at EU level as opposed to leaving action at national or sub-national level. The Union should act if and in so far as the objective of the action cannot be achieved sufficiently by Member States (at national, regional, and local levels). The analysis is reported in a subsidiarity grid annexed to all legislative politically significant and important proposals with an impact assessment, unless the Union has exclusive competence (European Commission, 2018). It has also its corollary in evaluations in the form of EU added value which looks for changes that are due to the EU intervention, over and above what could reasonably have been expected from national actions by Member States. If there is such value, the content and form of action are also critical: the action of the EU must be limited in its content and form to what is necessary to achieve the objectives of the treaty that it intends to implement. Hence proportionality is considered in the impact assessment but also in evaluations and fitness checks.

Principle of Subsidiarity

In areas in which the European Union does not have exclusive competence, the principle of subsidiarity, laid down in the Treaty on European Union (TEU)—Art. 5, defines the circumstances in which it is preferable for action to be taken by the Union, rather than the Member States (European Parliament, 2025).

4.2 *Apprehending the Final Impacts in a Multilevel System*

Another critical element concerns the completeness of analysis. The Commission produces an impact assessment to accompany its proposals with significant impacts and policy options, but during negotiations substantial amendments are added by co-legislators. Such amendments should be subject to an assessment, in line with the political commitment taken by the three institutions in the Interinstitutional Agreement on Better Law-Making. However, such assessment is not carried out by the EP and the Council. The President of the Commission has called to renew such agreement so that each institution assesses the impacts and costs of its amendments in the same way. This would address the concerns made by some that impact assessments are not dynamic, i.e. they do not take into consideration the breath of all expected final impacts (Letta E., 2024). Further, implementation at national and sub-national levels could also add additional requirements that might result in a complex regulatory framework, the so-called gold-plating. This concerns additional requirements added at national and sub-national levels exceeding the minimum (regulatory) requirements of a given act. The result is that the original analysis of expected impacts made by the Commission might no longer fully reflect its impacts when implemented.

Gold-Plating
'Gold plating' is a widely used term in the context of the implementation of the EU law, which refers to additional national obligations that go beyond EU requirements (European Commission, 2025).

4.3 *Higher Pace of Legislation*

The need to act swiftly to respond to crisis or political urgency and create the necessary legal framework requires evidence to be available at any point of time. The regular screening of the EU stock of legislation in stress tests will help to keep legislation under constant review and anticipate possible issues, rather than react to them. AI could play a role in this. The regular monitoring of the acquis could be supported by AI, allowing a broad mapping to identify more easily inefficiencies, redundancies, overlaps, and issues of implementation. AI could also help support consultation processes both in designing and processing contributions while keeping a close control over the output. It could help design legislation in a more user-friendly way, establishing closer links with existing legislation. A more efficient and agile system can also facilitate the handling of urgent situations. In the Commission work is under way on all these aspects.

5 Conclusions

The better regulation system is a dynamic, adaptive framework that balances evidence-based decision-making with stakeholder inclusivity. It needs to respond to current and future needs to ensure that it remains a catalyst for growth and innovation. An efficient and proportionate approach to better regulation, combined with a genuine and smarter consultation system, presents an opportunity to legislate in a way that is more attuned to current needs and improve the quality of legislation from the moment it is adopted by the Commission. The assessment of impacts of substantial amendments in the negotiation phase would help ensure that political decisions are based on due consideration of all significant impacts. An upcoming Communication will reflect on how to address these future challenges, in particular how to make the system more efficient and proportionate, ensure a smarter consultation approach and achieve simpler legislation.

References

Draghi, M. (2025). The future of European competitiveness. https://commission.europa.eu/topics/eu-competitiveness/draghi-report_en#paragraph_47059

European Commission. (2013). Commission communication on REFIT: COM(2013) 685 final of 2 October 2013.

European Commission. (2018). COM(2018) 703 final, "The principles of subsidiarity and proportionality: Strengthening their role in the EU's policymaking".

European Commission. (2021). Communication from the Commission to the European Parliament, the Council, the European and Social Committee and the Committee of the Regions, Better Regulation: Joining forces to make better laws, COM/2021/219 final, Brussels, 29.4.2021.

European Commission. (2023). Better regulation: guidelines and toolbox. https://commission.europa.eu/law/law-making-process/better-regulation/better-regulation-guidelines-and-toolbox_en and: https://eceuropaeu.sharepoint.com/sites/better-regulation/SitePages/better-regulation-guidelines-and-toolbox.aspx

European Commission. (2025). COM(2025) 47, communication on implementation and simplification.

European Parliament. (2025). The European Union's legal systems and decision-making procedures. https://www.europarl.europa.eu/factsheets/en/sheet/7/the-principle-of-subsidiarity

Letta, E. (2024). Much more than a market. https://single-market-economy.ec.europa.eu/news/enrico-lettas-report-future-single-market-2024-04-10_en

Organisation for Economic Co-operation and Development (OECD). (2025). Regulatory policy Outlook. https://www.oecd.org/en/publications/oecd-regulatory-policy-outlook-2025_56b60e39-en.html

Further Reading

A simpler and faster Europe: Communication on implementation sand simplification. https://commission.europa.eu/law/law-making-process/better-regulation/simplification-and-implementation_en

Interinstitutional Agreement between the European Parliament, the Council of the European Union and the European Commission on Better Law-Making, OJ L 123, 12.5.2016.

Antonina Cipollone is the Head of the unit SG. C2, which is the single contact point within the Secretariat-General for all aspects of better regulation, such as impact assessment, evaluations, stakeholder consultation as well as coordinating the whole work on simplification and burden reduction within the European Commission. She also acts as the Head of the Secretariat of the Regulatory Scrutiny Board, which is the Commission's oversight body. Previously she was dealing with competition policy within the Secretariat-General and in the Directorate for Competition. She holds a Master of Arts in European Political and Administrative Studies from the College of Europe and a post graduate Diploma in Management from the Vrije Universiteit of Brussel.

Outlook: The Ordinary Legislative Procedure—An Attempt to Look Ahead

Gerda Füricht-Fiegl, Alexander Burka, and Julia Kreyler-Valsky

The "Handbook on EU Lawmaking" provides a comprehensive analysis of the evolution and current state of legislative processes in the European Union, with a particular focus on the Ordinary Legislative Procedure (OLP) and its implications. Introduced by the Treaty of Lisbon in 2009, the OLP has evolved into the standard mechanism of EU lawmaking, reshaping the institutional balance of power and profoundly influencing the dynamics of policy-making within the Union.

One of the cornerstones of the OLP is the strengthened role of the European Parliament (EP), which has since assumed the position of co-legislator on an equal footing with the Council of the European Union. This development builds on earlier reforms, such as the co-decision procedure established by the Maastricht and Amsterdam Treaties, and reflects a broader trend toward democratization and institutional balance within the EU.

The handbook highlights the evolving scope of legislative acts and policy areas covered by the OLP. It sheds light on the increasing institutionalization of trilogues as a tool for interinstitutional coordination. Trilogues, as informal tripartite meetings between the EP, the Council and the Commission, are not mentioned in the EU Treaties, but have become de facto standard in EU lawmaking. These practices have reshaped the balance of power within the EU's legislative framework. However, they also raise concerns regarding transparency, accountability, and democratic legitimacy. Also met with different perspectives among the various actors involved in the lawmaking process are the Commission-driven Omnibus proposals, which are legal acts modifying several pieces of legislation with a compatible legal basis.

G. Füricht-Fiegl · A. Burka · J. Kreyler-Valsky (✉)
University of Applied Sciences Burgenland, Eisenstadt, Austria
e-mail: gerda.fuericht-fiegl@hochschule-burgenland.at;
alexander.burka@hochschule-burgenland.at; julia.kreyler-valsky@hochschule-burgenland.at

G. Füricht-Fiegl et al. (eds.), *Handbook on EU Law-making*, Professional Practice in Governance and Public Organizations, https://doi.org/10.1007/978-3-032-16559-6_30

The expansion of the EU from six Member States in 1957, when it was established as the European Economic Community, to twenty-seven by 2025 has introduced new complexities. The growing diversity of national interests, sovereignty concerns, and strategies for influencing EU institutions has made decision-making processes more intricate. The emergence of bottom-up regional groups (BURGs) within the Council further illustrates the evolving dynamics of coalition-building among Member States. These developments underscore the need for more effective coordination mechanisms to manage the growing number of actors with divergent interests, as well as the balance of political and economic influence among the Member States.

The handbook also examines the structural changes within the European Commission, particularly the evolving role of Vice-Presidents and the shift toward a more presidential model under the von der Leyen Commissions. This reflects a broader trend of centralizing authority within the Commission, with the president playing a more prominent role in shaping the EU's legislative and policy agenda. At the same time, the growing professionalism and influence of advisory bodies, such as the European Economic and Social Committee and the European Committee of the Regions, highlight the increasing importance of inclusive and participatory governance.

The role of non-institutional actors, such as lobbyists and NGOs, is another aspect of EU policy-making. Lobbying has become a defining feature of twenty-first-century democracy, influencing legislative processes at various stages. The handbook emphasizes the need for greater accountability and transparency to ensure fair representation of diverse interests while safeguarding against corruption. Transparency, it argues, should not merely be a punitive tool but a means to foster trust and partnership among stakeholders.

Looking ahead, the EU faces a range of challenges that will shape its legislative and policy priorities. The regulation of emerging technologies will require policymakers to balance the defense of European values with the need to minimize compliance burdens and maintain global competitiveness. The consolidation of existing regulatory frameworks and the fight against disinformation are crucial tasks for the future. The "Competitiveness Compass" outlined by the von der Leyen Commission II underscores the EU's commitment to market efficiency and regulatory simplification. This focus on competitiveness may sometimes conflict with socially progressive agendas, raising questions about the balance between economic growth and social harmonization.

The Commission's "better regulation" agenda offers a framework for addressing these challenges. By emphasizing evidence-based decision-making, stakeholder engagement, and the assessment of the impacts of legislative amendments, the EU can ensure that its laws are both effective and responsive to societal needs. A more holistic and innovative approach to regulation could enhance the quality of legislation and strengthen the EU's role as a global leader in governance.

Finally, the EU must confront a range of crises—geopolitical, environmental, economic, and democratic. In view of the current geopolitical situation (as of November 2025), marked by conflicts in and around Europe, the European Union will need to develop responses and action scenarios that will be reflected, not least, in its decision-making processes. As history has shown, the European project has consistently drawn its strength from times of adversity. By reaffirming its foundational values and addressing these challenges with unity and resolve, the EU has the potential to emerge stronger and more resilient. The future of EU law- and policy-making will depend on its ability to adapt to new realities while staying true to its core principles of democracy, transparency, and solidarity.

Gerda Füricht-Fiegl is a political scientist at the University of Applied Sciences Burgenland, where she heads the English-taught Master's programme European Studies—Management of EU Projects. She serves as Vice-Rector for Research and Innovation. Her teaching and research focus on the EU political system and political communication in the EU. She also brings extensive professional experience from the European Commission and the European Parliament.

Alexander Burka is a professor at the University of Applied Sciences Burgenland and co-founder and managing director of the CIVIC-Institute for International Education in Düsseldorf. He studied at the Free University Berlin and the Universites of Vienna and Helsinki and has worked for numerous national and international institutions worldwide in the areas of international competences, civic society, and democracy development. He also authors educational materials on international, political, and EU-related topics.

Julia Kreyler-Valsky is a lecturer at the University of Applied Sciences Burgenland and an expert in equal opportunities. She has held positions with the Austrian Minister for Women's Affairs, the OECD, and the financial sector in Central and Eastern Europe. Her research focuses on inclusive institutional structures and the effectiveness of anti-discrimination policies. Julia holds a Master's in Public Administration (LSE) and a PhD in Sociology (University of Vienna).

The manufacturer's authorised representative in the EU is Springer Nature Customer Service Centre GmbH, Europaplatz 3, 69115 Heidelberg, Germany. If you have any concerns regarding our products, please contact ProductSafety@springernature.com

Printed and bound by CPI Group (UK) Ltd, Croydon, CR0 4YY
17/09/2026
02218433-0012